Second Edition

CompTIA® CySA+

Guide to Cybersecurity Analyst

MARK CIAMPA, PH.D.

INFORMATION
SECURITY

⁛ Cengage

Australia • Brazil • Canada • Mexico • Singapore • United Kingdom • United States

CompTIA CySA+ Guide to Cybersecurity Analyst, Second Edition, Mark Ciampa

SVP, Higher Education & Skills Product: Erin Joyner

VP, Higher Education & Skills Product: Thais Alencar

Product Director: Mark Santee

Product Manager: Danielle Klahr

Product Assistant: Tom Benedetto

Executive Director, Learning Design: Natalie Skadra

Manager, Instructional Design: Erin Doppke

Learning Designer: Natalie Onderdonk

Senior Director, Content Creation: Rebecca von Gillern

Manager, Content Creation: Alexis Ferraro

Senior Content Manager and Content Manager: Anne Orgren and Michele Stulga

Director, Digital Production Services: Krista Kellman

Manager, Digital Services: Laura Ruschman

Digital Delivery Lead: Jim Vaughey

Vice President, Product Marketing: Jason Sakos

Director, Product Marketing: Danaë April

Marketing Manager: Mackenzie Paine

IP Analyst: Ashley Maynard

IP Project Manager: Nick Barrows

Technical Editor: Danielle Shaw

Developmental Editor: Lisa Ruffolo

Production Service/Composition: SPi

Creative Director: Jack Pendleton

Designer: Erin Griffin

Cover image Source: sollia/Shutterstock.com

Library of Congress Control Number: 2021944226

Student Edition: 978-0-357-67809-1
Loose-leaf Edition: 978-0-357-67812-1

Cengage
200 Pier 4 Boulevard
Boston, MA 02210
USA

Cengage is a leading provider of customized learning solutions with employees residing in nearly 40 different countries and sales in more than 125 countries around the world. Find your local representative at **www.cengage.com.**

To learn more about Cengage platforms and services, register or access your online learning solution, or purchase materials for your course, visit **www.cengage.com.**

Notice to the Reader
Publisher does not warrant or guarantee any of the products described herein or perform any independent analysis in connection with any of the product information contained herein. Publisher does not assume, and expressly disclaims, any obligation to obtain and include information other than that provided to it by the manufacturer. The reader is expressly warned to consider and adopt all safety precautions that might be indicated by the activities described herein and to avoid all potential hazards. By following the instructions contained herein, the reader willingly assumes all risks in connection with such instructions. The publisher makes no representations or warranties of any kind, including but not limited to, the warranties of fitness for particular purpose or merchantability, nor are any such representations implied with respect to the material set forth herein, and the publisher takes no responsibility with respect to such material. The publisher shall not be liable for any special, consequential, or exemplary damages resulting, in whole or part, from the readers' use of, or reliance upon, this material.

Printed in the United States of America
Print Number: 03   Print Year: 2022

BRIEF CONTENTS

TABLE OF CONTENTS

PREFACE

CompTIA® CySA+ Guide to Cybersecurity Analysis, 2nd edition, is intended to meet the needs of learners and professionals who are interested in mastering intermediate-level cybersecurity skills and knowledge. It is designed to prepare security analysts, threat intelligence analysts, and incident response handlers who will leverage intelligence and threat detection techniques, analyze and interpret data, identify and address vulnerabilities, suggest preventative measures, and effectively respond to and recover from incidents as they apply to an organization's data, applications, and digital infrastructure. Although there is no designated prerequisite, the *CompTIA® CySA+ Guide to Cybersecurity Analysis* is designed to build upon the CompTIA Security+ certification or equivalent experience. Those seeking to pass CompTIA's CySA+ certification exam will find the course's content, approach, and numerous projects and study questions especially helpful. For more information on CompTIA CySA+ certification, visit CompTIA's website at https://www.comptia.org/.

The course's pedagogical features are designed to provide a truly interactive learning experience and prepare you to face the challenges of cybersecurity. In addition to the information presented in the readings, each module includes the following:

- *Cybersecurity Today* opens each module with the details and explanations of a recent real-world cybersecurity event that introduces a topic in the module. This feature provides a real-world context for applying cybersecurity principles and skills.
- *Grow with Cengage Unlimited!* boxes throughout each module provide information for reviewing foundational topics and exploring the material presented in more depth.
- *Two Rights & a Wrong questions* at the end of every module section help learners with a quick assessment of the main points to ensure a complete understanding of the material.
- *Multiple case projects* are included in each module that direct learners into additional research and discussion of key topics of the module.
- *On the Job case project* concludes each module with a scenario of a challenging corporate decision that must be made based on the implications of a topic presented in the module.
- *Knowledge-based assessment questions and hands-on performance-based questions (PBQs)* that mimic those found on the CompTIA CySA+ certification exam are included in Appendix A. Many of these are presented in a scenario format to put the learner in a "you are there" setting when deciding which tools to use, why they should be used, and how to interpret and analyze the results. In addition, the answers to the Appendix A questions are found in a separate solution file so that learners can compare their knowledge and skills with the answers.

MODULE DESCRIPTIONS

The following list summarizes the topics covered in each module of this course:

Module 1, "Enterprise Threats and Vulnerabilities," looks at threats by exploring different types of attacks. In order for an enterprise to mount a successful defense, it must be aware not only of the attacker's threats but also of its own vulnerabilities. This module covers threats and vulnerabilities associated with technologies other than personal computers and data networks, such as mobile devices, embedded devices, and specialized devices.

Module 2, "Utilizing Threat Data and Intelligence," explores knowing both who the attackers are and how they attack. And because attacks continually evolve, it is also important to take advantage of all available threat intelligence information to know the very latest types of attacks and how to defend against them. This module also explores frameworks and threat research sources along with different modeling methodologies.

Module 3, "Vulnerability Management," focuses on a process known as infrastructure risk visibility and assurance, also called vulnerability management. Its purpose is to be an ongoing examination of the organization's security posture. This module looks at common vulnerabilities, how to configure vulnerability scanning tools, and how to report and remediate scan results.

Module 4, "Cloud Computing and Assessment Tools," introduces cloud computing and its vulnerabilities. It also looks beyond the cloud into vulnerabilities in software, infrastructures, and other assets, and explains the tools that can be used for assessing these vulnerabilities.

Module 5, "Infrastructure Controls," examines how it is necessary to direct influence over attacks through various methods of cybersecurity controls (countermeasures) that organizations implement to prevent, reduce, or counteract security risks. This module explores two broad categories of controls that relate to the infrastructure: infrastructure management controls and configuration controls.

Module 6, "Software and Hardware Assurance Best Practices," explores procedures that have been demonstrated by research and experience to produce optimal results and are used as standards that are suitable for widespread adoption.

Module 7, "Security Monitoring Through Data Analysis," looks at implementing proactive monitoring by using sophisticated data analysis tools. These tools can help detect attacks more quickly and enable defenders to respond promptly.

Module 8, "Security Operations," explores the enhanced automation that is becoming available to security personnel to streamline and speed up security processes. It also looks at a new change in philosophy about threat actors so that proactive security can be applied in seeking out and defending against attackers.

Module 9, "Incident Response Planning and Procedures," discusses how an organization can prepare for a cyber incident. This includes what type of planning is required in order to support meaningful communication, how the critical nature of data can be determined in order to protect it or respond if it is compromised, and what incident response procedures should be used for detection, analysis, containment, eradication, and recovery.

Module 10, "Responding to a Cyber Incident," looks at the steps that are taken in the aftermath of a cyber incident. These steps include identifying indicators of compromise on networks, endpoints, and applications as well as performing digital forensics.

Module 11, "Risk Mitigation," defines risk and explores methods for mitigating risks, especially through using policies, procedures, and frameworks.

Module 12, "Data Protection and Privacy," looks at the controls that organizations can use to protect data. It also discusses the topic of data privacy.

Appendix A contains tools for preparing for the CompTIA CySA+ CS0-002 certification exam. It provides knowledge-based assessment questions and PBQs that are designed to assess the test taker's skills in working with different cybersecurity tools.

Appendix B is a mapping of each CySA+ domain element, the module and section in which it is located, and how that material is covered based on Bloom's taxonomy.

Appendix C contains the answers to the "Two Rights & a Wrong" assessment questions.

FEATURES

To aid you in fully understanding cybersecurity analysis, this material includes many features designed to enhance your learning experience.

Cybersecurity Today. Each module opens with the details and explanation of a recent real-world cybersecurity event. This feature provides a real-world context for applying cybersecurity principles.

Module objectives. Each module lists the concepts to be mastered within that module. This list serves as a quick reference to the module's contents and a useful study aid.

Scenario-based practice questions. Practice questions, many of which are scenario based, help provide more of a real-world setting to help learners assess themselves.

Colorful illustrations, screenshots, tables, and bulleted lists. Numerous full-color diagrams illustrating abstract ideas and screenshots of cybersecurity tools help learners better visualize the concepts of cybersecurity. In addition, the many tables and bulleted lists provide details and comparisons of both practical and theoretical information that can be easily reviewed and referenced in the future.

Notes. Each module's content is supplemented with Note features that provide additional insight and understanding.

Cautions. The Caution features warn you about potential mistakes or problems and explain how to avoid them.

Cengage Unlimited cross-references. For those learners who have a Cengage Unlimited subscription, convenient cross-references to other publications with additional information on relevant concepts invite further study and exploration.

You're Ready prompts. At the end of each module, a "You're Ready" prompt appears that indicates the learner is ready for a specific project.

Key terms. Clickable key terms emphasize the core concepts of cybersecurity.

Module summaries. Each module reading concludes with a summary of the concepts introduced in that module. These summaries revisit the ideas covered in each module.

Two Rights & a Wrong. Each section of every module includes a series of questions that can serve as a quick self-assessment of the material. This helps to ensure a complete understanding of the material.

Case projects. Although it is important to understand the theory behind cybersecurity technology, nothing beats real-world experience. To this end, each module includes several case projects aimed at providing practical implementation experience as well as practice in applying critical thinking skills to the concepts learned throughout the module.

Instructor's Materials

Instructors, please visit cengage.com and sign in to access instructor-specific resources, which include the instructor manual, solutions manual, PowerPoint presentations, and figure files.

Instructor manual. The instructor manual that accompanies this course provides additional instructional material to assist in class preparation, including suggestions for classroom activities, discussion topics, and additional projects.

Solutions manual. Answers to the review questions, scenario-based practice questions, performance-based questions, case projects, and reflection activities are provided.

PowerPoint presentations. This course comes with Microsoft PowerPoint slides for each module. These are included as a teaching aid for classroom presentation, to make available to students on the network for module review, or to be printed for classroom distribution. Instructors, please feel at liberty to add your own slides for additional topics you introduce to the class.

Figure files. All of the figures in the course are reproduced on the Instructor Resource Site. Similar to the PowerPoint presentations, these are included as a teaching aid for classroom presentation, to make available to students for review, or to be printed for classroom distribution.

MINDTAP FOR CYSA+ GUIDE TO CYBERSECURITY ANALYSIS

MindTap is an online learning solution designed to help you master the skills you need in today's workforce. Research shows that employers need critical thinkers, troubleshooters, and creative problem solvers to stay relevant in our fast-paced, technology-driven world. MindTap helps you achieve this with assignments and activities that provide hands-on practice, real-life relevance, and certification test prep. MindTap guides you through assignments that help you master basic knowledge and understanding before moving on to more challenging problems. MindTap activities and assignments are tied to CompTIA CySA+ certification exam objectives. MindTap features include the following:

- *Live Virtual Machine labs* allow you to practice, explore, and try different solutions in a safe sandbox environment. Each module provides you with an opportunity to complete an in-depth project hosted in a live virtual machine environment. You implement the skills and knowledge gained in the module through real design and configuration scenarios in a private cloud created with OpenStack.

- The *Adaptive Test Prep (ATP)* app is designed to help you quickly review and assess your understanding of key IT concepts. Test yourself multiple times to track your progress and improvement by filtering results by correct answers, by all questions answered, or only by incorrect answers to show where additional study help is needed.
- *Pre- and Post-Quizzes* emulate the CySA+ certification exam.
- *Security for Life* assignments encourage you to stay current with what's happening in the IT field.
- *Reflection* activities encourage classroom and online discussion of key issues covered in the modules.

Instructors, MindTap is designed around learning objectives and provides analytics and reporting so you can easily see where the class stands in terms of progress, engagement, and completion rates. Use the content and learning path as is, or pick and choose how your materials will integrate with the learning path. You control what the students see and when they see it. Learn more at https://www.cengage.com/mindtap/.

STATE OF CYBERSECURITY IN INFORMATION TECHNOLOGY

The number of cyberattacks has reached epidemic proportions. According to one report, there are 375 threats per minute, and the total malware in existence now exceeds 1.2 billion instances. New malware targeting mobile devices has increased more than 70 percent annually. Disclosed incidents targeting the United States increased 61 percent in just one quarter. Most users expect that they will be recurring victims of cyberattacks throughout their lifetime.

To defend against these growing numbers of cyberattacks, annual cybersecurity spending by companies and governments worldwide is projected to grow from $146 billion in 2020 to $207 billion by 2024, an increase of almost 30 percent. Yet even though billions of dollars are spent each year on defenses, it appears to be having limited impact on the number of successful attacks.

This imbalance—large amounts of money spent on defenses that still do not stop threat actors—has caused many security professionals to call for a change in thinking about security defenses. Security professionals today must have the knowledge and expertise to analyze data about the different types of attacks. They must also be able to discover any vulnerabilities in the network and devices attached to it, and then strengthen them to resist attacks.

CERTIFICATIONS

To assist current and future security professionals, a security certification is now available to help security workers learn and practice new security skills. This certification is the Computing Technology Industry Association (CompTIA) Cybersecurity Analyst (CySA+). The CySA+ certification is designed for IT security analysts, vulnerability analysts, and threat intelligence analysts. The material covered in this certification helps security professionals apply behavioral analytics to networks in order to improve the overall state of security through providing an enhanced visibility of threats. The CySA+ certification will validate a cybersecurity professional's ability to proactively defend and continuously improve the security of an enterprise by leveraging intelligence and threat detection techniques, analyzing and interpreting data, identifying and addressing vulnerabilities, and recommending preventative measures.

The value of an IT professional who holds a security certification is significant. IT professionals who hold an IT certification earn 3.5 percent more than industry peers who do not have one. Professionals who hold a security certification earn 8.7 percent more than counterparts who do not have a security certification.

Certification provides job applicants with more than just a competitive edge over their noncertified counterparts competing for the same IT positions. Some institutions of higher education grant college credit to students who successfully pass certification exams, moving them further along in their degree programs. For those already employed, achieving a new certification increases job effectiveness, which opens doors for advancement and job security. Certification also gives individuals who are interested in careers in the military the ability to move into higher positions more quickly.

ABOUT THE AUTHOR

Dr. Mark Ciampa is Professor of Information Systems in the Gordon Ford College of Business at Western Kentucky University in Bowling Green, Kentucky. Previously, he was Associate Professor and Director of Academic Computing at Volunteer State Community College in Gallatin, Tennessee, for 20 years. Mark has worked in the IT industry as a computer consultant for businesses, government agencies, and educational institutions. He has published more than 25 articles in peer-reviewed journals and is also the author of over 30 technology textbooks, including *Security+ Guide to Network Security Fundamentals,* 7th Edition; *CWNA Guide to Wireless LANs*, 3rd Edition; *Guide to Wireless Communications, Security Awareness: Applying Practical Security In Your World*, 5th Edition; and *Networking BASICS*. Dr. Ciampa holds a PhD in technology management with a specialization in digital communication systems from Indiana State University, and he has certifications in security and healthcare.

ACKNOWLEDGMENTS

A large team of dedicated professionals all contributed to this project, and I am honored to be part of such an outstanding group of professionals. First, thanks go to Cengage Product Manager Danielle Klahr for providing me the opportunity to work on this project and for her continual support. Thanks also to Cengage Senior Content Manager Anne Orgren, Content Manager Michele Stulga, and Learning Designer Natalie Onderdonk for their valuable input, and to Danielle Shaw for her technical reviews. I would like to give special recognition to developmental editor Lisa Ruffolo. Once again, Lisa provided numerous helpful suggestions, made excellent comments, and continually kept me posted on upcoming deadlines. She expertly managed all the details, both large and small, so that I could stay focused. I also appreciate the significant contributions of the reviewers for this edition: Jeremy Derby, Fayetteville Technical Community College, Fayetteville, NC; Diego Tibaquira, Miami Dade College—Padron, Miami, FL; and Darlene Wood, Fayetteville Technical Community College, Fayetteville, NC. To everyone on the team, I extend my sincere thanks.

Finally, I want to thank my wonderful wife, Susan. Her love, patience, and support were, as always, there from the beginning to end. I could not have done it without her.

Dedication

To Braden, Mia, Abby, Gabe, Cora, Will, and Rowan.

READ THIS BEFORE YOU BEGIN

This book is designed to meet the needs of learners and professionals who want to master intermediate cybersecurity skills. A fundamental knowledge of computers and networks is required, along with a solid understanding of fundamental computer security. Those seeking to pass the CompTIA CySA+ certification exam will find the text's approach and content especially helpful; all CySA+ CS0-002 exam objectives are covered in the text (see Appendix B). The *CompTIA® CySA+ Guide to Cybersecurity Analysis* covers all aspects of network and computer security while satisfying the exam objectives.

The book's pedagogical features are designed to provide a truly interactive learning experience that helps prepare you for the challenges of network and computer security. In addition to the information presented in the text, each module includes one or more virtual lab activities that guide you through implementing practical hardware, software, network, and Internet security configurations step by step. Each module also contains case studies that place you in the role of problem solver, requiring you to apply concepts presented in the module to achieve successful solutions. Additional questions in Appendix A provide even more opportunities to practice using the necessary tools to master cybersecurity analysis.

EXTERNAL THREATS AND INTERNAL VULNERABILITIES

What is the first question that should be asked when protecting assets from a cyberattack? That initial question should be, "What external threats could exploit our internal vulnerabilities?" Without this knowledge of attacks and weaknesses, any cybersecurity efforts are doomed to fail. The modules in this first part explore how to identify these threats and vulnerabilities. Module 1 examines the common threats and vulnerabilities of an enterprise. Module 2 explores how to use threat data and intelligence sources to identify emerging threats. This data is then used to help identify vulnerabilities, which is the topic of Module 3. Finally, Module 4 examines cloud computing and tools for assessing vulnerabilities.

PART 1

MODULE 1
ENTERPRISE THREATS AND VULNERABILITIES

MODULE 2
UTILIZING THREAT DATA AND INTELLIGENCE

MODULE 3
VULNERABILITY MANAGEMENT

MODULE 4
CLOUD COMPUTING AND ASSESSMENT TOOLS

ENTERPRISE THREATS AND VULNERABILITIES

After completing this module, you should be able to do the following:

❶ Identify different types of common attacks

❷ Describe the risks associated with mobile devices

❸ Explain security issues of embedded and specialized devices

Cybersecurity Today

For the first 100 years of the automobile, wheeled motor vehicles were mechanical devices powered by internal combustion engines (ICE) with gearbox transmissions. Over the last 10 years, however, the car has undergone its most dramatic changes to date. Automobiles have moved from being mechanical devices to predominately electronic ones, providing dramatic increases in fuel economy, safety, and comfort as ICEs are replaced by electric engines with rechargeable batteries. The recent introduction of autonomous vehicles ("self-driving cars") has further revolutionized the automobile industry. It has been said that today's cars are primarily a battery, motor, and computer hardware and software—sometimes without even a driver.

It comes as no surprise that because automobiles rely so heavily on hardware and software that they have been targets of cyberattackers. The first record of car attacks dates back to 2010. By 2015, security researchers had demonstrated how they could remotely control a car from 10 miles away due to a software vulnerability. The researchers changed the air-conditioning settings and the radio, turned off and on the windshield wipers and sprayed wiper fluid on the windshield, and even prevented acceleration on a crowded interstate highway while disabling the brakes so the car ended up in a ditch.

It has been estimated that cyberattackers can take advantage of at least 10 vehicle attack vectors to control or disable a car while it is in motion. Recently, two other attack vectors have been added to the list.

The first additional attack vector is over-the-air (OTA) updates. Much like with today's computer operating systems (OSs), problems with car software can be addressed by patches that are pushed out to millions of cars through wireless transmissions. This saves automakers costly recalls that normally would require the owner to drive to an authorized car dealer for a possibly lengthy repair. It is estimated that by 2022, savings across the industry from OTA updates will reach $35 billion. In addition, OTA updates are not limited to fixing software: they can also address components that are governed by that software. In 2018, a national consumer magazine announced that it would not recommend the Tesla Model 3 due in part to inconsistent braking behavior. One week later, Tesla updated all Model 3 cars through an OTA update that reduced the stopping distance by nearly 20 feet (6 meters).

However, there are issues surrounding OTA updates. Automakers could quietly sidestep regulations requiring public disclosure of defects by silently applying an OTA update. These updates may also incentivize car makers to rush a car to market with poorly tested features, knowing that an OTA update can later solve any issues. There have already been at least two incidents of car makers pushing out defective OTA updates that rendered safety features, such as rear-view cameras and autopilot features, inoperable.

The more serious issue is that just as automakers can send OTA updates, so, too, can cybercriminals. Unless the wireless updates are sufficiently protected, cybercriminals could send their own malicious instructions to one car or millions of cars. In fact, security researchers have already demonstrated the ability to bypass OTA update security mechanisms designed to prevent this from occurring.

An equally alarming attack vector is the cameras in cars that read road signs. Known as machine vision, this feature is one of the most important features for self-driving cars and cars with a driver relying on an automated piloting system. These vehicles must be able to understand their environment and then react appropriately. The amount of free space between a car with machine vision and the cars ahead and behind must be monitored; solid objects have to be avoided; and all instructions—whether painted on the road itself or posted on signs—must be read, correctly interpreted, and obeyed. It turns out that machine vision, unlike the way humans identify images, can be easily fooled by extraneous markings on a sign that a human would know to dismiss. For example, a small sticker on a road sign would be ignored by someone who knows it is not part of the instructions being conveyed by the sign; a car using machine vision, however, can be tricked by that same sticker.

Security researchers placed small stickers on a stop sign that regular drivers saw but dismissed as the sign looking weathered. However, an autonomous car misread the same stop sign with the sticker as a speed limit sign. In a similar test, a slightly modified right turn sign was mistaken by a car's machine vision as a stop sign. In perhaps the most alarming test, a two-inch piece of black electrical tape was added across the middle of the "3" in the speed limit sign "35 MPH." The car mistook that sign as "85 MPH" and immediately began to accelerate to that speed. (The researchers, for safety's sake, intervened as the car continued to accelerate.)

Researchers have also experimented with injecting frames of an image on digital roadside billboards that are used for advertisements. They found that just displaying a small image of a stop sign for less than half a second—too fast for the human eye to detect—could trick a car's machine vision technology and cause the car to immediately stop. An attacker could hijack an Internet-connected billboard to display these images and cause massive traffic jams or deadly road accidents, all while leaving little if any evidence behind.

The thought of a remote attacker taking control of a 5,800-pound (2,630 kilogram) SUV as it barrels down the road with a helpless driver behind the wheel unable to control it has many security professionals calling for immediate improvements in automobile hardware, software, and connectivity. As one security organization said, "We need to accelerate discussions and awareness of the problems and steer the direction and development of next-generation technologies (puns intended)."

How many cyberattacks have occurred over the last 24 hours? Over the last hour? In the past minute? The number of attacks continues to grow exponentially and has reached unprecedented proportions. According to one report, there are 375 threats per minute. The total malware in existence now exceeds 1.2 billion instances. New malware targeting mobile devices has increased annually more than 70 percent while new macOS malware has increased by 51 percent. Disclosed incidents targeting the United States increased 61 percent, those targeting Great Britain increased 55 percent, and attacks directed at Canada increased 50 percent in just one quarter.[1] Cybercrime will cost the world $10.5 trillion annually by 2025, an increase from $3 trillion in 2015, representing the greatest transfer of economic wealth in human history.[2] And these attacks continue with no end in sight.

To defend against the growing numbers of cyberattacks, enterprises are spending a staggering amount of their budgets on cybersecurity. Annual cybersecurity spending by companies and governments worldwide is projected to grow from $146 billion in 2020 to $207 billion by 2024, an increase of almost 30 percent. In the financial services sector, spending on cyberdefenses equals $3,000 per full-time employee. Microsoft spends $1 billion annually on defenses, while the U.S. government spends $15 billion each year.[3] Yet even though billions of dollars are spent each year on defenses, the number of successful attacks continues to grow.

This imbalance—large amounts of money spent on defenses that still do not stop threat actors—has caused many security professionals to throw up their hands and scream "Enough!" Calls for a change in how cybersecurity is approached and practiced are resonating throughout enterprises of all types and sizes. As one security professional recently said, "It is time for a paradigm shift in the cybersecurity industry."[4]

While attackers have learned to evade traditional signature-based solutions, such as firewalls and antivirus software, a shift to an analytics-based approach is becoming increasingly important for enterprises. To assist future security professionals with this shift, an advanced security certification is now available. This certification is the Computing Technology Industry Association (CompTIA) Cybersecurity Analyst (CySA+). CompTIA CySA+ applies behavioral analytics to networks in order to improve the overall state of security through providing an enhanced visibility of threats. The CySA+ certification will validate a cybersecurity professional's ability to proactively defend and continuously improve the security of an enterprise by leveraging intelligence and threat detection techniques, analyzing and interpreting data, identifying and addressing vulnerabilities, and recommending preventative measures.

This part begins by looking at exploits. The noun "exploit" originally meant an attempt to capture something while on a military expedition. Today the word is often defined as a tool designed to take advantage of a flaw in a computer system, typically for malicious purposes. This definition well encompasses the current challenges of cybersecurity: threat actors are continually seeking to uncover flaws or vulnerabilities in the defenses of an enterprise and then use those to craft a malicious threat.

For an enterprise to mount a successful defense, it must be aware not only of the attacker's threats but also of its own vulnerabilities. To know the external threats without understanding its vulnerabilities is a formula for disaster, just as knowing its flaws but being ignorant of the threats is likewise a recipe for failure. Knowing both external threats and internal vulnerabilities is crucial.

This module looks at the threats by exploring different types of attacks. It also covers threats and vulnerabilities associated with technologies other than personal computers and data networks, such as mobile devices, embedded devices, and specialized devices.

TYPES OF ATTACKS

 CERTIFICATION

1.7 Given a scenario, implement controls to mitigate attacks and software vulnerabilities.

It is important to know the types of attacks that an enterprise faces today. These include attacks using malware, memory vulnerability attacks, web server application attacks, session hijacking, attacks on credentials, exploitation and penetration attacks, and social engineering attacks.

Attacks Using Malware

Malware (*mal*icious soft*ware*) is a "catchall" term for virtually any type of malicious software designed to harm or exploit a device, service, or network. It enters a computer system without the user's knowledge or consent and then performs an unwanted and harmful action. Although the total malware in existence now exceeds 1.2 billion instances, there is still no established standard for classifying the types of malware so that like malware can be grouped together for study.

NOTE 1

Just as there is no standard for classifying malware, there likewise is no standard for naming malware instances. Often malware is simply given a name by the security researcher who first discovered it, which has led to the malware names WannaCry, NotPetya, Cryptolocker, ILOVEYOU, Anna Kournikova, Heartbleed, Stuxnet, and Conficker. The Black Hat security conference annually gives out an award for the most memorable vulnerability name.

However, security professionals have created "container" categories for grouping malware. One such category is malware that attempts to evade detection or helps other malware stay hidden. For example, a *back door* gives access to a computer, program, or service that circumvents any normal security protections. Back doors installed on a computer allow the attacker to return later and bypass security settings. A *logic bomb* is computer code that is typically hidden in a legitimate computer program but lies dormant and evades detection until a specific logical event triggers it.

NOTE 2

The risks of rootkits in OSs are significantly diminished today due to protections built into modern OS software. These protections include preventing unauthorized kernel drivers from loading, stopping modifications to certain kernel areas used by rootkits to hide, and preventing rootkits from modifying the bootloader program.

Another example of malware that aids in evasion techniques is a rootkit. A rootkit is malware that can hide its presence and the presence of other malware on the computer. It does this by accessing the lower layers of the OS or even using undocumented functions. This renders the rootkit and any accompanying software undetectable by the OS and common antimalware scanning software designed to seek and find malware.

Memory Vulnerability Attacks

Several attacks are directed at vulnerabilities associated with how a program uses random access memory (RAM) and are often the result of poor techniques (or laziness) by the software developer. Some memory-related attacks attempt to manipulate memory contents. These types of attacks include buffer overflow attacks and integer overflow attacks.

Buffer Overflow

A storage buffer on a computer typically contains the memory location of the software program that was being executed when another function interrupted the process; that is, the storage buffer contains the "return address" where the computer's processor should resume once the new process has finished. Attackers can substitute their own "return address" to point to a different area in the computer's memory that contains their malware code.

A buffer overflow attack occurs when a process attempts to store data in RAM beyond the boundaries of a fixed-length storage buffer. This extra data overflows into the adjacent memory locations (a buffer overflow). Because the storage buffer typically contains the "return address," an attacker can overflow the buffer with a new address pointing to the attacker's malware code. A buffer overflow attack is shown in Figure 1-1.

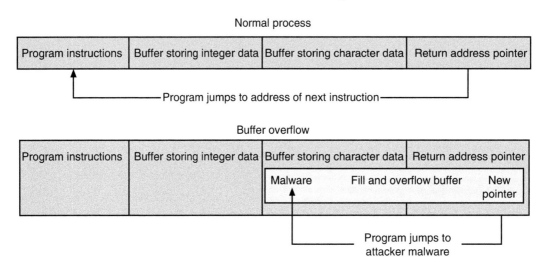

Figure 1-1   Buffer overflow attack

A buffer overflow attack can occur in one of two areas of computer memory. Memory is divided into the following four areas, as shown in Figure 1-2:

- *Data*. This area stores global variables that are separated into initialized and uninitialized variables.
- *Heap*. The heap is dynamic memory for the programmer to allocate as necessary.
- *Stack*. The stack stores local variables that the program uses.
- *Text*. Text stores the code that is being executed.

Each byte of computer memory has a unique address, beginning with zero (low address) to the largest possible address (high address). The *stack* area is near the top of memory with high addresses. Whenever a function is called by the computer program, a portion of stack memory is allocated. When new local variables are declared, more stack memory is automatically allocated. These allocations make the stack grow "down" (from higher memory addresses to

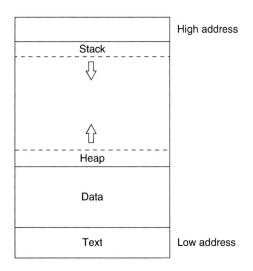

Figure 1-2   Computer memory areas

lower addresses). The *heap* area is allocated explicitly by the program and grows "up" (from lower addresses to higher addresses); it is not deallocated (freed) until the program explicitly mandates it. Because buffers are found in both the stack and heap areas, a buffer overflow attack can occur in either the stack (a *stack overflow*) or the heap (a heap overflow).

Integer Overflow

An integer overflow is the condition that occurs when the result of an arithmetic operation—such as addition or multiplication—exceeds the maximum size of the integer type used to store it. When this integer overflow occurs, the interpreted value then wraps around from the maximum value to the minimum value. For example, an eight-bit signed integer has a maximum value of 127 and a minimum value of –128. If the value 127 is stored in a variable and 1 is added to it, the sum exceeds the maximum value for this integer type and wraps around to become –128.

In an integer overflow attack, an attacker changes the value of a variable to something outside the range that the programmer had intended by using an integer overflow. This type of attack could be used by an attacker to create a buffer overflow. If an integer overflow could be introduced during the calculations for the length of a buffer when a copy is occurring, it could result in a buffer that is too small to hold the data. A large positive value in a bank transfer could also be wrapped around by an integer overflow attack to become a negative value, which could then reverse the flow of money: instead of adding this amount to the victim's account, it could withdraw that amount and later transfer it to the attacker's account.

NOTE 3

An extreme example of an integer overflow attack would be withdrawing $1 from an account that has a balance of 0, which could cause a new balance of $4,294,967,295!

Web Server Application Attacks

A web server provides services that are implemented as "web applications" through software programs running on the server. A typical web application infrastructure is shown in Figure 1-3. The client's web browser makes a request using the Hypertext Transfer Protocol (HTTP) to a web server, which may be connected to one or more web app servers. These application servers run the specific web apps, which in turn are directly connected to database servers on the internal network. Information from these database servers is retrieved and returned to the web server so that the information can be sent back to the user's web browser. A web application infrastructure is a tempting target for attackers for multiple reasons:

- A successful compromise could impact all web users who access the web server.
- An attack could provide a pathway into the enterprise's network infrastructure.
- The multiple elements in a web application infrastructure provide for a range of vulnerabilities that can be used as different attack vectors.

Two common application attacks are scripting attacks and injection attacks.

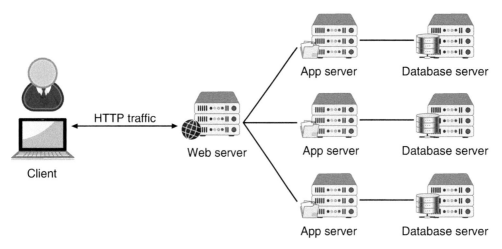

Figure 1-3 Web server application infrastructure

Scripting

Many websites—such as forums or message boards, blogging websites, and social networks—accept user input (visitor comments, web-based collaborations, etc.). The underlying web applications then use the input from users to create dynamic display content. For example, when a user enters CENGAGE into a search box, a webpage could be displayed to the user with the message *You are searching for: CENGAGE*. Or a user could enter a new topic about a recent player trade on a sports web forum that would then be displayed to subsequent users who access that same topic in the forum.

Threat actors can take advantage of this user input and display in a **cross-site scripting (XSS)** attack. The term "cross-site scripting" refers to an attack using scripting that originates on one site (the web server) to impact another site (the user's computer). XSS is essentially a client-side code injection attack using a web application. An attacker attempts to execute malicious scripts in the victim's web browser but not by directly injecting it into the user's web browser. Rather, the attacker inputs that malicious code on a website that accepts user input. The underlying web application that accepts the malicious code then becomes the vehicle to deliver the malicious script to every user's browser when he or she accesses that site. An XSS attack is shown in Figure 1-4.

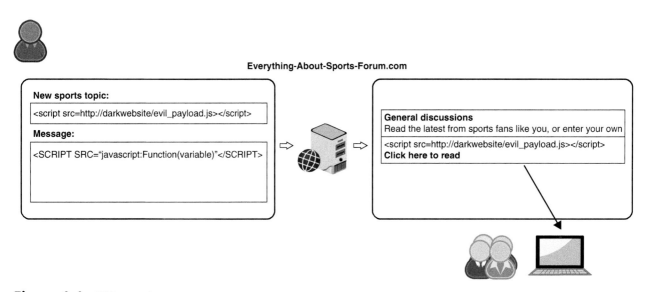

Figure 1-4 XSS attack

 **CAUTION** Malicious code in an XSS attack can be executed in the user's browser through VBScript, ActiveX, Flash, and even Cascading Style Sheets (CSS). However, it is most commonly executed in JavaScript because JavaScript is fundamental to most browsing experiences. Although web browsers run JavaScript in a tightly controlled environment with limited access to the OS and file system, it still has the potential to be misused by malware.

For a threat actor to launch an XSS attack, the attacker must identify a web application that accepts user input without validating it (called *sanitizing*) and then use that input in a response sent to the user. There are three main types of XSS attacks. These are summarized in Table 1-1.

Table 1-1   Types of XSS attacks

Name	Description	Comments
Reflected XSS	A user enters input into a web application that is then immediately displayed back ("reflected") to initiate the attack.	The simplest form of XSS attack
Persistent XSS	A threat actor enters input into a blog post or forum that is stored ("persistent") and an unsuspecting user later displays it to initiate the attack.	Also called Stored XSS or Second Order XSS
Document Object Model XSS	A web application writes data to the Document Object Model on the web server without proper sanitization and the attacker manipulates this data to include XSS content on the webpage.	The Document Object Model is a convention used to represent and work with objects in an HTML document (and other document types)

A threat actor who controls a script that is executed in the victim's browser through XSS could fully compromise that user. The attacker can do the following:

- Initiate interactions with other application users, including malicious attacks, that appear to originate from the trusted victim.
- Modify any information that the user is able to modify.
- Perform any action within the application that the user can perform.
- View any information that the user is able to view.

Injection

In addition to cross-site scripting attacks on web server applications, attacks called *injections* also introduce new input to exploit a vulnerability. One of the most common injection attacks, called **Structured Query Language (SQL) injection**, inserts statements to manipulate a database server. SQL is a language used to view and manipulate data that is stored in a relational database. SQL injection targets SQL servers by introducing commands into the server, much in the same way that XSS attacks inject malicious commands into a web application. However, with an SQL injection attack, the intent is to retrieve confidential information from the database and not inject malicious code.

An attacker using an SQL injection attack would begin by first entering a fictitious email address on a webpage that included a single quotation mark as part of the data, such as braden.thomas@fakemail.com'. If the message "Email Address Unknown" is displayed, it indicates that user input is being properly filtered and an SQL attack cannot be rendered on the site. However, if the error message "Server Failure" is displayed, it means that the user input is not being filtered and all user input is sent directly to the database. This is because the "Server Failure" message is due to a syntax error created by the additional single quotation mark in the fictitious email address.

Armed with the knowledge that input is sent unfiltered to the database, attackers understand that anything they enter as a username in the web form would be sent to and then processed by the SQL database. Now, instead of entering a username, the attackers would enter valid SQL statements that would be passed directly to the database for processing.

In addition to using SQL to view and manipulate data that is stored in a relational database, other types of databases not using SQL (called *NoSQL databases*) are used. One popular type of NoSQL database manipulates data using the *eXtensible Markup Language (XML)*. Like the markup language Hyper Text Markup Language (HTML) used for webpages, XML is not a processing language but instead is designed to store information. A NoSQL database that uses XML for data manipulation is also subject to an injection attack like SQL injection if the input is not sanitized. This is called an **eXtensible Markup Language (XML) attack**.

Grow with Cengage Unlimited!

If you'd like more information about this topic, use your Cengage Unlimited subscription to go to the CompTIA Security+ Guide to Network Security Fundamentals, 7th edition, open Module 3, and read the section titled "Application Attacks."
If you don't have a Cengage Unlimited subscription, you can find more information at cengage.com/unlimited.

Session Hijacking

A *session ID* is a unique value that a web server assigns a specific user for the duration of that user's visit (session). Most servers create complex session IDs by using the date, time of the visit, and other variables such as the device IP address, email, username, user ID, role, privilege level, access rights, language preferences, account ID, current state, last login, session timeouts, and other internal session details. Session IDs are usually at least 128 bits in length and hashed using a secure hash function like SHA-256. A sample session ID is *fa2e76d49a0475910504cb3ab7a1f626d174d2d*.

NOTE 4

Each time a website is visited, a new session ID is assigned and usually remains active as long as the browser is open. In some instances, after several minutes of inactivity, the server may generate a new session ID. Closing the browser terminates the active session ID, and it should not be used again.

Session IDs can be contained as part of a URL extension, by using "hidden form fields" in which the state is sent to the client as part of the response and returned to the server as part of a form's hidden data, or through cookies.

Session hijacking occurs when a threat actor takes over a user session. Different methods can be used for hijacking a session. One method involves intercepting the session ID. This can be done through XSS or a **man-in-the-middle (MITM)** attack (sometimes called an on-path attack) in which a communication between two systems is intercepted. In a typical HTTP transaction, a TCP connection is made between the endpoint and the server. Using different techniques, the attacker can divide the original TCP connection into two new connections, one between the client and the attacker and the other between the attacker and the server. The attacker can act as a proxy, being able to read, insert, and modify the information in the intercepted communication. Other methods include tricking the user into clicking a malicious link that contains a prepared session ID that the threat actor knows and can use or attempting to guess the session ID.

Attacks on Credentials

Authentication in information security is the process of ensuring that the person or system seeking access to resources is authentic (not an imposter). Seven recognized elements can be presented to prove this authenticity, since only the real or authentic person would uniquely possess one or more of these elements. These elements that prove authenticity, known as *authentication credentials*, are listed in Table 1-2.

Threat actors use a variety of techniques to attack credentials and gain access to protected systems. Because passwords (something you know) are the most common form of authentication credential, many of these attacks focus on attempting to compromise passwords.

One type of password attack uses "targeted guessing." A **password spraying attack** takes one or a small number of commonly used passwords (*Password1* or *123456*) and then uses this same password when trying to log in to several user accounts. Because this targeted guess is spread across many accounts and is not focused on attempting multiple

Table 1-2 Authentication credentials

Element	Description	Example
Somewhere you are	Restricted location	Restricted military base
Something you are	Unique biological characteristic that cannot be changed	Fingerprint reader
Something you have	Possession of an item that nobody else has	RFID card
Someone you know	Validated by another person	Adriano knows Li
Something you exhibit	Genetically determined characteristic	Red hair
Something you can do	Perform an activity that cannot be exactly copied	Signature
Something you know	Knowledge that nobody else possesses	Keys pressed on a keypad

password variations on a single account, it is much less likely to raise any alarms or lock out the user account from too many failed password attempts. Although password spraying may result in occasional success, it is not considered the optimal means for breaking into accounts.

Another attack takes advantage of the huge number of stolen passwords that have been posted online by threat actors. This treasure trove collection of passwords gives attackers a "head start" in credential attacks. Because users repeat their passwords on multiple accounts, attackers use these passwords in their attacks with a high probability of success. This is known as credential stuffing.

NOTE 5

Using stolen password collections as candidate passwords is the foundation of password cracking today, and almost all password cracking software tools accept these stolen "wordlists" as input. Websites host lists of these leaked passwords that attackers can download. One website boasts more than 1.45 *trillion* cracked password hashes.

Grow with Cengage Unlimited!

If you'd like more information about this topic, use your Cengage Unlimited subscription to go to the CompTIA Security+ Guide to Network Security Fundamentals, 7th edition; open Module 12; and read the section titled "Types of Authentication Credentials."

If you don't have a Cengage Unlimited subscription, you can find more information at cengage.com/unlimited.

Exploitation and Penetration Tactics

The goal of a threat actor is to exploit a vulnerability in order to penetrate a system. Generally, threat actors use these tactics for exploitation and penetration:

1. The threat actors first conduct reconnaissance against the systems, looking for vulnerabilities.
2. When a path to a vulnerability is exposed, they gain access to the system through the vulnerability.
3. Once initial access is gained, the threat actors attempt to escalate to more advanced resources that are normally protected from an application or user. This is called privilege escalation.
4. With the advanced privileges, they tunnel through the network, looking for additional systems they can access from their elevated position (called *lateral movement*). Threat actors may use a directory traversal attack that takes advantage of a vulnerability in a web application or web server software so that a user can move from the root directory to other restricted directories.
5. Threat actors install additional tools on the compromised systems to gain even deeper access to the network. They may also use vulnerabilities to enter commands to execute on a server; this is known as remote code execution (RCE).

6. Threat actors may install a back door that allows them repeated and long-term access to the system in the future. The back doors are not related to the initial vulnerability, so access remains even if the initial vulnerability is corrected.

7. Once the back door is installed, threat actors can continue to probe until they find their ultimate target and perform their intended malicious action—such as stealing research and development (R&D) information, password files, or customer credit card numbers.

 **CAUTION** The initial system that was compromised—the system through which the attackers first gained entry—most often is not the goal of the attack. Rather, this system only serves as a gateway for entry. Once they are inside the network, the threat actors then pivot or turn to other systems to be compromised, with the goal of reaching the ultimate target. This means they are not defeated if they cannot find a vulnerability on the target; rather, a vulnerability can be used to pivot to the ultimate target.

Social Engineering Attacks

Not all attacks rely on technology vulnerabilities; in fact, some cyberattacks use little if any technology to achieve their goals. *Social engineering* is a means of eliciting information (gathering data) by relying on the weaknesses of individuals. This information elicitation may be the goal of the attack, or the information may then be used for other attacks.

Social engineering impersonation (also called identity fraud) is masquerading as a real or fictitious character and then playing out the role of that person on a victim. For example, an attacker could impersonate a help desk support technician who calls the victim, pretends that there is a problem with the network, and asks for a valid username and password to reset the account. Sometimes the goal of the impersonation is to obtain private information, which is known as *pretexting*.

 **CAUTION** Common roles that are often impersonated include a repairperson, an IT support person, a manager, or a trusted third party. Often attackers will impersonate individuals whose roles are authoritative because victims generally resist saying no to anyone in power. Users should exercise caution when receiving a phone call or email from these types of individuals asking for something suspicious.

Grow with Cengage Unlimited!

If you'd like more information about this topic, use your Cengage Unlimited subscription to go to the CompTIA Security+ Guide to Network Security Fundamentals, 7th edition; open Module 1; and read the section titled "Social Engineering Attacks." If you don't have a Cengage Unlimited subscription, you can find more information at cengage.com/unlimited.

TWO RIGHTS & A WRONG

1. A rootkit is malware that can hide its presence and the presence of other malware on the computer.
2. The stack is dynamic memory for the programmer to allocate as necessary.
3. A Reflected XSS attack only affects the user who entered data into the website.

See Appendix C for the answer.

THREATS AND VULNERABILITIES OF SPECIALIZED TECHNOLOGY

✔ CERTIFICATION

1.5 Explain the threats and vulnerabilities associated with specialized technology.

The days are long past when threat actors focused only on file servers and desktop computers. Instead, just as individual users and large enterprises have shifted their focus to other technologies, so too have attackers. These technologies include embedded and specialized devices and mobile devices, and they each have specific security issues.

Embedded and Specialized Devices

Not all computing systems are desktop or mobile devices designed for human input. Computing capabilities can be integrated into a variety of different devices. An **embedded system** is computer hardware and software contained within a larger system designed for a specific function. A growing trend is to add these capabilities to devices that have never had computing power before.

Types of Devices

There are several categories of embedded and specialized devices. These include the hardware and software that can be used to create these devices, industrial systems, campus systems, Internet of Things devices, and specialized systems.

Hardware and Software   Hardware and software components are available for industrious users to create their own specialized devices. One of the most common hardware components is the Raspberry Pi. This is a low-cost, credit-card-sized computer motherboard, as shown in Figure 1-5. The Raspberry Pi can perform virtually the same tasks that a standard computer device can, such as browsing the Internet, playing high-definition video, creating spreadsheets, and playing games. However, it is most often used to control a specialized device.

Raspberry Pi Foundation

Figure 1-5   Raspberry Pi

A device similar to the Raspberry Pi is the Arduino. Unlike the Raspberry Pi, which can function as a complete computer, the Arduino is designed as a controller for other devices: it has an 8-bit microcontroller instead of a 64-bit microprocessor on the Raspberry Pi, a limited amount of RAM, and no OS but can only run programs that were compiled for the Arduino platform, most of which must be written in the C++ programming language.

Although the Raspberry Pi and Arduino are small motherboards, a field-programmable gate array (FPGA) is a hardware "chip" or integrated circuit (IC) that can be programmed by the user ("field programmable") to carry out one or more logical operations. (ICs on standard computers as well as on Raspberry Pis and Arduinos cannot be user-programmed.) Specifically, a FPGA is an IC that consists of internal hardware blocks with user-programmable interconnects to customize operations for a specific application. A user can write software that loads onto the FPGA chip and executes functions, and that software can later be replaced or deleted.

An even smaller component than the Raspberry Pi or Arduino is a system on a chip (SoC). An SoC combines all the required electronic circuits of the various computer components on a single IC chip (the Raspberry Pi and Arduino are tiny motherboards that contain ICs, one of which is an SoC). SoCs often use a real-time operating system (RTOS) that is a specifically designed OS for an SoC in an embedded or specialized system. Standard computer systems, such as a laptop with a mouse and a keyboard or a tablet with a touch screen, typically receive irregular "bursts" of input data from a user or a network connection. Embedded systems, on the other hand, receive very large amounts of data very quickly, such as for an aircraft preparing to land on a runway at night during a storm. The RTOS is tuned to accommodate very high volumes of data that must be immediately processed for critical decision making.

Industrial Systems Industrial control systems (ICSs) manage devices locally or at remote locations by collecting, monitoring, and processing real-time data so that machines can directly control devices such as valves, pumps, and motors without the need for human intervention. Multiple ICSs are managed by a larger supervisory control and data acquisition (SCADA) system. SCADA systems are crucial today for industrial organizations. They help to maintain efficiency and provide information on issues to help reduce downtime.

Many SCADA systems use the network communication protocol Modbus for transmitting information between devices. Developed in 1979, Modbus originally required a serial port for communication between a single controlling device and up to 247 subservient devices. The controlling device polls each subservient device in a defined sequence, essentially asking each device in turn, "Do you want to transmit?" A subservient device cannot "volunteer" its data but must instead wait until it is polled and approved before transmitting. A later variation to Modbus incorporated the TCP/IP protocol and uses a standard client/server architecture; this variation is called Modbus TCP/IP or Modbus TCP. Although standard Modbus has error-detection capabilities to protect against data corruption, it has no security protections against injected commands or the interception of data.

Campus Systems A "campus" is the grounds and buildings of a school, hospital, business, or similar institution. To decrease the demand on personnel to monitor and manage the many elements that even a single building requires—doors, lighting, HVAC (heating, ventilation, and air conditioning), and fire alarms, just to name a few—modern campuses use workflow and process automation systems. These systems interconnect all the various elements so that they can be centrally and automatically monitored and controlled. One common system is a building automation system that manages building elements, which often includes a physical access control system that can ensure doors are locked and unlocked at specific times for certain individuals.

Internet of Things (IoT) Devices The Telecommunication Standardization Sector of the International Telecommunication Union (ITU-T) defines the Internet of Things (IoT) as "A global infrastructure for the information society, enabling advanced services by interconnecting (physical and virtual) things based on existing and evolving interoperable information and communication technologies."[5] More simply, the IoT is connecting any device to the Internet for the purpose of sending and receiving data to be acted upon. Although this definition could encompass laptop computers and tablets, more often IoT refers to devices that heretofore were not considered as computing devices connected to a data network.

IoT devices include wearable technology and multifunctional devices as well as many everyday home automation items such as thermostats, coffee makers, tire sensors, slow cookers, keyless entry systems, washing machines, electric toothbrushes, headphones, and light bulbs, to name just a few. It is estimated that by 2025, there will be more than 25 billion IoT devices, of which more than half will be consumer devices.[6]

Specialized Systems   Several types of specialized systems are designed for specific applications. One example is a system that measures the amount of utilities consumed. Traditionally, households have had utilities such as electricity and water measured by an analog meter that records the amount of electricity or water being used. This requires an employee from the utility to visit each home and read from the meter the amount that was consumed for the month so that a bill can be sent to the occupant. These analog meters are being replaced by digital "smart meters." Smart meters have several advantages over analog meters. These are listed in Table 1-3.

Table 1-3   Analog meters vs. smart meters

Action	Analog meter	Smart meter
Meter readings	Employee must visit the dwelling each month to read the meter.	Meter readings are transmitted daily, hourly, or even by the minute to the utility company.
Servicing	Annual servicing is required in order to maintain accuracy.	Battery replacement every 20 years.
Tamper protection	Data must be analyzed over long periods to identify anomalies.	Can alert utility in the event of tampering or theft.
Emergency communication	None available	Transmits "last gasp" notification of a problem to utility company.

The last 20 years have seen a dramatic increase in specialized systems used for transportation. This includes vehicles and drones.

Vehicles.   The first automobile specialized systems appeared in mass-production vehicles in the mid-1970s in response to regulations calling for higher fuel economy and emission standards, and they handled basic functions such as engine ignition timing and transmission shifting. By the 1980s, more sophisticated computerized engine-management systems enabled the use of reliable electronic fuel-injection systems, and later active safety systems such as antilock braking and traction and stability control features were added, all controlled by specialized systems.

Initially, these automobile sensors and devices were connected through a complex set of "point-to-point" wiring schemes in which one sensor was directly connected to a monitoring device or to another sensor that required its input (called electronic control units or ECUs). However, it quickly became apparent that there needed to be an improved means for interconnecting the growing number of ECU devices. In 1986, Bosch, a German-based multinational engineering and technology company, introduced the controller area network (CAN) bus network for sending and receiving data. CAN essentially consists of two wires, CAN low and CAN high. Data broadcast through CAN from one ECU reaches all other ECUs, which then accept and evaluate the data to determine if it should be received or is unnecessary and can be ignored. A CAN bus is illustrated in Figure 1-6.

NOTE 9

CAN became an international standard in 1993 and data rates up to five megabits per second (Mbit/s) was standardized in 2016. CAN is also used outside of the automotive industry.

Today specialized systems in cars use sonar, radar, and laser emitters to control brakes, steering, and the throttle to perform functions such as blind-spot and pedestrian collision warnings, automated braking, safe distance keeping, and fully automated parking. Some of these specialized embedded systems in cars are shown in Figure 1-7.

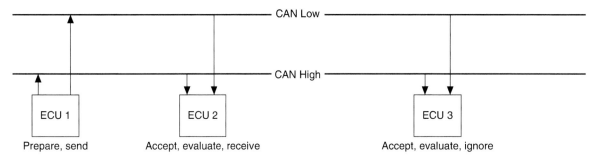

Figure 1-6   CAN bus

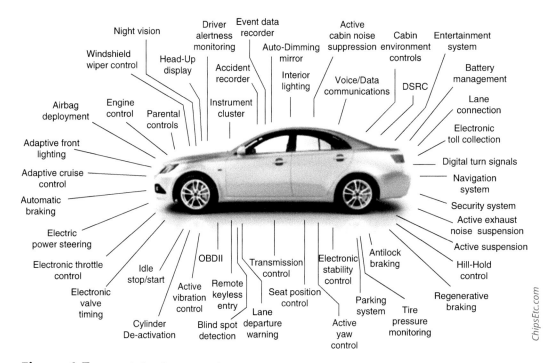

Figure 1-7   Specialized systems in cars

Figure 1-8   Drone

Drones.   An *unmanned aerial vehicle (UAV)*, better known as a drone, is an aircraft without a human pilot on board to control its flight. Drones can be controlled by a remote human operator, usually on the ground, or autonomously by preprogramming the onboard computers. While drones were originally used in military applications, today they have expanded into commercial, scientific, agricultural, and recreational uses. They are commonly used for policing and surveillance, product deliveries, aerial photography, infrastructure inspections, and even drone racing. A drone is seen in Figure 1-8.

NOTE 10

The term drone was first used to refer to unmanned aircraft that were used for target practice by battleships in the 1920s.

Security Issues

Despite the fact that embedded systems and specialized devices are widely used and will continue to grow exponentially, significant security issues surround these systems and devices. The lack of security in embedded systems and specialized devices can result in a wide range of attacks. For example, the vulnerable CAN bus has been a primary target for threat actors in manipulating vehicles.

Several constraints or limitations make security a challenge for these systems and specialized devices. These security constraints are listed in Table 1-4.

Table 1-4   Security constraints for embedded systems and specialized devices

Constraint	Explanation
Power	To prolong battery life, devices and systems are optimized to draw very low levels of power and thus lack the ability to perform strong security measures.
Compute	Due to their size, small devices typically possess low processing capabilities, which restricts complex and comprehensive security measures.
Network	To simplify connecting a device to a network, many device designers support network protocols that lack advanced security features.
Cryptography	Encryption and decryption are resource-intensive tasks that require significant processing and storage capacities that these devices lack.
Inability to patch	Few, if any, devices have been designed with the capacity for being updated to address exposed security vulnerabilities.
Authentication	To keep costs at a minimum, most devices lack authentication features.
Range	Not all devices have long-range capabilities to access remote security updates.
Cost	Most developers are concerned primarily with making products as inexpensive as possible, which means leaving out all security protections.
Implied trust	Many devices are designed without any security features but operate on an "implied trust" basis that assumes all other devices or users can be trusted.
Weak defaults	Usernames ("root," "admin," "support," etc.) and passwords ("admin," "888888," "default," "123456," "54321," and even "password") for accessing devices are often simple and well known.

NOTE 11

In one infamous security incident, a worm named Stuxnet attempted to gain administrative access to other computers through the network to control the SCADA system. It appears that Stuxnet's primary target was nuclear reactors at the Bushehr Nuclear Power Plant. Located in southwestern Iran near the Persian Gulf, Bushehr was a source of tension between Iran and the West (including the United States) because of fear that spent fuel from the reactor could be reprocessed elsewhere in the country to produce weapons-grade plutonium for use in nuclear warheads. Stuxnet was ultimately not successful in its attack.

Over several years, many industry-led initiatives have attempted to address security vulnerabilities in IoT and embedded devices. However, these initiatives were scattered and did not represent a comprehensive solution to the problem. To address security in these devices, governments have begun to propose or enact legislation to require stronger security on embedded systems and specialized devices. The *Internet of Things (IoT) Cybersecurity Improvement Act of 2019* was legislation introduced in the U.S. Senate in 2019. California and Oregon passed state laws addressing IoT security that went into effect in 2020. Both state laws require that connected devices be equipped with "reasonable security features" appropriate for the nature and function of the device and the information the device collects, contains, or transmits. Devices must be designed to protect both the device itself and any information contained within the device from unauthorized access, destruction, use, modification, or disclosure.

Mobile Device Risks

Few technologies can claim a growth rate that equals that of mobile devices. By 2022, 71 percent of the entire global population will be mobile users (5.7 billion). By that same year, mobile data traffic will reach an annual rate of 929.9 exabytes, up from 138.1 exabytes in 2017, and this mobile data traffic will be 113 times that of just 10 years earlier. The gigabyte equivalent of all movies ever made will cross mobile networks every five minutes by 2022.[7]

There is a wide array of mobile devices. These include the following:

- *Tablets*. Tablets are portable computing devices first introduced in 2010. Designed for user convenience, tablets are thinner, lighter, easier to carry, and more intuitive to use than other types of computers. Tablets generally lack a built-in keyboard or mouse. Instead, they rely on a touch screen that users manipulate with touch gestures to provide input.
- *Smartphones*. Smartphones are the most popular mobile devices. The popularity of a smartphone revolves around its OS, which allows it to run apps and access the Internet. Because it has an OS, a smartphone offers a broader range of functionality. Users can install apps to perform tasks for productivity, social networking, music, and so forth, much like a standard computer. Due to its ability to run apps, smartphones are essentially handheld personal computers that can also make phone calls.
- *Portable computers*. As a class, portable computers are devices that closely resemble standard desktop computers. Portable computers have similar hardware (keyboard, hard disk drive, and RAM, for example) and run the same OS (Windows, Apple macOS, or Linux) and applications (such as Microsoft Office and web browsers) as general-purpose desktop computers. The primary difference is that portable computers are smaller, self-contained devices that can easily be transported from one location to another while running on battery power.
- *Wearables*. The most popular wearable technology is a smart watch. A modern smart watch can receive notifications of phone calls and text messages, but it can also be used as a contactless payment system and safety monitor that calls emergency services if the watch detects the user has fallen. Figure 1-9 displays a smart watch.

Source: Alexey Boldin/Shutterstock.com

Figure 1-9 Smart watch

NOTE 12

Another popular type of wearable device is a fitness tracker. Originally designed to monitor and record physical activity, such as counting steps, they likewise have evolved into sophisticated health-monitoring devices. Modern fitness trackers can provide continuous heart rate monitoring, GPS tracking, oxygen consumption, repetition counting (for weight training), and sleep monitoring.

However, several risks are associated with mobile devices. These risks include device vulnerabilities, connection vulnerabilities, and accessing untrusted content.

Mobile Device Vulnerabilities

Mobile device vulnerabilities include physical security, limited updates, location tracking, and unauthorized recording.

Physical Security   The greatest asset of a mobile device—its portability—is also one of its greatest vulnerabilities. Mobile devices are frequently lost or stolen because, by their very nature, they are designed for use in a wide variety of locations, both public (coffee shops, hotels, and conference centers) and private (employee homes and cars). These locations are outside of the enterprise's normal protected physical perimeter of walls, security guards, and locked doors.

Unless properly protected, any data on a stolen or lost device could be retrieved by a thief. Of greater concern may be that the device itself can serve as an entry point into corporate data. On average, every employee at an organization has access to 17 million files and 1.21 million folders. The average organization has more than half a million sensitive files, and 17 percent of all sensitive files are accessible to each employee.

Limited Updates   Currently, there are two dominant OSs for mobile devices. Apple iOS, developed by Apple for its mobile devices, is a closed and proprietary architecture. Google Android is not proprietary but is open for any original equipment manufacturer (OEM) to install or even modify.

Security patches and updates for these two mobile OSs are distributed through firmware over-the-air (OTA) updates. Though these are called "firmware" OTA updates, they include modifying the device's firmware and updating the OS software. Apple commits to providing OTA updates for at least four years after the OS is released. However, OTA updates for Android OSs vary considerably. Mobile hardware devices developed and sold by Google receive Android OTA updates for three years after the device is first released. Other OEMs are required to provide OTAs for at least two years. However, after two years, many OEMs are hesitant to distribute Google updates because it limits their ability to differentiate themselves from competitors if all versions of Android start to look the same through updates. Also, because OEMs want to sell as many devices as possible, they have no financial incentive to update mobile devices that users would then continue to use indefinitely.

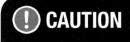 **CAUTION**   Whereas users once regularly purchased new mobile devices about every two years, that is no longer the case. Due to the high cost of some mobile devices, users are keeping their devices for longer periods of time. This can result in people using mobile devices that no longer receive OTA security updates and thus have become vulnerable.

Location Tracking   Mobile devices with Global Positioning System (GPS) capabilities typically support geolocation, or identifying the geographical location of the device. Location services are used extensively by social media, navigation systems, weather systems, and other mobile-aware applications. However, mobile devices using geolocation are at increased risk of targeted physical attacks. An attacker can determine where users with mobile devices are currently located and use that information to follow them and steal the mobile devices or inflict physical harm. In addition, attackers can craft attacks by compiling a list of people with whom the users associate and the types of activities they perform.

A related risk is GPS tagging (also called geo-tagging), which is adding geographical identification data to media such as digital photos taken on a mobile device. A user who, for example, posts a photo on a social networking site may inadvertently identify a private location to anyone who can access the photo.

Unauthorized Recording   Video cameras ("webcams") and microphones on mobile devices have been a frequent target of attackers. By infecting a device with malware, a threat actor can secretly spy on an unsuspecting victim and record conversations or videos.

Connection Vulnerabilities

Vulnerabilities in mobile device connections can also be exploited by threat actors. These vulnerabilities are summarized in Table 1-5.

Accessing Untrusted Content

Normally, users cannot download and install unapproved apps on their iOS or Android device. This is because users must access the Apple App Store or Google Play Store (or other Android store) to download an app to install on a mobile device; in fact, Apple devices can only download from the App store. However, users can circumvent the

Table 1-5 Connection vulnerabilities

Name	Description	Vulnerability
Tethering	A mobile device with an active Internet connection can be used to share that connection with other mobile devices through Bluetooth or Wi-Fi.	An unsecured mobile device may infect other tethered mobile devices or the corporate network.
USB On-the-Go (OTG)	An OTG mobile device with a USB connection can function as either a host (to which other devices may be connected such as a USB flash drive) for external media access or as a peripheral (such as a mass storage device) to another host.	Connecting a malicious flash drive that is infected with malware to a mobile device could result in an infection, just as using a device as a peripheral while connected to an infected computer could allow malware to be sent to the device.
Malicious USB cable	A USB cable could be embedded with a Wi-Fi controller that can receive commands from a nearby device to send malicious commands to the connected mobile device.	The device will recognize the cable as a human interface device (similar to a mouse or keyboard) giving the attacker enough permissions to exploit the system.
Hotspots	A hotspot is a location where users can access the Internet with a wireless signal.	Because public hotspots are beyond the control of the organization, attackers can eavesdrop on the data transmissions and view sensitive information.

installed built-in limitations on their smartphone (called *jailbreaking* on Apple iOS devices or *rooting* on Android devices) to download from an unofficial third-party app store (called *sideloading*) or even write their own custom firmware to run on their device. Because these apps have not been vetted, they may contain security vulnerabilities or even malicious code.

 **CAUTION** Jailbreaking and rooting give access to the underlying OS and file system of the mobile device with full permissions. For example, a jailbreak on an Apple iPhone will give users access to a UNIX shell that has root privileges, essentially allowing the user to do anything on the device.

Jailbreaking and rooting are not the same as carrier unlocking. Originally, almost all cell phones were connected ("locked") to a specific wireless carrier so that neither the phone nor the phone number could be transferred to another carrier. This restriction was enforced by a 2012 decision from the Library of Congress that cell phone unlocking was a violation of the Digital Millennium Copyright Act. However, in 2015, the Unlocking Consumer Choice and Wireless Competition Act, which approved carrier unlocking, was passed.

Another way untrusted content can invade mobile devices is through short message service (SMS), which are text messages of a maximum of 160 characters, or multimedia messaging service (MMS); which provides for pictures, video, or audio to be included in text messages; or rich communication services (RCS), which can convert a texting app into a live chat platform and supports pictures, videos, location, stickers, and emojis. Threat actors can send SMS messages that contain links to untrusted content or send a specially crafted MMS or RCS video that can introduce malware into the device.

Grow with Cengage Unlimited!

If you'd like more information about this topic, use your Cengage Unlimited subscription to go to the CompTIA Security+ Guide to Network Security Fundamentals, 7th edition; open Module 5; and read the section titled "Securing Mobile Devices."

If you don't have a Cengage Unlimited subscription, you can find more information at cengage.com/unlimited.

TWO RIGHTS & A WRONG

1. A field-programmable gate array (FPGA) is an integrated circuit (IC) that can be programmed by the user to carry out one or more logical operations.
2. A CAN bus is a network in a vehicle used for sending and receiving data.
3. Both Apple iOS and Google Android provide OTA updates for at least four years after the OS is released.

See Appendix C for the answer.

VM LAB You're now ready to complete the live, virtual machine labs for this module. The labs can be found in the Apply It folder in each MindTap module.

MODULE SUMMARY

- Malware, or malicious software, refers to any type of malicious software that is designed to harm or exploit a device, service, or network. It enters a computer system without the user's knowledge or consent and then performs an unwanted and harmful action. An example of malware that aids in evasion techniques is a rootkit, which is malware that can hide its presence and the presence of other malware on the computer. It does this by accessing the lower layers of the OS or even using undocumented functions.
- Several attacks are directed at vulnerabilities associated with how a program uses RAM. A storage buffer on a computer typically contains the memory location of the software program that was being executed when another function interrupted the process and is the "return address" where the computer's processor should resume once the new process has finished. A buffer overflow attack occurs when a process attempts to store data in RAM beyond the boundaries of a fixed-length storage buffer and overflows the buffer with a new address pointing to the attacker's malware code. A buffer overflow attack can occur in one of two areas of computer memory—either the stack or the heap. An integer overflow is the condition that occurs when the result of an arithmetic operation exceeds the maximum size of the integer type used to store it.
- A web server provides services that are implemented as "web applications" through software programs running on the server. A web application infrastructure is a tempting target for attackers. Many websites accept user input, and then underlying web applications use the input to create dynamic display content. Threat actors can take advantage of this user input and display in a cross-site scripting (XSS) attack. The term cross-site scripting refers to an attack using scripting that originates on one site (the web server) to impact another site (the user's computer). There are three main types of XSS attacks: Reflected XSS, Persistent XSS, and Document Object Model XSS. In addition to cross-site scripting attacks on web server applications, attacks called injections also introduce new input to exploit a vulnerability.
- One of the most common injection attacks, called Structured Query Language (SQL) injection, inserts statements to manipulate a database server. A NoSQL database that uses eXtensible Markup Language (XML) for data manipulation is also subject to an injection attack like SQL injection if the input is not sanitized. This is called an eXtensible Markup Language (XML) attack.
- A session ID is a unique value that a web server assigns a specific user for the duration of that user's visit (session). Session hijacking occurs when a threat actor takes over a user session. Different methods can be used for hijacking a session. One method involves intercepting the session ID. This can be done through XSS or a man-in-the-middle (MITM) attack in which a communication between two systems is intercepted.
- Threat actors use a variety of techniques to attack credentials and gain access to protected systems. Because passwords are the most common form of authentication credential, many of these attacks focus on attempting to compromise passwords. A password spraying attack uses one or a small number of commonly used passwords (Password1 or 123456) and then uses this same password when trying to log in to several different

user accounts. Another attack takes advantage of the very large number of stolen passwords that have been posted online by threat actors. Because users repeat their passwords on multiple accounts, attackers use these passwords in their attacks with a high probability of success. This is known as credential stuffing.

- Once initial access is gained into a system, threat actors attempt to escalate to more advanced resources that are normally protected from an application or user. This is called privilege escalation. Threat actors may use a directory traversal attack that takes advantage of a vulnerability in a web application or web server software so that a user can move from the root directory to other restricted directories. Threat actors install additional tools on the compromised systems to gain even deeper access to the network. They may also use vulnerabilities to enter commands to execute on a server known as remote code execution (RCE).

- Not all attacks rely on technology vulnerabilities; in fact, some cyberattacks use little if any technology to achieve their goals. Social engineering is a means of eliciting information (gathering data) by relying on the weaknesses of individuals. Social engineering impersonation is masquerading as a real or fictitious character and then playing out the role of that person on a victim.

- An embedded system is computer hardware and software contained within a larger system that is designed for a specific function. A growing trend is to add these capabilities to devices that have never had computing power before. Hardware and software components are available for industrious users to create their own specialized device. One of the most common hardware components is the Raspberry Pi. This is a low-cost, credit-card-sized computer motherboard. A device similar to the Raspberry Pi is the Arduino. Although the Raspberry Pi and Arduino are small motherboards, a field-programmable gate array (FPGA) is a hardware "chip" or integrated circuit (IC) that can be programmed by the user to carry out one or more logical operations. A system on a chip (SoC) combines all the required electronic circuits of the various computer components on a single IC chip. SoCs often use a real-time operating system (RTOS) that is a specifically designed OS for an SoC in an embedded or specialized system.

- Industrial control systems (ICSs) control devices locally or at remote locations by collecting, monitoring, and processing real-time data so that machines can directly control devices such as valves, pumps, and motors without the need for human intervention. Multiple ICSs are managed by a larger supervisory control and data acquisition (SCADA) system. Many SCADA systems use the network communication protocol Modbus for transmitting information between devices. Although standard Modbus has error-detection capabilities to protect against data corruption, it has no security protections against injected commands or the interception of data.

- A campus is the grounds and buildings of a school, hospital, business, or similar institution. In order to decrease the demand on personnel to monitor and manage the many elements of buildings on campus, modern campuses utilize workflow and process automation systems. These systems interconnect all the various elements so that they can be centrally and automatically monitored and controlled. One common system is a building automation system that manages building elements, which often includes a physical access control system that can ensure doors are locked and unlocked at specific times for certain individuals.

- The Internet of Things (IoT) is a global infrastructure for the information society, enabling advanced services by interconnecting (physical and virtual) things based on existing and evolving interoperable information and communication technologies. The IoT is connecting any device to the Internet for the purpose of sending and receiving data to be acted upon. IoT usually refers to devices that heretofore were not considered as computing devices connected to a data network.

- Several types of specialized systems are designed for specific applications. Automobiles have evolved into sophisticated systems with numerous sensors and electronic control units (ECUs). The controller area network (CAN) bus network is used for sending and receiving data in a vehicle. Data broadcast through CAN from one ECU reaches all other ECUs, which then accept and evaluate the data to determine if it should be received or is unnecessary and can be ignored. An unmanned aerial vehicle (UAV), or a drone, is an aircraft without a human pilot on board to control its flight. Drones can be controlled by a remote human operator, usually on the ground, or autonomously by preprogramming the onboard computers.

- Although embedded systems and specialized devices are widely used and will continue to grow exponentially, significant security issues surround these systems and devices. The lack of security in embedded systems and specialized devices can result in a wide range of attacks. Several constraints or limitations make security a challenge for these systems and specialized devices.

- Several risks are associated with mobile devices. The greatest asset of a mobile device—its portability—is also one of its greatest vulnerabilities. Mobile devices are frequently lost or stolen because, by their very nature, they are designed for use in a wide variety of locations outside of the enterprise's normal protected physical perimeter of walls, security guards, and locked doors. Unless properly protected, any data on a stolen or lost device could be retrieved by a thief.
- Security patches and updates for two mobile OSs are distributed through firmware over-the-air (OTA) updates. Apple commits to providing OTA updates for at least four years after the OS is released. However, OTA updates for Android OSs vary considerably from two to three years. Also, because OEMs want to sell as many devices as possible, they have no financial incentive to update mobile devices that users would then continue to use indefinitely.
- Mobile devices with Global Positioning System (GPS) capabilities typically support geolocation, which is identifying the geographical location of the device. Mobile devices using geolocation are at increased risk of targeted physical attacks. An attacker can determine where users with mobile devices are currently located and use that information to follow them and steal the mobile devices or inflict physical harm. Video cameras ("webcams") and microphones on mobile devices have been a frequent target of attackers. By infecting a device with malware, a threat actor can secretly spy on an unsuspecting victim and record conversations or videos. Vulnerabilities in mobile device connections can also be exploited by threat actors.
- Normally users cannot download and install unapproved apps on their iOS or Android device. This is because users must access the Apple App Store or Google Play Store (or other Android store) to download an app to install on a mobile device; in fact, Apple devices can only download from the App store. However, users can circumvent the installed built-in limitations on their smartphone (called jailbreaking on Apple iOS devices or rooting on Android devices) to download from an unofficial third-party app store (called sideloading) or even write their own custom firmware to run on their device. Because these apps have not been vetted, they may contain security vulnerabilities or even malicious code.

Key Terms

buffer overflow attack
building automation system
controller area network (CAN) bus
credential stuffing
cross-site scripting (XSS)
directory traversal
Document Object Model XSS
drone
embedded system
eXtensible Markup Language
  (XML) attack
field-programmable gate array
  (FPGA)

heap overflow
impersonation
industrial control system (ICS)
integer overflow attack
Internet of Things (IoT)
man-in-the-middle (MITM)
Modbus
password spraying attack
Persistent XSS
physical access control
privilege escalation
real-time operating system
  (RTOS)

Reflected XSS
remote code execution (RCE)
rootkit
session hijacking
Structured Query Language (SQL)
  injection
supervisory control and data
  acquisition (SCADA)
system on a chip (SoC)
workflow and process automation
  systems

Review Questions

1. Which of the following is FALSE about rootkits?
   a. A rootkit is malware that can hide the presence of other malware.
   b. Rootkits continue to be used extensively, and their usage has not diminished.
   c. Rootkits can be used to hide their own presence.
   d. Rootkits cannot be detected by either an OS or common antimalware scanning software.

2. What is the goal of a buffer overflow attack?
   a. To change the address in the buffer to the attacker's malware code
   b. To cause the computer to function erratically
   c. To steal data stored in RAM
   d. To link to an existing rootkit

3. Which area of computer memory is dynamic memory for the programmer to allocate as necessary?
   a. Text
   b. Stack
   c. Heap
   d. Data

4. Jan is explaining to his colleague the reasons why a web application infrastructure is a tempting target for attackers. Which of the following is NOT a reason Jan would give?
   a. A successful compromise could impact all web users who access the web server.
   b. An attack could provide a pathway into the enterprise's network infrastructure.
   c. An attack on a web application infrastructure is considered the easiest attack to create.
   d. The multiple elements in a web application infrastructure provide for a range of vulnerabilities that can be used as different attack vectors.

5. Which of the following is FALSE about a cross-site scripting (XSS) attack?
   a. The underlying web application that accepts the malicious code becomes the vehicle to deliver the malicious script to every user's browser when he or she accesses that site.
   b. An attacker attempts to execute malicious scripts in the victim's web browser by directly injecting it into the user's web browser.
   c. XSS is essentially a client-side code injection attack using a web application.
   d. The term cross-site scripting refers to an attack using scripting that originates on one site (the web server) to impact another site (the user's computer).

6. Ricardo is reviewing the different types of XSS attacks. Which attack only impacts the user who entered the text on the website?
   a. Reflected XSS
   b. Persistent XSS
   c. Document Object Model XSS
   d. Universal XSS

7. What is the goal of an SQL injection attack?
   a. To corrupt data in the database
   b. To manipulate a NoSQL database
   c. To extract data from a database
   d. To inject malware that will infect the web browsers of subsequent users

8. Bette is researching how a session hijacking attack could occur. Which of the following would she NOT find as a means for the attack to occur?
   a. MITM
   b. XSS
   c. Guessing the session ID
   d. MVFL

9. Which of the following is FALSE about a password spraying attack?
   a. It takes one or a small number of commonly used passwords in attempts to break into an account.
   b. Because it is spread across many different accounts, it is much less likely to raise any alarms.
   c. It is considered as the optimal means for breaking into accounts.
   d. It is a type of targeted guessing.

10. Why is credential stuffing effective?
    a. Because users repeat their passwords on multiple accounts
    b. Because it can circumvent all known password security protections
    c. Because it is the fastest known password cracking attack
    d. Because it is the oldest and most reliable attack on passwords

11. What is the goal of a directory traversal attack?
    a. It has no goal other than to silently look through files stored on a file server.
    b. Its goal is to move from the root directory to other restricted directories.
    c. Its goal is to identify a vulnerability in a server or endpoint so that access can be gained into a network.
    d. Its goal is to pivot to another server.

12. What is pretexting?
    a. Sending text messages to selected victims
    b. Obtaining private information
    c. Preparing to enter a network through a RCE vulnerability
    d. Moving laterally before entering a vulnerable endpoint

13. Which type of OS is found on an embedded system?
    a. RSTS
    b. SoC
    c. RTOS
    d. XRXS

14. Aiko has been asked by her friend if she should download and install an app that allows her to circumvent the built-in limitations on her Android smartphone. What is this called?
    a. Jailbreaking
    b. Side-caring
    c. Rooting
    d. Pivoting

15. Aiya wants a new notebook computer. She has asked a technician about a model that has USB OTG. Which of the following would the technician NOT tell Aiya about USB OTG?
    a. A device connected via USB OTG can function as a peripheral for external media access.
    b. A device connected via USB OTG can function as a host.
    c. Connecting a mobile device to an infected computer using USB OTG could allow malware to be sent to that device.
    d. USB OTG is only available for connecting Android devices to a subnotebook.

16. The organization for which Cho works has just purchased a manufacturing plant that has many machines using Modbus. Cho has been asked to research Modbus. Which of the following will Cho NOT find regarding Modbus?
    a. Many SCADA systems use Modbus.
    b. The original version of Modbus used serial ports.
    c. A later variation to Modbus incorporated the TCP/IP protocol.
    d. Modbus is robust security.

17. What is the network used in vehicles for communications?
    a. CAN
    b. ECU
    c. EDU
    d. M-BUS

18. Which of the following is NOT a security constraint for embedded systems and specialized devices?
    a. Power
    b. Compute
    c. Cost
    d. Patches

19. Which of the following is the greatest asset but also a security vulnerability of a mobile device?
    a. Low cost
    b. Portability
    c. Cameras
    d. Small screen

20. What is geo-tagging?
    a. Restricting where an app functions based on its location.
    b. Adding geographical identification data to media.
    c. Tracking a victim who is wearing a GPS-enabled wearable device.
    d. Using the GPS feature of a smartphone.

Case Projects

Case Project 1-1: Rootkits

Research how rootkits can evade detection from an OS or antimalware software. What techniques does it use to hide itself? How can it hide other malware? Besides hiding malware on a hard drive, where are other locations that rootkits can hide malware? Write a one-page paper on your research.

Case Project 1-2: Heap Overflow

Research heap overflows. How do they work? How can they be prevented? How common is this type of attack? Write a one-page paper on your research. Include a drawing of how RAM looks before and after a heap overflow attack.

Case Project 1-3: Document Object Model XSS

Search the Internet for information on Document Object Model XSS. What is a Document Object Model (DOM)? Where are DOMs found? How do threat attacks attempt to compromise them? How can they be used in an XSS attack? What is the defense against them? Write a one-page paper on your research.

Case Project 1-4: Real-Time Operating System (RTOS)

What features are found in a real-time operating system? How is it specifically designed for an SoC? What are its advantages? What are its disadvantages? Compare the features of three RTOSs, and create a table listing each along with its features. Write a one-page paper on your research.

Case Project 1-5: On the Job

Suppose you work for a company that has just hired a new senior vice president. After reviewing the budgets of all departments, the new VP went on record saying that the amount of money spent on cybersecurity is too large in proportion to the size of the company. She recommends an immediate 23 percent reduction in the cybersecurity budget. She has decided on this amount after informal conversations with other companies that have about the same number of employees. However, these other companies perform completely different functions: one company is in manufacturing while the other is a service organization, neither of which is the same as your company. The new VP says she will retract her recommendation if someone can prove that there have been no significant attacks due to the money spent on cyber defenses and not just because your company is unattractive to threat actors. Create a one-page memo to the senior vice president that explains your views on cybersecurity spending.

References

1. "McAfee Labs Threats Report," Jul. 2020, accessed Nov. 3, 2020, www.mcafee.com/enterprise/en-us/assets/reports/rp-quarterly-threats-july-2020.pdf.
2. "Cybercrime to Cost the World $10.5 Trillion Annually by 2025," *Cybersecurity Ventures*, accessed Dec. 30, 2020, www.globenewswire.com/news-release/2020/11/18/2129432/0/en/Cybercrime-To-Cost-The-World-10-5-Trillion-Annually-By-2025.html#:~:text=18%2C%202020%20(GLOBE%20NEWSWIRE),%243%20trillion%20USD%20in%202015.
3. Crawley, Kim, "Cybersecurity Budgets Explained: How Much Do Companies Spend on Cybersecurity?" *AT&T* Cybersecurity, May 5, 2020, accessed Nov. 3, 2020, https://cybersecurity.att.com/blogs/security-essentials/how-to-justify-your-cybersecurity-budget.
4. Moynahan, Matthew, "How Not to Waste a Trillion Dollars on Cybersecurity," *Forbes*, Nov. 9, 2018, accessed Apr. 21, 2019, www.forbes.com/sites/forbestechcouncil/2018/11/09/how-not-to-waste-a-trillion-dollars-on-cybersecurity/#75f16ed0df9a.
5. "Overview of the Internet of Things, Series Y: Global Information Infrastructure, Internet Protocol Aspects and Next-Generation Networks—Next Generation Networks—Frameworks and Functional Architecture Models," Jun. 2012, Retrieved May 18, 2017, www.itu.int/rec/T-REC-Y.2060-201206-I.
6. "Forecast Number of IoT Connected Objects Worldwide from 2018 to 2025, by Type," Statista, retrieved May 28, 2020, www.statista.com/statistics/976079/number-of-iot-connected-objects-worldwide-by-type/.
7. "VNI Mobile Forecast Highlights Tool," Cisco, accessed Nov. 6, 2020, www.cisco.com/c/m/en_us/solutions/service-provider/forecast-highlights-mobile.html.

UTILIZING THREAT DATA AND INTELLIGENCE

After completing this module, you should be able to do the following:

1 Identify different threat actors

2 Describe threat intelligence sources

3 Define frameworks and research sources

4 Explain modeling methodologies

Cybersecurity Today

Cybercrime is universally seen as relentless, undiminished, and unlikely to stop because it is just too easy and rewarding. One reason is that the chances of being caught and punished are almost negligible. Cybercriminals who operate in foreign nations can attack users and governments around the world with impunity because they know that their own government agencies reject any attempts to cooperate with law enforcement agencies in the victim's country and openly laugh at any attempts to extradite these criminals for prosecution. Often foreign governments take this approach to show open contempt against another nation or because the government itself is funding and supporting these attacks.

Another reason for unrestrained global cybercrime is that there has been a lack of a united global effort against it. A single nation in which the victims reside ("victim nation") must attempt to negotiate with the "attacking nation" for justice. Most attacking nations simply ignore these pleas, as they face few repercussions. If the victim nation breaks off diplomatic relations with the attacking nation or stops exporting its goods to them, the attacking nation will simply turn to another nation to import those same goods. This lack of unity among nations against cybercrime is one of the recognized reasons why cybercrime runs unabated.

However, two watershed events in recent years may have finally turned the tide against international attackers hiding behind foreign attacking nations. First, foreign governments, most notably Russia, have been identified as meddling in the democratic election processes of other nations. The United States, the Netherlands, Ukraine, and France have all been victims of foreign cyberattacks and operations to affect political campaigns, candidates, and open political discourse. Using sophisticated social media efforts as well as more traditional cybersecurity attacks on voter rolls and state electoral systems, these incidents have been designed as a concerted campaign to undermine democracy and weaken trust in the democratic process and institutions. These attacks have been directed at perceived opponents and other foreign governments to move support toward candidates who are more sympathetic to Russian interests.

The second watershed event was cyberattacks used to disrupt healthcare organizations fighting the COVID-19 pandemic. Security researchers have detected cyberattacks in Canada, France, India, South Korea, and the United States targeting prominent pharmaceutical companies and vaccine researchers directly involved in creating vaccines and treatments.

Threat actors have also attacked individual hospitals, the hospital system in Paris, the computer systems of Spain's hospitals, hospitals in Thailand, medical clinics in Texas, a healthcare agency in Illinois, and even international bodies such as the World Health Organization (WHO). These attacks are alleged to be the efforts of a group known as Strontium, an actor originating from Russia, and two actors—Zinc and Cerium—from North Korea.

These two watershed events have galvanized countries to take a unified stand against foreign nation-state actors. Knowing that many nations banding together can have much more influence than a single victim nation, several international efforts have recently been initiated as multi-stakeholder coalitions involving countries around the world to actively combat the attacks.

In 2019, the United Nations established a Group of Governmental Experts (GGE) on advancing responsible state behavior in cyberspace for cybersecurity. In 2020, three major efforts were begun. More than 65 healthcare-related organizations joined the Paris Call for Trust and Security in Cyberspace. These include pharmaceutical organizations working on vaccines, hospitals, and government health institutes. The Paris Call remains the largest multi-stakeholder coalition addressing these issues, and its first principle is the prevention of malicious cyber activities that threaten indiscriminate or systemic harm to people and critical infrastructures. In May 2020, a group of 36 of the world's most prominent international law experts, in what has become known as the Oxford Process, issued a statement making it clear that international law protects medical facilities at all times. In August of the same year, the Oxford Process issued a second statement emphasizing that organizations that research, manufacture, and distribute COVID-19 vaccines are also protected. Finally, the CyberPeace Institute and International Committee of the Red Cross led an effort by 40 international leaders calling on governments to stop the attacks on healthcare.

While the overall impact of these initiatives remains to be seen, one thing is clear. For the first time, nations from around the world are banding together to address cybersecurity threats in new ways.

There are no major sporting events today in which two teams playing for the championship do not know in advance who their opponent is. This is because enabling both teams to know their opponent in advance gives them time to study the strengths and weaknesses of the opposition and then craft a plan that leads to victory.

Likewise, in the competition known as cybersecurity, it is important to know both who the attackers are and how they attack. Because attacks continually evolve, it is also important to take advantage of all available threat intelligence information to know the very latest types of attacks and how to defend against them. With that information at hand, security can become more effective and efficient.

In this module, you will explore using threat data and intelligence. First, you will examine today's threat actors and their threats. You will then look at threat data and intelligence. Next, you will explore frameworks and threat research sources and, finally, study different modeling methodologies.

THREAT ACTORS AND THEIR THREATS

 **CERTIFICATION**

1.1 Explain the importance of threat data and intelligence.

"Know your enemy" is an oft-quoted statement, with applications ranging from military to sports. Knowing the cybersecurity attackers and their attacks is likewise important in creating a strong cyberdefense.

NOTE 1

The famous Chinese military strategist Sun Tzu said more than 1,500 years ago in *The Art of War*, "If you know the enemy and know yourself, you need not fear the result of a hundred battles. If you know yourself but not the enemy, for every victory gained you will also suffer a defeat. If you know neither the enemy nor yourself, you will succumb in every battle."

Who Are the Threat Actors?

In cybersecurity, a threat actor is a term used to describe individuals or entities who are responsible for cyber incidents against enterprises, governments, and users. The generic term *attacker* is also commonly used, as is *malicious actor*. In the past, the generic term *hacker* referred to a person who used advanced computer skills to attack computers. Yet because that title often carried with it a negative connotation, it was qualified in an attempt to distinguish between different types of hackers. The different types of hackers are summarized in Table 2-1.

Table 2-1   Types of hackers

Hacker type	Description
Black hat hackers	Threat actors who violate computer security for personal gain (such as to steal credit card numbers) or to inflict malicious damage (corrupt a hard drive)
White hat hackers	Also known as ethical attackers, they attempt to probe a system (with an organization's permission) for weaknesses and then privately provide that information back to the organization
Gray hat hackers	Attackers who attempt to break into a computer system without the organization's permission (an illegal activity) but not for their own advantage; instead, they publicly disclose the attack to shame the organization into taking action

However, these broad categories of hackers did not accurately reflect the differences among threat actors. The attributes, or characteristic features, of today's different groups of threat actors can vary widely. While some groups have a high level of capability and a massive network of resources, others are "lone wolves" who know how to acquire easy-to-use software like the one shown in Figure 2-1 to perform high-level attacks or know

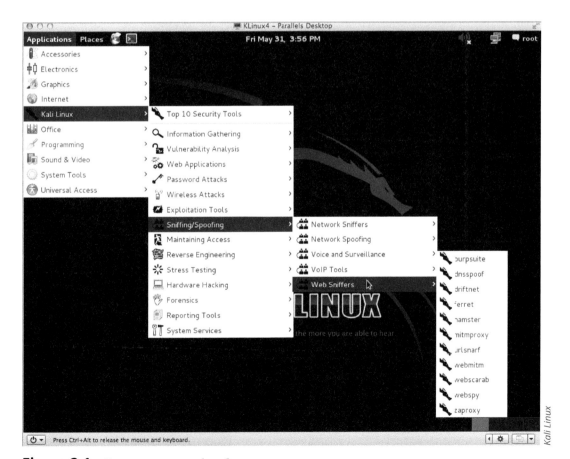

Figure 2-1   Easy-to-use attack software

where to purchase commodity malware, which is malware sold by other threat actors that can be customized for specific attacks. Whereas some threat actors work within the enterprise (internal), others are strictly from outside the organization (external). Finally, the intent or motivation—that is, the "why" behind the attacks—can vary widely.

Despite these differences, one element is common to all threat actors: they pose a serious threat to security. Threat actors who may not be as well educated in cyberattacks or may lack the "deep pockets" of funding sources nevertheless are a real threat. Many attackers have even modeled their work after modern economic theories, such as finding the optimum "price point" in which victims will pay a ransom. Some enterprising attackers who sell their commodity malware to other attackers now design these attack tools as a suite that receive regular updates and enhancements. It is a serious mistake to underestimate *any* modern threat actors.

Today threat actors are classified into distinct categories that address their capabilities, resources, and motivations. These include hactivists, nation-state actors, insider threats, and others.

Hactivists

A group that is strongly motivated by ideology (for the sake of their principles or beliefs) is hactivists (a combination of the words *hack* and *activism*). Most hactivists do not explicitly call themselves "hacktivists," but the term is commonly used by security researchers and journalists to distinguish them from other types of threat actors.

In the past, the types of attacks by hactivists usually involved defacing websites. They did so as a means of making a political statement (one hactivist group changed the website of the U.S. Department of Justice to read *Department of Injustice*) or performing retaliation (hactivists have disabled a bank's website because that bank stopped accepting online payments deposited into accounts belonging to groups supported by hactivists).

However, today most hactivists work through disinformation campaigns by spreading fake news and supporting conspiracy theories. As an example, hactivists were active during the coronavirus disease (COVID-19) pandemic of 2020. One large group of what were considered far-right neo-Nazi hactivists embarked on a months-long disinformation campaign designed to weaponize the pandemic by questioning scientific evidence and research. In another instance, thousands of breached email addresses and passwords from U.S. and global health organizations—including the U.S. National Institutes of Health, Centers for Disease Control and Prevention, and the WHO—were distributed on social media by these groups (called *doxing*). The intent was to encourage others to use this information to harass and distract the health organizations.

Nation-State Actors

Governments are increasingly employing their own state-sponsored attackers for launching cyberattacks against their foes. They are known as nation-state actors. Their foes may be foreign governments or even their own citizens that the government considers hostile or threatening. A growing number of attacks from state actors are directed toward businesses in foreign countries with the goal of causing financial harm or damage to the enterprise's reputation.

Many security researchers believe that nation-state actors might be the deadliest of any threat actors. When money motivates a threat actor, but the target's defenses are too strong, the attacker simply moves onto another promising target with less effective defenses. With nation-state actors, however, the target is very specific, and the attackers keep working until they are successful. These state-sponsored attackers are highly skilled and have enough government resources to breach almost any security defense.

Insiders

Another serious threat to an enterprise comes from its own employees, contractors, and business partners, called *insiders*, who pose an insider threat of manipulating data from the position of a trusted employee. The threats that come from insiders can be either intentional or unintentional.

Intentional Insiders   There are several reasons that insiders may intentionally steal or alter data that belongs to their organization. A healthcare worker, for example, who is disgruntled about being passed over for a promotion, might illegally gather health records on celebrities and sell them to the media. A securities trader who loses billions of dollars on bad stock bets could use knowledge of the bank's computer security system to conceal the losses through fake transactions. These attacks by intentional insiders are harder to recognize than other types of attacks because they come from within the enterprise, while defensive tools are usually focused on outside attackers.

Intentional insider attacks can be costlier than attacks from the outside. Six out of ten enterprises reported being a victim of at least one insider attack during 2019. The focus of these insiders were intellectual property (IP) theft (43 percent), sabotage (41 percent), and espionage (32 percent).[1] Because most IP thefts occur within 30 days of an employee resigning, it is thought that these insiders believe that either the IP belongs to them instead of the enterprise or that they were not properly compensated for their work behind the IP. In recent years, government insiders have stolen large volumes of sensitive information and then published it to alert its citizens of clandestine governmental actions.

Unintentional Insiders   Attacks are often the result of unintentional insiders. Although they may not have malicious intent, due to their action (or inaction), unintentional insiders can unwittingly cause harm (or increase the probability of serious future harm) to the organization's resources and assets. The reasons range from carelessness, too much multitasking, and low situational awareness. Consider the following actual events:

- HSBC, one of the largest banking and financial services institutions in the world, had to apologize in 2017 after an insider employee unintentionally emailed personal information about its customers to various account holders. The personal information contained names, email addresses, countries of residence, the name of the customers' relationship manager, and HSBC customer identification numbers. This error follows earlier incidents by HSBC of sending the details of 1,917 pension scheme members—including addresses, dates of birth, and national insurance numbers—and sending the details of 180,000 policyholders.
- Wells Fargo, when subpoenaed by an attorney for information related to a lawsuit, should have sent a few emails and selected documents. However, an insider unintentionally sent 1.4 gigabytes of confidential information about 50,000 of the bank's wealthiest clients. The information included customers' names and Social Security numbers along with financial details such as the size of their investment portfolios and the fees the bank charged them.

NOTE 2

The response by Wells Fargo to this incident was, "This was the unfortunate result of an unintentional human error involving a spreadsheet."

Data supports evidence of the harm that is caused by unintentional insiders. Almost two out of every three organizations found that a careless employee or contractor was the root cause of most insider incidents. Misdelivery, or sending sensitive information to a recipient who is not authorized to receive it, is the fourth most frequent action that results in data breaches across all businesses and was the cause of 35 percent of all data breaches in 2019.[2]

NOTE 3

Insider carelessness often involves the employee not considering the consequences of an action. For example, more than half of all employees admit to allowing a friend or family member to use employee-issued technology equipment while at home, which could expose access to highly sensitive data such as the organization's proprietary information or private customer data.

Other Threat Actors

In addition, there are other categories of threat actors. These are summarized in Table 2-2.

Table 2-2 Descriptions of other threat actors

Threat actor	Description	Explanation
Competitors	Launch attack against an opponent's system to steal classified information.	Competitors may steal new product research or a list of current customers to gain a competitive advantage.
Brokers	Sell their knowledge of a weakness to other attackers or governments.	Individuals who uncover weaknesses do not report it to the software vendor but instead sell them to the highest bidder, who is willing to pay a high price for the unknown weaknesses.
Cyberterrorists	Attack a nation's network and computer infrastructure to cause disruption and panic among citizens.	Targets may include a small group of computers or networks that can affect the largest number of users, such as the computers that control the electrical power grid of a state or region.
Organized crime	Moving from traditional criminal activities to more rewarding and less risky online attacks.	Organized criminal syndicates are usually run by a small number of experienced online criminal networks who do not commit crimes themselves but act as entrepreneurs.
Shadow IT	Employees become frustrated with the slow pace of acquiring technology, so they purchase and install their own equipment or resources in violation of company policies.	Installing personal equipment, unauthorized software, or using external cloud resources can create a weakness or expose sensitive corporate data.

Classifying Threats

At a U.S. Department of Defense (DoD) news briefing in 2002, the Secretary of Defense Donald Rumsfeld was asked a question regarding the lack of evidence linking a foreign government with the supply of weapons of mass destruction to terrorist groups. Secretary Rumsfeld responded:

> *Reports that say that something hasn't happened are always interesting to me, because as we know, there are known knowns; there are things we know we know. We also know there are known unknowns; that is to say, we know there are some things we do not know. But there are also unknown unknowns— the ones we don't know we don't know. And if one looks throughout the history of our country and other free countries, it is the latter category that tend to be the difficult ones.*[3]

Secretary Rumsfeld's statement is considered the first time the general public was exposed to the concept of *known knowns*, *known unknowns*, and *unknown unknowns*. However, national security and intelligence professionals had for several years used a similar approach based on an analysis technique created in the mid-1950s. This technique was developed to help individuals understand their relationship with others and themselves. The technique is called the *Johari window* and is shown in Figure 2-2.

NOTE 4

At the time that Secretary Rumsfeld made his comments, he was criticized because some individuals felt that the comments did not make sense and were an unnecessarily complex way of explaining the issues around security intelligence. However, as time passed, his observation was considered insightful.

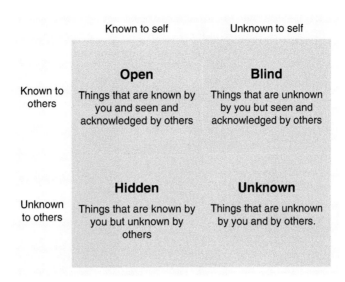

Figure 2-2   Johari window

Today cybersecurity professionals have adopted the Johari window as one means of classifying cybersecurity threats, particularly **known threats vs. unknown threats**, or classifying threats by comparing the knowledge of the threat actor to security personnel. Figure 2-3 applies the Johari window to these cybersecurity threats.

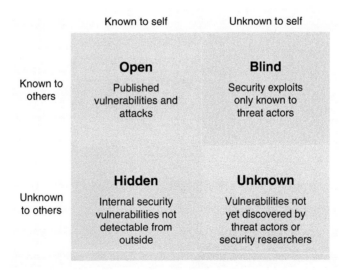

Figure 2-3   Johari window cybersecurity threats

The four categories of these threats are as follows:

- *Known knowns.* These are threats that both threat actors and security personnel are aware of, such as a virus that has been active for several years. The defense against these threats is established technologies and devices such as antivirus solutions and firewalls.
- *Known unknowns.* Known unknowns refer to vulnerabilities that the organization is aware of in their systems but outside threat actors have not discovered. A defense against these are actions taken by the organization to address the vulnerability.

- *Unknown knowns*. These are threats that are known to threat actors but not to security professionals. Often called zero-day attacks, these are unknown vulnerabilities and give victims no time (*zero days*) to prepare or defend against the attacks. There is no defense strategy against unknown knowns.
- *Unknown unknowns*. Unknown unknowns are security threats that currently are hidden from both threat actors as well as security professionals. There is no indication when—or if—they will be found. Like unknown knowns, there is no specific defense against these.

NOTE 5

Although the Johari window is a common means of classifying threats, there are others as well.

A particularly ominous threat that has emerged in recent years must also be classified. Nation-state actors are known for being well-resourced and highly trained attackers. They often are involved in multiyear intrusion campaigns targeting very sensitive economic, proprietary, or national security information. These threat actors have created a new class of attacks called advanced persistent threats (APTs). They use innovative attack tools (*advanced*), and once a system is infected, they silently extract data over an extended period of time (*persistent*). APTs are most commonly associated with nation-state actors.

TWO RIGHTS & A WRONG

1. Hactivists are responsible for the class of attacks called advanced persistent threats.
2. Hactivists are strongly motivated by ideology.
3. Brokers sell their knowledge of a weakness to other attackers or a government.

See Appendix C for the answer.

THREAT DATA AND INTELLIGENCE

✓ CERTIFICATION

1.1 Explain the importance of threat data and intelligence.

1.2 Given a scenario, utilize threat intelligence to support organizational security.

Threat data and intelligence has become a vital source today for organizations attempting to defend against emerging attacks. Using threat data and intelligence involves understanding what constitutes threat data and intelligence, knowing the intelligence cycle, and understanding the categories and sources of threat intelligence.

What Is Threat Data and Intelligence?

At one time, organizations were reluctant to share information about attacks on their networks and endpoints, often because they were concerned about "bad publicity" that might arise from the disclosure. Not sharing details about threats (threat data and intelligence) only crippled cybersecurity defenses. Organizations had data and intelligence on threats that affected only that organization, which resulted in a limited volume of details. In addition, they could not address emerging or zero-day attacks.

Today, however, that is no longer the case. Organizations are pooling their experiences and knowledge gained about the latest attacks with the broader security community. Sharing this type of information has become an important aid to help other organizations shore up their defenses.

An example of the type of information that is shared is the evidence of an attack. Most organizations monitor their networking environment to determine what normally occurs. This data is then used to create a database of *key risk indicators (KRIs)*. A KRI is a metric of the upper and lower bounds of specific indicators of normal network activity. These indicators may include the total network logs per second, the number of failed remote logins, network bandwidth, and outbound email traffic. When a KRI exceeds its normal bounds, it could be (but is not always) evidence of an indicator of compromise (IoC). An IoC shows that a malicious activity is occurring but is still in the early stages of an attack.

Making IoC information available to others can prove to be of high value, as it may indicate a common attack that other organizations may also be experiencing or will soon experience. This information aids others in their predictive analysis or discovering an attack before it occurs.

NOTE 6

Like radar that shows the enemy approaching, predictive analysis helps determine when and where attacks may occur.

In addition to identifying an imminent attack by sharing IoCs, threat intelligence sharing can also aid in other areas such as incident response (handling a cyberattack or data breach), vulnerability management (identifying and addressing security vulnerabilities), risk management (controlling threats to assets), security engineering (building systems to resist attacks), and detection and monitoring (uncovering and managing vulnerabilities).

The Intelligence Cycle

What is the difference between *data, information,* and *knowledge*? Although these terms are often used synonymously, they vary significantly. Table 2-3 provides definitions and examples that illustrate the differences between these terms.

Table 2-3 Differences between data, information, and knowledge

Element	Definition	Example
Data	Discrete, objective facts	141, 700, A, 701, B
Information	Organized data that has been processed so it has meaning and value	Course 141-700 is offered in the A-Term
Knowledge	Expert skills and experience applied to information in order to make informed decisions	Enrollment in CIS 141/700 A-Term has increased over CIS 141/701 in the B-Term

NOTE 7

Another element that could be added is *wisdom*, which may be defined as administering knowledge.

When a cyber incident occurs, the data about it can be captured, such as the type of attack, the target, the time of day it occurred, and the IP address of the source. However, the data is only discrete facts and, in this form, has limited value. The data needs to be "processed" to become useful information. The process through which raw cybersecurity data becomes useful threat intelligence information can be illustrated by the intelligence cycle, also called the *threat intelligence lifecycle*. Figure 2-4 illustrates an intelligence cycle. This cycle is considered a multi-step cyclical process: more than one step is involved, and the process continues to cycle with no endpoint.

 **CAUTION** A multitude of intelligence cycles relate to cybersecurity, each with any number of steps using different terminology. The intelligence cycle presented here is the core of most intelligence cycles.

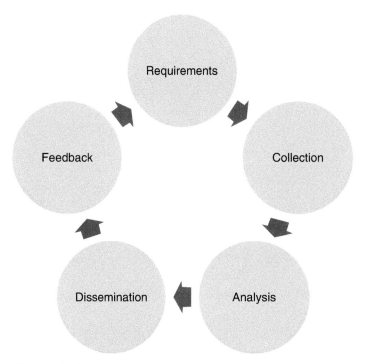

Figure 2-4   Intelligence cycle

The steps of the intelligence cycle are as follows:

- *Requirements*. The **requirements** phase of the intelligence cycle sets the high-level goals for the threat intelligence program. This involves determining the information assets and business processes that need to be protected, the potential impacts of losing those assets or interrupting those processes, and the priorities of what order to provide protection. This phase helps determine the types of threat intelligence that are needed to protect assets and respond to threats. For example, if a goal is to understand likely threat actors, this could be framed as a question such as, "Which actors on underground forums are actively soliciting data concerning our organization?"

- *Collection*. **Collection** is the process of gathering information to address the most important intelligence requirements. Numerous sources provide this threat information. An organization can gather log information and metadata from internal networks and security devices by conducting targeted interviews with knowledgeable security sources, scanning security news and blogs, harvesting information from user forums, scraping attacker data posted on public sites (called "pastes"), and even infiltrating threat actor closed sources. An increasing number of organizations are subscribing to threat data feeds from industry organizations and cybersecurity vendors for threat intelligence.

- *Analysis*. The data gathered at the collection stage typically will be a combination of finished information (such as intelligence reports from cybersecurity experts and vendors) along with raw data (like malware signatures or pasted leaked credentials). This data must be processed into a format usable by the organization in the **analysis** phase. Different collection methods often require different means of processing. For example, an analysis may involve extracting IP addresses from a security vendor's report or extracting indicators from an email before enriching them with other information.

- *Dissemination*. The results of the analysis phase will drive decisions about how this information should be acted upon and distributed to where it needs to go (**dissemination**). Typical decisions involve whether to investigate a potential threat, what actions to take immediately to stop an attack (such as communicating with endpoint protection tools for automated blocking), how to strengthen security controls, or how much investment in additional security resources may be needed. These decisions then drive how the threat intelligence is disseminated.

NOTE 8

Most organizations have multiple security-related teams that need threat intelligence. The process of dissemination should be determined in advance by asking the teams how best to provide the information to them. There are several questions that could be asked: What threat intelligence do you need? How can external information support your activities? How should the intelligence be presented to make it easily understandable and actionable for you? How often should we provide updates and other information? Through what media should the intelligence be disseminated?

- *Feedback.* The final phase is feedback regarding how effective the threat intelligence was. Feedback can be viewed as answering the basic question, "What did we do right, and what did we do wrong?" The answers then become input back into the requirements phase to improve the overall intelligence cycle.

Categories of Threat Intelligence Sources

There are two broad categories of threat intelligence sources. These are open source and closed source intelligence.

Open Source Intelligence

Threat intelligence that is freely available, often called open source intelligence (OSINT), has become a vital resource. The most basic level of OSINT typically consists of public lists of threat indicators that anyone can download. This type of threat intelligence, sometimes called "abuse feeds" and "blacklists," is curated by one or more security professionals as a service (or sometimes just as a hobby) to the larger security community. Users of these public lists are also encouraged to upload their own malware samples to be analyzed.

A more formalized level of OSINT sharing is conducted through trusted communities where official membership is required and the members exchange their own threat information. This information is often collected and then disseminated through public information sharing centers. A typical sharing center is the U.S. Department of Homeland Security (DHS) Cyber Information Sharing and Collaboration Program (CISCP). The CISCP "enables actionable, relevant, and timely unclassified information exchange through trusted public-private partnerships across all critical infrastructure sectors." With the DHS serving as the coordinator, the CISCP enables its members (called "partners") to not only share threat and vulnerability information but also take advantage of the DHS's cyber resources. Some of the CISCP services include the following:

- *Analyst-to-analyst technical exchanges.* Partners can share and receive information on the tactics used by threat actors and emerging trends.
- *CISCP analytical products.* A portal can be accessed through which partners can receive analysis of products and threats.
- *Cross-industry orchestration.* Partners can share lessons learned and their expertise with peers across common sectors.
- *Digital malware analysis.* Suspected malware can be submitted to be analyzed and then generate malware analysis reports to mitigate threats and attack vectors.

NOTE 9

The CISCP program is free to join and use. Those interested must agree to a Cyber Information Sharing and Collaboration Agreement (CISCA), which enables DHS and its partners to exchange anonymized information. Once partners sign the agreement, DHS coordinates an on-boarding session to customize how DHS and the organization can exchange information.

The final level of OSINT is composed of similar organizations that share information that may be unique to their specific industry. These include the areas of healthcare, financial services, aviation, government, and critical infrastructure. The organizations that share OSINT are called information sharing and analysis communities.

One challenge of OSINT is that because the data comes from a variety of sources, it may be in a variety of formats. To overcome this obstacle, OpenIoC (Open Indicators of Compromise) was developed as an open framework for sharing OSINT in a machine-readable format. The data is formatted in the eXtensible Markup Language (XML) and comes with 500 predefined base indicators, which can be easily customized for adding intelligence. An example of an OpenIoC feed is shown in Figure 2-5.

```
<OpenIOC xmlns:xsd="http://www.w3.org/2001/XMLSchema" xmlns:xsi="http://www.w3.org/200
  <metadata>
    <short_description>LAZARUS GROUP CAMPAGN TARGETNG THE CRYPTOCURRENCY VERTICAL</sho
    <description>LAZARUS GROUP CAMPAGN TARGETING THE CRYPTOCURRENCY VERTICAL</descripti
    <keywords/>
    <authored_by>343XCR-Guy OTX</authored_by>
    <authored_date>2020-09-28T18:31:07</authored_date>
    <links>
      <link rel="https://labs.f-secure.com/assets/BlogFiles/f-secureLABS-tlp-white-laz;
      <link rel="https://otx.alienvault.com/pulse/5f44efcd13c6da6b9fd3d3f7" href="http:
    </links>
  </metadata>
  <criteria>
    <Indicator id="86fd3c88-d4d8-4002-a299-4e46da7a0ccb" operator="OR">
      <IndicatorItem id="1f5c5543-679d-4e66-a658-d88b4199250c" condition="contains" pr
        <Context document="DnsEntryItem" search="DnsEntryItem/Host" type="mir"/>
        <Content type="string">googledrive.download</Content>
      </IndicatorItem>
      <IndicatorItem id="ab5a5446-e685-4b51-b301-6d02b2e570c4" condition="contains" pr
        <Context document="DnsEntryItem" search="DnsEntryItem/Host" type="mir"/>
        <Content type="string">antlercap.com</Content>
      </IndicatorItem>
```

Figure 2-5 OpenIoC example

However, several concerns surround public information sharing centers. Is the intelligence applicable and helpful (**relevancy**) and is the data correct (**accuracy**) are questions that are often raised. In addition, the privacy of shared information and the timeliness of the shared information are concerns.

Privacy Another concern about using public information sharing centers is that of privacy. An organization that is the victim of an attack must be careful that any proprietary or sensitive information is not shared when providing IoCs and attack details. As a safeguard, most public information sharing centers have protections in place to prevent the disclosure of protected information. For example, Table 2-4 lists the privacy protections of the CISCP.

Table 2-4 CISCP privacy protections

Protection	Explanation	Example
Cybersecurity Information Sharing Act (CISA)	CISA is a federal law passed in 2015 that provides authority for cybersecurity information sharing between the private sector, state and local governments, and the federal government.	CISA requires a non-federal entity to remove any information from a cyber threat indicator that it knows at the time of sharing to be personal information of a specific individual or information that identifies a specific individual that is not directly related to a cybersecurity threat.
Freedom of Information Act (FOIA)	FOIA was passed in 1967 and provides the public the right to request access to records from any federal agency.	Although federal agencies are required to disclose any information requested under the FOIA, there are nine exemptions, one of which protects interests such as personal privacy.
Traffic-Light Protocol (TLP)	TLP is a set of designations used to ensure that sensitive information is shared only with the appropriate audience.	TLP uses four colors (red, amber, green, and white) to indicate the expected sharing limitations to be applied by the recipients.
Protected Critical Infrastructure Information (PCII)	The PCII Act of 2002 protects private sector infrastructure information that is voluntarily shared with the government for the purposes of homeland security.	To qualify for PCII protections, information must be related to the security of the critical infrastructure, voluntarily submitted, and not submitted in place of compliance with a regulatory requirement.

Timeliness   It is critical that threat intelligence information be distributed as quickly as possible to others. To rely on email alerts that require a human to read them and then react takes far too much time. As an alternative, *Automated Indicator Sharing (AIS)* can be used instead. AIS enables the exchange of cyber threat indicators between parties through computer-to-computer communication, not email communication. Threat indicators such as malicious IP addresses or the sender address of a phishing email can be quickly distributed to enable others to repel these attacks.

Two tools facilitate AIS. **Structured Threat Information Expression (STIX)** is a language and format used to exchange cyber threat intelligence. All information about a threat can be represented with objects and descriptive relationships. STIX information can be visually represented for a security analyst to view or stored in a lightweight format to be used by a computer. **Trusted Automated Exchange of Intelligence Information (TAXII)** is an application protocol for exchanging cyber threat intelligence over Hypertext Transfer Protocol Secure (HTTPS). TAXII defines an application protocol interface (API) and a set of requirements for TAXII clients and servers.

Closed Source Intelligence

Closed source intelligence is the opposite of open source intelligence. It is *proprietary*, meaning that it is owned by an entity that has an exclusive right to it. Organizations that are participants in closed source information are part of private information sharing centers that restrict both access to data and participation. Whereas private sharing centers are similar to public sharing centers in that members share threat intelligence information, insights, and best practices, private sharing centers are restrictive regarding who may participate. All candidates must go through a vetting process and meet certain criteria. Usually, a security vendor collects the threat intelligence from all members, curates the information, and then redistributes it along with a detailed analysis of the information to all other members. Participation in a closed source intelligence community requires the members to pay a high annual fee to participate.

> **NOTE 10**
>
> Those participating in AIS generally are connected to a managed system controlled by the public information sharing center that allows bidirectional sharing of cyber threat indicators. Not only do participants receive indicators but they can also share indicators they have observed in their own network defenses to the public center, which then distributes them out to all participants.

> **NOTE 11**
>
> AIS is used more extensively with public information sharing centers than private centers.

Sources of Threat Intelligence

Several sources of threat intelligence are useful. These include the following:

- *Vulnerability databases.* A *vulnerability database* is a repository of known vulnerabilities and information about how they have been exploited. These databases create "feeds" of the latest cybersecurity incidences. Common cybersecurity data feeds include *vulnerability feeds* that provide information on the latest vulnerabilities and *threat feeds* that outline current threats and attacks. The *adversary tactics, techniques, and procedures (TTP)* is a database of the behavior of threat actors and how they orchestrate and manage attacks.
- *Threat maps.* A cybersecurity *threat map* illustrates cyber threats overlaid on a diagrammatic representation of a geographical area. Figure 2-6 illustrates a threat map. Threat maps are promoted as helping to visualize attacks and provide a limited amount of context of the source and the target countries, the attack types, and historical and near real-time data about threats. Although threat maps may look impressive, in reality they provide limited valuable information. Many maps are simply a playback of previous attacks, and because threat maps show anonymized data, it is impossible to know the identity of the attackers or the victims. As a result, many cybersecurity professionals question the true value of threat maps.
- *File and code repositories.* Another source of threat intelligence is *file and code repositories*. Victims of an attack can upload malicious files and software code that can then be examined by others to learn more about these attacks and craft their defenses. Often samples of recently discovered malware variants are uploaded to malware aggregation repositories along with published detailed malware analysis reports (MARs) containing IoCs for each malware variant.

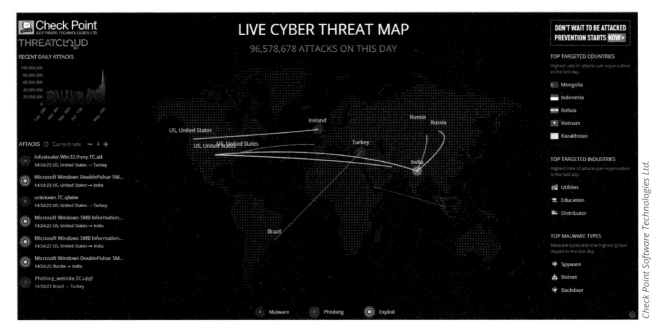

Figure 2-6 Threat map

- *Dark web*. The *dark web* is considered to be part of the web that is the domain of threat actors and beyond the reach of a normal search engine. Using special software such as *Tor* or *I2P (Invisible Internet Project)*, this software will mask the user's identity to allow for malicious activity such as selling drugs and stolen personal information and buying and selling malicious software used for attacks. Some security professionals and organizations use the dark web on a limited basis to look for signs that information critical to that enterprise is being sought out or sold on the dark web.

 **CAUTION** Finding information on the dark web is difficult. First, it requires using Tor or I2P, which prevents a device's IP address being traced. Second, although there are some dark web search engines, they are unlike regular search engines such as Google. The dark web search engines are difficult to use and notoriously inaccurate. One reason is because merchants who buy and sell stolen data or illicit drugs are constantly on the run, and their dark websites appear and then suddenly disappear with no warning. Finally, dark websites use a naming structure that results in dark website URLs like *p6f47s5p3dq3qkd.onion*. All of these are hurdles that keep out anyone who does not understand these inner workings.

TWO RIGHTS & A WRONG

1. A key risk indicator (KRI) is a metric of the upper and lower bounds of specific indicators of normal network activity.
2. Two tools that facilitate the privacy of OSNIT are STIX and TAXII.
3. The adversary tactics, techniques, and procedures (TTP) is a database of the behavior of threat actors and how they orchestrate and manage attacks.

See Appendix C for the answer.

FRAMEWORKS AND THREAT RESEARCH

 **CERTIFICATION**

1.2 Given a scenario, utilize threat intelligence to support organizational security.

Taking advantage of attack frameworks can provide an in-depth look into the thinking and tactics of threat actors. In addition, conducting threat research can also help support threat data and intelligence.

Studying Attack Frameworks

A cybersecurity framework is a series of documented processes used to define policies and procedures for implementation and management of security controls in an enterprise environment. Just as a cybersecurity framework, or series of documented processes, can be used to define policies and procedures for implementing and managing security controls in an enterprise environment, frameworks of how attacks occur can also be studied. These are called attack frameworks or *exploitation frameworks* and serve as models of the thinking and actions of today's threat actors.

The following are three of the most common attack frameworks:

- *MITRE ATT&CK*. MITRE ATT&CK is a knowledge base of attacker techniques that have been broken down and contain classification in detail. The attacks are offensively oriented actions that can be used against particular platforms. The focus of ATT&CK is not on the tools and malware that attackers use but instead looks at how they interact with systems during an operation. These techniques are arranged into a set of tactics to help explain and provide context for the technique. Figure 2-7 displays a sample of the ATT&CK framework.

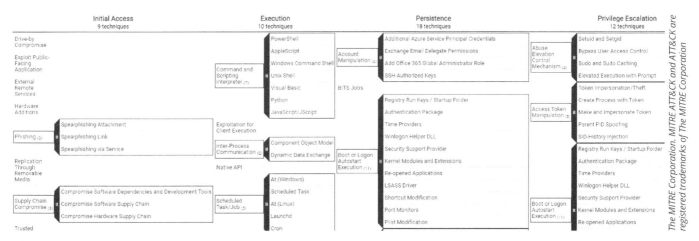

Figure 2-7   MITRE ATT&CK framework

- *The Diamond Model of Intrusion Analysis*. The Diamond Model of Intrusion Analysis is a framework for examining network intrusion events. This framework derives its name and shape from the four core interconnected elements that comprise any event: adversary, infrastructure, capability, and victim. Analyzing security incidents involves piecing together the Diamond using information collected about these four facets to understand the threat in its full context. Figure 2-8 illustrates the Diamond Model.

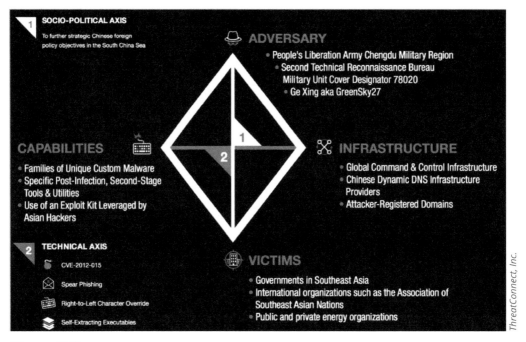

Figure 2-8 Diamond Model of Intrusion Analysis

- *Cyber Kill Chain*. A *kill chain* is a military term used to describe the systematic process to target and engage an enemy. An attacker who attempts to break into a web server or computer network actually follows these same steps. Known as the **Cyber Kill Chain**™, it outlines the steps of an attack. Figure 2-9 shows the Cyber Kill Chain. The underlying purpose of the Cyber Kill Chain is to illustrate that attacks are an integrated and end-to-end process like a "chain." Disrupting any one of the steps will interrupt the entire attack process, but the ability to disrupt the early steps of the chain is the most effective and least costly.

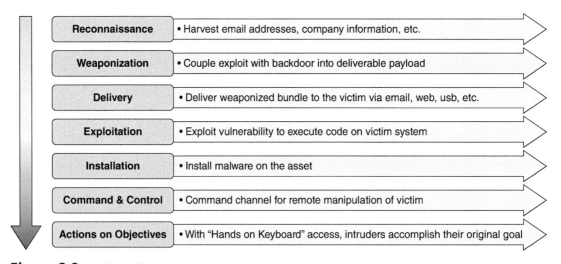

Figure 2-9 Cyber Kill Chain

Grow with Cengage Unlimited!

Conducting Threat Research

In addition to studying attack frameworks, there can be value in conducting more in-depth research into potential threats. Although often time consuming, researching threats can lead to new sources that contain valuable information. Threat research includes reputational research and behavioral research. It also involves prioritizing threats.

Reputational Research

Consider a typical website that an employee has accessed but resulted in an attack directed at the enterprise. Is this an isolated security failure, or is it part of a pattern of poor security of that website or even underlying malicious behavior? Looking into past actions, which is called reputational research, can help answer this question. Some security vendors compile domain-reputation databases that track the credibility of web domains by assigning a reputation score. This score may be based on factors such as the age of a website, historical location changes, and indications of suspicious activities. This information can then be used to block users from accessing infected or even malicious websites.

NOTE 12

To increase accuracy and reduce false positives, much website reputational research assigns reputation scores to specific pages or links within sites instead of classifying or blocking the entire website. This is because often only parts of legitimate sites are compromised.

Behavioral Research

Most efforts to improve cybersecurity focuses primarily on developing new technologies to thwart attackers. However, even though large numbers of new technologies have been introduced and utilized over the past 20 years, attacks continue unabated. Security researchers are beginning to recognize that that a key element for improvement involves acknowledging the importance of human behavior when designing, building, and using cybersecurity technology. This is known as behavioral research.

Consider phishing attacks. Although users have received training regarding phishing schemes, many users continue to click malicious links or open infected attachments. Behavioral research now shows that phishing emails use psychological techniques to trick recipients to succumb to the phishing email. Table 2-5 lists the principles of influence, or how to get someone to do something.

Table 2-5 Principles of influence

Principle	Explanation
Reciprocation	Return of a favor or kind gesture
Commitment and consistency	Honor a pledge
Social proof	Do things we see other people doing
Authority	Obey someone in command
Liking	Persuaded by people we like
Scarcity	Limited quantity or time

Threat actors have long ago learned that incorporating these principles of influence into their phishing emails can increase the rate at which victims "fall for" the phishing attack. While all six of these can increase the rates of victims clicking on a phishing email, "scarcity" and "authority" were the principles that had a higher impact upon older users, while "reciprocation" and "liking" had a higher impact upon younger email recipients. Behavioral research can assist in understanding this human element in cybersecurity and be used to improve security awareness training and designing more secure systems and processes.

Common Vulnerability Scoring System (CVSS)

Many new security personnel are surprised to learn *it is rarely possible, and often not desirable, to address all vulnerabilities*. Not all vulnerabilities are as potentially damaging as others. Also, although a scanner might assign a medium rating to a vulnerability, not all organizations will react to the rating in the same way. To one company, this vulnerability may be critical, but to another it is not worth the effort to fix. Because many vulnerabilities are complex to unravel and take an extended amount of time to address, there may not be enough time to solve all of them. So, beginning with the high vulnerabilities and working down through the low ones may not always be the best plan of action.

Instead, vulnerabilities need to be prioritized so that the most important ones are addressed early on, while others wait until later or are not even addressed. Several criteria are used for prioritizing vulnerabilities.

First, a numeric score is usually assigned to a vulnerability based on the **Common Vulnerability Scoring System (CVSS)**. These numeric scores are generated using a complex formula that considers such variables as the access vector, attack complexity, authentication, confidentiality of the data, and the system's integrity and availability. The vulnerabilities with the highest numeric CVSS scores are generally considered to require early attention.

However, the vulnerabilities with higher CVSS scores may not always be the ones that should be addressed first. Instead, it is important to look at scores and the entire vulnerability scan in the context of the organization. These questions about a vulnerability may help in identifying which ones need early attention:

- Can the vulnerability be addressed in a reasonable amount of time, or would it take several days or even a week to fix?
- Can the vulnerability be exploited by an external threat actor, or would exploitation require that the person be sitting at a computer in a vice president's office?
- If the vulnerability led to a threat actor infiltrating the system, would she be able to pivot to more important systems, or would she be isolated?
- Is the data on the affected device sensitive, or is it public?
- Is the vulnerability on a critical system that runs a core business process, or is it on a remote device that is rarely used?

NOTE 13

Prioritizing vulnerabilities is an inexact and sometimes difficult process. However, attention should first be directed toward vulnerabilities deemed to be critical (those that can cause the greatest degree of harm to the organization). Another part of prioritizing is making sure that the difficulty and time for implementing the correction is reasonable.

TWO RIGHTS & A WRONG

1. The focus of ATT&CK is on the tools and malware that attackers use.
2. The Cyber Kill Chain™ outlines the steps of an attack.
3. The principle of social proof is to do things we see other people doing.

See Appendix C for the answer.

THREAT MODELING

 **CERTIFICATION**

1.2 Given a scenario, utilize threat intelligence to support organizational security.

Consider the following principles about a cyberattack:

- Defenders cannot always assume the most likely course of action by the threat actor.
- Defenders must take into account all unlikely events and be prepared for them.
- Given the same tool, different adversaries may have different capabilities to use it.
- Only the attacker knows when an attack starts and ends.

- Principles in the physical world may not always translate into the cyber world.
- Some attacks can be from an individual while others can be from a large group.
- There is a wide spectrum of the adversaries' abilities, capabilities, and goals.

These principles illustrate the difficulty in not only anticipating attacks but also being able to defend against them. One method that has gained increasing popularity in cybersecurity defense is threat modeling. Once a theoretically interesting concept, threat modeling has now moved into a cybersecurity standard of significant value to enterprises. Threat modeling involves defining the concept, knowing the components of the modeling process, and understanding different threat modeling methodologies.

Definition of Threat Modeling

At its core, threat modeling is a proactive strategy for evaluating risks. It involves identifying potential threats and developing tests to detect and respond to those threats. Threat modeling has several advantages:

- *Address new threats.* When performed routinely, threat modeling can also help security teams ensure that protections are in line with evolving threats.
- *Become more proactive.* Threat modeling enables enterprises to perform a proactive cybersecurity threat assessment. Security teams can use threat modeling insights to evaluate risks.
- *Develop a deeper level of understanding.* Threat modeling helps an enterprise understand how threats may impact systems, how to better classify threats, and how and why to apply appropriate countermeasures.
- *Prioritize threats and mitigation.* Security teams can use threat modeling to prioritize threats to ensure that resources and attention are distributed effectively for mitigation. Because it is a model, the prioritization can be applied during planning, design, and implementation of cybersecurity to ensure that the solutions are effective.

Components of a Threat Modeling Process

Several components must be considered when performing threat modeling. These components are listed in Table 2-6.

Table 2-6   Threat modeling components

Component	Definition	Explanation
Adversary capability	Assessing the attacker's intent, ability, capability, skills, tenacity, and available resources	Nation-state actors have a higher adversary capability than unintentional insiders
Total attack surface	The sum total of the number of different attack points	Typically, larger enterprises have a higher total attack surface
Attack vector	The method used to compromise a vulnerability	Examples include weak authentication credentials, misconfigurations, malware, and poorly implemented cryptography
Impact	The effect or influence of the attack on the enterprise	Includes reputational damage, fines by government or regulatory agencies, and loss of customers
Likelihood	The probability of an attack occurring and being successful	Can range from low to very high

Threat Modeling Methodologies

An enterprise can design its own threat modeling process that encompasses the necessary components. One of the first threat modeling methodologies that an enterprise could create had the basic goals of better understanding who the attackers are, why they attack, and what types of attacks might occur. This early threat modeling often built scenarios of the types of threats that assets can face by the construction of an *attack tree*, which is a visual image of the attacks that may occur against an asset. Drawn as an inverted tree structure, an attack tree displays the goal of the attack, the types of attacks that may occur, and the techniques used in the attacks.

NOTE 14

The concept of attack trees was developed by Counterpane Internet Security.

Figure 2-10 shows a partial attack tree for an attacker who is attempting to log in to a restricted account. The attacker may attempt to learn the password (Level 2) by looking for one that is written down and stored under a mouse pad in an office (Level 3). He could also try to get the password from the user (Level 3) by installing a keylogger on the computer or by shoulder surfing (Level 4). An alternative approach may be to steal the password digest file to use offline cracking (Level 2). Attack trees help list the types of attacks that can occur and trace how and from where the attacks may originate.

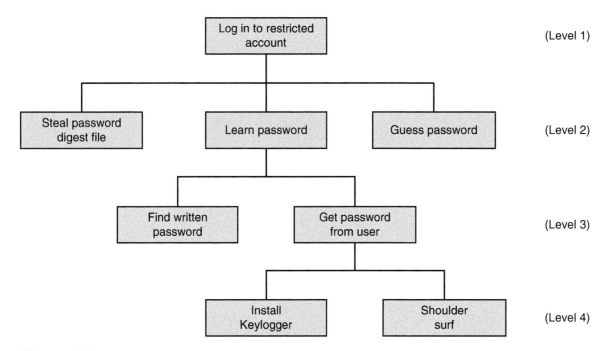

Figure 2-10 Attack tree

Although originally helpful, attack trees were too simplistic to be of real value to an enterprise. Today several threat modeling methodologies can be used. Many of these have a specific focus. The most popular modeling methodologies (with the focus in parentheses) are the following:

- *OCTAVE (Practice)*. The Operationally Critical Threat, Asset, and Vulnerability Evaluation methodology (OCTAVE) was one of the first created specifically for cybersecurity threat modeling. The OCTAVE threat modeling methodology is designed for assessing nontechnical organizational risks that may result from compromised data. Using OCTAVE, an organization's information assets are identified and the datasets they contain are assigned attributes based on the type of data stored. The drawbacks to OCTAVE are the documentation can become very large and it lacks scalability as more users and applications are added.
- *Trike (Acceptable risk)*. Trike threat modeling is an open-source threat modeling process that is designed to satisfy the security auditing process from a cyber risk management perspective. The foundation of Trike is a

"requirements model" that ensures the assigned level of risk for each asset is acceptable to the various stakeholders. Once the requirements model is in place, a data flow diagram (DFD) is then developed to illustrate how data moves through the system and the actions users can perform within it. However, Trike requires an overall view of the entire system before conducting an attack surface analysis. This can be difficult to scale to larger systems.

- *PASTA (Attacker)*. The Process for Attack Simulation and Threat Analysis is a relatively new threat modeling methodology. PASTA provides a seven-step process for risk analysis that does not depend upon which platform is being used. The goal of PASTA is to align business objectives with technical requirements while taking into account business impact analysis and compliance requirements. The PASTA threat modeling methodology combines an attacker-centric perspective on potential threats with risk and impact analysis. PASTA requires a significant investment in training.

- *STRIDE (Developer)*. STRIDE stands for Spoofing Tampering Repudiation Information Message Disclosure Denial of Service and Elevation of Privilege. The goal of STRIDE is to ensure that an application meets the security properties of Confidentiality, Integrity, and Availability (CIA), along with Authorization, Authentication, and Non-Repudiation. Once the security subject matter experts construct the DFD threat model, system engineers or other subject matter experts check the application against the STRIDE threat model classification scheme. STRIDE is most useful when creating a risk-aware corporate culture and is very customizable to an organization's specific security objectives and risk environment.

- *VAST (Enterprise)*. The Visual, Agile, and Simple Threat modeling (VAST) methodology was developed to address the weaknesses and implementation challenges in the other threat modeling methodologies. The founding principle is that threat modeling must scale across the infrastructure and entire application development (DevOps) library and provide actionable, accurate, and consistent outputs for developers, security teams, and senior executives. A fundamental difference of the VAST threat modeling methodology is its practical approach. Recognizing the security concerns of development teams are distinct from those of an infrastructure team, this methodology calls for two types of threat models.

When choosing a threat model methodology, there are three primary considerations. First, the outputs of the model should be considered. While all threat modeling methodologies may be capable of identifying potential threats, the number and type of threats identified will vary significantly, as will the quality, consistency, and value from those threat models.

Another consideration should be scalability. At the enterprise level, the ability to scale across hundreds or even thousands of threat models must be taken into consideration.

The final consideration is the overall goal. Some enterprises are looking for a model that will generate relevant financial and productivity reports for executive financial reporting. Other enterprises may have the goal of reducing the organization's overall threat profile, attack surface, and risk portfolio.

TWO RIGHTS & A WRONG

1. At its core, threat modeling is a proactive strategy for evaluating risks and involves identifying potential threats and developing tests to detect and respond to those threats.
2. The total attack surface is the sum total of the number of different attack points.
3. The threat model methodology STRIDE has its primary focus on the enterprise.

See Appendix C for the answer.

⤤ VM LAB

You're now ready to complete the live, virtual machine labs for this module. The labs can be found in the Apply It folder in each MindTap module.

MODULE SUMMARY

- A threat actor is a term used to describe individuals or entities who are responsible for cyber incidents against enterprises, governments, and users. In the past, the generic term hacker referred to a person who used advanced computer skills to attack computers. It was qualified in an attempt to distinguish between different types of hackers. However, these broad categories of hackers did not accurately reflect the differences among threat actors. The attributes, or characteristic features, of the different groups of threat actors can vary widely.

- A group that is strongly motivated by ideology (for the sake of their principles or beliefs) is hactivists. In the past, the types of attacks by hactivists usually involved defacing websites. Today most hactivists work through disinformation campaigns by spreading fake news and supporting conspiracy theories. Governments are increasingly employing their own state-sponsored attackers for launching cyberattacks against their foes. These are known as nation-state actors. Their foes may be foreign governments or even their own citizens that the government considers hostile or threatening. Many security researchers believe that nation-state actors might be the deadliest of any threat actors. These state-sponsored attackers are highly skilled and have enough government resources to breach almost any security defense.

- Another serious threat to an enterprise comes from its own employees, contractors, and business partners, called insiders, who pose an insider threat of manipulating data from the position of a trusted employee. Insiders may intentionally steal or alter data that belongs to their organization for several reasons. These attacks by intentional insiders are harder to recognize than other types of attacks. That is because they come from within the enterprise while defensive tools are usually focused on outsider attackers. Attacks are often the result of unintentional insiders. Although they may have no malicious intent, due to their action (or inaction), unintentional insiders can unwittingly cause harm (or increase the probability of serious future harm) to the organization's resources and assets. Organized criminal syndicates involved in cyberattacks are usually run by a small number of experienced online criminal networks who do not commit crimes themselves but act as entrepreneurs.

- It is important to identify known threats vs. unknown threats, which is classifying threats by comparing the knowledge of the threat actor to security personnel. The four categories of these threats are known knowns, known unknowns, unknown knowns, and unknown unknowns. A particularly ominous threat that has emerged in recent years is called advanced persistent threat (APT). APTs use innovative attack tools, and once a system is infected, they silently extract data over an extended period of time. APTs are most commonly associated with nation-state actors.

- At one time, organizations were reluctant to share information about attacks on their networks and endpoints, often because they were concerned about "bad publicity" that might arise from this disclosure. This lack of sharing of details about threats (threat data and intelligence) only crippled cybersecurity defenses. Today, however, organizations are pooling their experiences and knowledge gained about the latest attacks with the broader security community. In addition to identifying an imminent attack by sharing indicator of compromise (IoC) data, threat intelligence sharing can also aid in other areas such as incident response (handling a cyberattack or data breach), vulnerability management (identifying and addressing security vulnerabilities), risk management (controlling threats to assets), security engineering (building systems to resist attacks), and detection and monitoring (uncovering and managing vulnerabilities).

- When a cyber incident occurs, the data about it can be captured. However, the data needs to be "processed" to become useful information. The process through which raw cybersecurity data becomes useful threat intelligence information can be illustrated by the intelligence cycle, also called the threat intelligence lifecycle. The intelligence lifecycle has five phases: requirements, collection, analysis, dissemination, and feedback.

- There are two broad categories of threat intelligence sources. Threat intelligence that is freely available is called open source intelligence (OSINT). Many organizations share OSINT (called information sharing and analysis communities). OpenIoC (Open Indicators of Compromise) was developed as an open framework for sharing OSINT in a machine-readable format. The data is formatted in the eXtensible Markup Language (XML) and comes with 500 predefined base indicators, which can be easily customized for adding intelligence.

- A concern about using public information sharing centers is that of privacy. An organization that is the victim of an attack must be careful that any proprietary or sensitive information is not shared when providing IoCs and attack details. As a safeguard, most public information sharing centers have protections in place to prevent the disclosure of protected information. Also, it is critical that threat intelligence information be distributed as quickly as possible to others. Automated Indicator Sharing (AIS) enables the exchange of cyber threat indicators between parties through computer-to-computer communication. Two tools facilitate AIS. Structured Threat Information Expression (STIX) is a language and format used to exchange cyber threat intelligence. Trusted Automated Exchange of Intelligence Information (TAXII) is an application protocol for exchanging cyber threat intelligence over Hypertext Transfer Protocol Secure (HTTPS).

- Closed source intelligence is the opposite of open source intelligence. It is proprietary, meaning that it is owned by an entity that has an exclusive right to it. Organizations that are participants in closed source information are part of private information sharing centers that restrict both access to data and participation. There are several sources of threat intelligence. These include vulnerability databases, threat maps, file and code repositories, and the dark web.

- A cybersecurity framework is a series of documented processes used to define policies and procedures for implementation and management of security controls in an enterprise environment. Just as a cybersecurity framework, or series of documented processes, can be used to define policies and procedures for implementing and managing security controls in an enterprise environment, frameworks of how attacks occur can also be studied. Attack frameworks or exploitation frameworks serve as models of the thinking and actions of today's threat actors. Three of the most common attack frameworks include MITRE ATT&CK, Diamond, and Cyber Kill Chain. In addition to studying attack frameworks, there can be value in conducting more in-depth research into potential threats. Although often time consuming, researching threats can frequently lead to new sources that contain valuable information. Threat research includes reputational research and behavioral research.

- Vulnerabilities need to be prioritized so that the most important ones are addressed early on, while others wait until later or are not even addressed. Several criteria are used for prioritizing vulnerabilities. First, a numeric score is usually assigned to a vulnerability based on the Common Vulnerability Scoring System (CVSS). These numeric scores are generated using a complex formula that considers such variables as the access vector, attack complexity, authentication, confidentiality of the data, and the system's integrity and availability. The vulnerabilities with the highest numeric CVSS scores are generally considered to require early attention.

- At its core, threat modeling is a proactive strategy for evaluating risks. It involves identifying potential threats and developing tests to detect and respond to those threats. Several components must be considered when performing threat modeling. These components include adversary capability, total attack surface, attack vector, impact, and likelihood. An enterprise can design its own threat modeling process that encompasses the necessary components. Today several threat modeling methodologies can be used. These include OCTAVE, Trike, PASTA, STRIDE, and VAST.

Key Terms

accuracy
advanced persistent threat (APT)
adversary capability
analysis
attack frameworks
attack vector
behavioral research
closed source intelligence
collection
commodity malware
Common Vulnerability Scoring
  System (CVSS)

Cyber Kill Chain™
detection and monitoring
Diamond Model of Intrusion
  Analysis
dissemination
feedback
framework
hactivists
impact
incident response
indicator of compromise (IoC)

information sharing and analysis
  communities
insider threat
intelligence cycle
known threats vs. unknown
  threats
likelihood
MITRE ATT&CK
nation-state actors
open source intelligence (OSINT)
OpenIoC

organized crime
relevancy
reputational research
requirements
risk management
security engineering

Structured Threat Information
   Expression (STIX)
threat actor
threat data and intelligence
threat modeling
total attack surface

Trusted Automated Exchange of
   Intelligence Information (TAXII)
vulnerability management
zero-day attacks

Review Questions

1. Which type of hacker attempts to probe a system with an organization's permission for weaknesses and then privately reports back to that organization?
   a. Gray hat hackers
   b. Black hat hackers
   c. White hat hackers
   d. Green hat hackers

2. What is the name for malware that is sold by attackers to other attackers and can be customized?
   a. Custom malware
   b. Proprietary malware
   c. Commodity malware
   d. ATTACK malware

3. Parvin is conducting research on hactivists. Which of the following would she NOT find about hactivists?
   a. The name is a combination of the words "hack" and "activism."
   b. Hactivists proudly wear the name "hactivist."
   c. Hactivists have defaced websites in order to make a political statement.
   d. Disinformation campaigns are a favorite tactic of hacktivists.

4. Which is not a category of threats based on the Johari window of cybersecurity threats?
   a. Known knowns
   b. Unknown unknowns
   c. Unknown knowns
   d. Knowns

5. Which of the following is NOT correct about an advanced persistent threat (APT)?
   a. APTs are most commonly associated with nation-state actors.
   b. APTs use innovative attack tools.
   c. Once a system is infected by an ATP, it silently extracts data over an extended period of time.
   d. APTs require the use of SQL injection attacks.

6. Which of the following is NOT a step of the intelligence cycle?
   a. Analysis
   b. Dissemination
   c. Data processing
   d. Collection

7. Which phase of the intelligence cycle feeds back into the requirements phase?
   a. Dissemination
   b. Analysis
   c. Financial
   d. Feedback

8. Shahnaz is researching security appliances and needs the devices to accept threat data and intelligence using a standard machine-readable open framework. Which technology would Shahnaz require to be a feature of the security appliance?
   a. OpenIoC
   b. XRML
   c. SQL
   d. NoSQL

9. Which of the following enables the exchange of cyber threat indicators between parties through computer-to-computer communication?
   a. AKI
   b. PKI
   c. AIS
   d. TLP

10. Which of the following is a language and format used to exchange cyber threat intelligence?
    a. TAXII
    b. BRICK
    c. STIX
    d. FLOWII

11. Which of the following is NOT a source of threat intelligence?
    a. Database vulnerability repositories (DVR)
    b. File and code repositories
    c. Dark web
    d. Vulnerability databases

12. Which attack framework is a knowledge base of attacker techniques that have been broken down and contain classification in detail?
    a. MITRE ATT&CK
    b. Diamond Model of Intrusion Analysis
    c. Cyber Kill Chain
    d. AXITI

13. Hyat has been asked to research the variables that are used as a basis for the Common Vulnerability Scoring System (CVSS). Which of the following is NOT a variable used in CVSS?
    a. Access vector
    b. Attack complexity
    c. Time of attack
    d. Confidentiality of data

14. What is threat modeling?
    a. A proactive strategy for evaluating risks
    b. Using CVS data as input into a threat engine
    c. Using old threat intelligence data to create new threat intelligence data
    d. A standard for assigning a qualitative label to a threat

15. Which of the following components is the sum total of the number of different attack points?
    a. Fault aggregation
    b. Vulnerability platform
    c. Total attack surface
    d. Attack vector

16. Which threat model has the developer as its primary focus?
    a. MAGELLAN
    b. STRIDE
    c. Trike
    d. PASTA

17. Which of the following is NOT correct about nation-state actors?
    a. Governments are increasingly employing their own state-sponsored attackers.
    b. The foes of nation-state actors are only foreign governments.
    c. Nation-state actors are considered the deadliest of any threat actors.
    d. These attackers are highly skilled and have deep resources.

18. What is the name of attackers that sell their knowledge of a weakness to other attackers or to governments?
    a. Trustees
    b. Dealers
    c. Investors
    d. Brokers

19. Which of the following categories describes a zero-day attack?
    a. Known unknowns
    b. Unknown knowns
    c. Unknown unknowns
    d. Known knowns

20. What is a KRI?
    a. A metric of the upper and lower bounds of specific indicators of normal network activity
    b. A measure of vulnerability applied to a DVSS
    c. A level of IoC
    d. A label applied to an XSS

Case Projects

Case Project 2-1: Nation-State Actors

Research the current state of nation-state actors. Which countries are recognized as having nation-state actors? What attacks have these actors launched? Why? What is being done to address nation-state actors? Write a one-page paper on your research.

Case Project 2-2: Intelligence Cycle

Research different intelligence cycles. Create and label a cycle that is different than that presented in this module. Include a description of each of the steps.

Case Project 2-3: TAXII and STIX

Search the Internet for information on TAXII and STIX. Write a two-paragraph explanation of each technology, how it is used, and its strengths and weaknesses.

Case Project 2-4: Threat Models

Select one of the threat models (OCTAVE, Trike, PASTA, STRIDE, or VAST), and use the Internet to research this model. How is it used? What are its advantages? What are its disadvantages? Write a one-page paper on your research.

Case Project 2-5: On the Job

Suppose you work for a company where you are trying to convince your team leader of the advantages of both reputational research and behavioral research. Use the Internet to research these two types of research and find examples of how they are used and how they would be of value. Create a one-page memo to your team leader about these types of research.

References

1. "2019 Insider Threat Report," *NucleusCyber*, retrieved Apr. 21, 2020, https://info.nucleuscyber .com/2019-insider-threat-report.
2. Eliyahu, Tal, "Insider Threats: From Malicious to Unintentional," *SentinelOne*, Aug. 22, 2019, accessed Nov. 15, 2020, www.sentinelone.com/blog/insider-threats-from-malicious-to-unintentional/#:~:text=An%20 unintentional%20insider%20threat%20(UIT,substantially%20increases%20the%20probability%20of.
3. "Known and Unknown: Author's Note," *The Rumsfeld Papers*, retrieved Dec 2, 2020, https://papers .rumsfeld.com/about/page/authors-note.

VULNERABILITY MANAGEMENT

After completing this module you will be able to do the following:

1 List common vulnerabilities

2 Explain the reasons for conducting a vulnerability scan

3 Describe the different scanning decisions

4 Explain how to run a vulnerability scan

5 Describe how to remediate vulnerabilities

Cybersecurity Today

Cybersecurity threat data and intelligence, also simply known as threat intelligence (TI), is a booming segment within the cybersecurity industry. The commercial market for TI products and services is valued at more than $5 billion globally. And it is predicted to triple over the next five years.

TI helps address a major challenge facing all organizations, namely identifying and understanding all relevant cybersecurity threats. Some TI can be extracted from an organization's security devices, such as a firewall log that captures the external IP addresses of a threat actor attempting a brute force attack on passwords or a spam filter that can identify emails that contain a phishing URL. These IP addresses and URLs, known as indicators of compromise (IoCs), can then be fed into the organization's Security Event and Information Management (SIEM) tool or an intrusion detection system (IDS) to ward off the attacks. But these "local" IoCs are only a fraction of the total threat landscape at any given moment. Instead of relying upon their own TI, most organizations turn to external sources that can not only provide a broader range of attacks but also can extract more information from the data to reveal new patterns and trends.

There are three major sources of TI. Open source threat intelligence typically consists of public lists of indicators, sometimes called abuse feeds or blacklists. Shared TI is a collaboration between trusted communities in which the members exchange their own threat information. The third source is paid TI. This source not only provides TI information as electronic feeds into security appliances but also typically gives in-depth research and even specialized services for a specific market sector, such as government or financial services. A recent survey of security professionals in North America and the United Kingdom found that 44 percent of respondents say that paid TI is the primary source of threat intelligence for their organization.

How accurate is this data from paid TI providers? These companies do not openly share their information with outsiders or researchers so that it can be compared and evaluated. In fact, they rarely even advertise the cost of their services (estimates range up to $650,000 annually, depending upon the size of the organization). However, security researchers were recently able to analyze and compare paid TI.[1] What they found was surprising.

When comparing TI feeds from different paid TI sources, the researchers discovered little if any overlap; that is, a threat identified from one paid TI source was not identified by another TI source. In fact, only 1.3 percent of the IoCs of Paid IT Source #2 were found in Paid IT Source #1. In one analysis, the researchers tracked 22 threat actors in two separate feeds and found only 2.5 to 4.0 percent of the indicators were in both TI feeds. Even the highest overlap was only 21 percent, which was the IP address of a specific threat actor. The researchers concluded that each paid TI source observes unique indicators of cybersecurity incidents, and that helps to explain why information from one TI source is not found in the feed from another TI source.

When they looked at the timeliness of the TI, they found that one TI paid source identified a threat one month earlier than another source, which could leave organizations subscribing to the second source unprotected for 30 days. Although it could be assumed that paid TI sources would provide the information more quickly than other types of sources, they were faster in only half of the analyzed cases. That means that half of the time, the open source and shared TI were quicker in getting their alerts out.

Another surprising insight was how the subscriber organizations use the data. Many organizations highly value the more selective and curated TI from a paid source—but not just because it is used for network detection of attacks. Rather, they value the TI because it decreases the time that their internal analysts must spend poring over the data. Open source and shared TI usually contain large volumes of data and are not vetted.

While TI data is important for organizations to protect themselves from cybersecurity attacks, the researchers concluded that the true value of TI data from paid TI sources may not be as high as it should be. Given that 44 percent of organizations use paid TI as their primary source, this could result in gaping holes in their defenses.

Threat modeling, a proactive strategy for evaluating risks, involves identifying potential threats and developing tests to detect and respond to those threats. This testing can be performed by *penetration testing*, which attempts to exploit vulnerabilities just as a threat actor would. However, pen testing is a significant undertaking. It requires a substantial amount of time to properly plan and implement so that vulnerabilities can be exploited in the same way as a threat actor. Pen testing may also impact the daily operations of the organization if the test is being conducted by third-party security professionals on the organization's production system. Because of this, a pen test is considered a major event and is often recommended to be performed only once per year or when required by a regulatory agency.

But what about the software or hardware vulnerabilities that arise between the pen tests? Waiting up to a year before the next scheduled pen test can leave an organization thinking it has a strong level of security when new vulnerabilities have made it ripe for an attack. What should an organization do?

The answer lies in a process known as *vulnerability management*. Also called *infrastructure risk visibility and assurance*, its purpose is to be an ongoing examination of the organization's security posture instead of an annual event. While it may not expose the deep vulnerabilities that a pen test can, it nevertheless provides an ongoing evaluation of the protections in place. Vulnerability management seeks to answer questions such as *Where are we exposed? What should we prioritize? Are we reducing our exposure over time? How do we compare with our peers?*

In this module, you will examine the security vulnerability management process. First, you will study common vulnerabilities. Then, you will explore what is a vulnerability scan, how to configure scanning tools, and how to report and remediate scan results.

COMMON VULNERABILITIES

CERTIFICATION

1.7 Given a scenario, implement controls to mitigate attacks and software vulnerabilities.

Several categories of common vulnerabilities may be found in an organization. These include improper software exception and error handling, insecure external components and functions, faulty configurations, broken authentication, and inadequate monitoring.

Improper Software Exception and Error Handling

Several software coding techniques should be used to create secure applications and limit sensitive data exposure, or disclosing sensitive data to attackers. However, vulnerabilities in software are often the result of poor coding on the part of the software developers. This is commonly the case when a program does not properly check for exceptions that may occur when the program is running.

Some software may not properly trap an error condition, potentially providing an attacker with access to the underlying operating system (OS). This is known as improper error handling. Suppose an attacker enters a string of characters that is much longer than expected. Because the software has not been designed for this event, the program could crash or suddenly halt its execution and then display an underlying OS prompt, giving an attacker broad access to the computer.

Another improper exception handling situation involves a pointer. A value (such as a number or text) is stored in a specific computer memory address. To access the value, computer programming languages use pointers that contain a numeric memory address. These pointers "point" to the memory address containing the value. When the program needs to access the value stored in memory (that the pointer points to), it dereferences the pointer. When an application dereferences a pointer that it expects to be valid but instead has a value of NULL, it typically causes a program to crash or exit. A NULL pointer/object dereference can occur through a number of flaws, including simple programming omissions.

A NULL pointer/object dereference can also be the result of a race condition. A race condition in software occurs when two concurrent threads of execution access a shared resource simultaneously, resulting in unintended consequences. For example, in a program with two threads that have access to the same location in memory, Thread #1 stores the value *A* in that memory location. But since Thread #2 is also executing, it may overwrite the same memory location with the value *Z*. When Thread #1 retrieves the value stored, it is then given Thread #2's *Z* instead of its own *A*. The software checks the state of a resource before using it, but the resource's state can change between the check and the use in a way that invalidates the results of the check. Known as a *Time Of Check/Time Of Use* race condition, this condition is often security relevant: a threat actor who can influence the state of the resource between check and use can negatively impact a number of shared resources such as files, memory, or variables in multithreaded programs.

An insecure object reference occurs when an application externally exposes a reference to an internal object. For example, a website may ask a user to enter a customer number and then pass that number to an internal database by crafting a URL with that information:

http://vulnerable_website.org/customer_account?customer_number=11302002

A threat actor could easily modify the *customer_number* value to retrieve any customer information.

Insecure External Software Components

In addition to attacking the software directly, threat actors also target external software components that may be insecure. These include the following:

- *Application program interface (API)*. An *application program interface (API)* is a link provided by an OS, web browser, or other platform that allows a developer access to resources at a high level. An example of an API is when a user visits a website and the message "This site wants to know your location" appears. The website is attempting to the use the geolocation API available in the web browser. APIs relieve the developer from having to write code for specific hardware and software. Because APIs provide direct access to data and an entry point to an application's functions, they are attractive targets for attackers searching for vulnerabilities.

NOTE 1

The common application attacks of scripting attacks and injection attacks are both examples of not properly checking for exceptions. These allow the user to enter data but have improper input-handling features that do not filter or validate user input to prevent a malicious action. Scripting attacks and injection attacks are covered in Module 1.

NOTE 2

API vulnerabilities are particularly attractive because they can have a broad impact and may take a long time to discover. In 2018, Facebook found a vulnerability in its API code that had made it possible for attackers to steal access tokens and take over the accounts of 30 million users. It took Facebook 14 months before it discovered the API vulnerability. It is predicted that by 2022, API abuses will become the most common type of web application attack resulting in a data breach.[2]

- *Device driver.* A *device driver* is software that controls and operates an external hardware device that is connected to a computer. Device drivers are specific to both the OS and the hardware device. Threat actors may attempt to alter a device driver for use in an attack (called *device driver manipulation*). An attacker may use shimming, or transparently adding a small coding library that intercepts calls made by the device and changes the parameters passed between the device and the device driver. This refactoring (changing the design of existing code) can be difficult to detect yet serves as a real threat.
- *Dynamic link library (DLL).* A *dynamic link library (DLL)* is a repository of both code and data that can be used by more than one program at the same time. For example, in the Windows operating system, the Comdlg32.DLL performs common dialog box related functions. Attackers use a technique called *DLL injection* for inserting code into a running process through a DLL to cause a program to function in a different way than intended.

Insecure Internal Functions

Programmers who choose internal programming language functions can likewise introduce vulnerabilities. For example, the programming language C has an internal function `strcpy` that can be used to copy a string to a destination buffer. However, this function does not check the length of the destination buffer into which the string is being copied and could overwrite a portion of memory to perform a memory vulnerability attack. The solution is to use the more secure internal function *strlcpy* that cannot overflow into the destination buffer.

NOTE 3

Memory vulnerability attacks are covered in Module 1.

Faulty Configurations

Modern hardware and software platforms provide a wide array of features and security settings, which must be properly configured to repel attacks. However, the configuration settings often are not properly implemented, resulting in weak configurations. Table 3-1 lists several weak configurations that can result in vulnerabilities.

Table 3-1 Weak configurations

Configuration	Explanation	Example
Default configurations	Default settings are predetermined by the vendor for usability and ease of use (and not security) so the user can immediately begin using the product.	A router comes with a default password that is widely known.
Open ports and services	Devices and services are often configured to allow the most access so that the user can then close those that are specific to that organization.	A firewall comes with FTP ports 20 and 21 open.
Unsecured root accounts	A root account can give a user unfettered access to all resources.	A misconfigured cloud storage repository could give any user access to all data.
Open permissions	Open permissions are user access over files that should have been restricted.	A user could be given *Read, Write*, and *Execute* privileges when she should have only been given *Read* privileges.
Unsecure protocols	Also called *insecure protocols,* unsecure protocols for telecommunications do not provide adequate protections.	A network administrator could use devices that run services with unsecure protocols like *Telnet* or *SNMPv1*.
Weak encryption	Weak encryption results from choosing a known vulnerable encryption mechanism.	A system administrator user could select an encryption scheme that has a known weakness or a key value that is too short.
Errors	Errors are human mistakes in selecting one setting over another without considering the security implications.	A user could use deprecated settings instead of current configurations.

Broken Authentication

Vulnerabilities introduced by poor authentication practices (broken authentication) can open a broad pathway for a threat actor to exploit. When the topic of broken authentication is raised, it is common to point a finger at user practices—selecting a weak password, reusing passwords on multiple sites, and not using a password manager to generate, store, and autofill passwords at login prompts—as the culprit. While these user practices can weaken authentication, often network administrators can also contribute to broken authentication. Typical network-based poor authentication practices include the following:

- Storing user credentials using general-purpose hash algorithms like MD5 and SHA instead of using key stretching algorithms like bcrypt and PBKDF2
- Exposing session IDs in a URL
- Failing to force session values to expire after a set period of time or at logout
- Reusing session IDs after a successful login
- Sending passwords, session IDs, and other credentials sent over unencrypted connections

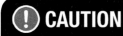 **CAUTION** Researchers recently examined the internal password-generation feature of several well-known password managers by generating 147 million passwords by these password managers to evaluate the strength of the generated passwords. One test was to determine when the user chose to have specific characters included in the password (lowercase letters, uppercase letters, digits, and/or symbols) if this impacted the randomness of the generated password. Surprisingly, researchers found that in some instances, some password managers created weaker passwords when specific character sets were chosen. For example, when using one password manager and requiring that both a letter and a digit be part of the password, it then generated a truly random password; however, any other required combinations (such as letter and symbol, symbol and digit, etc.) created nonrandom passwords.[3]

Grow with Cengage Unlimited!

If you'd like more information about this topic, use your Cengage Unlimited subscription to go to the CompTIA Security+ Guide to Network Security Fundamentals, 7th edition; open Module 12; and read the section titled "Types of Authentication Credentials."

If you don't have a Cengage Unlimited subscription, you can find more information at cengage.com/unlimited.

Inadequate Monitoring and Logging

While generating audit logs to identify changes made to sensitive data or critical systems is an important element of cybersecurity, monitoring those logs for signs of potential cybersecurity threats can be difficult. The sheer volume of raw log data makes it impossible to manually uncover meaningful insights. This sometimes causes organizations to practice insufficient monitoring and logging. The solution is to automate the logging and monitoring processes to trigger alerts and then, if necessary, manually examine logs for the specific information.

NOTE 4

Inadequate logging and monitoring is not a direct cause of an attack but instead affects the ability to react quickly and effectively to threats.

VULNERABILITY SCANNING

 **CERTIFICATION**

1.3 Given a scenario, perform vulnerability management activities.

As its name implies, *vulnerability scanning* is an examination of the organization's security posture to uncover vulnerabilities. Unlike a penetration test that may be an annual event intended to expose deep vulnerabilities, vulnerability scanning is a higher-level ongoing evaluation of the protections in place. Vulnerability scanning is an important tool that organizations should regularly use to protect their assets. Vulnerability scanning involves understanding what a vulnerability scan is, knowing the decisions that must be made regarding scans, running a scan, analyzing scan reports, and remediating uncovered vulnerabilities.

What Is a Vulnerability Scan?

One useful means of defining a vulnerability scan is to compare it to a penetration test; although these contain similarities, in reality, they are very different. Knowing the reasons for conducting a scan can also help define a vulnerability scan. However, there are also challenges associated with a vulnerability scan.

Vulnerability Scan vs. Penetration Test

Consider Bob, who sees his doctor for an annual physical but only because it is required by his employer. Bob's blood pressure is taken, and it is just barely below the upper limits that would require intervention. Bob leaves the office satisfied that he is in good health (and happy that he does not have to start regular exercise), that he has met the requirements mandated by his employer, and that he can wait another year before returning for the next physical.

Now consider Serafina, who likewise visits her physician for her annual physical. However, she does so because she is concerned about maintaining good health, not just meeting an employer requirement. Her blood pressure is taken in the doctor's office and is in the normal range. Serafina also uses a wearable fitness tracker so that her blood pressure is continually and automatically monitored, and she views the results every evening with an app on her smartphone.

Which patient has a higher probability of detecting a sudden and prolonged spike in their blood pressure and then immediately taking steps to manage it? Is it Bob, who has it checked manually once per year at the doctor's office, or Serafina, who has it continually monitored?

Obviously, Serafina has a much higher probability of catching a change in her blood pressure than Bob does. This is because Serafina is continually and automatically monitoring her health, while Bob is only having it reviewed annually. In addition, because Serafina is genuinely concerned about maintaining good health and is not just having her vital signs taken to meet a requirement, this attitude in itself will play a role in a more proactive approach to good health.

The difference between Bob and Serafina in this scenario is similar to the difference between a penetration test and a vulnerability scan. A penetration test is a single event using a manual process that is too often performed only to comply with regulatory requirements. However, much like Bob, once the pen test is over, it is forgotten about until the next time it is required. A vulnerability scan, on the other hand, is like Serafina's behaviors: it is a frequent and ongoing process that is automated to continuously identify vulnerabilities and monitor cybersecurity progress. In other words, a vulnerability assessment is a cyclical and continual process of ongoing scanning and continuous monitoring to reduce the attack surface. Table 3-2 contrasts a vulnerability scan with a penetration test.

Table 3-2   Vulnerability scan vs. Penetration test

	Vulnerability scan	Penetration test
Purpose	Reduce attack surface	Identify deep vulnerabilities
Procedure	Scan to find weaknesses and then mitigate	Act like a threat agent to find vulnerabilities to exploit
Frequency	Usually ongoing scanning and continuous monitoring	When required by regulatory body or on a predetermined scheduled
Personnel	Internal security personnel	External third parties or internal security personnel
Process	Usually automated with handful of manual processes	Entirely manual process
Goal	Identify risks by scanning systems and networks	Gain unauthorized access and exploit vulnerabilities
Final report audience	Executive summary for less technical audience, technical details for security professionals	Several different audiences

A vulnerability scan and a penetration test share some similarities. For example, both should be conducted following a data breach, the launch of a new application, or a major change to the network. However, since a vulnerability scan is continuous, it may only need to focus on the new application or changes to the network.

Reasons for Conducting a Scan

There are several reasons for conducting a vulnerability scan besides provide continuous monitoring. These include meeting regulatory requirements and following corporate policies.

Meet Regulatory Requirements   Conducting a vulnerability scan is necessary to meet regulatory requirements, which is following specific actions mandated by an external regulatory body. Examples of regulatory compliance laws and regulations include the Dodd–Frank Act, Payment Card Industry Data Security Standard (PCI DSS), Health Insurance Portability and Accountability Act (HIPAA), the Federal Information Security Management Act (FISMA), and the Sarbanes–Oxley (SOX) Act.

 **CAUTION**   Although aligning with regulatory standards is important, the primary goal of a vulnerability scan or pen test should never be just to meet compliance standards. Some compliance cybersecurity standards are considered absolute minimal protection. It is therefore essential for cybersecurity professionals to continually remind their organizations that compliance does not equal security!

The PCI DSS regulatory requirements, called a compliance standard, are typical. These were introduced to provide a minimum degree of security for handling customer card information. The Requirement 11 of the latest standard (PCI DSS 3.2.1) states that organizations must *regularly test security systems and processes* using both vulnerability scans and penetration tests. A partial list of the PCI DSS Requirement 11 standards is contained in Table 3-3.

Table 3-3   PCI DSS requirement 11 standards

Standard	Description	Frequency
11.1	Implement processes to test for the presence of wireless access points (802.11) and detect and identify all authorized and unauthorized wireless access points.	Quarterly
11.2	Run internal and external network vulnerability scans to address vulnerabilities and perform rescans as needed, until passing scans are achieved. External scans must be performed by an Approved Scanning Vendor (ASV) while scans conducted after network changes and internal scans may be performed by internal staff.	At least quarterly and after any significant change in the network
11.3	Develop and implement a methodology for penetration testing that includes external and internal penetration testing. If segmentation is used to reduce PCI DSS scope, perform penetration tests to verify the segmentation methods are operational and effective. Service providers using segmentation must confirm PCI DSS scope by performing penetration testing on segmentation controls.	At least annually and after any significant upgrade or modification. Service providers must perform penetration testing at least every six months and after making changes to controls.

NOTE 5

Many of the controls in the current PCI DSS standard date back more than a decade. Major changes have not been made to the standard since 2015. An updated PCI DSS 4.0 is now scheduled to be released in 2021. Because of the length of time since the standards were last updated, many industry insiders anticipate that the changes in the new PCI DSS 4.0 will be significant.

Follow Corporate Policies   Different terms are used to describe the "rules" for an organization. A *standard* is a collection of requirements specific to the system or procedure that must be met by everyone. For example, a standard might describe how to secure a computer at home that remotely connects to the organization's network. Users must follow this standard if they want to be able to connect. A *guideline* is a collection of suggestions that should be implemented. These are not requirements to be met but are strongly recommended. A *policy* is a document that outlines specific requirements or rules that must be met. A policy generally has these characteristics: it communicates a consensus of judgment, defines appropriate behavior for users, identifies what tools and procedures are needed, provides directives for human resources actions in response to inappropriate behavior, and may be helpful if it is necessary to prosecute violators.

At its core, a *security policy* is a recorded document that states how an organization plans to protect the company's information technology assets. The policy outlines the protections that should be enacted to ensure that the organization's assets face minimal risks. A security policy—along with the accompanying procedures, standards, and guidelines—is key to implementing information security in an organization. Having a written security policy empowers an organization to take appropriate action to safeguard its data. A policy is considered the correct tool for an organization to use when establishing security because a policy applies to a wide range of hardware or software (it is not a standard) and is required (it is not just a guideline).

NOTE 6

If the question "What is a security policy?" were posed to a manager and a security technician, the answers would likely be different. A manager might say that a security policy is a set of management statements that defines an organization's philosophy of how to safeguard its information. A security technician might respond that a security policy is the cybersecurity configuration settings in a system. These two responses are not conflicting but complementary: a written policy dictates what technology configuration settings should be used.

To adhere to corporate policies, a vulnerability scan may be necessary. The ongoing scanning and continuous monitoring features of such a scan can meet the goals of an organization as outlined in its security policy.

Grow with Cengage Unlimited!

If you'd like more information about this topic, use your Cengage Unlimited subscription to go to the CompTIA Security+ Guide to Network Security Fundamentals, 7th edition; open Module 14; and read the section titled "Policies."

If you don't have a Cengage Unlimited subscription, you can find more information at cengage.com/unlimited.

Vulnerability Scanning Challenges

Despite its importance, several challenges are associated with vulnerability scanning. Some of these can even be considered as risks and include the following:

- *Volume of scan data.* Vulnerability scans can produce a large amount of information that must be analyzed.
- *Identification of the vulnerability.* A vulnerability scanner must be able to perform two tasks. It must locate and identify devices, software, open ports, and other system information and then correlate that information with known vulnerabilities from one or more vulnerability databases. Not every identified system element may be an actual vulnerability, and if a system element is not part of the vulnerability database, then a weakness may be overlooked.
- *Remediation of the vulnerability.* Due to several factors, such as a high cost to remediate or a very low risk of exploitation, not all identified vulnerabilities may be addressed. The process for making these determinations can often be challenging and highly debated.
- *Technical limitations.* Vulnerability scanning that is configured to be aggressive or intrusive can impair performance or even the stability of the systems being scanned. Scanning could also cause bandwidth issues on networks. These technical limitations of a vulnerability scan could have an effect on the timeliness and usefulness of the scan.

Scanning Decisions

Several decisions must be made prior to conducting a scan if the scan is to be effective. Often the decisions are dictated by regulatory requirements. These prerequisite decisions include determining what should be scanned, how it should be scanned, and when the scan should occur.

What Should Be Scanned?

One of the first decisions before conducting a scan is to determine what should be scanned. This includes data and the assets (devices) that contain the data. As threat actors have enhanced their ability for making lateral movements after penetrating a network, a scan must look at how well the network has been segmented.

Data Classification   Before performing a vulnerability scan, it is important to know the value of specific data. This is because not all data is the same: some data is critical and must be protected at all costs (such as research and development data), while other data is of lesser importance (like marketing data). Understanding the value of the data can determine the type of vulnerability scans and their frequency on the data. A vulnerability scan can be made to primarily focus on the critical data elements while not neglecting other data elements.

Assigning labels to like types of data based on their importance is a process known as data classification. Commercial (corporate) environments do not have standards for data classification. Some organizations simply use *public* and *confidential* as the only data classifications. However, using multiple data classification levels can help provide greater clarification of the importance of the data and prevent data that is "mostly public but a little confidential" from being mislabeled. Table 3-4 lists a typical commercial data classification from the lowest level to the highest level.

NOTE 7

The measure of the importance of data can often be gauged by asking the basic question, *What would an unexpected loss or disclosure of this information mean to us?*

Table 3-4   Commercial data classification levels (lowest to highest)

Classification level	Description
Public	Data that is the least sensitive and would cause only a small amount of harm if disclosed, such as the number of current employees
Proprietary	Data that is disclosed outside the company on only a limited basis to trusted third parties; an unexpected disclosure could reduce the company's competitive advantage, such as the nontechnical specifications for a new product
Private	Data that, while it may not harm the company itself, could cause damage to others, such as human resources data of employees
Confidential	Data that is used internally within the company, but a public disclosure would cause significant harm to the organization, such as an impending merger or acquisition
Sensitive	Data that could cause catastrophic harm to the company if disclosed, such as the technical specifications for a new product

NOTE 8

When considering which classification a data element should be assigned, not only should the confidentiality of the data be considered but also the integrity and availability.

Government data classifications have continued to evolve. Whereas at one time the classification levels of *top secret, secret, confidential, sensitive but unclassified (SBU),* and *unclassified* were used, currently only the first three levels are now used (*top secret, secret,* and *confidential*). The level of sensitivity is based upon a calculation of the damage to national security that the disclosure of the information would cause.

Asset Criticality   In addition to knowing the relative value of the data, knowing the location of that data is important (**asset criticality**). This ensures that specific assets with high-value data can be scanned more frequently. Table 3-5 lists the types of vulnerability scans that can be made over common assets that typically contain or transmit important data.

Table 3-5   Types of vulnerability scans over assets

Asset	Description
Network	Scans can identify possible network security attacks and vulnerable systems on wired networks.
Endpoint	Scans can locate and identify vulnerabilities in servers, workstations, or other network endpoints and provide visibility into the configuration settings and patch history of the endpoints.
Wireless network	Scans can identify rogue access points and validate that the wireless network is secure.
Database	Scans may identify the weak points in a database.
Applications	Web applications and other software assets can be scanned to detect known software vulnerabilities and erroneous configurations.

However, to create this list of assets to be scanned, an asset inventory or listing of all significant assets needs to be consulted. Organizations that maintain an up-to-date asset inventory through regular asset management can review the asset inventory to identify the systems that should be scanned. However, what if no asset inventory is available, or it is out of date so that it cannot be trusted as being accurate?

Although it is possible to use a vulnerability scanning tool to run a full vulnerability scan of all devices on the entire network, this can take a significant amount of time to find assets and assess their vulnerabilities. Fortunately, most vulnerability scanning tools allow for an inventory scan that only searches for devices attached to the network instead of conducting a full vulnerability scan that looks for vulnerabilities. Figure 3-1 shows the hardware asset management screen of the vulnerability scanner Nessus. Software assets can also be identified. Figure 3-2 shows the Nessus software asset management screen.

Source: Tenable

Figure 3-1   Nessus hardware asset management

Source: Tenable

Figure 3-2   Nessus software asset management

Network Segmentation   The work of threat actors to penetrate a system often follows a similar pattern. The threat actors first conduct reconnaissance against the system, looking for vulnerabilities. When a path to a vulnerability is exposed, they gain access to the system through the vulnerability. Once initial access is gained, the threat actors attempt to escalate to more advanced resources that are normally protected from an application or user (called privilege escalation). With the advanced privileges, they tunnel through the network looking for additional systems they can access from their elevated position (known as lateral movement).

NOTE 9

The exploitation and penetration tactics of threat actors are covered in Module 1.

To thwart lateral movement by threat actors, network **segmentation** must be followed. Network segmentation is designed to architect a network so that parts can be cordoned off or segmented into isolated sections. This allows an organization to treat each segment of the network differently based on the classification of the data in that segment: low-risk segments may have fewer restrictions, while high-risk segments are more heavily protected.

NOTE 10

Using a virtual local area network (VLAN) is one means of performing network segmentation.

Vulnerability scans and penetration testing can identify vulnerabilities in network segmentation. Several regulatory requirements, such as the PCI DSS, mandate that segmentation controls be scanned.

How Should It Be Scanned?

Another scanning decision involves how the data and assets should be scanned. Two categories of options include active vs. passive scanning and internal vs. external scanning.

Active vs. Passive Scanning   A vulnerability scan needs to collect data on the assets that will be examined. For example, data such as the device name, IP address, OS version, installed software, and patches applied are all needed to determine if there is a vulnerability. Extracting this data is called **enumeration** and is intended to build a picture of the endpoint and the network (**mapping**).

There are two approaches to gathering this data. **Active scanning** sends test traffic transmissions into the network and monitors the responses of the endpoints. **Passive scanning**, on the other hand, does not send any transmissions but instead only listens for normal traffic to learn the needed information.

A primary advantage of conducting active scanning over passive scanning is that active scanning can accelerate the collection of the data; it is not necessary to wait for normal network traffic to or from each asset to generate a complete profile of information. In addition, not all parts of a network may always be available, which can limit the ability to passively monitor traffic.

NOTE 11

Some active scanners can also immediately take action if a serious vulnerability is uncovered (such as blocking an open port) or even launch a simulated attack to observe the response.

However, there are disadvantages to active scanning. These disadvantages include the following:

- Smaller networks can become overloaded with high volumes of test traffic.
- Sending test traffic increases the risk of the endpoints malfunctioning if incompatible queries are sent.
- Some devices such as Internet of Things (IoT) devices may not be able to perform their normal tasks while receiving and returning test traffic and could become overloaded.
- Many IoT devices are proprietary and may react differently to test traffic.

Internal vs. External   Another option regarding how the assets should be scanned involves the "vantage point" of the scan. An **internal vulnerability scan** is performed from the vantage point of inside the internal network; that is, it is launched and then conducted from inside the corporate network. An internal vulnerability scan typically has the primary benefit of identifying at-risk systems.

An **external vulnerability scan** is performed from the vantage point of outside the network. It targets specific IP addresses that are within the network to identify vulnerabilities. An external scan can also detect open ports and protocols.

NOTE 12

An external vulnerability scan is in some ways similar to a penetration test.

When Should It Be Scanned?

Another consideration is when and how frequently a vulnerability scan should be conducted. The optimum frequency for vulnerability scanning is continual: all systems are scanned all the time. However, different constraints call for scanning on a routine basis instead of around the clock. These constraints include the following:

- *Technical constraints.* Limitations based on technology (technical constraints) can dictate how frequently a scan may be performed. For an organization with a large network with many devices, it simply may not be possible to scan the entire network within a desired time period. Other technical constraints include limitations on network bandwidth and vulnerability scan software license limitations. When dealing with technical constraints, spreading out the scans to run at specific times may be a necessary alternative.
- *Workflow interruptions.* Continual vulnerability scans may interfere with the response time of a system so that the daily workflow or normal business processes are hindered. Moving the scans to "off hours" such as nights or weekends can limit the interruptions.
- *Regulatory requirements.* Specific regulations can dictate how frequently a vulnerability scan must be performed. For example, PCI DSS states how often vulnerability scans must be conducted.
- *Risk appetite.* A final consideration is the organization's tolerance for exposure to a vulnerability (*risk appetite*). The risk appetite for each system may be different: systems with sensitive data for which there is a low risk appetite may be scanned more frequently than systems that contain only public data and have a high risk appetite.

>  **CAUTION** When determining the risk appetite, longer intervals between scans result in a greater risk for a vulnerability to be exploited.

Running a Vulnerability Scan

Several tools can be used to run a vulnerability scan. Running the vulnerability scan itself generally involves updating the vulnerability scan software, configuring the software, and then executing the scan.

Updating the Scan Software

After selecting a vulnerability scanning tool, the software needs to be updated. As with any software today, updates are available to enhance its functionality or provide stronger security. Vulnerability scan software is no exception. In addition to the usual software updates, vulnerability scan software updating includes plug-in updates and vulnerability feeds.

Plug-In Updates   As attacks continue to evolve, vulnerability scan software must be "nimble" so that information regarding new attacks can be regularly added and updated. Many vulnerability scan products are modular instead of contained in a single enormous software package. These module updates, known as *plug-ins*, can be downloaded and installed as needed.

However, plug-ins generally go beyond basic updates. Many plug-ins contain advanced vulnerability information, a set of remediation actions, and updated algorithms to test for the presence of the security issue.

Vulnerability Feeds   Vulnerability scanning software looks for the presence of a vulnerability by comparing scanned software against a set of known vulnerabilities. This is known as signature-based monitoring because it compares activities against a predefined signature. Signature-based monitoring requires access to an updated database of signatures along with a means to actively compare and match current software against a collection of signatures.

NOTE 13

Plug-ins are similar to penetration testing exploitation frameworks.

NOTE 14

The number of plug-ins continues to grow exponentially. In an almost 18-month period, the number of Nessus vulnerability scanner plug-ins grew from 131,363 to 149,780.

NOTE 15

One of the weaknesses of signature-based monitoring is that the signature databases must be constantly updated, and as the number of signatures grows, the behaviors must be compared against an increasingly large number of signatures.

To provide a set of vulnerabilities to vulnerability scan software, various **vulnerability feeds**, which are ongoing streams of data related to potential or current threats, provide this data. Some of the best-known vulnerability feeds are the following:

- NIST National Vulnerability Database (NVD)
- MITRE Common Vulnerabilities and Exposures (CVE)
- CERT Vulnerability Notes Database
- VulnDB

NOTE 16

Several once-popular vulnerability feeds have closed, most notably the U.S. Defense Information System Agency's (DISA) Information Assurance Vulnerability Alerts (IAVAs), Security Tracker, and Open Source Vulnerability Database (OSVDB).

Configuring the Scan Software

Configuring vulnerability scan software involves setting specific parameters so that the scan meets the intended objective. These parameters include the scope, sensitivity levels, and data types.

Scope The **scope** of a vulnerability scan defines the target devices to be scanned. This generally will include a range of hosts or subnets, as shown in Figure 3-3. The scope of a scan should be designed to meet the intended goals of the scan. If a specific vulnerability for Windows 10 computers is being targeted in the scan, for example, then it makes sense to only scan those systems running that OS.

Figure 3-3   Vulnerability scan scope

NOTE 17

Limiting the scope can also reduce the impact on the overall performance of the network.

Sensitivity Level   While the scope represents the breadth of the scan, the sensitivity level is the depth of a scan. That is, what type of vulnerabilities are being searched for? While a general scan may search for all vulnerabilities, often a scan is looking for a specific type of vulnerability. The sensitivity configuration variable can be used to limit how deeply a system is examined.

Data Type   Another configuration setting specifies the data types to be scanned. Like the sensitivity level, this can be used to "drill down" when searching for a specific vulnerability in a known file type instead of searching all files on a system.

Executing the Scan

When executing the scan, types of scanner options can impact running the scan. These are server-based vs. agent-based scans and credentialed vs. non-credentialed scans. However, before attempting a scan, the scanner permissions and access should be reviewed. It is also important to properly configure other network appliances when running a scan.

Scanner Permissions and Access   A well-protected network ideally should hinder or even block a scanner from performing a vulnerability scan, just as it would prevent threat actors from conducting their own scans for reconnaissance. In such cases, the network security would prevent the vulnerability scanner from accurately examining the devices on the network. Network security may need to add appropriate scanner permissions so that it can access the devices on the network.

Just as the scanner needs permissions to access the network, from another standpoint, an additional set of scanner permissions are also needed. These are permissions for a user to access and use the scanner itself.

It is no surprise that a vulnerability scanner may uncover significant vulnerabilities that if executed on a system not owned by the organization, they would allow the tester access to the system. This obviously raises serious legal and ethical issues. Testers using a vulnerability scanner should have permissions from internal supervisors to use the software, and this software should only be used to access approved systems.

Server-Based vs. Agent-Based Scans   Suppose you want to invite a group of your friends out to share a pizza late one night at a new restaurant. You open your smartphone, bring up a web browser, and search for the time that the restaurant closes. Once you find that information, you post it on your social media account so that your friends will see it.

You have just used the two means of accessing Internet information. *Pull* is when you are seeking information, such as answer to a question, so you *pull* that information into you. *Push* is when you are using the Internet in a more passive way and content comes to you. By posting the information about the restaurant's closing time in your social media account, it is then *pushed* to your friends.

Vulnerability scanners have traditionally used a pull approach: a scanner manager connects to a scanner engine that probes each system for information that is then gathered (pulled) back for analysis. This is known as a server-based (pull) scanner technology, as shown in Figure 3-4.

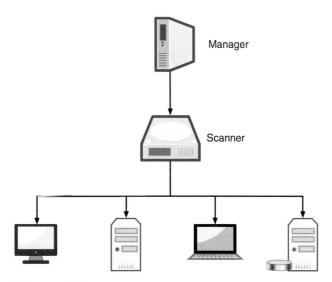

Figure 3-4   Server-based scanner technology

However, today a push option is becoming increasingly popular. Software agents that reside on a system send (push) their information back to the manager. This is known as agent-based (push) scanner technology. Agent-based scanner technology is shown in Figure 3-5. Agent-based scanners tend to have less impact on network performance. However, the software agents could become the target of threat actors so that they would not accurately report the true status of a compromised computer.

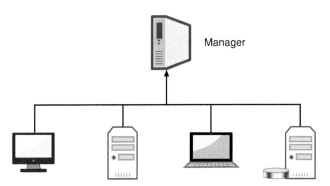

Figure 3-5 Agent-based scanner technology

Credentialed vs. Non-credentialed Scan   Threat actors who can compromise a network can cause a significant degree of harm. Yet threat actors who can compromise a network and have in their possession valid authentication credentials (such as usernames and passwords, certificates, and public keys) can potentially cause catastrophic harm. Which of these should a vulnerability scan imitate: a threat actor who does not have stolen credentials or one who does?

Fortunately, most vulnerability scanners allow for both types of scans. A credentialed scan is a scan for which valid authentication credentials are supplied to the vulnerability scanner to mimic the work of a threat actor who possesses these credentials, while a non-credentialed scan provides no such authentication information. Figure 3-6 shows the credentials that can be entered for a credentialed scan.

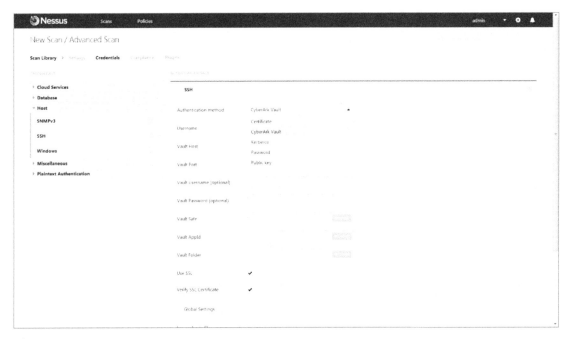

Figure 3-6   Credentialed scan

Non-credentialed scans run faster because they are performing fundamental actions such as looking for open ports and finding software that will respond to requests. Credentialed scans are slower but can provide a deeper insight into the system by accessing a fuller range of software installed on the system and examining the software's configuration settings and current security posture.

Network Appliance Configurations Vulnerability scanners should set off alarms on security appliances such as intrusion detection systems (IDSs), intrusion prevention systems (IPSs), and firewalls. One approach is to mitigate these alarms by instructing the IDS/IPS to ignore attacks originating at the vulnerability scanner and to also configure the vulnerability scanner to correspond to the IDS/IPS.

However, a preferred approach is to use a scan as an opportunity to validate the behavior of the vulnerability scanner and IDS/IPS. By knowing that the vulnerability scanner should set off alarms on other security appliances, it is possible to predict the behavior of the IDS/IPS in response to the vulnerability scanner. By analyzing the behavior of both devices, this can serve as a check to ensure that they are operating properly.

NOTE 18

If you choose to have the IDS/IPS not ignore the vulnerability scanner, you should configure the IDS/IPS to record the predicted events but set them to a low priority for generating alerts.

Analyzing Vulnerability Scans

Once the vulnerability scan is completed, the results need to be first validated and then reported.

Validation

When examining results of a vulnerability scan, it is important to validate its results for accuracy. Has the vulnerability scan identified genuine vulnerabilities and not missed any? If the scan were 100 percent accurate, then the organization would know that a future attack would accurately trigger an alarm (**true positive**) while the absence of an attack would not trigger an alarm (**true negative**). However, it is possible that the scan could generate an error. There are two particular types of errors:

- *False positive*. A **false positive** is an alarm that is raised when there is no problem
- *False negative*. A **false negative** is the failure to raise an alarm when there is an issue.

NOTE 19

The mathematical formula for calculating the accuracy of the validation is (true positive + true negative)/(true positive + true negative + false positive + false negative).

Vulnerability scans may produce false positives for several reasons; for example, scan options may not be well defined or may have been missed in a configuration review, or the scanner might not recognize a control that is already in place to address an existing vulnerability. A false positive in a vulnerability scan results in unnecessary work looking for a vulnerability when none exists. Security professionals should attempt to identify false positives in a scan report, especially those that would require extensive effort to address.

The result of a false negative, however, is more serious: the scan overlooked an existing vulnerability that a threat actor may find and exploit. One means of identifying false positives is for the vulnerability scan data to be correlated with several internal data points. The most common are related log files. Because a log is simply a record of events, system event logs document any unsuccessful events and the most significant successful events. The types of information recorded might include the date and time of the event; a description of the event; its status, error codes, and service name; and the user or system that was responsible for launching the event. Log reviews, or an analysis of log data, can be used to identify false positives.

NOTE 20

Logs can be particularly helpful internal data points when correlating with vulnerability scan results. For example, if a scan indicates that a vulnerability in a software application was found on a specific device but a follow-up investigation revealed that the application was no longer vulnerable, log files could indicate whether that program's configuration had been changed between the time of the scan and the follow-up analysis.

Reporting

Usually, different levels of available reports should be distributed to different audiences. Table 3-6 illustrates the report types and audiences.

Table 3-6   Vulnerability scan reporting

Audience	Level of report	Explanation
Management	A general report that outlines the impact to the organization	Management is interested in how the latest scan compares with previous scans, how serious are the vulnerabilities, and how long it will take to address these latest vulnerabilities.
System and network engineers	A technical report that outlines what needs to be addressed	Engineers want a listing of the devices with vulnerabilities and specific details regarding how to fix the problems.
Application developers	A report that lists the applications that contain vulnerabilities and what those vulnerabilities are	Developers want to know which of their applications are vulnerable and as much as possible the location of that vulnerability in their code.
Security teams	A very specific report as it relates to the technical security details	Security teams want to know what systems were vulnerable, the details as to why they could be exploited, and what remediation steps are necessary.

NOTE 21

Today vulnerability scan software can provide extensive information through reporting to assist different audiences. For example, for a website that contains an SQL injection vulnerability, the vulnerability scan software can provide application developers with the name of the application, the input to the web application that triggered the vulnerability and the corresponding output, and even the specific variable within the application that resulted in the compromise.

There are also different means for distributing reports. Reports can be distributed automatically via email to specific audiences. They also can be sent at different times, such as when a scan is completed or once each week. Another option is for individuals to be given direct access to the vulnerability scan software so that they can read the reports on demand as a type of manual report distribution.

Addressing Vulnerabilities

The final step in executing a vulnerability scan is to address any issues that were uncovered. This involves remediating vulnerabilities. It also includes being aware of inhibitors to remediation.

Remediating Vulnerabilities

To remediate vulnerabilities, the first step is to prioritize the vulnerabilities. Then action steps should be taken to address those vulnerabilities that have been identified as most important.

Prioritizing Vulnerabilities   Consider a vulnerability scan that produces the results as shown in Figure 3-7, which lists 20 vulnerabilities. Although there are (thankfully) no critical vulnerabilities, nevertheless, there are multiple high, medium, and low vulnerabilities. But where do you begin? Do you start with the high vulnerabilities and work your way down through all the low vulnerabilities? Or is there a better approach to take?

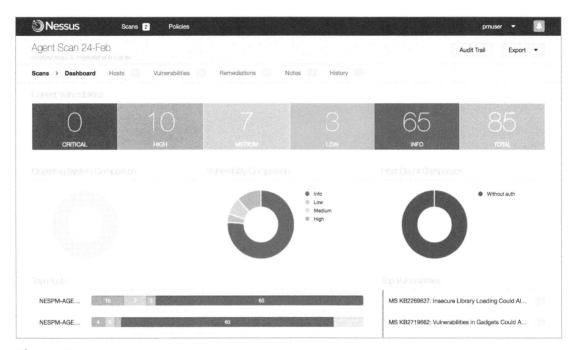

Figure 3-7 Results of vulnerability scan

Remember the principle that *it is rarely possible, and often not desirable, to address all vulnerabilities*. Not all vulnerabilities are as potentially damaging as other vulnerabilities. Despite the rating of medium given to a vulnerability by a scanner, to one organization this vulnerability may be critical, while to another it is not worth the effort to fix. Also, because many vulnerabilities are complex to unravel and take an extended amount of time to address, there may not be enough time to solve all of them. Beginning with the high vulnerabilities and working down through the low vulnerabilities may not always be the best plan of action.

Instead, vulnerabilities need to be prioritized so that the most important vulnerabilities are addressed early on, while others can wait until later or not even be addressed. Several criteria are used for prioritizing vulnerabilities. The numeric score assigned to a vulnerability based upon the Common Vulnerability Scoring System (CVSS) can serve as a starting point. These numeric scores are generated using a complex formula that accounts for variables such as the access vector, attack complexity, authentication, confidentiality of the data, and the integrity and availability of the system. Vulnerabilities with the highest numeric CVSS score generally are considered as requiring early attention.

NOTE 22

CVSS is covered in Module 2.

Prioritizing vulnerabilities is an inexact and sometimes difficult process. However, attention should first be directed toward those that are determined to be critical (can cause the greatest degree of harm) to the specific organization and that the difficulty and time for implementing the correction is reasonable.

Action Steps Once the vulnerabilities are prioritized, a series of action steps can be taken to actively address the uncovered vulnerabilities. These action steps include the following:

- *Patch and harden.* Vulnerabilities should first be addressed by patching systems that are missing existing software updates. This is the easiest, quickest, and most economical approach and generally addresses a high number of exposed vulnerabilities. After patching, the systems should be hardened as necessary with new hardware or software.
- *Address difficult vulnerabilities.* Some vulnerabilities that need to be addressed will not have a quick and easy solution; instead, the options are difficult or impractical. In these cases, it may be necessary to determine an alternative action (**compensating control**), such as removing an endpoint from the network. In other cases, it may simply be necessary to acknowledge that the risk exists and take no further action (**risk acceptance**).
- *Verify mitigation.* It is important to corroborate that the vulnerabilities have indeed been properly addressed. In addition, once the changes have been approved and applied to the production system, these changes need to be formally communicated and recorded. This is a process known as change control (also called change management) and refers to a methodology for modifying a system and keeping track of those changes.

NOTE 23

In too many instances, changes to network or system configurations are made haphazardly to alleviate a pressing security vulnerability. However, no proper documentation of the changes is made. This results in future changes negating or diminishing a previous change or even unknowingly creating a security vulnerability. Change management seeks to approach changes systematically and provide the necessary documentation of the changes.

- *Create configuration baseline.* After steps have been taken to address the vulnerabilities, it is important to create an updated foundation-level configuration (configuration baseline) that is then applied to all systems. This becomes the standard to which all existing and newly installed systems must maintain.

Inhibitors to Remediation

At first, the idea seems unthinkable of someone or something inhibiting a change to a system to address a vulnerability. However, external factors may impact how, when, or even if a change can be made to address a vulnerability.

Often inhibitors are due to interoperability agreements, or formal contractual relationships. These agreements include the following types:

- A service level agreement (SLA) is a service contract between a vendor and a client that specifies what services will be provided, the responsibilities of each party, and any guarantees of service.
- A memorandum of understanding (MOU) describes an agreement between two or more parties. It demonstrates a "convergence of will" between the parties so that they can work together. An MOU generally is not a legally enforceable agreement but is more formal than an unwritten agreement.
- An *interconnection security agreement (ISA)* is an agreement that is intended to minimize security risks for data transmitted across a network. Examples of network interconnections usually include corporate virtual private network (VPN) tunnels that are used to connect to a network. The ISA ensures the adequate security of both entities as they share data across networks.
- A *nondisclosure agreement (NDA)* is a legal contract between parties that specifies how confidential material will be shared between the parties but restricted to others. An NDA creates a confidential relationship between the parties to protect any type of confidential and proprietary information.

NOTE 24

Any of these formal relationships may hinder addressing a vulnerability. For example, an MOU may state that specific changes will not be made to a remote system, even if a vulnerability is discovered on that system.

Another inhibitor can be the organizational governance of the company. Organizational governance is defined as the system by which an organization makes and then implements decisions. While the ideal would be for everyone at the organization to agree with the necessity of addressing cybersecurity vulnerabilities, this is not always the case. Due to infighting, multiple levels of bureaucracy, and extensive "red tape," it is not uncommon to delay correcting a vulnerability for an extended period, particularly if the correction may interrupt the normal business processes.

On some occasions, addressing a vulnerability may change or even eliminate a function of an application for the sake of making it more secure. This is known as degrading functionality and may invoke stiff resistance when users have been accustomed to a function or option. One means of addressing degrading functionality is to remind users of the relationship between *security* and *convenience*: as security is increased, convenience is often decreased. That is, the *more* secure something is, the *less* convenient it may become to use. (Security is said to be "inversely proportional" to convenience.)

Another "pushback" from the organization to implementing tighter security by addressing vulnerabilities is the reluctance of the organization to make any changes to a system that is properly functioning. Today businesses and industrial processes function in a "just-in-time" environment in which processing time has been significantly reduced to increase overall efficiency. This essentially results in no "slack" in the system. There may be objections to bringing the key critical devices (priority systems) offline to address vulnerabilities when this could impair the entire production system. In many instances, these are older systems with specialized software that cannot be easily replaced (legacy systems), and thus, there is no alternative for bringing them offline. This is known as business process interruption. It is not uncommon for higher levels of management to lack support in addressing vulnerabilities if doing so may interrupt normal functions.

Advanced Vulnerability Scanning

The concept of all an organization's servers residing in an on-premise data center that serves resources to desktop computers is a historical relic. Computer servers, networks, and endpoints have evolved more rapidly over the last decade than perhaps in any time in the history of information technology. Cloud computing, mobile smartphones, virtual machines, and Internet of Things (IoT) devices, to name a few, have dramatically increased today's enterprise's IT capabilities—and correspondingly have dramatically increased its attack surface. This is shown in Figure 3-8.

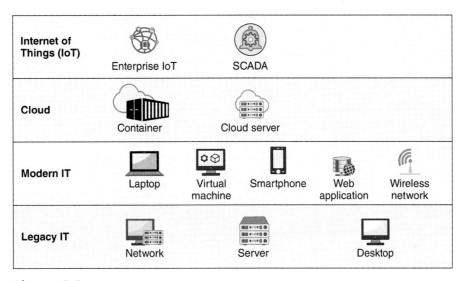

Figure 3-8 Today's enterprise IT

However, performing static vulnerability scans, in the eyes of many security professionals, may no longer provide the *visibility* into system and network vulnerabilities that it once did. Legacy scans that are ad hoc and siloed are usually labor intensive and expensive, resulting in limited deployments and incomplete visibility. These scans often lack comprehensive, continuous, and accurate visibility into where vulnerabilities reside and how businesses might be affected. Without this visibility, it is difficult or even impossible to prioritize and manage risks.

Among the specific limitations of legacy vulnerability management are the following:

- *Focus on traditional assets.* Legacy vulnerability scanning focuses on traditional IT assets such as network infrastructures, servers, and desktop computers. These tools are not always designed to discover and scan new assets such as cloud instances, containers, web applications, and IoT devices.
- *Reliance on active scanning technologies.* Active vulnerability scanning tools, while essential, can only capture a snapshot at a single point in time. They often entirely miss devices that are not always connected to the corporate network or that do not have static IP addresses (such as smartphones or remote employees' laptop computers), short-lived assets such as containers, and resources like cloud repositories. Vulnerability scanning was simply not designed for today's dynamic assets and does not always give an accurate picture of their security.
- *Limitations of scanning.* Active vulnerability scanning tools should not be used on all systems. For example, many industrial control systems, IoT devices, and medical devices have not been designed to be scanned, so scanning may cause disruption or even an entire outage.
- *Lack of insight and prioritization.* A legacy scan gives a large amount of detail on assets and their vulnerabilities. Yet it does not provide tailored information and actionable steps that allow security personnel to quickly prioritize remediation efforts. In addition, it lacks data analytics that can be used to evaluate and manage the overall cyber risk more easily.

As a result, advanced vulnerability scanning tools and processes have recently been introduced to reflect the changes in IT. A new category of security tools, sometimes called *cyber exposure platforms*, is specifically designed to continuously perform asset inventory and then assess not only traditional IT infrastructures and devices but also cloud, mobile, IoT, and other assets across the entire organization. In addition, these tools can help quickly evaluate vulnerabilities, prioritize issues, take appropriate corrective steps, and finally measure and report on the vulnerability from both a technical and business perspective.

TWO RIGHTS & A WRONG

1. Unlike a penetration test, a vulnerability scan is designed to identify deep vulnerabilities.
2. There are five types of vulnerability scans over assets: network, endpoint, wireless network, database, and applications.
3. Active scanning sends test traffic transmissions into the network and monitors the responses of the endpoints.

See Appendix C for the answer.

VM LAB   You're now ready to complete the live, virtual machine labs for this module. The labs can be found in the Apply It folder in each MindTap module.

MODULE SUMMARY

- Vulnerability management is also called infrastructure risk visibility and assurance. Its purpose is to be an ongoing examination of the organization's security instead of a specifically scheduled or even annual event. It is not designed to expose the deep vulnerabilities as a pen test can, but it provides an ongoing evaluation of the protections in place.
- Several categories of common vulnerabilities may be found in an organization. Software coding techniques that should be used to create secure applications and limit sensitive data exposure or disclosing sensitive data to attackers are often implemented incorrectly by software developers. Some software may not properly trap an error condition, potentially providing an attacker with access to the OS. This is known as improper error handling. Another improper exception handling situation is an insecure pointer/object dereference caused by an invalid dereference, which is used to obtain from a pointer the address of a data item held in another location. A race condition in software occurs when two concurrent threads of execution access a shared resource simultaneously, resulting in unintended consequences. An insecure object reference occurs when an application externally exposes a reference to an internal object.
- In addition to attacking the software directly, threat actors also target external software components that may be insecure. An application program interface (API) is a link provided by an OS, web browser, or other platform that allows a developer access to resources at a high level. Because APIs provide direct access to data and an entry point to an application's functions, they are attractive targets for attackers looking for vulnerabilities. A device driver is software that controls and operates an external hardware device connected to a computer. Threat actors may attempt to alter a device driver for use in an attack (called device driver manipulation). A dynamic link library (DLL) is a repository of both code and data that can be used by more than one program at the same time. Attackers use a technique called DLL injection for inserting code into a running process through a DLL to cause a program to function in a different way than intended.

- Programmers who choose internal programming language functions can likewise introduce vulnerabilities. The programming language C has an internal function strcpy that can be used to copy a string to a destination buffer but could also be used to overwrite a portion of memory to perform a memory vulnerability attack. Modern hardware and software platforms provide a wide array of features and security settings, and these must be properly configured to repel attacks. However, often the configuration settings are not properly implemented, resulting in weak configurations. Vulnerabilities introduced by poor authentication practices (broken authentication) can open a broad pathway for a threat actor to exploit. The sheer volume of raw log data makes it virtually impossible to manually uncover meaningful insights. This sometimes causes organizations to practice insufficient monitoring and logging.

- One useful means of defining a vulnerability scan is to compare it to a penetration test. A penetration test is a single event using a manual process that is too often performed only to comply with regulatory requirements. A vulnerability scan is a frequent and ongoing process that is automated to continuously identify vulnerabilities and monitor cybersecurity progress. A vulnerability assessment is a cyclical and continual process of ongoing scanning and continuous monitoring.

- There are different reasons for conducting a vulnerability scan. Several government and industry regulatory requirements call for vulnerability scans to be conducted on a regular basis. Examples of regulatory compliance laws and regulations include the Dodd–Frank Act, Payment Card Industry Data Security Standard (PCI DSS), Health Insurance Portability and Accountability Act (HIPAA), the Federal Information Security Management Act (FISMA), and the Sarbanes–Oxley (SOX) Act. To adhere to corporate policies, a vulnerability scan may be necessary. The ongoing scanning and continuous monitoring features of such a scan can meet the goals of an organization as outlined in its security policy. Despite its importance, several challenges are associated with vulnerability scanning.

- Several decisions must be made prior to conducting a scan if the scan is to be effective. One of the first decisions is to determine what should be scanned. This involves knowing the value of specific data. Assigning labels to like types of data based on their importance is known as data classification. Commercial (corporate) environments do not have standards for data classification; the government data classifications are top secret, secret, and confidential. In addition to knowing the relative importance of the data, also knowing its location is important so that specific systems with high-value data can be scanned more frequently. However, to create a list of assets to scan, an asset inventory or listing of all significant assets needs to be consulted or produced. To thwart lateral movement by threat actors, it is important that network segmentation be followed. Network segmentation is designed to architect a network so that parts can be cordoned off or segmented into isolated sections. Vulnerability scans and penetration testing can be used to identify vulnerabilities in network segmentation.

- Another scanning decision involves how the data and assets should be scanned. Extracting important endpoint and network data is called enumeration and is intended to build a picture of the endpoint and network (mapping). There are two approaches to gathering this data. Active scanning sends test traffic transmissions into the network and monitors the responses of the endpoints. Passive scanning, on the other hand, does not send any transmissions but only listens for normal traffic to learn the needed information. Another option regarding how the assets should be scanned involves the "vantage point" of the scan. An internal vulnerability scan is performed from the vantage point of inside the internal network, while an external vulnerability scan is performed from the vantage point of outside the network.

- Another consideration is when and how frequently a vulnerability scan should be conducted. Some constraints call for scanning on a routine basis instead of around the clock. These include technical constraints, workflow interruptions, regulatory requirements, and risk appetite.

- Several tools can be used for conducting a vulnerability scan. After selecting a vulnerability scanning tool, the software needs to be updated. Many vulnerability scan products are modular instead of contained in a single enormous software package. These module updates, known as plug-ins, can be downloaded and installed as needed. Vulnerability scanning software looks for the presence of a vulnerability by comparing software that is scanned against a set of known vulnerabilities. Various vulnerability feeds provide sets of vulnerabilities to vulnerability scan software.

- Configuring vulnerability scan software involves setting specific parameters so that the scan meets the intended objective. The scope of a vulnerability scan is the target devices to be scanned. This generally includes a range of hosts or subnets. The sensitivity level is the depth of a scan: that is, what type of vulnerabilities are being searched for? While a general scan may search for all vulnerabilities, often a scan is looking for a specific type of vulnerability. Another configuration setting specifies the data types to be scanned.

- When executing the scan, different scanner options can impact running the scan. A well-protected network ideally should hinder or even block a scanner from performing a vulnerability scan, just as it would prevent threat actors from conducting their own scans for reconnaissance. Network security may need to add appropriate scanner permissions so that can access the devices on the network. Vulnerability scanners have traditionally used a "pull" approach in that a scanner manager connects to a scanner engine that probes each system for information and then gathers (pulls) it back for analysis. This is called a server-based (pull) scanner technology. Today a push option is becoming increasingly popular. Software agents that reside on a system send (push) their information back to the manager. This is known as agent-based (push) scanner technology.

- In a credentialed scan, valid authentication credentials are supplied to the vulnerability scanner to mimic the work of a threat actor who possesses these credentials, while a non-credentialed scan provides no such authentication information. Vulnerability scanners should set off alarms on security appliances such as intrusion detection systems (IDSs), intrusion prevention systems (IPSs), and firewalls. One approach is to mitigate these alarms by instructing the IDS/IPS to ignore attacks originating at the vulnerability scanner. However, a preferred approach is to use this as an opportunity to validate the behavior of both the vulnerability scanner and IDS/IPS.

- Once the vulnerability scan is completed, the results need to be validated and then reported. Validating a scan involves looking for two types of errors: false positives and false negatives. Different levels of reports should be distributed to separate audiences. There are also different means for distributing reports. Reports can be distributed automatically via email to specific audiences at different times, such as when a scan is completed or once each week. Another option is for individuals to be given direct access to the vulnerability scan software so that they can read the reports on demand.

- The final step in executing a vulnerability scan is to remediate any uncovered vulnerabilities. Not all vulnerabilities are as potentially damaging as other vulnerabilities. Despite the rating of medium given to a vulnerability by a scanner, to one organization this vulnerability may be critical, while to another it is not worth the effort to fix. Because many vulnerabilities are complex to unravel and take an extended amount of time to address, there may not be enough time to solve all of them. Vulnerabilities need to be prioritized so that the most important vulnerabilities are addressed early on, while others can wait until later or not even be addressed. Several criteria are used for prioritizing vulnerabilities.

- Once a priority order of addressing vulnerabilities is established, the next step is to work toward correcting the vulnerabilities. This includes patching, hardening, addressing difficult vulnerabilities, verifying mitigation, and creating a new configuration baseline. External factors often impact how, when, or even if a change can be made to address a vulnerability. As a result, advanced vulnerability scanning tools and processes have recently been introduced to reflect the changes in IT. A new category of security tools, sometimes called cyber exposure platforms, is specifically designed to continuously perform asset inventory and then assess not only traditional IT infrastructures and devices but also cloud, mobile, IoT, and other assets across the entire organization.

Key Terms

active scanning
agent-based scanner technology
asset criticality
broken authentication
business process interruption
compensating control
configuration baseline
credentialed scan

default configuration
degrading functionality
dereference
enumeration
external vulnerability scan
false negative
false positive
improper error handling

insecure object reference
insufficient monitoring and logging
internal vulnerability scan
legacy systems
mapping
memorandum of understanding (MOU)
non-credentialed scan

organizational governance
passive scanning
priority systems
race condition
regulatory requirements
risk acceptance
scope

segmentation
sensitive data exposure
sensitivity level
server-based scanner technology
service level agreement (SLA)
strcpy
technical constraints

true negative
true positive
types of data
vulnerability feed
vulnerability scan
weak configuration
workflow

Review Questions

1. Aegeus has been asked to create a report outlining the security risk of improper error handling. Which of the following would Aegeus include on his report?

   a. It can slow down the overall system so that security appliances cannot be used to monitor its processes.

   b. It could potentially provide an attacker to the underlying OS.

   c. It will cause error messages to appear on the screen that could contain fake instructions telling the user to perform an insecure action.

   d. It can result in all other applications that are currently running to abort and send erroneous data across the network.

2. Alexsanteri is holding a coding workshop for employees interested in advanced IT positions at his organization. The topic under discussion is dereferences. How would Alexsanteri define a dereference?

   a. To dereference a pointer is to access the value stored in memory that the pointer is pointing to.

   b. To dereference a memory location is to access the value stored in memory that the pointer is pointing to.

   c. To dereference a string is to access the value stored in memory that contains the string.

   d. To dereference a number is to access the corresponding string value stored in memory that the pointer is pointing to.

3. Callister is evaluating a software application that is not providing the correct output. He is able to determine that two concurrent threads of execution are accessing a shared resource simultaneously. What has Callister uncovered?

   a. A RAM memory conflict (ARMC)

   b. A race condition

   c. A resource allocation conflict (RAC)

   d. A worm trigger

4. An application has inadvertently externally exposed a reference to an internal object. What is this called?

   a. Unmasking attack

   b. Token manipulation (T-Man)

   c. URL stuffing

   d. Insecure object reference

5. Which of the following is NOT an external software component that could be targeted in an attack?

   a. API

   b. DLL

   c. ORP

   d. Device driver

6. Dimitri is studying the programming language C and wants to use the internal function *strcpy*. What is the problem associated with using this function?

   a. Programmers should never copy into a memory location directly but should dereference it instead.

   b. This function does not check the length of the destination buffer into which the string is being copied.

   c. *Strcpy* is no longer available but has been replaced with *strlencpy.*

   d. The *strcpy* function has been compromised by threat actors infecting it with malware.

7. Which of the following is NOT a weak configuration that can result in vulnerabilities?

   a. Default configurations

   b. Open ports and services

   c. Unsecured root accounts

   d. Using current configurations instead of deprecated settings

8. Which of the following is NOT a network-based poor authentication practice?

   a. Not using a password manager to generate, store, and autofill passwords

   b. Storing user credentials using general-purpose hash algorithms like MD5 and SHA

   c. Reusing session IDs after a successful login

   d. Exposing session IDs in a URL

9. Evgeni has been asked to perform a vulnerability scan. Which of the following steps would he perform first?
   a. Determine data classifications.
   b. Update the scan software.
   c. Configure the scan software.
   d. Set the sensitively levels.

10. Which of the following is NOT a reason to conduct a vulnerability scan?
    a. Have continuous monitoring.
    b. Meet regulatory requirements.
    c. Adhere to corporate policies.
    d. Perform an in-depth analysis of the vulnerabilities.

11. Which of the following does NOT apply to a vulnerability scan?
    a. Identify vulnerabilities by scanning systems and networks.
    b. Scan to find weaknesses and then mitigate.
    c. Usually automated with a handful of manual processes.
    d. Act like a threat actor to find vulnerabilities to exploit.

12. Which of the following is NOT a regulatory compliance law or regulation that requires a vulnerability scan?
    a. Payment Card Industry Data Security Standard (PCI DSS)
    b. Federal Information Security Management Act (FISMA)
    c. Federal Education Rights and Privacy Act (FERPA)
    d. Health Insurance Portability and Accountability Act (HIPAA)

13. Gregson has just completed a vulnerability scan that has identified several vulnerabilities in software applications. To whom should Gregson send this report so that they can be quickly addressed?
    a. System and network engineers
    b. Application developers
    c. Security team
    d. Management

14. Chiara is reviewing different types of vulnerability scanners, and she finds one type that uses pull technology. Which of the following types uses pull technology?
    a. Server-based
    b. Agent-based
    c. Credential-based
    d. Software-based

15. How can the impact of a vulnerability scan on workflow be mitigated?
    a. Perform the scans at night.
    b. Alternate the scans so they run every other hour.
    c. Execute scans after completing a pen test.
    d. It is not possible to mitigate its impact.

16. Which of the following do plug-ins NOT contain?
    a. Advanced vulnerability information
    b. A listing of vulnerable local IP addresses
    c. Remediation actions
    d. Updated algorithms

17. Nikita needs to specify which devices need to be included in the next vulnerability scan. What parameter must she set?
    a. Sensitivity level
    b. Region
    c. Scope
    d. NET-SCAN

18. When prioritizing vulnerabilities, what system will assign a numeric score to a vulnerability?
    a. CRCV
    b. DSS
    c. RDV
    d. CVSS

19. What is an SLA?
    a. A service contract between a vendor and a client that specifies what services will be provided, the responsibilities of each party, and any guarantees of service
    b. An agreement between two or more parties that demonstrates a "convergence of will" between the parties so that they can work together
    c. A legal contract between parties that specifies how confidential material will be shared between the parties but restricted to others
    d. A regulatory platform that is the foundation of businesses that use IT

20. What is the first step that should be taken after deciding which vulnerability scanning tool to use?
    a. Set the scope.
    b. Determine the sensitivity level.
    c. Update the plug-ins.
    d. Execute the scan.

Case Projects

Case Project 3-1 Data Classification Levels

Create a table of the five different types of commercial data classification levels. For each type, indicate one example of your personal data that would fit into each category. Next, indicate one example of data at your school or place of employment that would fit into each category. How difficult is it to assign labels to data types? Would more labels make the exercise easier or more difficult? Why?

Case Project 3-2 Vulnerability Feed

Visit the website abuse.ch and research the different features that are available for a vulnerability feed. How up to date does the information appear to be? How many malware instances have been submitted? What strengths are there of this feed? What weaknesses exist? And how could a threat actor use this site? Write a one-page paper on your research.

Case Project 3-3 Nessus

Perhaps the best-known and most widely used vulnerability scanner is Nessus, which contains a wide array of pre-built templates. Nessus advertises that new plug-ins are available as soon as 24 hours after a new vulnerability is disclosed. Visit the Nessus website at www.tenable.com/products/nessus and read the information on Nessus. Write a one-page paper on your research about Nessus. You can also download the free Nessus Essentials software and run a vulnerability scan on a maximum of 16 IP addresses.

Case Project 3-4 Scanning Decisions

Identify a network at your school, business, or a personal network to evaluate and develop the scanning decisions if you were to perform a vulnerability scan on it. Include what should be scanned (data classification, asset criticality, and network segmentation), how should it be scanned (active vs. passive scanning and internal vs. external), and when should it be scanned. For each of these, have a justification as to why you made this decision and the weakness of the alternative. Create a one-page paper on your scanning decisions.

Case Project 3-5 On the Job

Suppose you work for a company that is resisting implementing changes to vulnerabilities identified by a vulnerability scan. Your company states that the business process interruption would be significant and could potentially cause significant downtime to address a vulnerability that possibly would never even be exploited. Create a one-page memo to your manager about the importance of addressing vulnerabilities and your recommendations for balancing business processes and cybersecurity.

References

1. Bouwman, Xander; Griffioen, Harm; Egbers, Jelle; Doerr, Christian; Klievink, Bram; and van Eeten, Michel, "A Different Cup of TI? The Added Value of Commercial Threat Intelligence," *29th USENIX Security Symposium*, retrieved Aug. 8, 2020, www.cyber-threat-intelligence.com/publications/Usenix2020-PaidCTI.pdf.
2. Zumerle, Dioisio; D'Hoinne, Jeremy; and O'Neill, Mark, "How to Build an Effective API Security Strategy," Gartner Research, Dec. 8, 2017, accessed May 12, 2020, www.gartner.com/en/documents/3834704.
3. Oesch, Sean, and Ruoti, Scott, "That Was Then, This Is Now: A Security Evaluation of Password Generation, Storage, and Autofill in Thirteen Password Managers," *USENIX Security 2020,* accessed Aug. 8, 2020, https://arxiv.org/pdf/1908.03296.pdf.

CLOUD COMPUTING AND ASSESSMENT TOOLS

After completing this module, you should be able to do the following:

1. Define the cloud and explain how it is used and managed
2. List different cloud vulnerabilities
3. Describe the features of tools used for assessing vulnerabilities

Cybersecurity Today

With increasing frequency, government data is under attack from threat actors. The Center for Strategic and International Studies maintains a record of cyberattacks directed against governments, and for the first 11 months of 2020, at least 46 attacks were reported.[1] These included Iranian attacks targeting state election websites to download voter registration information and conduct a voter intimidation campaign; Greek hactivists who defaced the website of the Turkish Parliament and 150 Azerbaijani government websites that supported Armenia; North Korean nation-state attackers conducting cyber espionage campaigns against government entities in South Korea, Japan, and the United States with the purpose of collecting intelligence on national security issues related to the Korean peninsula, sanctions, and nuclear policy; and unknown attackers targeting the U.S. Census Bureau in a possible attempt to collect bulk data, alter registration information, and compromise the census infrastructure.

As governments, like all organizations, continue to migrate more of their data to the cloud, concern is growing that important government data in the cloud will increasingly become under attack. Because of the potential security issues related to cloud storage and a lack of robust cloud security controls, cloud-based government data may not always be as secure as data stored in a government data center. The potential to incite broad social unrest by manipulating government data makes securing this information particularly important.

To protect government cloud data, some cloud providers have started offering special high-level secure cloud environments for governments only. For example, Microsoft has launched specialized cloud environments exclusively for governments that use its Azure cloud services. In addition to its standard Azure for commercial entities, Microsoft created the Azure Government cloud environment. Azure Government is advertised as a dedicated and mission-critical cloud. It provides an additional layer of protection by using special "contractual commitments" that only store data on domestic servers (and not on international servers located in other countries) to support U.S. export control regulations. Only U.S. federal, state, local, and tribal governments and their partners can have access to Azure Government. In addition, the internal cloud operations are controlled only by screened U.S. citizens.

On the heels of Azure Government, Microsoft launched Azure Government Secret, which is an enhanced version of Azure Government. Azure Government Secret is designed for the unique requirements of the critical national security workloads used by the Department of Defense (DoD), Intelligence Community (IC), and U.S. government partners working within "Secret Enclaves." Azure Government Secret stores data across three dedicated regions located more than 500 miles apart. This is to enable applications to continue to function in the face of a disaster. In addition, Azure Government Secret cloud resources can be accessed using dedicated connections instead of through the "standard" Internet. Government agencies with direct connections through U.S. government classified networks can connect directly (natively) to Azure Government Secret. Agencies can also connect over a private and dedicated connection.

In late 2020, Microsoft announced the Azure Government Top Secret cloud environment. It is designed to serve government agencies that handle highly sensitive and classified data. Microsoft is currently working with the U.S. government on accreditation for this latest service to ensure that it meets mandated high-level security standards.

The COVID-19 pandemic of 2020 is generally recognized as accelerating migrations that were already in progress, albeit at a more moderate pace. For example, consider online delivery and pickup of grocery orders. In August 2019, prior to the pandemic, online grocery sales totaled $1.2 billion. Yet a little more than one year later, in the midst of the pandemic, total sales were $5.9 billion, as almost 39 million shoppers placed at least one online grocery order. Sales continued to grow as orders in November 2020 increased 3.6 percent from August of that same year.[2] Clearly, the pandemic accelerated a migration that had already started and was underway.

It is also recognized that the pandemic has accelerated the growth of cloud computing. As more employees transitioned to working from home, it was essential for them to have remote access to corporate data. This forced organizations to speed up their migration to using the cloud. It is now estimated that, due to COVID-19, all organizations will be running 75 percent of their workload on cloud platforms by 2022.[3]

However, despite the rapid migration to the cloud, potential security vulnerabilities that could be exploited by threat actors remain. In this module, you will explore cloud computing and its vulnerabilities. To identify the vulnerabilities for not only the cloud but also software, infrastructures, and other assets, a variety of tools can be used for assessing these vulnerabilities. You will also explore several of these tools.

CLOUD THREATS AND VULNERABILITIES

 **CERTIFICATION**

1.6 Explain the threats and vulnerabilities associated with operating in the cloud.

Understanding cloud threats and vulnerabilities first involves an overall introduction to cloud computing. It also involves looking at vulnerabilities of a cloud environment.

Introduction to Cloud Computing

Understanding cloud computing involves knowing what cloud computing, the different types of clouds, cloud architectures, and cloud models are.

What Is Cloud Computing?

Although various definitions of cloud computing have been proposed, the definition from the National Institute of Standards and Technology (NIST) may be the most comprehensive: "Cloud computing is a model for enabling convenient, on-demand network access to a shared pool of configurable computing resources (e.g., networks, servers, storage, applications, and services) that can be rapidly provisioned and released with minimal management effort or service provider interaction."[4]

Cloud computing is a much more flexible approach to computing resources. All cloud resources are available online so that users from virtually anywhere around the world can access them. This access is achieved simply through opening a web browser without needing to install additional software. Cloud computing allows an almost endless array of servers, software, and network appliances to be quickly and easily configured as needed. It is also a pay-per-use computing model in which customers pay only for the online computing resources they need. As computing needs increase or decrease, cloud computing resources can be quickly scaled up or scaled back. Table 4-1 lists advantages of cloud computing.

Table 4-1 Cloud computing advantages

Characteristic	Explanation
On-demand self-service	The consumer can make changes, such as increasing or decreasing computing resources, without requiring any human interaction from the service provider.
Universal client support	Virtually any networked device (desktop, laptop, smartphone, tablet, etc.) can access the cloud computing resources.
Invisible resource pooling	The physical and virtual computing resources are pooled together to serve multiple, simultaneous consumers, which are dynamically assigned or reassigned based on the consumers' needs; the customer has little or no control or knowledge of the physical location of the resources.
Immediate elasticity	Computing resources can be increased or decreased quickly to meet demands.
Metered services	Fees are based on the computing resources used.

NOTE 1

Entities that offer cloud computing are called cloud service providers.

Cloud computing significantly reduces—and in some instances eliminates—the need for an organization to invest in *provisioning*. Provisioning is the process of setting up an information technology (IT) infrastructure of networks, appliances, servers, and related devices. Provisioning also refers to the steps required to manage access to these assets and data to make them available to users and systems. Provisioning traditional IT is a time-consuming and costly process, requiring the physical setup of the hardware, installation and configuration of software, and connection to networks and storage, all performed by qualified IT personnel.

NOTE 2

While virtualization can reduce provisioning, it nevertheless still requires time and energy to repeat the work multiple times for every new deployment, and it does not provide a means for tracking changes to prevent any inconsistencies of the deployments.

Grow with Cengage Unlimited!

If you'd like more information about this topic, use your Cengage Unlimited subscription to go to the CompTIA Security+ Guide to Network Security Fundamentals, 7th edition; open Module 10; and read the section titled "Virtualization."
If you don't have a Cengage Unlimited subscription, you can find more information at cengage.com/unlimited.

NOTE 3

Cloud computing involves shifting the bulk of the costs from *capital expenditures* (CapEx)—or purchasing and installing servers, storage, networking, and related infrastructure—to *operating expenses* (OpEx) in which the costs are only for the usage of these resources.

However, cloud computing can significantly reduce provisioning. Because the cloud service provider is responsible for installing and maintaining all hardware and networking connections, the organization is relieved of this responsibility and only needs to request the resources. Even the process of procuring the cloud resources can be simplified through Infrastructure as Code (IaC). IaC enables software developers to effectively "order up" the needed infrastructure from the cloud service provider by simply executing a script.

Types of Clouds

There are different types of clouds. A public cloud is one in which the services and infrastructure are offered to all users with access provided remotely through the Internet. Unlike a public cloud that is open to anyone, a community cloud is open only to specific organizations that have common concerns. For example, because of the strict data requirements of the Health Insurance Portability and Accountability Act of 1996 (HIPAA), a community cloud open only to hospitals may be used. A private cloud is created and maintained on a private network. Although this type offers the highest level of security and control (because the company must purchase and maintain all the software and hardware), it also reduces cost savings. A hybrid cloud is a combination of public and private clouds.

Cloud Architecture

Many elements make up a cloud architecture. Here is a sampling of these elements:

- *Thin client.* A thin client is a computer that runs from resources stored on a central cloud server instead of a localized hard drive. Thin clients connect remotely to the cloud computing environment where applications and data are stored and where the processing takes place.
- *Transit gateway.* A transit gateway is an Amazon Web Services (AWS) technology that allows organizations to connect all existing virtual private clouds (VPCs), physical data centers, remote offices, and remote gateways into a single managed source. The transit gateway gives full control over all the resources, including network routing and security, VPCs, shared services, and other resources that may even span multiple AWS accounts. Transit gateways can consolidate edge connectivity and route it through a single cloud entry point.

NOTE 4

A transit gateway is considered a "hub-and-spoke" network topology that enables the user to monitor all activity.

- *Serverless infrastructure.* "Serverless" is actually a misnomer. While there are servers performing a critical function (somewhere), a serverless infrastructure is one in which the capacity planning, installation, setup, and management are all invisible to the user because they are handled by the cloud provider. Because the server resources of the cloud are inconspicuous to the user, this type of infrastructure is called "serverless."

NOTE 5

Serverless essentially means that provisioning, deploying, and managing a physical server disappears from a list of concerns.

Cloud Models

There are several service models in cloud computing. These are Software as a Service, Platform as a Service, Infrastructure as a Service, and Function as a Service.

Software as a Service (SaaS) A typical enterprise must manage many sets of software licenses for the various software applications it uses. These applications typically include human resources, finance, and customer relationship management (CRM)—along with OSs, productivity software, utilities, and many others. Significant costs are associated with purchasing these desktop or service licenses, installing and upgrading the software, distributing patches, and managing them.

What if, as an alternative, the enterprise paid a low monthly or annual fee per user for an external service to host the software on their own hardware? And what if it was then made available through a web browser to users? Not only would the enterprise be relieved of the burden of purchasing and maintaining the software, but because it could be accessed via a browser, all authorized users could access it from any number of endpoints without needing to install specialized software.

This is the definition of **Software as a Service (SaaS)**. SaaS is a cloud computing hosted software environment. SaaS eliminates any software purchase, installation, maintenance, upgrades, and patches; instead, the cloud computing provider centrally manages the software on a per-user basis. SaaS usually includes provisions for a fixed amount of bandwidth and storage.

NOTE 6

SaaS offers commercial and well-known software to users, without any technical intervention from the IT staff. The software is offered as a complete *service* to users.

Platform as a Service (PaaS)   Platform as a Service (PaaS) provides a software *platform* on which the enterprise or users can build their own applications and then host them on the PaaS provider's infrastructure. The software platform can be used as a development framework to build and debug the app and then deploy it.

Unlike SaaS, in which everything is transparent to the enterprise, PaaS allows a moderate degree of control for the enterprise over the cloud computing environment. However, the enterprise does not always need to monitor usage and manually add resources; rather, the cloud provider can guarantee elasticity and scalability.

NOTE 7

PaaS can also provide "middleware" services like database and component services for use by the applications.

⚠ CAUTION   Not all applications developed for a traditional enterprise network may seamlessly migrate to PaaS. Often the most success is from new applications that are developed specifically on and for the cloud.

Infrastructure as a Service (IaaS)   Infrastructure as a Service (IaaS) provides unlimited "raw" computing, storage, and network resources that the enterprise can use to build its own virtual infrastructure in the cloud. The number of CPU processors and their speed, the amount of memory, the volume of storage, and the desired virtual networking resources like routers and switches can all be arranged to create the necessary virtual infrastructure. Enterprises can then load their own OSs (or "rent" them from the cloud provider) along with software, web services, and database applications. Scaling and elasticity are not always automatically provided as with PaaS. Instead, it is the enterprises' responsibility to monitor and request additional services.

How much of an enterprise's network architecture should be migrated to the cloud—and how much should remain on-prem? A traditional three-tier on-prem architecture is illustrated in Figure 4-1. (Note that for simplicity, no security appliances are illustrated.) This multitiered design helps control connections, provide scaling, and increase security. An enterprise could migrate *Tier 1—Web servers* and *Tier 2—Application servers* to a cloud computing provider but keep *Tier 3—Database servers* on-prem for security. However, it could just as easily migrate all three tiers to the cloud computing provider. Such a decision will need to be based on several factors.

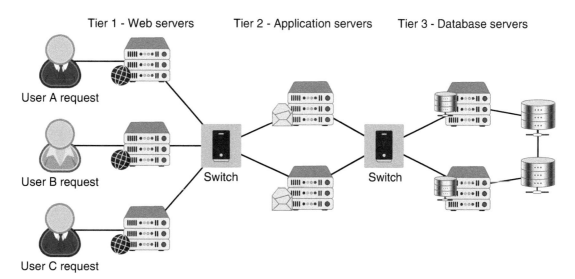

Figure 4-1   Three-tier architecture

Another question with IaaS involves using Layer 2 (switching) or Layer 3 (routing) when connecting to the virtual cloud network. Whereas Layer 2 is the simpler mode, in which the Ethernet MAC address and Virtual LAN (VLAN) information is used for forwarding, the disadvantage of Layer 2 networks is scalability. Using Layer 2 addressing and connectivity can result in a "flat" topology, which is unrealistic with a large number of endpoints. Instead, using routing and subnets to provide segmentation for the appropriate functions provides greater flexibility but at a cost of forwarding performance and network complexity.

Function as a Service (FaaS)   Function as a Service (FaaS) is a serverless approach to execute modular pieces of code. Traditionally, programmers would write software code that was interwoven into one large system (called a monolithic architecture). Changes to a monolithic architecture, even minor modifications, required a significant investment of time since the entire software program had to be modified, recompiled, and redeployed.

Instead of a monolithic architecture, an application can be constructed out of multiple modular components (called a microservices architecture). Dividing an application into microservices allows developers to create smaller "chunks" of code that can be more easily integrated into the application. Any modifications only impact those specific microservices. From the user's perspective, an application built with microservices has a single interface and functions identically to an application with a monolithic architecture. Behind the scenes, however, each microservice has its own database and runs separately from the rest of the application. A comparison of monolithic architecture and microservices architecture is illustrated in Figure 4-2.

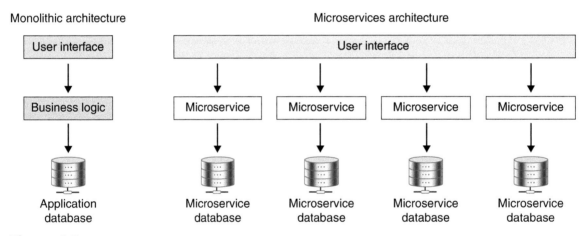

Figure 4-2   Monolithic vs. microservices architecture

NOTE 8

Using a microservices architecture allows a single application to be written in different programming languages and use different libraries.

Using FaaS, developers can better focus on writing the application code. The cloud service provider is responsible for server allocation and the backend services.

A comparison of the IT responsibilities in the different cloud computing models is shown in Table 4-2.

Table 4-2   Cloud computing comparisons

Model	IT responsibilities	Explanation
SaaS	Low	The organization contracts with the cloud service provider for access to software, relieving the IT staff of any responsibilities.
PaaS	Medium	The IT staff has moderate duties of creating the platform, but once completed, the duties diminish.
IaaS	High	Designing, building, and monitoring the virtual environment rely on IT staff.
FaaS	Low	The cloud service provider manages microservice databases and backend services.

NOTE 9

A broad category of subscription services related to cloud computing is called Anything as a Service (XaaS). XaaS is essentially any IT function or digital component that can be transformed into a service for enterprise or user consumption. Today a growing number of products, tools, and technologies are being delivered as a service over the Internet. Examples of IT-based services include Security as a Service (SECaaS), which provides security services all delivered from the cloud to the enterprise, Communication as a Service (CaaS), Desktop as a Service (DaaS), and Healthcare as a Service (HaaS). One example of a non-IT service is ridesharing like Uber and Lyft and is called Transportation as a Service (TaaS).

Cloud Vulnerabilities

Despite its advantages, cloud computing has several potential security issues. These are listed in Table 4-3.

Table 4-3   Cloud security issues

Security issue	Description
Unprotected storage	Improper cloud security configurations can result in data being left exposed.
Logging and monitoring invisibility	Organizations generally cannot access or have limited or no visibility into the security mechanisms of the cloud provider and thus cannot monitor and verify the effectiveness of security controls or view logging records.
Insecure application program interfaces (APIs)	While APIs help cloud customers customize their PaaS by providing data recognition, access, and effective encryption, any vulnerable API can be exploited by threat actors.
Compliance regulations	Maintaining compliance requires that an organization know where their data is, who can access it, and how it is protected, but this can be difficult in an opaque cloud system where the transparency is lacking.
System vulnerabilities	A cloud infrastructure is prone to system vulnerabilities due to complex networks and multiple third-party platforms.

A particularly serious potential cloud vulnerability regards a lack of key management. In a microservices architecture, each microservice manages its own database, generates its own logs, and handles user authentication by using microservices APIs and specialized APIs called REST APIs. The microservices need to communicate among themselves. However, the cloud-based microservices must have the keys including authentication credentials for accessing the other microservices, such as API keys, passwords, certificates, encryption keys, and tokens. How should these "secrets" be passed or accessed securely in a cloud environment? Embedding the keys as part of the software code (*hard-coding*) is not a secure option, nor is trying to hide the keys in the cloud. This lack of key management for cloud applications can result in compromised data that has been encrypted to protect it, but the keys are left exposed.

NOTE 10

In mid-2019, a former Amazon Web Services (AWS) employee used an improperly configured web application firewall (WAF) to launch a Server-Side Request Forgery (SSRF) attack to retrieve the authentication credentials from an AWS metadata API. The employee then ran a simple program of only three lines of code to extract 30 GB of credit application data from a cloud data server. This incident compromised the data of 100 million people in the United States and six million in Canada. The data stolen included 140,000 Social Security numbers and 80,000 bank account numbers on U.S. consumers, and roughly one million Social Insurance Numbers (SINs) for Canadian credit card customers.

TWO RIGHTS & A WRONG

1. Invisible resource pooling is an advantage of cloud computing.
2. "Serverless" means that an application is running on a virtual machine.
3. A serverless infrastructure is one in which the capacity planning, installation, setup, and management are all invisible to the user because they are handled by the cloud provider.

See Appendix C for the answer.

VULNERABILITY DIAGNOSTIC TOOLS

 **CERTIFICATION**

1.4 Given a scenario, analyze the output from common vulnerability assessment tools.

NOTE 11

Other examples of polysemy are mouse (a small rodent and a computer pointing device), bank (a financial institution and a synonym for relying upon something), and man (the human species and adult males of the human species).

Polysemy is from two Greek words (*many sign*) and is defined as the capacity for a word or phrase to have multiple meanings. For example, a *book* can be a printed work of individual pages bound within two covers. The same word can also be used to record an action (*The criminal was booked by the police.*). In the world of cybersecurity, no better example of polysemy can be found in the term *vulnerability assessment*. In the eyes of some security professionals, a vulnerability assessment consists of a basic automated software scan used to identify flaws within a system. Yet to other professionals, a vulnerability assessment goes much deeper: it is a major process that comprises a range of subprocesses that deal with identifying, quantifying, and ranking discovered vulnerabilities as well as mitigating or eliminating the vulnerabilities.

Due to the confusion and sometimes overlapping definitions of assessments and related words like scans and enumerations, it is sometimes best to use a different word altogether. The word *diagnostics* can be substituted for this act of "hunting" for vulnerabilities. Several tools can be used for this process, which vary depending upon the asset being examined. These assets include software, infrastructures, web applications, networks, wireless networks, and cloud infrastructures.

 **CAUTION**   The CompTIA CySA+ CS0-002 exam objectives state that a test taker should be able to analyze the output from the common vulnerability assessment tools listed in this section. Because of the number of tools, an in-depth evaluation of each tool and its output is not possible. It is important for those taking the CS0-002 exam to spend time becoming familiar with the different outputs. Additional practice on several of these tools is available in Appendix A.

Software

Examining software for unintentional vulnerabilities has long been considered important. However, today software and "apps" are also being examined for intentional malware. While at one time commercial software packages were considered as untainted by malware because they were written by trusted software engineers, that is no longer the case. Software programs are being increasingly developed by nation-state actors and other threat actors so that the software appears benign but actually contains malware.

There are two types of software analysis for vulnerabilities and malware: static analysis and dynamic analysis.

Static Analysis

Typically, the software development process involves software engineers writing *source code* using a *programming language* that is then *compiled* into binary *machine code.* When looking for vulnerabilities, the testing of the software should occur before the source code is compiled. These tests are called a static analysis. Figure 4-3 illustrates an automated static code analysis tool.

Figure 4-3   Automated static analysis tool

NOTE 12

Automated static code analysis may also be accompanied by manual peer reviews in which the software engineers and developers paired together or in larger teams laboriously examine each line of source code, looking for vulnerabilities.

Dynamic Analysis

Security testing can also be performed after the source code is compiled, though it is more difficult to find flaws. This is called dynamic analysis or *run-time verification* when all components are integrated and running. This analysis is typically achieved using a tool or suite of pre-built attacks or testing tools that specifically monitor the application's behavior for memory corruption, user privilege issues, and other critical security problems.

Some of the most common dynamic code analysis tools use a process called fuzzing. Fuzzing provides random input to a program to attempt to trigger exceptions, such as memory corruption, program crashes, or security breaches. An advantage of fuzzing is that it produces a record of what input triggered the exception so that it can be reproduced to track down the problem within the code. Fuzzing test software consists of an *execution engine* and an *input generator*, which usually allows the tester to configure the types of inputs. This is seen in Figure 4-4.

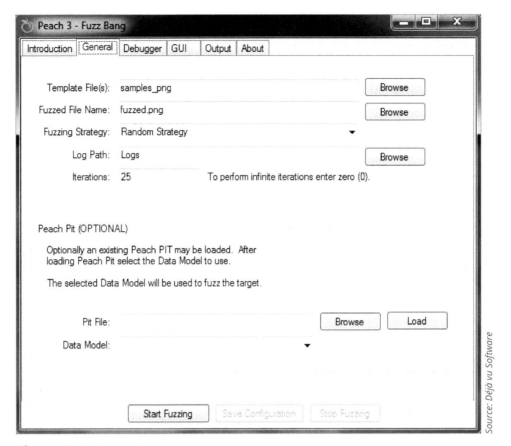

Source: Déjà vu Software

Figure 4-4   Fuzzer input generator

NOTE 13

A single pass of a fuzzer is unlikely to find all exceptions in software, due to the randomness in the fuzzing process. This is because the mutation of the inputs relies on randomness to determine where to mutate input and what to mutate. Fuzzers require multiple trials and statistical tests.

However, how can an organization that has purchased or leased software examine the compiled code to determine if it contains malware? In this case, dynamic analysis can also be used. Instead of relying on a suite of pre-built attack tools to look for vulnerabilities, **reverse engineering** can be performed. Reverse engineering is disassembling and analyzing a product. Software tools are available to reverse-engineer or transform compiled binary code into a text form. A *disassembler* maps processor instruction codes into instruction mnemonics on a one-to-one basis. A *decompiler* can also create text from binary code, though the code is at a much higher level and is more concise and easier to analyze. Figure 4-5 illustrates the output from a decompiler that converts compiled binary code in the left pane to a more readable "pseudocode" in the right pane.

Infrastructure

Although several tools are available for examining an infrastructure for vulnerabilities, Tenable's **Nessus** is one of the most popular and highly regarded infrastructure vulnerability scanning tools. Nessus's advantages include the following:

- Nessus is an open source vulnerability scanner that uses the Common Vulnerability Scoring System (CVSS).
- It has a modular architecture consisting of centralized servers, which conduct scanning, and remote client agents, which interact with the servers.
- Nessus uses the Nessus Attack Scripting Language (NASL), which is a basic language that can be used for describing individual threats and potential attacks.

```
IDA View-A                                           □  ⊟  ×    Pseudocode-A
.text:0041662C 070 04 00 46 AC   sw    $a2, (buffer+4 - 0x100036B0)($v0)    ^   int monitor_printf(const char *a1, ...)
.text:00416630 070 08 00 47 AC   sw    $a3, (buffer+8 - 0x100036B0)($v0)        {
.text:00416634 070 14 00 00 10   b     loc_416688                                 int *v2; // $s1
.text:00416638 070 0C 00 48 AC   sw    $t0, (buffer+0xC - 0x100036B0)($v0)        size_t v3; // $s2
.text:0041663C                   #                                                int i; // $s0
.text:0041663C                                                                    int result; // $v0
.text:0041663C                   loc_41663C:        # CODE XREF: monitor_printf+5C↑j   struct timeval v6; // [sp+28h] [-38h] BYREF
.text:0041663C 070 44 00 A2 8F   lw    $v0, 0x60+var_1C($sp)                      struct tm v7; // [sp+30h] [-30h] BYREF
.text:00416640 070 18 80 84 8F   la    $a0, dword_10000000                        va_list va; // [sp+74h] [+14h] BYREF
.text:00416644 070 1C 80 85 8F   la    $a1, unk_490000
.text:00416648 070 9C FF 42 24   addiu $v0, -0x64                                va_start(va, a1);
.text:0041664C 070 10 00 A2 AF   sw    $v0, 0x60+var_50($sp)                     if ( gettimeofday(&v6, 0) >= 0
.text:00416650 070 38 00 A2 8F   lw    $v0, 0x60+var_28($sp)                         && localtime_r(&v6.tv_sec, &v7) )
.text:00416654 070 40 00 A7 8F   lw    $a3, 0x60+var_20($sp)                     {
.text:00416658 070 20 83 99 8F   la    $t9, sprintf                                 sprintf(
.text:0041665C 070 14 00 A2 8F   lw    $v0, 0x60+var_4C($sp)                           buffer,
.text:00416660 070 34 00 A2 8F   lw    $v0, 0x60+var_2C($sp)                           "%02d.%02d.%02d %02d:%02d:%02d",
.text:00416664 070 3C 00 A6 8F   lw    $a2, 0x60+var_24($sp)                           v7.tm_mday,
.text:00416668 070 B0 36 84 24   addiu $a0, (buffer - 0x10000000)  # s               v7.tm_mon + 1,
.text:0041666C 070 18 00 A2 AF   sw    $v0, 0x60+var_48($sp)                           v7.tm_year - 100,
.text:00416670 070 30 00 A2 8F   lw    $v0, 0x60+var_30($sp)                           v7.tm_hour,
.text:00416674 070 28 18 A5 24   addiu $a1, (a02d02d02d02d02 - 0x490000)  # "%02     v7.tm_min,
.text:00416678 070 01 00 E7 24   addiu $a3, 1                                        v7.tm_sec);
.text:0041667C 070 09 F8 20 03   jalr  $t9 ; sprintf                             }
.text:00416680 070 1C 00 A2 AF   sw    $v0, 0x60+var_44($sp)                     else
.text:00416684 070 20 00 BC 8F   lw    $gp, 0x60+var_40($sp)                     {
.text:00416688                                                                      strcpy(buffer, "00.00.00 00:00:00");
.text:00416688                   loc_416688:        # CODE XREF: monitor_printf+98↑j }
.text:00416688 070 18 80 84 8F   la    $a0, dword_10000000                       v2 = &monitor_conns;
.text:0041668C 070 28 88 99 8F   la    $t9, vsnprintf                            v3 = vsnprintf(
.text:00416690 070 21 30 00 02   move  $a2, $s0  # format                           &buffer[17],
.text:00416694 070 C1 36 84 24   addiu $a0, (buffer+0x11 - 0x10000000)  # s          0x3EFu,
0001667C 0041667C: monitor_printf (Synchronized with Pseudo v                        a1,
<                                                         >    0001667C monitor_printf:15 (41667C (Synchroniz
```

Figure 4-5   Decompiler output

- It can detect security vulnerabilities in local or remote hosts and identify missing security updates and patches by simulating attacks to pinpoint vulnerabilities.
- Nessus is compatible with a variety of different computers and servers and supports Windows, macOS, Linux, and Unix operating systems.

NOTE 14

Because different vulnerability scanners produce different output results, this section uses Nessus as one example.

The basic steps for installing and running a vulnerability scan on Nessus are as follows:

- *Download Nessus software.* Nessus software consists of the vulnerability scanning manager Nessus Essentials (a free version for schools or hobbyists), Professional (for security practitioners), or Nessus Manager (an enterprise-based package for managing numerous Nessus Agents). An alternative is to use Tenable.io, which is a subscription-based cloud service that allows different teams to share scanners, schedules, scan policies, and scan results. Nessus

NOTE 15

Nessus can also be downloaded on a virtual machine.

Agents can also be downloaded to provide a flexible way of scanning hosts without the need to provide authentication, and the agents enable scans to be carried out even when the hosts are offline.
- *Install Nessus.* By default, Nessus is installed and managed using the Hypertext Transfer Protocol Secure (HTTPS) and Secure Sockets Layer (SSL) through port 8834. It may be necessary to allow Nessus to operate through a firewall and any installed antivirus software product. Because the installation of Nessus uses a self-signed SSL certificate, a security warning of "Untrusted Site" or "Unsecure Connection" may appear in the installation web browser; these warnings can be dismissed.

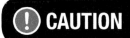 **CAUTION**   To avoid a warning about the self-signed Nessus SSL certificate, a customized SSL certificate specific to the organization can be created instead.

- *Download plug-ins.* As information about new vulnerabilities is discovered, programs to detect these vulnerabilities are created. These programs are called plug-ins and are written in NASL. The plug-ins contain vulnerability information, a simplified set of remediation actions, and the algorithm to test for the presence of the security issue. In addition to new plug-ins, updated plug-ins are also available, as shown in Figure 4-6.

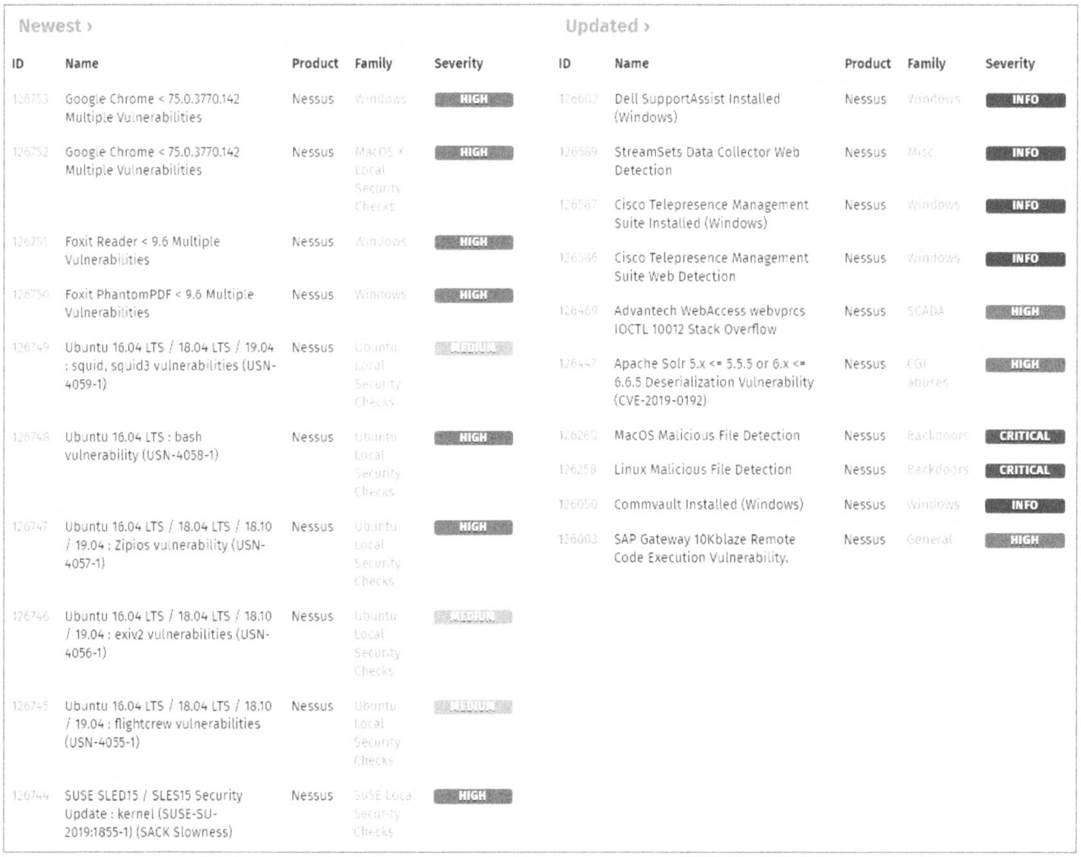

Newest ›

ID	Name	Product	Family	Severity
126753	Google Chrome < 75.0.3770.142 Multiple Vulnerabilities	Nessus	Windows	HIGH
126752	Google Chrome < 75.0.3770.142 Multiple Vulnerabilities	Nessus	MacOS X Local Security Checks	HIGH
126751	Foxit Reader < 9.6 Multiple Vulnerabilities	Nessus	Windows	HIGH
126750	Foxit PhantomPDF < 9.6 Multiple Vulnerabilities	Nessus	Windows	HIGH
126749	Ubuntu 16.04 LTS / 18.04 LTS / 19.04 : squid, squid3 vulnerabilities (USN-4059-1)	Nessus	Ubuntu Local Security Checks	MEDIUM
126748	Ubuntu 16.04 LTS : bash vulnerability (USN-4058-1)	Nessus	Ubuntu Local Security Checks	HIGH
126747	Ubuntu 16.04 LTS / 18.04 LTS / 18.10 / 19.04 : Zipios vulnerability (USN-4057-1)	Nessus	Ubuntu Local Security Checks	HIGH
126746	Ubuntu 16.04 LTS / 18.04 LTS / 18.10 / 19.04 : exiv2 vulnerabilities (USN-4056-1)	Nessus	Ubuntu Local Security Checks	MEDIUM
126745	Ubuntu 16.04 LTS / 18.04 LTS / 18.10 / 19.04 : flightcrew vulnerabilities (USN-4055-1)	Nessus	Ubuntu Local Security Checks	MEDIUM
126744	SUSE SLED15 / SLES15 Security Update : kernel (SUSE-SU-2019:1855-1) (SACK Slowness)	Nessus	SUSE Local Security Checks	HIGH

Updated ›

ID	Name	Product	Family	Severity
126603	Dell SupportAssist Installed (Windows)	Nessus	Windows	INFO
126569	StreamSets Data Collector Web Detection	Nessus	Misc.	INFO
126587	Cisco Telepresence Management Suite Installed (Windows)	Nessus	Windows	INFO
126586	Cisco Telepresence Management Suite Web Detection	Nessus	Windows	INFO
126469	Advantech WebAccess webvprcs IOCTL 10012 Stack Overflow	Nessus	SCADA	HIGH
126447	Apache Solr 5.x <= 5.5.5 or 6.x <= 6.6.5 Deserialization Vulnerability (CVE-2019-0192)	Nessus	CGI abuses	HIGH
126260	MacOS Malicious File Detection	Nessus	Backdoors	CRITICAL
126258	Linux Malicious File Detection	Nessus	Backdoors	CRITICAL
126050	Commvault Installed (Windows)	Nessus	Windows	INFO
126003	SAP Gateway 10Kblaze Remote Code Execution Vulnerability.	Nessus	General	HIGH

Source: Tenable

Figure 4-6 Nessus plug-ins

- *Select scan template.* Vulnerability scans can be facilitated by using Nessus *scan templates*, which are predefined scan configurations. There currently are over 20 different templates that cover different levels of scans (*Advanced Scan, Basic Network Scan, Malware Scan, Mobile Device Scan, Web Application Tests*), scans that meet regulatory requirements (*Internal PCI Network Scan, PCI Quarterly External Scan, Policy Compliance Auditing, SCAP and OVAL Auditing*), scans that look for specific widespread vulnerabilities (*Bash Shell-shock Detection, Credentialed Patch Auditing*), and scans that target the latest vulnerabilities (*Shadow Brokers Scan, Spectre and Meltdown Scan, WannaCry Ransomware Scan*).
- *Determine scan settings.* Scan templates can be further tweaked by configuring specific scan settings, such as scheduling the scan frequency (*Once, Daily, Weekly, Monthly,* or *Yearly*), who is to be notified when the scan is completed and what report type is distributed, the scan type (*Quick, Normal, Thorough,* or *Custom*), the discovery methods (such as for *Port Scanning* for determining the port range to be scanned), and the accuracy of the scan, among other settings.

Once the scan is configured, it can be executed. For example, Figure 4-7 shows selecting a Basic Network scan. When the scan is completed, a summary dashboard is displayed as an overview of the results, as shown in Figure 4-8. A more detailed report on each vulnerability can be viewed, as shown in Figure 4-9.

Each vulnerability from the Nessus vulnerability scan can then be explored in greater detail by selecting that vulnerability. Figure 4-10 displays the details for a single vulnerability.

New Scan / Basic Network Scan
‹ Back to Scan Templates

Settings   Credentials   Plugins ⊚

BASIC   Name   Basic Network Scan
   General
   Schedule   Description
   Notifications
DISCOVERY
ASSESSMENT   Folder   My Scans   ▼
REPORT
ADVANCED   Targets   192.168.9.0/24

                         Upload Targets   Add File

Save ▼   Cancel

Launch

Source: Tenable

Figure 4-7   Nessus basic network scan

Basic Network Scan   Configure
‹ Back to My Scans

Hosts 4   Vulnerabilities 125   Remediations 2   History 1

Filter ▼

   Host   Vulnerabilities   %   Scan Details
                                                                 Name: Basic Network Scan
   192.168.9.131   6   117   100%   Status: Running
                                                                 Policy: Basic Network Scan
   192.168.9.133   29   100%   Scanner: Local Scanner
                                                                 Start: Today at 1:32 AM
   192.168.9.2   13   100%
                                                                 Vulnerabilities
   192.168.9.1   9   100%
                                                                      ● Critical
                                                                      ● High
                                                                      ● Medium
                                                                      ● Low
                                                                      ● Info

Source: Tenable

Figure 4-8   Scan summary

Figure 4-9   Scan details

Figure 4-10   Vulnerability details

The vulnerabilities details page displays a *Description* of the vulnerability and a *Solution* to the problem in the center pane. The right pane gives the *Plugin Details* such as its *Severity*, *Version*, and dates *Published* and *Modified*. It also contains an area called *Risk Information*. This information is of primary importance and lists two numeric scores:

- *CVSS Base Score*. The *Base Score* represents the characteristics (Nessus calls these *intrinsic qualities*) of the vulnerability when it was first discovered.
- *CVSS Temporal Score*. The *Temporal Score* reflects the current characteristics of a vulnerability that may have changed over time. As mitigations for a vulnerability become more widespread, such as being included as part of an operating system software patch, its characteristics may diminish, resulting in a lower CVSS Temporal Score.

NOTE 16

CVSS is covered in Module 3.

Multiple measurements (*metrics*) make up the CVSS score, and they are provided as input to a complex series of algorithms to produce these scores. The metrics are divided into three main categories: Base Score Metrics, Temporal Score Metrics, and Environmental Score Metrics, as shown in Figure 4-11.

An explanation of the CVSS Base Score Exploitability Metrics is found in Table 4-4.

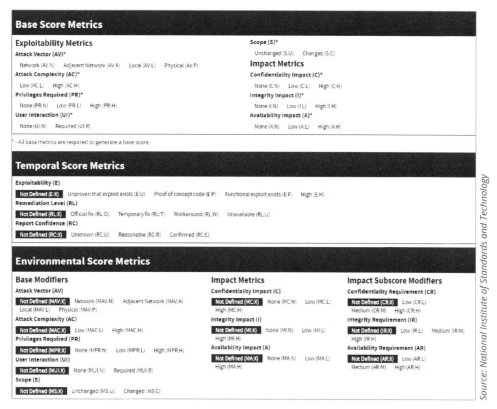

Source: National Institute of Standards and Technology

Figure 4-11   CVSS metrics

Table 4-4   CVSS base score exploitability metrics

Metric	Description	Values	Explanation	Impact on Base Score
Attack Vector (AV)	The type of network access necessary to exploit a vulnerability	Network (AV:N) Adjacent Network (AV:A) Local (AV:L) Physical (AV:P)	This is based on how close or remote must a threat actor be in order to successfully launch an attack.	The AV metric will be higher the more remote a threat actor can be in order to launch the attack.
Attack Complexity (AC)	The conditions beyond the threat actor's control that must exist in order to exploit the vulnerability	Low (AC:L) High (AC:H)	This is based on conditions that may require the threat actor to gather more information about the target.	Less complex attacks generate a higher score.
Privileges Required (PR)	The level of privileges that are necessary for exploiting the vulnerability	None (PR:N) Low (PR:L) High (PR:N)	This metric describes the level of privileges the threat actor must have before successfully exploiting the vulnerability.	The highest score is when no privileges are required.
User Interaction (UI)	The requirement for a user other than the treat actor to participate in the successful compromise of the vulnerability	None (UI:N) Required (UI:R)	This is based on whether the vulnerability can be exploited exclusively by the threat actor or if a separate user must also be involved.	When no user interaction is required, this generates a higher score.
Scope	The ability for the vulnerability in one software component to impact other resources	Unchanged (S:U) Changed (S:C)	Whenever the impact of a vulnerability breaches a security boundary and impacts other components, a Scope change occurs.	When a Scope change occurs, a higher score is generated.

In addition to Exploitability Metrics in the CVSS Base Score, there are also Impact Metrics. These are *Confidentiality Impact (C), Integrity Impact (I),* and *Availability Impact (A).* Each of these has one of three values: *None, Low,* and *High.* For example, a description of the values for the Confidentiality Impact are *No impact on confidentiality, Low loss so that access to restricted information is obtained but the threat actor has no control over what information,* and *High loss of all confidentiality so that all resources are divulged to the threat actor.*

Each value of a metric has its own set of definitions. Table 4-5 explains the values of the attack vector (AV) metric.

Table 4-5 CVSS attack vector base score exploitability metrics

Metric value	Description	Example
Network (AV:N)	The vulnerability is bound to the network stack and can be exploited at the protocol level across one or more routers. This is a vulnerability that is remotely exploitable so that the set of possible threat actors includes the entire Internet.	A threat actor causes a denial of service (DoS) by sending a specially crafted TCP packet across a wide area network.
Adjacent (AV:A)	The vulnerable component is bound to the network stack, but the attack is limited at the protocol level to a logically adjacent topology. An attack must be launched from the same shared physical (Bluetooth or 802.11) or logical (local IP subnet) network, or from within a secure or otherwise limited administrative domain (such as a secure VPN to a restricted network zone).	An ARP (IPv4) or neighbor discovery (IPv6) flood leads to a DoS on the local LAN segment.
Local (AV:L)	The vulnerability is not bound to the network stack, and the threat actor exploits the vulnerability by accessing the target system locally (by accessing the system's keyboard), remotely (through SSH), or through interacting directly with the user.	A social engineering attack sends a malicious email attachment and then tricks the user into opening it.
Physical (AV:P)	The attack requires the threat actor to physically manipulate the vulnerable component; the interaction could be either brief or persistent.	A threat actor gains access to disk encryption keys after physically accessing the target system.

Figure 4-12 illustrates a CVSS score based on selected values for the Base Score.

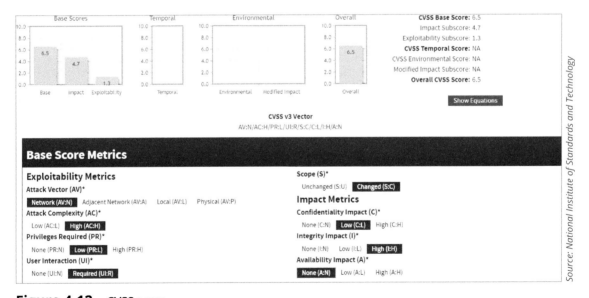

Source: National Institute of Standards and Technology

Figure 4-12 CVSS score

NOTE 17

An online calculator from the National Institute of Standards and Technology provides detailed information on each metric and demonstrates how a score is calculated. The calculator is at *https://nvd.nist.gov/vuln-metrics/cvss/v3-calculator*.

In addition to Nessus are several other tools that can be used for conducting an infrastructure vulnerability diagnosis. Some of the most popular include the following:

- *Open Vulnerability Assessment Scanner (OpenVAS).* OpenVAS is considered a full-featured vulnerability scanner that currently includes more than 50,000 vulnerability tests. It receives daily vulnerability feeds. OpenVAS has been maintained by Greenbone Networks since 2009 and serves as part of Greenbone's proprietary vulnerability management system. However, OpenVAS itself is open source under the GNU General Public License (GNU GPL).
- *Nexpose.* Nexpose is a well-known vulnerability scanner from Rapid7. A Nexpose Community Edition is a scaled-down version of Rapid7's more comprehensive vulnerability scanner. The Community Edition will run on physical machines under either Windows or Linux and is also available as a virtual appliance to run within a virtual machine. However, the Community Edition has several limitations: only a maximum of 32 IP addresses can be scanned, and it can only be used for 12 months.
- *Qualys.* The infrastructure vulnerability scanner Qualys can detect vulnerabilities on virtually any networked assets, including servers; network devices such as routers, switches, and firewalls; and peripherals and endpoints. Qualys can assess any device that has an IP address. It is unique in its delivery platform. Qualys is a cloud-based Software-as-a-Service (SaaS) delivery model, allowing users to access Qualys from any web browser. For organizations that require an on-premise solution, a private cloud can be set up in the organization's own data center.

Web Applications

Vulnerabilities in web applications continue to be a leading attack vector today; in fact, by some estimates, vulnerabilities in web applications may account for almost half of all successful security incidents. Several tools can be used to diagnose vulnerabilities in web applications. These tools take a variety of approaches:

- *Passive scanning.* A web application vulnerability diagnostic tool that performs passive scanning examines each page of the web application delivered by the web server and then looks at the HTML in responses from the web application. Passive scanning does not change responses in any way and is considered safe; in addition, it is performed in a background thread and will not impact the response of the application to other users. Passive scanning is effective in finding some vulnerabilities and in assessing the basic security state of a web application to locate where more investigation may be warranted.
- *Active scanning.* Active scanning attempts to find other vulnerabilities by using known attacks against the selected targets. It attacks all the discovered pages by testing their functionality and parameters. Because active scanning is an attack on those targets and can put them at risk, its usage must be controlled so as not to harm the web server and its applications.
- *Dynamic analysis.* Dynamic analysis searches for flaws from the outside of the application with no knowledge of the software's structure or source code.
- *Static analysis.* Static analysis examines the web application code from the inside to look for common vulnerabilities such as SQL injection and cross-site scripting, as well as coding errors like buffer overflows and unhandled error conditions.

The OWASP Zed Attack Proxy (ZAP) is considered the premiere open source tool for diagnosing web applications. ZAP is a Java-based tool with a highly usable graphical interface that allows testers to perform fuzzing, scripting, and other actions to attack web apps. Because it is a Java tool, ZAP can run on most OSs that support Java. An example of ZAP output is shown in Figure 4-13.

> ### NOTE 18
>
> The Open Web Application Security Project (OWASP) is a vendor-neutral nonprofit group of volunteers who work to make web applications more secure.

Other web application vulnerability diagnostic tools include Burp Suite (a tool that performs both a static and dynamic analysis), Nikto (a command-line open source tool), and Arachni (a modular open source tool).

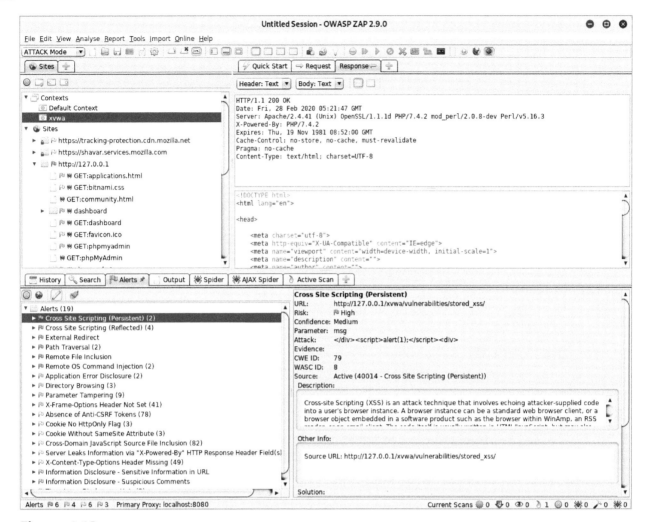

Figure 4-13   OWASP ZAP output

Networks

When diagnosing networks for vulnerabilities, the actions can be in one of two states:

- *Passive.* Passive actions are by definition "watching and listening" but are not performing any overt actions against the network.
- *Active.* Active actions involve taking some type of action against the network or network server. This generally includes causing packets to come into contact with the network.

Searching for network vulnerabilities involves enumeration. The general definition of enumeration is *the act of making a list of items one after another.* In cybersecurity, enumeration is defined as the process of extracting a list of usernames, machine names, network resources, shares, and services from a network system. By creating an active connection to the network and then performing directed queries to gain this information, the gathered information is used to identify the vulnerabilities that can be exploited.

When conducting enumeration, several network utility tools can be used. These include utilities that are native to the OS as well as third-party tools.

Operating System Tools

As its name implies, netstat (*net*work *stat*istics) provides detailed information about current network connections. It is a command-line utility included in virtually all OSs (Windows, macOS, Linux, etc.) and provides network protocol statistics as well as network connections for the Transmission Control Protocol (TCP), network interfaces, and routing tables. Netstat commands can be tailored by using one or more parameters called "switches" (such as *netstat -a*). Table 4-6 lists some of the most commonly used netstat switches.

Table 4-6   Common netstat switches

Switch	Description
-a	All active connections and the ports that the computer is listening on
-e	Ethernet data such as number of bytes and packets sent and received
-g	Multicast group membership data
-n	Active TCP connections (addresses and port numbers displayed numerically)
-r	Contents of routing table
-s	Statistics by protocol
-n	Redisplays data every *n* seconds until Ctrl+C is pressed

NOTE 19

All operating systems also have unique netstat switches. For example, you can use the *-o* switch in Windows to include the process ID, and you can use the *-t* switch in Linux to display only TCP connections.

In addition to netstat, other OS system tools can be useful in gathering network information:

- *ipconfig* (*ifconfig* in Linux). *I*nternet *P*rotocol *config*uration (ipconfig) is a tool that displays TCP/IP network connection data, such as the IP address, subnet mask, and default gateway for all network adapters. It also displays DNS information.
- *tracert* (*traceroute* in Linux). This tool can give basic information about the path that a packet takes.
- *ping.* The ping tool is a networking program to test whether a particular host can be reached.
- *nslookup* (*dig* in Linux). The nslookup (*n*ame *s*erver *lookup*) tool can be used to obtain the IP address or domain name of a host.

Third-Party Tools

In addition to network utilities that are part of the OS, third-party tools can be useful in reconnaissance. One of the best-known tools is **nmap** (*n*etwork *map*per), which is an open source utility for network discovery and security auditing. Using IP packets, nmap can determine what hosts are available on a network; what services the hosts are offering, such as application name and version; and what types of packet filters or firewalls are in use. Nmap can also be used for OS fingerprinting as well as discovering characteristics of a specific host computer (*host scanning*). One of the advantages of nmap is its ability to quickly scan very large networks. Table 4-7 shows several common commands in the command-line version of nmap.

Table 4-7   Common nmap commands

Command	Description
nmap www.cengage.com	Scan one host
nmap 192.168.1.1	Scan one IP address
nmap 192.168.1.1-20	Scan a range of IP addresses
nmap 192.168.1.0/24	Scan an entire subnet
nmap -p 22 192.168.1.1	Scan one port
nmap -p 1-100 192.168.1.1	Scan a range of ports
nmap -p- 192.168.1.1	Scan all 65535 ports
nmap -A 192.168.1.1	Detect the operating system and services on the specific host computer
nmap -sV 192.168.1.1	Detect the services on the host computer
nmap -sV --version-intensity 5 192.168.1.1	Conduct an aggressive service detection scan

A graphical user interface (GUI) version of nmap called Zenmap is also available, as shown in Figure 4-14. Zenmap can also be used for creating a visual map of a network, as shown in Figure 4-15.

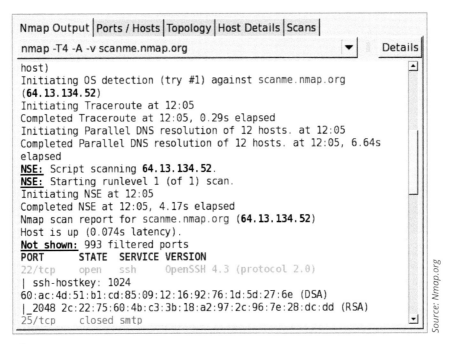

Figure 4-14 Zenmap

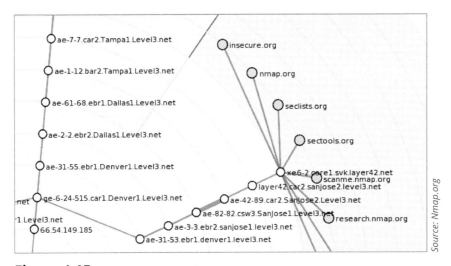

Figure 4-15 Zenmap network map

Other third-party network tools include hping (a command-line TCP/IP packet assembler and analyzer) and responder (a tool that can manipulate name resolution services to uncover sensitive information).

Wireless Networks

In a traditional wired network, a well-defined boundary or "hard edge" protects data and resources. There are two types of hard edges. The first is a network hard edge. A wired network typically has one point (or a limited number of points) through which data must pass from an external network to the secure internal network. This single data entry point makes it easier to defend against attacks because any attack must likewise pass through this one point. Security appliances can be used to block attacks from entering the network. The combination of a single entry point plus security appliances that can defend it make up a network's hard edge, which protects important data and resources. The second hard edge is made up of the walls of the building that house the enterprise. Because these walls keep out unauthorized personnel, attackers cannot access the network. In other words, the walls serve to physically separate computing resources from attackers.

The introduction of wireless local area networks (WLANs) in enterprises, however, has changed these hard edges to "blurred edges." Instead of a network hard edge with a single data entry point, a WLAN can contain multiple entry points. The radio frequency (RF) signals from access points (APs) create several data entry points into the network through which attackers can inject attacks or steal data. This makes it difficult to create a hard network edge. In addition, because RF signals extend beyond the boundaries of the building, the walls cannot be considered as a physical hard edge to keep away attackers. A threat actor sitting in a car well outside of the building's security perimeter can still easily pick up a wireless RF signal to eavesdrop on data transmissions or inject malware behind the firewall. An AP whose security settings have not been set or have been improperly configured can allow attackers access to the network, resulting in several different wireless attacks directed at the enterprise. These include rogue access points, evil twins, intercepting wireless data, and wireless denial-of-service attacks and are illustrated in Figure 4-16.

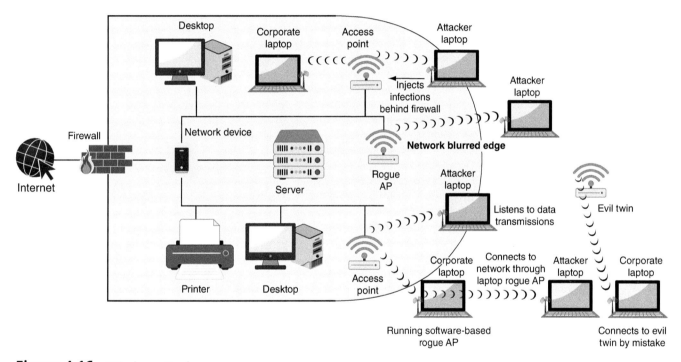

Figure 4-16   Wireless attacks

Grow with Cengage Unlimited!

If you'd like more information about this topic, use your Cengage Unlimited subscription to go to the CompTIA Security+ Guide to Network Security Fundamentals, 7th edition; open Module 11; and read the section titled "Vulnerabilities of WLAN Security."

If you don't have a Cengage Unlimited subscription, you can find more information at cengage.com/unlimited.

Different tools can be used to diagnose or exploit wireless vulnerabilities. One exploitation tool that can be used on data exfiltrated from a wireless network is Hashcat. Hashcat is a tool for cracking password hashes and is seen in Figure 4-17. Other wireless tools include Aircrack-ng (a tool for capturing wireless packets and attacking wireless networks) and Reaver (a tool for cracking Wi-Fi Protected Setup (WPS) PINs).

```
hashcat (v6.0.0) starting...

CUDA API (CUDA 10.2)
====================
* Device #1: GeForce GTX 1080, 7982/8112 MB, 20MCU

Minimum password length supported by kernel: 4
Maximum password length supported by kernel: 256

Hashes: 1 digests; 1 unique digests, 1 unique salts
Bitmaps: 16 bits, 65536 entries, 0x0000ffff mask, 262144 bytes, 5/13 rotates

Applicable optimizers:
* Single-Hash
* Single-Salt
* Brute-Force
* Slow-Hash-SIMD-LOOP

Watchdog: Temperature abort trigger set to 90c

Host memory required for this attack: 1725 MB

$bitlocker$1$16$3038323434393732373135333330333732$10...09e60e:20200615

Session..........: hashcat (Brain Session/Attack:0xdd79fcf8/0xc2bc45aa)
Status...........: Cracked
Hash.Name........: BitLocker
Hash.Target......: $bitlocker$1$16$3038323434393732373135333330333732$10...09e60e
Time.Started.....: Mon Jun 15 16:20:12 2020 (44 secs)
Time.Estimated...: Mon Jun 15 16:20:56 2020 (0 secs)
Guess.Mask.......: ?d?d20?d?d?d?d [8]
Guess.Queue......: 1/1 (100.00%)
Speed.#1.........:     1426 H/s (57.15ms) @ Accel:1 Loops:4096 Thr:1024 Vec:1
Recovered........: 1/1 (100.00%) Digests
Progress.........: 184320/1000000 (18.43%)
Rejected.........: 0/184320 (0.00%)
Brain.Link.All...: RX: 16 B, TX: 51 B
Brain.Link.#1....: RX: 16 B (0.00 Mbps), TX: 51 B (0.00 Mbps), idle
Restore.Point....: 0/100000 (0.00%)
Restore.Sub.#1...: Salt:0 Amplifier:2-3 Iteration:1036288-1040384
Candidates.#1....: 22206007 -> 27203992
Hardware.Mon.#1..: Temp: 77c Fan: 49% Util:100% Core:1759MHz Mem:4513MHz Bus:1

Started: Mon Jun 15 16:19:45 2020
Stopped: Mon Jun 15 16:20:57 2020
```

Source: Hashcat

Figure 4-17   Hashcat

CAUTION   The CompTIA CS0-002 CySA+ exam objectives list oclHashcat as a wireless assessment tool. However, oclHashcat is no longer available and has been replaced by Hashcat. Hashcat can also be used in a variety of settings beyond wireless networks.

Cloud Infrastructure

Several tools can be used to identify vulnerabilities in cloud platforms. These include the following:

- *Prowler*. **Prowler** is a command-line tool for diagnosing vulnerabilities in services using the AWS cloud. It looks at cloud configurations and compares them with more than 150 cloud security best practices. The output from a Prowler assessment is shown in Figure 4-18.
- *Scout Suite*. **Scout Suite** is an open source multi-cloud security-auditing tool. It can be used to assess the security posture assessment of different cloud environments. Scout Suite uses the APIs that are exposed by the cloud providers to gather configuration data for manual inspection and highlight areas of risk. Scout Suite supports Amazon Web Services (AWS), Microsoft Azure, Google Cloud Platform, Alibaba Cloud, and Oracle Cloud.
- *Pacu*. **Pacu** is an exploitation framework for AWS. It has more than 35 modules that range from reconnaissance, persistence, privilege escalation, enumeration, data exfiltration, log manipulation, and miscellaneous general exploitation.

NOTE 20

Pacu is named after a type of piranha fish that lives in the Amazon River in South America.

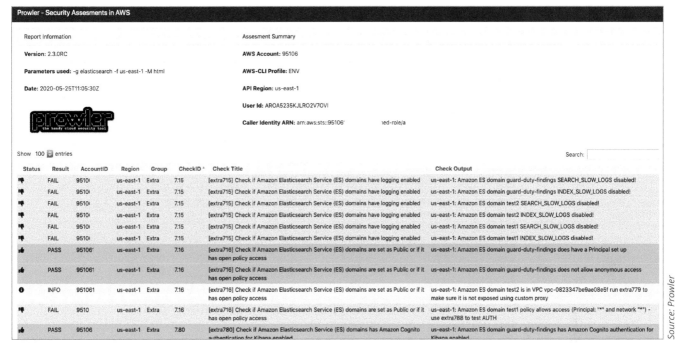

Source: Prowler

Figure 4-18   Prowler

TWO RIGHTS & A WRONG

1. There are two types of software analysis for vulnerabilities and malware: static analysis and dynamic analysis.
2. OpenVAS is a wireless vulnerability scanner.
3. Cybersecurity enumeration is defined as the process of extracting a list of usernames, machine names, network resources, shares, and services from a network system.

See Appendix C for the answer.

 **VM LAB**   You're now ready to complete the live, virtual machine labs for this module. The labs can be found in the Apply It folder in each MindTap module.

MODULE SUMMARY

- Cloud computing is a popular and flexible approach to computing resources. All cloud resources are available online from virtually anywhere, and access is achieved through a web browser without needing to install additional software. Cloud computing allows an almost endless array of servers, software, and network appliances to be quickly and easily configured as needed, and then as computing needs increase or decrease, these resources can be quickly scaled up or scaled back. As a pay-per-use computing model, customers pay only for the online computing resources they need.
- A public cloud is one in which the services and infrastructure are offered to all users with access provided remotely through the Internet. A community cloud is open only to specific organizations that have common concerns. A private cloud is created and maintained on a private network. Although this type offers the highest

level of security and control (because the company must purchase and maintain all the software and hardware), it also reduces cost savings. A hybrid cloud is a combination of public and private clouds.

- Many elements make up a cloud architecture. A thin client is a computer that runs from resources stored on a central cloud server instead of a localized hard drive. A transit gateway is a technology that allows organizations to connect all existing virtual private clouds (VPCs), physical data centers, remote offices, and remote gateways into a single managed source. A serverless infrastructure is one in which the capacity planning, installation, setup, and management are invisible to the user because they are handled by the cloud provider.

- There are several service models in cloud computing. Software as a Service (SaaS) is a cloud computing hosted software environment. Platform as a Service (PaaS) provides a software platform on which the enterprise or users can build their own applications and then host them on the PaaS provider's infrastructure. Infrastructure as a Service (IaaS) provides unlimited "raw" computing, storage, and network resources that the enterprise can use to build its own virtual infrastructure in the cloud. Function as a Service (FaaS) is a serverless approach to execute modular pieces of code.

- Cloud computing has several potential security issues. These include unprotected storage, logging and monitoring invisibility, and insecure APIs. A particularly serious potential cloud vulnerability regards a lack of key management, or protecting API keys, passwords, certificates, encryption keys, and tokens that must be passed between microservices.

- Examining software for unintentional vulnerabilities has long been considered important. However, today software and "apps" are also being examined for intentional malware. There are two types of software analysis for vulnerabilities and malware. When looking for vulnerabilities, the testing of the software should occur before the source code is compiled. These tests are called a static analysis. Security testing can also be performed after the source code is compiled, although it is more difficult to find flaws. This is called dynamic analysis or run-time verification when all components are integrated and running.

- Although several tools are available for examining an infrastructure for vulnerabilities, Tenable's Nessus is one of the most popular and highly regarded vulnerability scanning tools. Other popular tools include OpenVAS, Nexpose, and Qualys.

- Vulnerabilities in web applications continue to be a leading attack vector. A web application vulnerability diagnostic tool that performs passive scanning examines each page of the web application delivered by the web server and then looks at the HTML in responses from the web application. Active scanning attempts to find other vulnerabilities by using known attacks against the selected targets. It attacks all the discovered pages by testing their functionality and parameters. Dynamic analysis searches for flaws from outside the application with no knowledge of the software's structure or source code. Static analysis examines the web application code from the inside to look for common vulnerabilities such as SQL injection and cross-site scripting, as well as coding errors like buffer overflows. The OWASP Zed Attack Proxy (ZAP) is considered the premiere open source tool for diagnosing web applications. Other web application vulnerability diagnostic tools include Burp Suite (a tool that performs both a static and dynamic analysis), Nikto (a command-line open source tool), and Arachni (a modular open source tool).

- Searching for network vulnerabilities involves enumeration. The general definition of enumeration is the act of making a list of items one after another. In cybersecurity, enumeration is defined as the process of extracting a list of usernames, machine names, network resources, shares, and services from a network system. When conducting enumeration, several network utility tools can be used. Some tools are native to the OS. Others are third-party tools. One of the best-known tools is nmap (network mapper), which is an open source utility for network discovery and security auditing. Other third-party network tools include hping (a command-line TCP/IP packet assembler and analyzer) and responder (a tool that can manipulate name resolution services to uncover sensitive information).

- The introduction of wireless local area networks (WLANs) in enterprises has introduced several potential vulnerabilities. Different tools can be used to diagnose or exploit wireless vulnerabilities. One exploitation tool that can be used on data exfiltrated from a wireless network is Hashcat. Hashcat is a tool for cracking password hashes. Other wireless tools include Aircrack-ng (a tool for capturing wireless packets and attacking wireless networks) and Reaver (a tool for cracking Wi-Fi Protected Setup (WPS) PINs).

- Several tools can be used to identify vulnerabilities in cloud platforms. Prowler is a command-line tool for diagnosing vulnerabilities in services using the AWS cloud. Scout Suite is an open source multi-cloud security-auditing tool. Pacu is an exploitation framework for AWS.

Key Terms

active	Infrastructure as Code (IaC)	Platform as a Service (PaaS)
Aircrack-ng	Infrastructure as a Service (IaaS)	private cloud
Arachni	insecure application program	Prowler
Burp Suite	interfaces (APIs)	public cloud
cloud computing	lack of key management	Qualys
community cloud	logging and monitoring invisibility	Reaver
dynamic analysis	Nessus	responder
enumeration	Nikto	reverse engineering
Function as a Service (FaaS)	nmap	Scout Suite
fuzzing	OpenVAS	serverless infrastructure
Hashcat	OWASP Zed Attack Proxy (ZAP)	Software as a Service (SaaS)
hping	Pacu	static analysis
hybrid cloud	passive	unprotected storage

Review Questions

1. Which of the following is NOT a characteristic of cloud computing?
   a. Metered services
   b. Immediate elasticity
   c. Universal client support
   d. Visible resource pooling

2. Qiang is creating a report for his supervisor about the cost savings associated with cloud computing. Which of the following would he NOT include on the report on the cost savings?
   a. Reduction in broadband costs
   b. Resiliency
   c. Scalability
   d. Pay-per-use

3. Fai is the company HR manager and wants to create a type of cloud that would only be accessible to other HR managers. Which type of cloud would best fit Fai's need?
   a. Public cloud
   b. Group cloud
   c. Hybrid cloud
   d. Community cloud

4. Which of the following is a serverless approach to executing modular pieces of code?
   a. FaaS
   b. IaaS
   c. PaaS
   d. CaaS

5. Chen is frustrated that there are so many different cloud services that his company is using that span multiple cloud provider accounts and even from different cloud providers. He wants to implement a technology to give full control and visibility over all the cloud resources, including network routing and security. What product does Chen need?
   a. Thin virtual visibility appliance (TVVA)
   b. SWG
   c. CASB
   d. Transit gateway

6. What does the term "serverless" mean in cloud computing?
   a. The cloud network configuration does not require any servers.
   b. Server resources of the cloud are inconspicuous to the end user.
   c. Servers are run as VMs.
   d. All appliances are virtual and do not interact with physical servers.

7. Which of the following questions correctly defines "lack of key management"?
   a. How should authentication credentials be passed or accessed securely in a cloud environment?
   b. Who should be given responsibility for uploading keys to the cloud?
   c. How can virtual keys be stored securely on a flash drive?
   d. How often should keys be duplicated for PKIs?

8. Which cloud model requires the highest level of IT responsibilities?
   a. IaaS
   b. SaaS
   c. PaaS
   d. RaaS

9. What type of analysis occurs before source code has been compiled?
   a. Dynamic analysis
   b. Static analysis
   c. Compiled analysis
   d. Decompiled analysis

10. Which of the following is NOT a cloud computing security issue?
    a. System vulnerabilities
    b. Insecure APIs
    c. Compliance regulations
    d. Bandwidth utilization

11. Which of the following is NOT correct about fuzzing?
    a. Fuzzing is used with static analysis.
    b. Fuzzing provides random input to a program to attempt to trigger exceptions.
    c. An advantage of fuzzing is it produces a record of what input triggered the exception so that it can be reproduced in order to track down the problem within the code.
    d. Fuzzing test software consists of an execution engine and an input generator.

12. Which of these is NOT created and managed by a microservices API?
    a. User experience (UX)
    b. Database
    c. Logs
    d. Authentication

13. Which of the following is NOT true about Nessus?
    a. Nessus is an open source vulnerability scanner that uses the Common Vulnerability Scoring System (CVSS).
    b. Nessus has a modular architecture consisting of centralized servers, which conduct scanning, and remote client agents, which interact with the servers.
    c. Nessus can detect security vulnerabilities in local or remote hosts and identify missing security updates and patches by simulating attacks to pinpoint vulnerabilities.
    d. Nessus only runs on the Linux/Unix OS.

14. Which of the following is true about the CVSS Temporal Score?
    a. The Temporal Score represents the characteristics (intrinsic qualities) of the vulnerability when it was first discovered.
    b. The Temporal Score cannot be determined until there are 100,000 incidents based on the vulnerability.
    c. The Temporal Score does not consider attack vectors (AVs).
    d. The Temporal Score reflects the current characteristics of a vulnerability that may have changed over time.

15. Which infrastructure diagnostic tool is a cloud-based Software-as-a-Service (SaaS) delivery model, allowing users to access it from any web browser?
    a. Qualys
    b. Net-Expose
    c. OpenVAS
    d. Cloud-AX

16. Which of the following is NOT a means of analysis that web application vulnerability scanners use?
    a. Recursive scanning
    b. Passive scanning
    c. Static analysis
    d. Dynamic analysis

17. Which tool can be used for network mapping?
    a. Zenmap
    b. Nslookup
    c. Ipconfig/ifconfig
    d. Tracert/traceroute

18. Which of the following tools is NOT native to an OS?
    a. Netstat
    b. Nmap
    c. Ping
    d. Nslookup

19. Which third-party network tool can manipulate name resolution services to uncover sensitive information?
    a. hping
    b. responder
    c. ZEN-X
    d. APX

20. Which tool is used to crack password hashes?
    a. Hashcat
    b. Reaver
    c. Pacu
    d. Prowler

Case Projects

Case Project 4-1: Secrets Management Systems

Cloud computing providers typically offer their own proprietary secrets management systems, and there are several third-party systems available. Identify two proprietary secrets management systems from cloud providers and two third-party systems. Research each and then create a document outlining how they are used, their strengths, and their weaknesses.

Case Project 4-2: Insecure Application Program Interfaces (APIs)

Insecure Application Program Interfaces (APIs) have become a prime target today. Use the Internet to research APIs. How are they used? How can they be manipulated? What is being done to secure APIs? What should be done? Write a one-page paper on your research.

Case Project 4-3: Comparing Disassemblers and Decompilers

Use the Internet to identify three disassemblers and three decompilers. Compare the features of each. What are their advantages? What are their disadvantages? How specific is the output from a decompiler? What legal issues surround their use? Is it legal to reverse-engineer software code? Write a one-page paper on your research.

Case Project 4-4: Hashcat

Hashcat is considered the premiere password hashing cracking tool. Research hashcat and write a one-page paper on its features, its strengths, its weaknesses, and how it can be used.

Case Project 4-5: On the Job

Suppose you work for a company that has just discovered that an employee has been using vulnerability scanning tools on networks and systems other than those belonging to the company. One senior vice president said that since the employee was not caught by anyone outside the company, the employee should be told to discontinue the scans, but no further action should be taken. However, another senior vice president said that the employee should be terminated, and the companies that he scanned should be contacted about what happened as a means of full disclosure. This senior VP feels that this is the ethical approach and he also wants to prevent a future scandal if any of the outside companies were to discover later that the scans came from this company. Where do you stand? Should the incident be forgotten, or should there be full transparency? Write a one-page memo about what you think should be done and why.

References

1. "Significant Cyber Incidents," *Center for Strategic and International Studies*, accessed Dec. 12, 2020, www.csis.org/programs/strategic-technologies-program/significant-cyber-incidents.
2. Melton, James, "US Consumers Made Almost 63 Million Online Grocery Orders in November," *DigitalCommerce360*, Dec. 10, 2020, accessed Dec. 12, 2020, www.digitalcommerce360.com/article/coronavirus-impact-online-retail/.
3. "Accelerating into the Cloud," *Cognizant*, accessed Dec. 12, 2020, https://reprints.forrester.com/#/assets/2/346/RES122882/reports.
4. Mell, Peter, and Grance, Tim, "The NIST Definition of Cloud Computing," NIST Computer Security Division Computer Security Resource Center. Oct. 7, 2009, accessed Apr. 2, 2011, http://csrc.nist.gov/groups/SNS/cloud-computing/.

CONTROLS AND BEST PRACTICES

After identifying threats and vulnerabilities, the next logical step is to implement countermeasures to counteract any cybersecurity risks. These countermeasures involve implementing controls and following best practices to reduce attacks or their severity. The modules in this part examine these various types of controls and best practices. Module 5 examines the controls as they relate to the infrastructure and configurations of devices. Module 6 looks at specific software and hardware best practices.

MODULE 5
INFRASTRUCTURE CONTROLS

MODULE 6
SOFTWARE AND HARDWARE ASSURANCE BEST PRACTICES

PART 2

INFRASTRUCTURE CONTROLS

After completing this module, you should be able to do the following:

1 Define cybersecurity controls

2 List infrastructure management controls

3 Describe different configuration controls

Cybersecurity Today

Suppose that an organization needs to keep a crucial network or endpoint from being compromised. It could "lock down" network devices to only allow the barest minimum of required packets into the network or install on endpoints the most potent antimalware software available. However, because virtually all networks and endpoints are connected to an external network or support connections from other devices, this serves as an open invitation for threat actors to access these devices.

The solution is to completely isolate the network or endpoint from all external sources. This includes separating the network infrastructure from all other networks—especially the Internet—and disabling USB connectors or even filling them with glue so that USB flash drives cannot be inserted. This extreme isolation is called an "air gap" because the devices to be protected have a separation between them and any other device that consists of air and nothing else. Air gaps are often used in environments in which computers that control pumps and valves must be completely isolated. (Manipulating a critical valve could cause an explosion or release raw sewage into the drinking water system.) Another example of an air gap is when a user works with a separate Linux-based computer only for accessing an online financial site. This prevents using an already infected computer from capturing login information to the financial site.

It is not uncommon for sophisticated threat actors such as nation-state actors to employ sophisticated and innovative techniques to bridge an air gap. For example, the infamous Stuxnet worm was introduced into an air-gapped network at an Iranian nuclear power plant. The attackers infected USB flash drives with their malware and then left several of these flash drives scattered in a parking lot. Unsuspecting employees picked up the flash drives while walking into the secure facility and then inserted them into their computers to discover the owner of the "lost" flash drive (or they were just curious about what was stored on the drive). However, this introduced the malware into this air-gapped network.

Air gaps are also used for networks or endpoints in which it is essential to prevent data theft (exfiltration): by isolating the network or device, threat actors cannot reach the data to steal it. However, researchers have demonstrated that data on an air-gapped computer can still be exfiltrated in mind-boggling ways.

Mordechai Guri, the head of Research and Development and his team at the Ben-Gurion University Cybersecurity Research Center of the Negev in Israel, has demonstrated different methods for sending data from air-gapped computers to the outside world without being detected. And these techniques do not involve planting malware on computers to steal the data. Instead, they take advantage of normal and innocuous computer actions. A list of the names of some of the techniques and their descriptions include the following:

AirHopper: Use the local graphics utility unit (GPU) card to emit electromagnetic signals to a nearby mobile phone.
BitWhisper: Exfiltrate data from non-networked computers using heat emanations.
BRIGHTNESS: Steal data from air-gapped systems using variations in monitor screen brightness.
DiskFiltration: Use read/write hard disk drive (HDD) operations to steal data via sound waves.
Fansmitter: Exfiltrate data from air-gapped endpoints by using sounds from a computer's GPU fan.
LED-it-Go: Steal data through an HDD's activity light-emitting diode (LED) light.
MOSQUITO: Swipe data using attached speakers and headphones.
PowerHammer: Exfiltrate data through power cords.
USBee: Force a USB data bus to give out electromagnetic emissions.

The university's team recently discovered that the vibrations generated by a computer's fans (such as CPU fans, GPU fans, and power supply fans) can be used to steal data. By controlling the fan's speed, an attacker can vary the frequency of the vibrations that result from the fan. Called the AiR-ViBeR technique, a nearby attacker can then record these vibrations to later decode the data from the vibration patterns. Even if the attackers cannot control the fans, they can target employees of the company with a "special offer" to download a smartphone app. However, this is also an infected app (Trojan) that can pick up these vibrations on behalf of the attacker. This is possible because the accelerometer sensors in modern smartphones can be accessed by any app without requiring the user's permission.[1]

To control (verb) is to direct influence over something. A horse trainer on a ranch works to have control over a wild stallion. Firefighters spray hundreds of gallons of water on a wildfire to bring it under control. Citizens are strongly encouraged to be vaccinated in order to control a spreading pandemic. A baseball pitcher uses a certain grip of the ball to control its flight as it streaks across the plate within the strike zone. Thus, *a control* (noun) is that which influences, regulates, or governs, such as a horse trainer, water, vaccine, or grip.

In cybersecurity, it is likewise necessary to direct influence over attacks through various methods. That is, it is important to control attacks by using different controls. These cybersecurity controls are often said to be "countermeasures" that organizations implement to prevent, reduce, or counteract security risks.

There are any number of ways to categorize controls. In this module, you will explore two broad categories of controls that relate to the infrastructure, namely, infrastructure management controls and configuration controls.

INFRASTRUCTURE MANAGEMENT SOLUTIONS AND CONTROLS

 **CERTIFICATION**

2.1 Given a scenario, apply security solutions for infrastructure management.

Several solutions and controls relate to managing the infrastructure. These include general management concepts and controls that apply to the cloud, virtualization, identity and access management, certificate management, and networking.

General Concepts

Several general concepts relate to infrastructure management solutions and controls. These concepts can apply to a broad range of controls and include active defense and change and asset management.

Active Defense

One general concept is to engage in an **active defense** against threat actors. In the military, active defense is often used on the battlefield. It consists of steps to make an attack more difficult for the enemy to carry out. For example, an army may build obstacles to slow down or even prevent armored vehicles or tanks from entering an area. These obstacles, when constructed of concrete, are called dragon's teeth; when constructed of metal, they are known as Czech hedgehogs and are illustrated in Figure 5-1. Slowing down or derailing the attackers so they cannot advance or complete their attack also increases the likelihood that the attackers will make a mistake and expose their presence or reveal their attack plans.

Source: Vasek.x1/Shutterstock.com

Figure 5-1   Czech hedgehogs

NOTE 1

It is important to devise an active defense so that it cannot then be turned around by the attacker as part of its attack. For example, during World War II, Czech hedgehogs that were implanted to prevent Allied tanks from entering the beach at Normandy on D-Day were later removed and welded to the front of Allied tanks to be used as plows for clearing away trees and hedgerows to expose the enemy.

When defending against cyberattacks, active defense can also prove beneficial. Active defense techniques can raise the cost for the attacker in terms of wasted time and processing power. One basic example is using encryption: an attacker who spends large amounts of time and energy hunting for specific data can be thwarted—and frustrated—by finding that the data is encrypted.

More common active defenses include deceptions. These are designed to detect attackers early in their attack cycle by obfuscating the attack surface and setting up attractive bait as a realistic decoy that only misdirects the attack. In many instances, a deception tricks the attackers into engagement and leads them to think they are escalating their attack, when, in fact, they are not only wasting their time and processing power but may actually be providing the defender with counterintelligence. Deceptions require strict **monitoring and logging** to watch and record the actions of the threat actors.

 **CAUTION**   Active defense should be viewed as only one part of a cyber defense. Whereas it may frustrate some threat actors who are looking for "low-hanging fruit" and then move onto other targets, it rarely will defeat dedicated threat actors like nation-state actors. While active defense can prove beneficial in some instances, it should not be relied upon as the key element in a defense strategy.

Change and Asset Management

Proper management is another general concept and includes the following:

- *Change management.* Change management refers to a formal process for making modifications to a system and keeping track of those changes. A change management policy is a written document that defines the types of changes that can be made and under what circumstances.
- *Change control.* Change control stipulates the processes to follow for implementing system changes. It involves communicating the changes to relevant stakeholders and reviewing the processes for validating a change. Change control should be made following the standards set in the change management policy.
- *Asset management.* Asset management is the procedure of procuring and protecting assets. An asset management policy provides the guidelines and practices that govern decisions about how assets should be acquired, maintained, and disposed. Asset management typically includes asset tagging, which is affixing physical tags to hardware and creating an approved listing of software that can be installed.

Cloud Controls

Securing the resources in the corporate data center is much different from securing data held and processed in the cloud (cloud vs. on-premises). When securing cloud resources, some controls are inherent to the cloud computing platforms and offered by the cloud computing providers to their customers (cloud native controls) while other security controls are available from external sources (third-party solutions). Securing cloud computing involves using controls such as the following:

NOTE 2

The decision regarding how much of an enterprise's network architecture should be migrated to the cloud and how much should remain on-prem is covered in Module 4.

- *Conducting audits.* A cloud security audit is an independent examination of cloud service controls. Once completed, the auditor renders an objective assessment of the security. A cloud auditor can evaluate the services provided by a cloud provider in terms of security controls, privacy impact, availability, and performance.
- *Utilizing regions and zones.* Highly available systems are reliable because they can continue operating even when critical components fail. These systems are also resilient, meaning that they can handle failure without service disruption or data loss, and seamlessly recover from such a failure. In a cloud computing environment, reliability and resiliency are achieved through duplicating processes across one or more geographical areas.
- *Enforce functional area mitigations.* Cloud computing has three functional areas: storage, network, and compute. Each of these has its own set of security mitigations that should be applied.
- *Implement secrets management.* A solution to the problem of insecure application program interfaces (APIs) is to use secrets management. Secrets management enables strong security and improved management of a microservices-based architecture. It allows the entire cloud infrastructure to remain flexible and scalable without sacrificing security. A secrets manager provides a central repository and single source to manage, access, and audit secrets across a cloud infrastructure. Typical features of a secrets management system are listed in Table 5-1. Cloud computing providers typically offer their own proprietary secrets management systems, and several third-party systems are available.

Table 5-1   Secrets management features

Feature	Description
Limited and automated replication	While secret data and secret names are "project-global" resources, the secret data is stored in regions, which the user can specify or the cloud provider can designate.
Secret-specific versioning	A secret can be pinned to a specific version of the code (like "v3.2").
Audit logging	Every interaction generates an audit entry in a log file that can be used to find abnormal access patterns that may indicate possible security breaches.
Default encryption	Data is encrypted in transit and at rest with AES-256-bit encryption keys.
Extensibility	The system is able to extend and integrate into other existing secret management systems.

Grow with Cengage Unlimited!

If you'd like more information about this topic, use your Cengage Unlimited subscription to go to the CompTIA Security+ Guide to Network Security Fundamentals, 7th edition; open Module 1; and read the section titled "Cloud Security." If you don't have a Cengage Unlimited subscription, you can find more information at cengage.com/unlimited.

While securing the functional areas of the cloud (storage, networking, and compute) is universally considered as important, an area often overlooked is protecting applications. There are several common misperceptions, ranging from application security being entirely the cloud computing provider's responsibility to the native "out-of-the-box" security of the applications being licensed as providing adequate security. However, misconfigurations of the application setup and insecure APIs or interfaces can provide vulnerabilities for threat actors to exploit.

One of an organization's security protections for cloud computing application security is to use a **cloud access security broker (CASB)**. A CASB is a set of software tools or services that resides between an enterprise's on-prem infrastructure and the cloud provider's infrastructure. Acting as the gatekeeper, a CASB ensures that the security policies of the enterprise extend to its data in the cloud. For example, if the enterprise has a policy for encrypting data, a CASB can enforce that control and ensure that data is encrypted when it is copied from the cloud to a local device.

Virtualization

Virtualization is a means of managing and presenting computer resources by function without regard to their physical layout or location. One type of virtualization in which an entire operating system (OS) environment is simulated is known as host virtualization. Instead of using a physical computer, a virtual machine (VM), which is a simulated software-based emulation of a computer, is created instead. The host system (the OS installed on the computer's hardware) runs a VM monitor program that supports one or more guest systems (a foreign virtual OS) that runs applications. For example, a computer that boots to Windows 10 (host) could support a VM of Linux (guest) as well as another Windows 10 (guest) system. The VM monitor program is called a hypervisor, which manages the VM OSs. Hypervisors use a small "layer" of computer code in software or firmware to allocate resources in real time as needed, such as input/output functions and memory allocations.

NOTE 3

Virtualization is not new. It was first developed by IBM in the 1960s for running multiple software "contexts" on its mainframe computers. It has gained popularity over the last 20 years as on-prem data centers used it for migrating away from physical servers to more economical VMs.

An even more reduced instance of virtualization is a *container*. With hypervisors, the entire guest OS must be started and fully functioning before an application can be launched. A container, on the other hand, holds only the necessary OS components (such as binary files and libraries) that are needed for that specific application to run. In some instances, containers can even share binary files and libraries. This not only reduces the necessary hard drive storage space and random access memory (RAM) needed but also allows for containers to start more quickly because the entire OS does not have to be started. Using containers (**containerization**) means the necessary OS components can be easily moved from one computer to another. A container is illustrated in Figure 5-2.

Another application of VMs is known as **Virtual Desktop Infrastructure (VDI)**. VDI is the process of running a user desktop inside a VM that resides on a server. This enables personalized desktops for each user to be available on any computer or device that can access the server so that users' personalized desktops and files can be accessed as if they were sitting at their own computer. VDI allows centralized management as opposed to the need for technical support personnel to access a system remotely or even visit a user's desk to troubleshoot, saving substantial time and money.

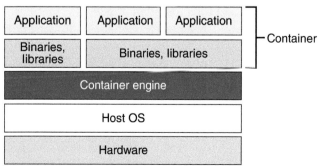

Figure 5-2   Container

Host virtualization also has several security-related advantages:

- The latest security updates can be downloaded and run in a VM to determine compatibility, or the impact on other software or even hardware. This is used instead of installing the update on a production computer and then being forced to "roll back" to the previous configuration if it does not work properly.
- A snapshot of a state of a VM can be saved for later use. A user can make a snapshot before performing extensive modifications or alterations to the VM, and then the snapshot can be reloaded so that the VM is at the beginning state before the changes were made. Multiple snapshots can be made, all at different states, and loaded as needed.
- Testing the existing security configuration, known as security control testing, can be performed using a simulated network environment on a computer using multiple VMs. For example, one VM can virtually attack another VM on the same host system to determine vulnerabilities and security settings. This is possible because all the VMs can be connected through a virtual network.
- VMs can promote security segregation and isolation. Separating VMs from other machines can reduce the risk of infections transferring from one device to another.
- A VM can be used to test for potential malware. A suspicious program can be loaded into an isolated VM and executed. If the program is malware, it will impact only the VM, and it can easily be erased and a snapshot reinstalled.

NOTE 4

Threat actors have learned that when their malware is run in a VM, it most likely is being examined by a security professional. Many modern instances of malware will refuse to function and will self-destruct if they detect they are being run in a VM.

However, there are security concerns for virtualized environments:

- Not all hypervisors have the necessary security controls to keep out determined attackers. If a single hypervisor is compromised, multiple virtual servers are at risk.
- Traditional security tools—such as antivirus, firewalls, and IDS—were designed for single physical servers and do not always adapt well to multiple VMs. Instead, "virtualized" versions can be used instead, such as a firewall virtual appliance that is optimized for VMs.
- VMs must be protected from both outside networks and other VMs on the same physical computer. In a network without VMs, external devices such as firewalls and IDSs that reside between physical servers can help prevent one physical server from infecting another physical server, but no such physical devices exist between VMs.
- VMs may be able to "escape" from the contained environment and directly interact with the host OS. It is important to have virtual machine escape protection so that a VM cannot directly interact with the host OS and potentially infect it, which could then be transmitted to all other VMs running on the host OS.
- Because VMs can easily and quickly be created and launched, this has led to virtual machine sprawl, or the widespread proliferation of VMs without proper oversight or management. It is often easy for a VM to be created and then forgotten. A guest OS that has remained dormant for a period may not contain the latest security updates, even though the underlying host OS has been updated. When the guest is launched, it will be vulnerable until properly updated. One option for combating VM sprawl is to install a virtual machine manager, which can provide a dashboard of the status of the VMs. A virtual machine manager is seen in Figure 5-3.

In addition to protecting VMs, container security is also important. Best practices for securing a container include the following:

- Always manage container-based processes using non-privileged user accounts.
- Use trusted images to create a container because a compromised image can more easily circumvent existing security measures.
- Use tools such as Security-Enhanced Linux (SELinux) to harden the hosts.

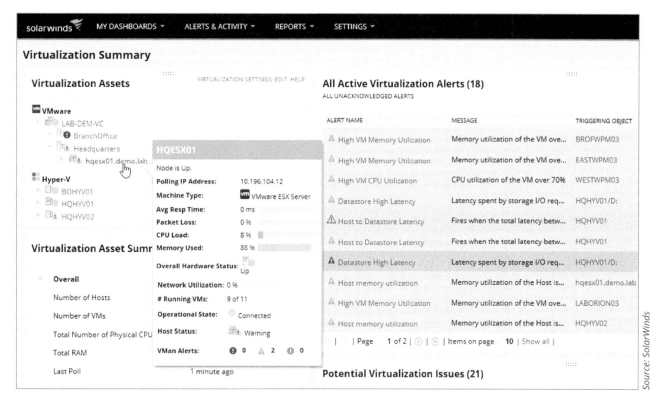

Figure 5-3   Virtual machine manager

Identity and Access Management (IAM)

Identity and access management (IAM) is an umbrella term that describes the various products, processes, and policies for managing a user's identity and regulating access to resources. In today's global environment, "users" are not limited to only current employees but also include third-party partners, suppliers, contractors, and even customers. "Access" can include not only contact with a resource but also what can be done with that resource. (For example, a user may be given access to view a data file but not have access to change the file contents.)

> **NOTE 5**
>
> IAM typically is used to identify, authenticate, and authorize users.

While any number of components can be involved in IAM, most often it includes three primary elements:

- A database that contains users' identities and access privileges
- Tools used by a system administrator for creating, monitoring, modifying, and deleting access privileges
- A system for auditing user logins and access history

IAM provides several controls for restricting unauthorized users while permitting approved users. These include multifactor authentication (MFA), single sign-on (SSO), and access control schemes.

Multifactor Authentication (MFA)

At least seven elements, known as *authentication credentials*, can be presented to an IT system to verify the genuineness of the user. Three of these elements (something you know, something you have, and something you are) are called *factors* while the remaining four (somewhere you are, something you can do, something you exhibit, and someone you know) are called *attributes*. The element *something you exhibit* is often linked to more specialized attributes and may even include neurological traits that can be identified by specialized medical equipment. Because only the real or "authentic" person possesses one or more of these elements, these can be considered as types of authentication, or proof of genuineness. Although any of these elements can be used as an authentication credential, the most common in IT are something you know, something you have, something you are, and something you can do.

> **NOTE 6**
>
> Authentication credentials are covered in Module 1.

When an IAM requires more than one type of authentication credential to be presented, this is called multifactor authentication (MFA). Using just one type of authentication is called *single-factor authentication* and using two types is called *two-factor authentication (2FA)*. The most common items used for MFA are passwords combined with specialized devices, smartphones, or security keys. Requiring multiple authentication credentials can serve as a control and thwart a threat actor who, for example, has stolen a user's password but does not have access to the user's smartphone.

Single Sign-On (SSO)

One problem facing users today is having multiple accounts across multiple platforms that all should use a unique username and password. The difficulty in managing these authentication credentials frequently causes users to compromise and select the least burdensome password and then use it for all accounts. A solution to this problem is to have one username and password to gain access to all accounts so that the user has only one authentication credential to remember.

This is the idea behind identity management, which is using a single authentication credential that is shared across multiple networks. When those networks are owned by different organizations, it is called federation (or sometimes called federated identity management, or FIM). One application of federation is single sign-on (SSO), or using one authentication credential to access multiple accounts or applications. SSO holds the promise of reducing the number of usernames and passwords that users must memorize (potentially, to just one).

There are several current technologies for federation systems. These are listed in Table 5-2.

Table 5-2 Federation systems technologies

Name	Description	Explanation
OAuth (Open Authorization)	Open source federation framework	OAuth 2.0 is a framework to support the development of authorization protocols.
Open ID	Open standard decentralized authentication protocol	Open ID is an authentication protocol that can be used in OAuth 2.0 as a standard means to obtain user identity.
Shibboleth	Open source software package for designing SSO	Shibboleth uses federation standards to provide SSO and exchanging attributes.

Access Control Schemes

Consider a system administrator who needs to assign privileges to users. This includes new users as well as those whose duties have changed. With hundreds of thousands of files scattered across many servers, and with users given different access privileges to each file (for example, a user can view one file but not edit it, but for a different file, the user can edit but not delete), controlling access can prove to be a daunting task. Coupled with this burden are periodic manual reviews of privileges. These reviews often require matching users with human resource (HR) data, reviewing their current privileges, identifying new personnel, and contacting existing users to encourage them to complete their access reviews. The entire manual review process must also be completed within specific audit timelines.

However, this job is made easier when the hardware and software have a predefined framework that the administrator can use for controlling access. This framework, called an *access control scheme*, is embedded in the software and hardware. The administrator can use the appropriate scheme to configure the necessary level of control. Using these schemes is part of privileged management, which is the technologies and strategies for controlling elevated (privileged) access and permissions. Three common access control schemes are Mandatory Access Control, Role-Based Access Control, and Attribute-Based Access Control.

Mandatory Access Control (MAC)   Mandatory Access Control (MAC) assigns users' access controls strictly according to the data custodian's desires. This is considered the most restrictive access control scheme because the user has no freedom to set controls or distribute access to other subjects. MAC has two key elements:

- *Labels.* In a system using MAC, every entity is an object (laptops, files, projects, and so on) and is assigned a classification label. These labels represent the relative importance of the object, such as *confidential, secret*, and *top secret*. Subjects (users, processes, and so on) are assigned a privilege label (sometimes called a *clearance*).
- *Levels.* A hierarchy based on the labels is also used, both for objects and subjects. *Top secret* has a higher level than *secret*, which has a higher level than *confidential.*

MAC grants permissions by matching object labels with subject labels based on their respective levels. To determine if a file can be opened by a user, the object and subject labels are compared. The subject must have an equal or greater level than the object to be granted access. For example, if the object label is *top secret*, yet the subject has only a lower *secret* clearance, access is denied. Subjects cannot change the labels of objects or other subjects to modify the security settings.

Role-Based Access Control   Role-Based Access Control (RBAC) is sometimes called *Non-Discretionary Access Control*. RBAC is considered a more "real-world" access control than the other schemes because the access under RBAC is based on a user's job function within an organization. Instead of setting permissions for each user or group, the RBAC scheme assigns permissions to particular roles in the organization and then assigns users to those roles. Objects are set to be a certain type, to which subjects with that particular role have access. For example, instead of creating a user account for Ahmed and assigning specific privileges to that account, the role *Business_Manager* can be created based on the privileges an individual in that job function should have. Then Ahmed and all other business managers in the organization can be assigned to that role. The users and objects inherit all the permissions for the role.

Attribute-Based Access Control   Attribute-Based Access Control (ABAC) uses flexible policies that can combine attributes. These policies can take advantage of many types of attributes, such as object attributes, subject attributes, and environment attributes. ABAC rules can be formatted using an *If-Then-Else* structure so that a policy can be created, such as *If this subject has the role of manager, then grant access else deny access.*

Table 5-3 summarizes the features of the three access control schemes.

Table 5-3   Access control schemes

Name	Explanation	Description
Mandatory Access Control (MAC)	User cannot set controls	Most restrictive scheme
Role-Based Access Control (RBAC)	Assigns permissions to particular roles in the organization and then users are assigned to roles	Considered a more "real-world" approach
Attribute-Based Access Control (ABAC)	Uses policies that can combine attributes	Most flexible scheme

NOTE 9

Access control schemes are variously referred to as access control models, methods, modes, techniques, or types. They are used by data custodians/stewards for access control but are neither created nor installed by them. Instead, these schemes are already part of the software and hardware.

NOTE 10

In the original MAC scheme, all objects and subjects were assigned a numeric access level, and the access level of the subject had to be higher than that of the object for access to be granted. For example, if EMPLOYEES.XLSX was assigned Level 500 while SALARIES.XLSX was assigned level 700, then a user with an assigned level of 600 could access EMPLOYEES.XLSX (Level 500) but not SALARIES.XLSX (Level 700). This scheme was later modified to use labels instead of numbers.

Certificate Management

One of the strongest controls for protecting data is cryptography. Dating back to the ancient Greeks, cryptography (which is from Greek words meaning *hidden writing*) is the practice of transforming information so that it cannot be understood by unauthorized parties, and is thus secure. This is usually accomplished through "scrambling" the information in such a way that only approved recipients (either human or machine) can understand it. When using cryptography, the process of changing the original text into a scrambled message is known as encryption. (The reverse process is *decryption*, or changing the message back to its original form.)

NOTE 11

A digital certificate is basically a container for a public key. It can be used to identify objects other than users, such as servers and applications. Typically, a digital certificate contains information such as the owner's name or alias, the owner's public key, the name of the issuer, the digital signature of the issuer, the serial number of the digital certificate, and the expiration date of the public key. It can contain other user-supplied information, such as an email address, postal address, and basic registration information.

Asymmetric cryptography (also called public key cryptography) uses a pair of related keys. The public key can be distributed and shared with anyone, while the corresponding private key must be kept confidential by the owner. Asymmetric cryptography has two uses: it can encrypt or decrypt a set of data, and it can be used as a proof to verify a "signature" of the sender. A digital certificate is a technology used to associate a user's identity to a public key that has been digitally signed by a trusted third party. This third party verifies the owner and that the public key belongs to that owner.

Multiple entities make up strong certificate management, or controlling digital certificates. These include a certificate repository and a means for certificate revocation.

Certificate Repository (CR)

A *certificate repository (CR)* is a publicly accessible centralized directory of digital certificates that can be used to view the status of a digital certificate. This directory can be managed locally by setting it up as a storage area connected to the CA server.

Certificate Revocation

Digital certificates normally have an expiration date. However, some circumstances might cause the certificate to be revoked before it expires. Some reasons might be benign, such as when the certificate is no longer used or the details of the certificate, such as the user's address, have changed. Other circumstances could be more dangerous. For example, if attackers steal a user's private key, they could impersonate the victim through using digital certificates without the other users being aware of it. In addition, what would happen if digital certificates were stolen? The thieves could then issue certificates to themselves that would be trusted by unsuspecting users. It is important that a published list of approved certificates as well as revoked certificates be generated in a timely fashion; otherwise, it could lead to a situation in which security may be compromised.

 **CAUTION** There have been several incidences of digital certificates being stolen. The thieves can then trick unsuspecting users into connecting with an imposter site, thinking it is a legitimate site. There have also been charges that nation-state actors have stolen digital certificates to trick their own citizens into connecting with a fraudulent email site to monitor their messages and to locate and crack-down on dissidents.

The status of a certificate can be checked by one of two means to see if it has been revoked. The first method is to use a Certificate Revocation List (CRL), which is a list of certificate serial numbers that have been revoked. Many certificate authorities maintain an online CRL that can be queried by entering the certificate's serial number. In addition, a local computer receives updates on the status of certificates and maintains a local CRL, as illustrated in Figure 5-4.

The second method is an Online Certificate Status Protocol (OCSP), which performs a real-time lookup of a certificate's status. OCSP is called a request-response protocol. The browser sends the certificate's information to a trusted entity like the CA, known as an *OCSP Responder*. The OCSP Responder then provides revocation information on that one specific certificate.

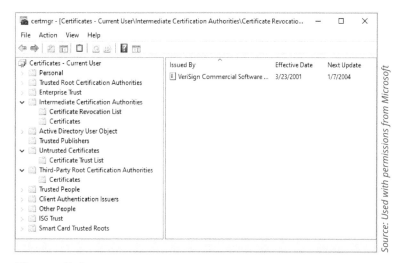

Figure 5-4   Certificate Revocation List (CRL)

A variation of OCSP is called OCSP stapling. OCSP requires the OCSP Responder to provide responses to every web client of a certificate in real time, which may create a high volume of traffic. With OCSP stapling, web servers send queries to the Responder OCSP server at regular intervals to receive a signed, time-stamped OCSP response. When a client's web browser attempts to connect to the web server, the server can include (*staple*) in the handshake with the web browser the previously received OCSP response. The browser can then evaluate the OCSP response to determine if it is trustworthy. OCSP stapling is illustrated in Figure 5-5.

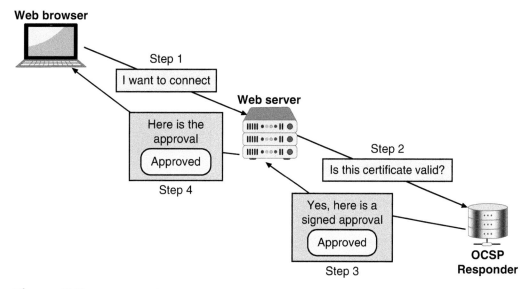

Figure 5-5   OCSP stapling

 **CAUTION**   Determining the revocation status of certificates presented by websites is an ongoing problem in web security. Initially, modern web browsers (Chrome, Firefox, Internet Explorer, Safari, and Opera) used OCSP. However, if the web browser cannot reach the OCSP Responder server, such as when the server is down, then the browser receives a notification of a network error (called a *soft-fail*) and the revocation check is simply ignored. Also, online revocation checking by web browsers can be slow. For these reasons, web browsers have implemented a range of solutions to reduce or eliminate the need for online revocation checking by instead "harvesting" lists of revoked certificates from CAs and then pushing them to the user's browser.

Networking

The final category of infrastructure management solutions and controls are those that relate to a network. They can be categorized as those pertaining to the network architecture, network segmentation, and honeypots.

Network Architecture

For traditional physical networks found in a data center on-prem, various technologies relate to the secure architectural design of the network to provide controls. However, as more networks make the transition from physical to virtual, these new network architectures can provide even more controls. One example is a *serverless* infrastructure in which no server is physically present but is virtually available. Network architecture controls include software-defined networks, virtual private networks, and virtual private clouds.

> **NOTE 12**
>
> Serverless infrastructures are covered in Module 4.

Software Defined Network (SDN)   Virtualization has been an essential technology in changing the face of computing over the last decade. Racks of individual physical servers running a single application have been replaced by only a few hardware devices running multiple VMs, simulated software-based emulations of computers. VMs have made cloud computing possible; as computing needs increase or decrease, cloud computing resources on VMs can be quickly scaled up or back. Networks can also be configured into logical groups to create a *virtual* LAN (VLAN). A VLAN allows scattered users to be logically grouped together even though they are physically attached to different switches. The computing landscape today would simply not be possible without virtualization.

Yet VMs and virtual LANs run into a bottleneck: the physical network. Dating back more than 40 years, networks comprised of physical hardware like bridges, switches, and routers have collided with the world of VMs and VLANs.

Consider this problem. A network manager needs to make sure the VLAN used by a VM is assigned to the same port on a switch as the physical server that is running the VM. But if the VM needs to be migrated, the manager must reconfigure the VLAN every time that a virtual server is moved. In a large enterprise, whenever a new VM is installed, it can take hours for managers to perform the necessary reconfiguration. In addition, these managers must configure each vendor's equipment separately, tweaking performance and security configurations for each session and application. This process is difficult to do with conventional network switches because the *control logic* for each switch is bundled together with the *switching logic*.

What is needed is for the flexibility of the virtual world to be applied to the network. This would allow the network manager to add, drop, and change network resources quickly and dynamically.

The solution is a software defined network (SDN). An SDN virtualizes parts of the physical network so that it can be reconfigured more quickly and easily. This is accomplished by separating the *control plane* from the *data plane*, as illustrated in Figure 5-6. The control plane consists of one or more SDN servers and performs complex functions such as routing and security checks. It also defines the data flows through the data plane.

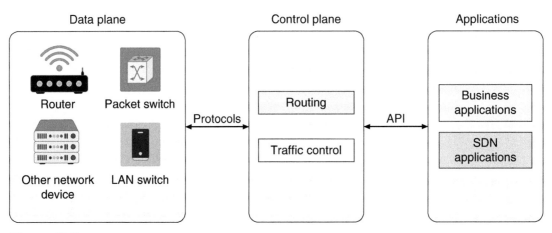

Figure 5-6   Software defined network

NOTE 13

In an SDN, the control plane is essentially an application running on a computer that can manage the physical plane.

If traffic needs to flow through the network, it first receives permission from the SDN controller, which verifies that the communication is permitted by the network policy of the enterprise. Once approved, the SDN controller computes a route for the flow to take and adds an entry for that flow in each of the switches along the path. Because all the complex networking functions are handled by the SDN controller, the switches simply manage "flow tables" whose entries are created by the controller. The communication between the SDN controller and the SDN switches uses a standardized protocol and API.

NOTE 14

The architecture of SDNs is very flexible, using different types of switches from different vendors at different protocol layers. SDN controllers and switches can be implemented for Ethernet switches (Layer 2), Internet routers (Layer 3), Transport (Layer 4) switching, or Application layer switching and routing.

With the decoupling of the control and data planes, SDN enables applications to deal with one "abstracted" network device without any care for the details of how the device operates. This is because the network applications see only a single API to the controller. This makes it possible to quickly create and deploy new applications to orchestrate network traffic flow to meet specific enterprise requirements for performance or security.

NOTE 15

From a security perspective, SDNs can provide strong controls. SDN technology can simplify extending VLANs beyond just the perimeter of a building, which can help secure data. Also, an SDN can ensure that all network traffic is routed through a firewall. Because all network traffic flows through a single point, it can help capture data for intrusion prevention systems.

Virtual Private Network (VPN)   A virtual private network (VPN) is a security technology that enables authorized users to access an unsecured public network, such as the Internet, as if it were a secure private network. It does this by encrypting all data transmitted between the remote endpoint and the network and not just specific documents or files. There are two common types of VPNs. A remote access VPN is a user-to-LAN connection used by remote users. The second type is a site-to-site VPN, in which multiple sites can connect to other sites over the Internet. Some VPNs allow the user to always stay connected instead of connecting and disconnecting from it. These are called always-on VPNs.

NOTE 16

Software-based VPNs are often used on mobile devices and offer the most flexibility in how network traffic is managed. However, hardware-based VPNs, typically used for site-to-site connections, are more secure, have better performance, and can offer more flexibility.

Using a VPN involves two options depending upon which traffic is to be protected. When all traffic is sent to the VPN concentrator and protected, this is called a full tunnel. However, not all traffic—such as web surfing or reading personal email—may need to be protected through a VPN. In this case, a split tunnel, or routing only some traffic over the secure VPN while other traffic directly accesses the Internet, may be used instead. This can help to preserve bandwidth and reduce the load on the VPN concentrator.

NOTE 17

A variety of protocols can be used for VPNs. The most common are IPsec and SSL or the weaker TLS. The Layer 2 Tunneling Protocol (L2TP) is a VPN protocol that does not offer any encryption or protection, so it is usually paired with IPSec (L2TP/IPSec). The current version of HTML, HTML5, can be used as a "clientless" VPN on an endpoint so that no additional software must be installed. Other popular VPN protocols include OpenVPN, SoftEther, WireGuard, SSTP, and IKEv2/IPSec.

Virtual Private Cloud (VPC) A virtual private cloud (VPC) is a cloud-based service that creates a logically isolated virtual network. Using a VPC, an organization can create a public-facing subnet for web servers that have access to the Internet. VPCs also can be used for "backend systems," such as databases or application servers, in a private-facing subnet that has no Internet access. Administrators have complete control over the virtual networking environment, including selecting their own IP address range, creating subnets, and configuring route tables and network gateways.

Network Segmentation

Dividing a network into small elements (segmentation) can provide the controls of separation and quarantining (system isolation), thus preventing threat actors from freely roaming on an infected network to look for targets. Physical segmentation involves using separate physical networks and infrastructures. Examples of physical segmentation are using VLANs and a demilitarized zone (DMZ). Virtual segmentation uses VMs to separate network functions. Two examples of network segmentation are a jump box and an air gap.

Jump Box How should a DMZ be configured so that trusted administrators can securely access the hardware and software in a DMZ but not provide access to threat actors? If a pathway is enabled for administrators to enter the zone, that same pathway, if compromised, can provide access to threat actors back to the secure network.

NOTE 18

VPCs are often used for cloud-based disaster recovery.

A common approach is to use a jump box (sometimes called a *jump server* or *jump host*), as shown in Figure 5-7. A jump box is a minimally configured administrator server (either physical or virtual) within the DMZ. Running only essential protocols and ports, it connects two dissimilar security zones while providing tightly restricted access between them. An administrator accesses the jump box, which is connected to the administrative interface of the devices within the DMZ.

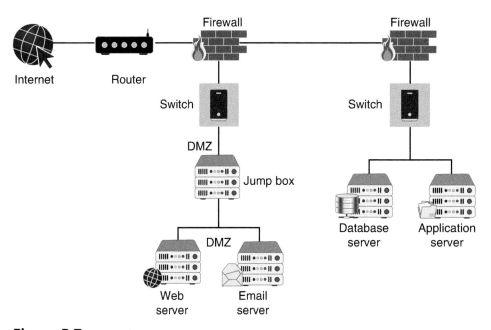

Figure 5-7 Jump box

 **CAUTION** To further limit the vulnerabilities of a jump box, administrators should ensure that all jump box software is regularly updated, limit the programs that can run on a jump box, implement multi-factor authentication for logins, not allow outbound access or severely restrict access from the jump box, and use ACLs to restrict access to specific authorized users.

In recent years, an additional security configuration has been used to limit risks when administering a DMZ. Instead of an administrator connecting to a jump box from any computer, only a dedicated *secure admin workstation (SAW)* can be used to connect to the jump box. Using a SAW prevents an administrator's infected computer from compromising the jump box.

Air Gap   To keep a crucial network or endpoint from being compromised by infection or data exfiltration, an **air gap** can be used. This solution completely isolates the network or endpoint from all external sources, including any network connections or external ports (like a USB port) into which external media can be attached. This isolation is called an "air gap" because the devices to be protected have a separation between them and all other devices that only consists of air. Air gaps are often used in manufacturing environments in which computers that control pumps and valves need to be completely isolated.

> 🛈 **CAUTION**   As noted in the *Cybersecurity Today* opener to this module, air gaps are not foolproof.

Honeypot

Deception is the act of causing someone to accept as true that which is false. Deception can be used as a security defense: by directing the focus of threat actors away from a valuable asset to something that has little or no value, threat actors can be tricked into thinking what they are attacking is truly valuable when in reality it is not or thinking their attack is successful when it is not.

A common deception instrument is a **honeypot**, which is a computer located in an area with limited security that serves as "bait" to threat actors. The honeypot is intentionally configured with security vulnerabilities so that it is open to attacks. Security personnel generally have two goals when using a honeypot:

NOTE 19

Niccolò Machiavelli, an Italian Renaissance diplomat and philosopher who is often called the father of modern political science, once said, "Never attempt to win by force what can be won by deception."

- *Deflect.* A honeypot can deflect or redirect threat actors' attention away from legitimate servers by encouraging them to spend their time and energy on the decoy server, distracting their attention from the data on the actual server.
- *Discover.* A honeypot can trick threat actors into revealing their attack techniques. Once these techniques are discovered, it can then be determined if actual production systems could thwart such an attack.

Figure 5-8 shows the results from a honeypot dashboard; it lists attacker probes by time and country.

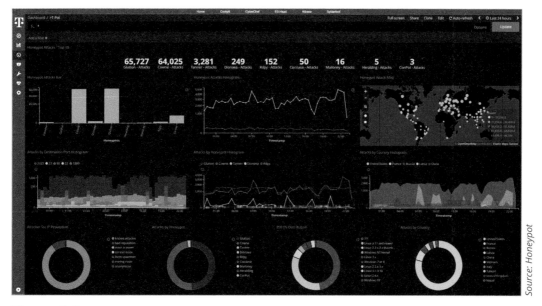

Source: Honeypot

Figure 5-8   Honeypot dashboard

There are different types of honeypots. A low-interaction honeypot may only contain a login prompt. This type of honeypot only records login attempts and provides information on the threat actor's IP address of origin. A high-interaction honeypot is designed for capturing much more information from the threat actor. It usually is configured with a default login and loaded with software, data files that appear to be authentic but are actually imitations of real data files (honeyfiles), and fake telemetry. (Telemetry is the collection of data such as how certain software features are used, application crashes, and general usage statics and behavior.) A high-interaction honeypot can collect much more valuable information from threat actors about attack techniques or the particular information they are seeking from the organization.

NOTE 20

The number of attempts against a honeypot is staggering. In one study,10 honeypots around the world were created that simulated the Secure Shell (SSH) service. One of the honeypots started receiving login attempts just *52 seconds* after it went online. After all 10 of the honeypots were discovered, a login attempt was made about every *15 seconds on each one*. At the end of one month, more than five million attacks had been attempted on these honeypots.[2]

Similar to a honeypot, a *honeynet* is a network set up with intentional vulnerabilities. Its purpose is also to invite attacks so that the attacker's methods can be studied; that information can then be used to increase network security. A honeynet typically contains one or more honeypots.

 **CAUTION** Setting up a honeypot to attract threat actors can be dangerous. It is critical that there be no connection between the honeypot and the production network. A safer approach is to use a cloud service provider for setting up a honeypot.

TWO RIGHTS & A WRONG

1. Active defense is considered too weak to be of any value in cybersecurity defenses.
2. A CASB is a set of software tools or services that resides between an enterprise's on-prem infrastructure and the cloud provider's infrastructure.
3. VDI is the process of running a user desktop inside a VM that resides on a server.

See Appendix C for the answer.

CONFIGURATION CONTROLS

3.2 Given a scenario, implement configuration changes to existing controls to improve security.

Controls can not only be added, but they can also be more strongly configured to increase security. These configuration controls can be divided into authorization and hardware controls.

Authorization

Different elements of authorization controls can be strengthened. These include the following:

- *Permissions.* A permission is preapproval to perform an activity. Permissions can be assigned to file access (such as read, write, and execute), to user accounts, and to other elements.

 **CAUTION** There are two primary issues around granting permissions. Incorrectly granting permissions can give unauthorized access to confidential material. A second weakness is that with some types of access control, a subject's permissions will be "inherited" by any programs that the subject executes. Threat actors often take advantage of this inheritance because users frequently have a high level of privileges. Malware downloaded onto a user's computer would then run at the same high level as the user's privileges.

- *Whitelisting.* An increasingly popular approach to security is to employ whitelisting, particularly for applications and websites. Whitelisting (also known as an allow list) is approving in advance only specific applications to run so that any item not approved is either restricted or denied ("default-deny").
- *Blacklisting.* The inverse of whitelisting is blacklisting (also known as a blocklist). Blacklisting is creating (in advance) a list of unapproved software or websites so that any item not on the list of blacklisted applications can run or websites can be accessed ("default-allow").

Hardware

Strengthening configuration controls for hardware can be divided into the categories of network appliances and network technologies.

Network Appliances

Configuration settings for network appliances include firewalls and intrusion prevention system rules.

Firewalls   Both national and local building codes require commercial buildings, apartments, and other similar structures to have a *firewall*. In building construction, a firewall is usually a brick, concrete, or masonry wall positioned vertically through all stories of the building. Its purpose is to contain a fire and prevent it from spreading. A computer firewall serves a similar purpose: it is designed to limit the spread of malware.

A firewall performs bidirectional inspection by examining both outgoing and incoming network packets. It allows approved packets to pass through but can take different actions when it detects a suspicious packet. The actions are based on specific criteria or rules; these firewalls are called *rule-based firewalls*. The firewall rules can contain parameters such as the following:

- *Source address.* The source address is the location of the origination of the packet (where the packet is *from*). Addresses generally can be indicated by a specific IP address or range of addresses, an IP mask, the MAC address, or host name.
- *Destination address.* This is the address the connection is attempting to reach (where the packet is going *to*). These addresses can be indicated in the same way as the source address.
- *Source port.* The source port is the TCP/IP port number being used to send packets of data through. Options for setting the source port often include a specific port number or a range of numbers.
- *Destination port.* This setting gives the port on the remote computer or device that the packets will use. Options include the same as for the source port.
- *Protocol.* The protocol defines the network protocol (such as *TCP, UDP, TCP or UDP, ICMP,* or *IP*) being used when sending or receiving packets of data.
- *Direction.* This is the direction of traffic for the data packet (*Incoming, Outgoing,* or *Both*).
- *Priority.* The priority determines the order in which the rule is applied.
- *Time.* Rules can be set to be active only during a scheduled time.
- *Context.* A rule can be created that is unique for specific circumstances (contexts). For example, different rules may be in effect depending on whether a laptop is on the campus or is remote (sometimes called geographical consideration).

NOTE 21

The elite Tailored Access Operations (TAO) section of the National Security Agency (NSA) is responsible for compromising networks owned by hostile nations to spy on them. The head of the TAO spoke at a security conference about the best practices of security from the NSA's perspective (in his own words, "What can you do to defend yourself to make my life hard?"). One of the most important steps was to employ whitelisting for the software that runs on servers. A similar step is to whitelist a predefined set of websites to which users can connect to prevent malware from accessing a C&C or to exfiltrate stolen information.[3]

- *Action.* The action setting indicates what the firewall should do when the conditions of the rule are met. Typical firewall rule actions are listed in Table 5-4.

Table 5-4 Typical firewall rule actions

Action	Description	Example	Comments
Allow	Explicitly allows traffic that matches the rule to pass	Permit incoming Address Resolution Protocol (ARP) traffic	Allow implicitly denies all other traffic unless explicitly allowed
Bypass	Allows traffic to bypass the firewall	Bypass based on IP, port, traffic direction, and protocol	Designed for media-intensive protocols or traffic from a trusted source
Deny	Explicitly blocks all traffic that matches the rule	Deny traffic from IP address	Deny generally drops the packet with no return message to the sender
Force Allow	Forcibly allows traffic that would normally be denied by other rules	Useful for determining if essential network services are able to communicate	Traffic will still be subject to inspection by other security appliances
Log Only	Logs traffic but no other action is taken	Bypass rules do not generate log files but Log Only will	Log Only occurs if the packet is not stopped by a Deny rule or an Allow rule that excludes it

Older firewalls often had each rule as a separate instruction that was processed in sequence so that firewall rules were essentially an *if-then* construction: *if* these rule conditions are met, *then* the action occurs. This made it important to consider not only the rules but also the sequencing of the rules. For example, if Rule #13 allowed an FTP connection to a specific address but later Rule #27 was added to deny all FTP traffic, then FTP packets meeting Rule #13 would be allowed because it occurred first. More modern firewalls allow a priority order to be created to eliminate the confusion that often surrounded multiple conflicting rules.

A more flexible type of firewall than a rule-based firewall is a *policy-based firewall.* This type of firewall allows for using more generic statements instead of specific rules. For example, the policy statement *Allow management traffic from trusted networks* could translate into specific rules that allow traffic from *192.2.0.0/24* to *TCP Port 22* and *192.2.100.0/24* to *TCP Port 3389*.

NOTE 22

In addition to filtering based on packets, firewalls can also apply content/URL filtering. The firewall can be used to monitor websites accessed through HTTP to create custom filtering profiles. The filtering can be performed by assessing webpages by their content category and then creating whitelists and blacklists of specific URLs. This type of filtering is often available with consumer-oriented firewalls and advertised as a parental control feature that is easily configurable.

Most modern firewalls have a wide array of settings that can be configured to provide a granular degree of security. These should be fully—but carefully—used as a hardware configuration control.

Intrusion Prevention System (IPS) Rules While firewalls examine the Network and Transport layers of a packet (such as IP, TCP, and UDP), intrusion prevention system (IPS) rules examine payloads in the Session and Application layers of the packet (such as DNS, HTTP, SSL, and SMTP). These rules also look at the sequence of the packets according to those higher-layer protocols. Traffic is scanned using IPS rules that are enabled and configured. When traffic matches an IPS rule, the agent handles it as a possible or confirmed attack. Action is then taken based on the configuration settings, such as replacing specifically defined or suspicious byte sequences, dropping packets, or resetting the connection.

NOTE 23

IPS rules can generally be created from scratch, modified from existing rules, or imported.

Network Technologies

Configuration settings for network technologies include network access control, data loss prevention, and sinkholing.

Network Access Control Network access control (NAC) examines the current state of an endpoint before it can connect to the network. Any device that does not meet a specified set of criteria, such as having the most current antivirus signature or the software firewall properly enabled, is denied access to the network, given restricted access to computing resources, or connected to a "quarantine" network where the security deficiencies are corrected, after which the endpoint is connected to the normal network. The goal of NAC is to prevent computers with suboptimal security from potentially infecting other computers through the network.

An example of the NAC process is illustrated in Figure 5-9:

> **NOTE 24**
>
> NAC also can be used to ensure that systems not owned by the organization—such as those owned by customers, visitors, and contractors—can be granted access without compromising security.

1. The client performs a self-assessment using a System Health Agent (SHA) to determine its current security posture.
2. The assessment, known as a Statement of Health (SoH), is sent to a server called the Health Registration Authority (HRA). This server enforces the security policies of the network. It also integrates with other external authorities such as antivirus and patch management servers to retrieve current configuration information.
3. If the client is approved by the HRA, it is issued a Health Certificate.
4. The Health Certificate is then presented to the network servers to verify that the client's security condition has been approved.
5. If the client is not approved, it is connected to a quarantine network where the deficiencies are corrected, and then the computer is allowed to connect to the network.

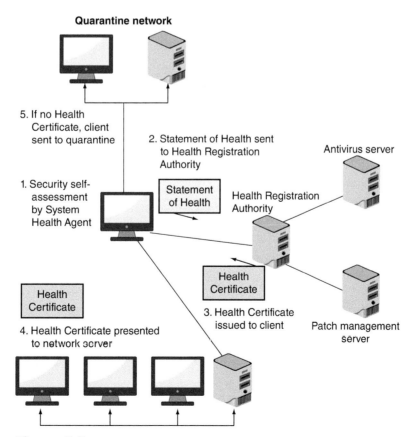

Figure 5-9 Network access control (NAC) process

NOTE 25

Surprisingly, research has shown that security awareness training has not had an impact on employee mishandling of sensitive data. The percentage of employees who admit to sending misdirected emails is the highest in organizations that provide security awareness training most frequently. And these same employees are almost twice as likely to send company data to their personal email accounts.

NOTE 26

One drawback of DLP is that rules must be continually created and maintained as new employees, third-party agent contractors, and customers are added and new data sets are created. Machine learning (ML) increasingly is used by DLP to continually create and modify the criteria for protecting data.

Data Loss Prevention (DLP)

Keeping corporate data secure is a challenge for all organizations. While the threat of data theft from outside threat actors remains high, inside employees increasingly are being careless or make mistakes when handling confidential corporate data. Employee carelessness with data has been identified in two primary areas. First, against company policy, many employees routinely send confidential data to their own private email accounts so they can easily access it when needed. About one-third of employees admit to sending corporate data to their personal email accounts up to three times each month. Second, sensitive data is often sent to an approved third-party as an email attachment—but to the wrong recipient. Almost three-fourths of employees admit to sending data to the wrong recipient once per month.[4]

One means of securing internal corporate data is through data loss prevention (DLP). DLP is considered as rights management, or the authority of the owner of the data to impose restrictions on its use. DLP is a system of security tools used to recognize and identify data critical to the organization and ensure it is protected. This protection involves monitoring who is using the data and how it is being accessed. Data considered confidential or critical to the organization can be tagged as such. A user who then attempts to access the data to disclose it to an unauthorized user will be prevented from doing so.

Most DLP systems use *content inspection*. Content inspection is a security analysis of the transaction within its approved context. Content inspection looks at not only the security level of the data, but also who is requesting it, where the data is stored, when it was requested, and where it is going. DLP systems also can use *index matching*. Documents that have been identified as needing protection, such as the program source code for a new software application, are analyzed by the DLP system and complex computations are conducted based on the analysis. Thereafter, if even a small part of that document is leaked, the DLP system can recognize the snippet as being from a protected document.

DLP begins with an administrator creating DLP rules based on the data (what is to be examined) and the policy (what to check for). DLPs can be configured to look for specific data (such as Social Security and credit card numbers), lines of computer software source code, words in a sequence (to prevent a report from leaving the network), maximum file sizes, and file types. In addition, whitelists and blacklists can be created to prevent specific files from being scanned. These rules are then loaded into a DLP server.

When a policy violation is detected by the DLP agent, it is reported back to the DLP server. Different actions can then be taken. They could include blocking the data, redirecting it to an individual who can examine the request, quarantining the data until later, or alerting a supervisor of the request.

Sinkholing

Another technique used for both deception and mitigation is a sinkholing. A sinkhole is essentially a "bottomless pit" designed to steer unwanted traffic away from its intended destination to another device, deceiving the threat actor into thinking the attack is successful when the sinkhole is actually providing information about the attack. One type of sinkhole is a DNS sinkhole. A DNS sinkhole changes a normal DNS request to a pre-configured IP address that points to a firewall that has a rule of *Deny* set for all packets so that every packet is dropped with no return information provided to the sender.

NOTE 27

DNS sinkholes are commonly used to counteract DDoS attacks. Many enterprises contract with a DDoS mitigation service that helps identify DDoS traffic so that it is sent to a sinkhole while allowing legitimate traffic to reach its destination. Sinkholes are also used by law enforcement to stop a widespread ongoing attack by redirecting traffic away from the attacker's command and control (C&C) server to a sinkhole. As an added step, the sinkhole can save these packets for further examination in an to attempt to identify the threat actors.

TWO RIGHTS & A WRONG

1. Blacklisting is approving in advance only specific applications to run so that any item not approved is either restricted or denied ("default-deny").
2. "Force Allow" is a firewall rule that is useful for determining if essential network services are able to communicate.
3. NAC examines the current state of an endpoint before it can connect to the network.

See Appendix C for the answer.

VM LAB   You're now ready to complete the live, virtual machine labs for this module. The labs can be found in the Apply It folder in each MindTap module.

MODULE SUMMARY

- Cybersecurity controls are countermeasures that organizations implement to prevent, reduce, or counteract security risks. Several general concepts relate to infrastructure management solutions and controls. When defending against cyberattacks, active defense can prove marginally beneficial. Active defense techniques can raise the cost for the attacker in terms of wasted time and processing power. Change management refers to a formal process for making modifications to a system and keeping track of those changes. Asset management is the procedures for procuring and protecting assets. Asset management typically includes asset tagging, which is affixing physical tags to hardware and creating an approved listing of software that can be installed.

- Securing the resources in the corporate data center is different from securing data held and processed in the cloud. When securing cloud resources, some controls are inherent to the cloud computing platforms and offered by the cloud computing providers to their customers (cloud native controls) while other security controls are available from external sources (third-party solutions). Cloud controls include conducting audits, using regions and zones, enforcing functional area mitigations, and implementing secrets management. A cloud access security broker (CASB) is a set of software tools or services that resides between an enterprise's on-prem infrastructure and the cloud provider's infrastructure. Acting as the gatekeeper, a CASB ensures that the security policies of the enterprise extend to its data in the cloud.

- Virtualization is a means of managing and presenting computer resources by function without regard to their physical layout or location. One type of virtualization in which an entire OS environment is simulated is known as host virtualization. An even more reduced instance of virtualization is a container. A container holds only the necessary OS components (such as binary files and libraries) needed for a specific application to run. Another application of VMs is known as Virtual Desktop Infrastructure (VDI). VDI is the process of running a user desktop inside a VM that resides on a server. Host virtualization has several security-related advantages but there are security concerns as well.

- Identity and access management (IAM) is an umbrella term that describes the various products, processes, and policies used to manage a user's identity and to regulate access to resources. When an IAM requires more than one type of authentication credential to be presented, this is called multifactor authentication (MFA). One of the problems facing users is having multiple accounts across multiple platforms that all should use a unique username and password. A solution to this problem is to have one username and password to gain access to all accounts so that the user has only one credential to remember. That is the foundation of identity management, which is using a single authentication credential that is shared across multiple networks. When those networks are owned by different organizations, it is called federation. One application of federation is single sign-on (SSO), or using one authentication credential to access multiple accounts or applications.

- To facilitate assigning user accounts and permissions, hardware and software have a predefined framework that the administrator can use for controlling access. This framework, called an access control scheme, is embedded in the software and hardware. The administrator can use the appropriate scheme to configure the necessary level of control. Using these schemes is part of privileged management, which is the technologies and strategies for controlling elevated (privileged) access and permissions. Mandatory Access Control (MAC) assigns users' access controls strictly according to the data custodian's desires. Role-Based Access Control (RBAC) is based on a user's job function within an organization. Instead of setting permissions for each user or group, the RBAC scheme assigns permissions to particular roles in the organization, and then assigns users to those roles. Attribute-Based Access Control (ABAC) uses flexible policies that can combine attributes. These policies can take advantage of many types of attributes, such as object attributes, subject attributes, and environment attributes.

- Multiple entities make up strong certificate management or controlling digital certificates. These include a certificate repository and a means for certificate revocation. As more networks make the transition from physical to virtual, these new network architectures can provide even more controls. A software defined network (SDN) virtualizes parts of the physical network so that it can be more quickly and easily reconfigured. This is accomplished by separating the control plane from the data plane. A virtual private network (VPN) is a security technology that enables authorized users to use an unsecured public network, such as the Internet, as if it were a secure private network. It does this by encrypting all data transmitted between the remote endpoint and the network and not just specific documents or files. A virtual private cloud (VPC) is a cloud-based service that creates a logically isolated virtual network.

- Dividing a network into small elements (segmentation) can provide system isolation, thus preventing threat actors from freely roaming on an infected network to look for targets. Physical segmentation involves using separate physical networks and infrastructures by using VLANs and a demilitarized zone (DMZ). Virtual segmentation uses VMs to separate network functions. A jump box is a minimally configured administrator server (either physical or virtual) within the DMZ. Running only essential protocols and ports, it connects two dissimilar security zones while providing tightly restricted access between them. To keep a crucial network or endpoint from being compromised by infection or data exfiltration, an air gap can be used. This solution completely isolates the network or endpoint from all external sources, including any network connections or external ports (like a USB port) into which external media can be attached. A common deception instrument is a honeypot, which is a computer located in an area with limited security that serves as "bait" to threat actors. The honeypot is intentionally configured with security vulnerabilities so that it is open to attacks.

- Controls can not only be added, but they can also be more strongly configured to increase security. Elements of authorization controls can be strengthened, including permissions, whitelisting, and blacklisting. Whitelisting is approving in advance only specific applications to run so that any item not approved is either restricted or denied. The inverse of whitelisting is blacklisting. Blacklisting is creating (in advance) a list of unapproved software or websites so that any item not on the list of blacklisted applications can run or websites can be accessed.

- A firewall performs bidirectional inspection by examining both outgoing and incoming network packets. It allows approved packets to pass through but can take different actions when it detects a suspicious packet. The actions are based on specific criteria or rules; these firewalls are called rule-based firewalls. A more flexible type of firewall is a policy-based firewall. This type of firewall uses more generic statements instead of specific rules. While firewalls examine the Network and Transport layers of a packet (such as IP, TCP, and UDP), intrusion prevention system (IPS) rules examine payloads in the Session and Application layers of the packet (such as DNS, HTTP, SSL, and SMTP). These rules also look at the sequence of the packets according to those higher-layer protocols. Traffic is scanned using IPS rules that are enabled and configured.

- Network access control (NAC) examines the current state of an endpoint before it can connect to the network. Any device that does not meet a specified set of criteria, such as having the most current antivirus signature or the software firewall properly enabled, is denied access to the network, or given restricted access to computing resources, or connected to a "quarantine" network where the security deficiencies are corrected, after which the endpoint is connected to the network. Data loss prevention (DLP) is a system of security tools used to recognize and identify data that is critical to the organization and ensure that it is protected. This protection involves monitoring who is using the data and how it is being accessed. Another technique used for both deception and mitigation is sinkholing. A sinkhole is essentially a "bottomless pit" designed to steer unwanted traffic away from its intended destination to another device, deceiving the threat actor into thinking the attack is successful when the sinkhole is actually providing information about the attack.

Key Terms

active defense
air gap
asset management
asset tagging
Attribute-Based Access Control
   (ABAC)
blacklisting
certificate management
change management
cloud access security broker (CASB)
cloud vs. on-premises
containerization
data loss prevention (DLP)
encryption
federation

firewall
honeypot
identity and access management
   (IAM)
intrusion prevention system (IPS)
   rules
jump box
Mandatory Access Control (MAC)
manual reviews
monitoring and logging
multifactor authentication (MFA)
network access control (NAC)
permission
physical networks
physical segmentation

privileged management
Role-Based Access Control
   (RBAC)
single sign-on (SSO)
sinkholing
software defined network
   (SDN)
system isolation
Virtual Desktop Infrastructure
   (VDI)
virtual private cloud (VPC)
virtual private network (VPN)
virtual segmentation
virtualization
whitelisting

Review Questions

1. Which of the following is NOT a firewall rule parameter?
   a. Time
   b. Context
   c. Visibility
   d. Action

2. Daichi is preparing a presentation about active defense. Which of the following would he NOT include on the report as an advantage of active defense?
   a. Active defense can cause the attacker to waste time and processing power.
   b. Active defense can cause a frustrated and weak-willed attacker to seek another target.
   c. Active defense can replace multiple other security defenses at a lower cost.
   d. Active defense can cause attackers to reveal their attack plans.

3. What is a formal process for making modifications to a system and keeping track of those changes?
   a. Change control
   b. Change tracking
   c. Change management
   d. Change regulation

4. Which firewall rule action is useful for determining if essential network services are able to communicate?
   a. Allow
   b. Log only
   c. Force Deny
   d. Force Allow

5. Which of the following contains honeyfiles and fake telemetry?
   a. High-interaction honeypot
   b. Telemetry honeypot
   c. Honeypotnet
   d. Honeyserver

6. Aito is looking into solutions for DDoS mitigations. Which of the following should he consider?
   a. DDoS Prevention System (DPS)
   b. DNS sinkhole
   c. DDoS pit
   d. IP filter

7. Which of the following is NOT an NAC option when it detects a vulnerable endpoint?
   a. Deny access to the network.
   b. Give restricted access to the network.

    c. Update Active Directory to indicate the device is vulnerable.

    d. Connect to a quarantine network.

8. Which of the following is NOT a cloud control for cybersecurity?

    a. Implement secrets management.

    b. Avoid utilizing regions and zones.

    c. Enforce functional area mitigations.

    d. Conduct audits.

9. Which of these is a list of preapproved applications?

    a. Whitelist

    b. Greenlist

    c. Redlist

    d. Blacklist

10. Which of the following would an administrator use to access a server in a DMZ?

    a. Air gap

    b. SDN

    c. DNS

    d. Jump box

11. Which of the following virtualizes parts of a physical network?

    a. SDA

    b. SDS

    c. SDX

    d. SDN

12. Which of the following is a set of software tools or services that resides between an enterprise's on-prem infrastructure and the cloud provider's infrastructure and acts as the gatekeeper?

    a. ASB

    b. CASB

    c. BSAC

    d. CBCB

13. Kouki is discussing with his supervisor the advantages of containerization. Which of the following would Kouki NOT give as an advantage?

    a. Containerization eliminates the need for an OS.

    b. Containerization allows containers to be easily moved between computers.

    c. Containerization can share binary files and libraries.

    d. Containerization reduces hard drive space and RAM requirements.

14. Which of these is NOT a host virtualization security advantage?

    a. VMs can promote security segregation and isolation.

    b. Analyzing malware in a VM is much faster because all processes run more quickly in a VM.

    c. Testing the existing security configuration, known as security control testing, can be performed using a simulated network environment on a computer using multiple VMs.

    d. A snapshot of a state of a VM can be saved for later use.

15. What is an umbrella term that describes the various products, processes, and policies that are used to manage a user's identity and to regulate access to resources?

    a. IAM

    b. MIA

    c. AIM

    d. MAI

16. What is a federation?

    a. A system of networks that are owned by different organizations

    b. A system of networks that are owned by the same organization

    c. A system of networks that require the use of SSO

    d. A system of networks that prohibits the use of SSO

17. Which access control model uses flexible policies that can combine attributes?

    a. MAC

    b. ABAC

    c. RBAC

    d. RXAX

18. What is a publicly accessible centralized directory of digital certificates that can be used to view the status of a digital certificate?

    a. DR

    b. CR

    c. RC

    d. XR

19. Which of the following is NOT correct about SDN?

    a. It virtualizes parts of the physical network so that it can be more quickly and easily reconfigured.

    b. It separates the action plane from the data plane.

    c. It utilizes flow tables.

    d. The communication between the SDN controller and the SDN switches uses a standardized protocol and API.

20. Which of the following is NOT correct about a VPC?

    a. An organization can create a public-facing subnet for web servers that have access to the Internet.

    b. It can be used for "backend systems," such as databases or application servers, in a private-facing subnet that has no Internet access.

    c. Administrators have little control over the virtual networking environment.

    d. VPCs are often used for cloud-based disaster recovery.

Case Projects

Case Project 5-1: Data Loss Prevention Comparison

Research at least four data loss prevention (DLP) products from four different vendors. Create a table that compares at least six different functions and options. Based on your research, which would you choose? What features make this product the best? Why? Write a short paragraph that summarizes your research.

Case Project 5-2: Cloud-Based Honeypots

Research cloud-based honeypots. What are their advantages? What are their disadvantages? When should they not be used? How could one be set up? Create a one-page paper of your research.

Case Project 5-3: Hardening a Jump Box

How should a jump box be configured? Create a list of configurations that you would use to set up a jump box that had the fewest risks.

Case Project 5-4: Air Gaps

Use the Internet to research how air gaps are used. In which environments are they used? What are some ways in which they have been circumvented? How would you air-gap a network? Write a one-page paper on your research.

Case Project 5-5: On the Job

Suppose you work for a company that has been the victim of a significant cyberattack that resulted in the loss of revenue and customers and generated ill will and a lack of trust in the organization. An angry senior vice president says that the organization should deploy an active defense, which includes tracking down the culprits and then retaliating against them. As support for her argument, she says that this is a common practice used by the government, and as long as there is no price to pay by the attackers, then these attacks will continue. Where do you stand? Should organizations be involved in retaliation? What are the advantages? What are the risks? Write a one-page memo about what you think should be done and why.

References

1. Cimpanu, Catalin, "Academics Steal Data from Air-Gapped Systems Using PC Fan Vibrations," *ZDNet*, Apr. 17, 2020, retrieved Dec. 28, 2020, www.zdnet.com/article/academics-steal-data-from-air-gapped-systems-using-pc-fan-vibrations.
2. Boddy, Matt, "Exposed: Cyberattacks on Cloud Honeypots," *Sophos*, Apr. 9, 2019, accessed June 5, 2019, www.sophos.com/en-us/press-office/press-releases/2019/04/cybercriminals-attack-cloud-server-honeypot-within-52-seconds.aspx.
3. Horowitz, Michael, "The Head of NSA TAO Advises on Defensive Computing for Networks," *Computerworld*, Feb. 1, 2016, accessed May 11, 2017, www.computerworld.com/article/3028025/security/defending-a-network-from-the-nsa.html.
4. "The State of Data Loss Prevention 2020: What You Need to Know," *Tessian*, May 28, 2020, accessed Jun. 26, 2020, www.tessian.com/blog/the-state-of-data-loss-prevention-2020-what-you-need-to-know/.

SOFTWARE AND HARDWARE ASSURANCE BEST PRACTICES

After completing this module, you should be able to do the following:

1 Define assurance best practices

2 List software assurance best practices

3 Explain DevSecOps procedures

4 Describe hardware assurance best practices

Cybersecurity Today

Where is the best place to plant malware on a computer? It has to be somewhere that the malware remains persistent and can continue its malicious activity over a long period of time. It also must be stealthy and hard to find, perhaps somewhere users do not even think of as a location for malware. Where would such a place be? The answer for the ideal location for malware is arguably the UEFI (Unified Extensible Firmware Interface). And that is exactly where attackers are starting to plant their malware.

Personal computers are designed to be able to start when powered on without external assistance from other devices. This booting process on early personal computers used firmware called the BIOS (Basic Input/Output System), which was a chip integrated into the computer's motherboard. However, the BIOS had several limitations, such as the inability to boot from a hard drive larger than 2.1 terabytes (TB). The UEFI was developed to replace the BIOS and add other functionality.

Recently, security researchers have uncovered an attack in which the threat actors used the persistence and stealth capabilities of the UEFI. The UEFI firmware was infected with malware so that whenever the computer was booted, the firmware checked to see if a malicious file named IntelUpdate.exe was inside the Windows startup folder. If it was missing, the UEFI image would copy the file to the folder. The IntelUpdate.exe file then launched when the computer finished booting, contacted the attacker's command and control (C&C) server, and downloaded several malware-based files onto the computer. Some security researchers have started calling this type of malware a "bootkit" because, like a rootkit, it does a great job of hiding its presence so that it cannot be found.

How did the threat actors infect the UEFI in the first place? It turns out that attackers took advantage of a little-known feature built into UEFIs dating back to 2014. This feature was used to track stolen computers. An antitheft device known as Absolute Computrace had a module that embedded itself inside the UEFI. This module regularly communicated with an Absolute Computrace C&C server. If a computer was lost or stolen, the server could remotely control the computer; determine the computer's current IP address; and, if necessary, wipe the hard drive of any data. Because the module ran inside the UEFI, the tracking system worked even if the computer's hard drive had been replaced. In 2018, attackers repurposed the Absolute Computrace firmware by extracting it and then overwriting it with their own malicious code. Instead of connecting to the Absolute Computrace C&C server, it connected to the attackers' C&C for its commands.

Evidently, the threat actors were able to infect the UEFI because its firmware can be updated. Perhaps the attackers gained physical access to the targeted computers and then inserted a USB flash drive, rebooted the computer, accessed the UEFI, and instructed the computer to reboot again but this time boot from the USB flash drive. The flash drive contained an update to the UEFI firmware that installed the malware.

One of the more interesting elements of these UEFI attacks is the victims. So far, there have only been two known victims, and both were government diplomatic figures located in Asia. This may indicate that the attack is highly specialized and is the work of nation-state actors. However, with their many advantages, UEFI attacks may soon become more widespread. Users can protect against an attack by setting a strong password on the UEFI. Another defense is to use full disk encryption (FDE) to prevent the UEFI firmware from writing anything to the hard drive.

Although often used interchangeably, the terms *cybersecurity* and *information assurance* are different. Cybersecurity usually refers to the ability to defend against cyberattacks, protect resources, and prevent future attacks by focusing on defending endpoints, networks, and communication. Information assurance, on the other hand, covers both the technical and managerial aspects of controlling and securing information. These measures are designed to ensure the confidentiality, integrity, authenticity, availability, and utility of information and the systems on which the information resides. Cybersecurity has a narrower and more technical focus and is considered a subset of information assurance.

The goal of information assurance centers around the word assurance. Assurance is certainty, confidence, and conviction. Thus, information assurance attempts to ensure that information is protected. There are several advertised best practices for information assurance. A "best practice" is a procedure that has been demonstrated by research and experience to produce optimal results and is used as a standard suitable for widespread adoption.

This module explores best practices for information assurance. These can be classified as practices relating to computer software and those that involve hardware.

SOFTWARE BEST PRACTICES

2.2 Explain software assurance best practices.

NOTE 1

These platforms are covered in Module 1.

Several software assurance best practices can be used to protect a variety of platforms including mobile and client/server platforms. These practices also encompass more specialized hardware such as an embedded system, system on a chip (SoC), and firmware. The platforms run a wide variety of software, ranging from Internet-based web applications to apps to IoT programs.

Software best practices include those for service-oriented architectures and application development.

Service-Oriented Architectures (SOAs)

Several software assurance best practices are related to service-oriented architectures. These include Security Assertions Markup Language (SAML), Simple Object Access Protocol (SOAP), and Representational State Transfer (REST). First, it is important to understand service-oriented architectures.

What Is Service-Oriented Architecture?

The first 50 years of business software development can be summarized by the words *integrated* and *isolated*. Programs accessing data that was housed in another system required that code for a specific task be embedded within the specific program. Complex point-to-point integration from the program to the data was necessary. When a second program also needed similar access to the data, it too required a new development project to achieve the integration. Because of the complex integration needed for each program, the code was isolated and unusable for other programs. This resulted in duplication of labor and additional time needed to complete or modify projects, and it provided an avenue for the introduction of coding errors and vulnerabilities.

By the late 1990s, a new approach to business software development emerged that could be summarized by the words *modular* and *reusable*. This approach defined a way to make software components reusable through "service interfaces." These interfaces used common communication standards in such a way that they could be incorporated into new applications quickly and easily without the need to perform complex and deep point-to-point integration each time. This is called a service-oriented architecture (SOA).

Each service in an SOA combines (embodies) both the code and necessary data integrations required to execute a complete and discrete business function. For example, a specific service might calculate a monthly loan payment. The service interfaces support and provide "loose coupling." Loose coupling means that these services can be called with little or no required knowledge of how the integration is implemented. The services serve as "black boxes" that simply perform their tasks without requiring understanding of how the functionality occurs. The services are "exposed" using standard network protocols that send requests to read or update data. Finally, the services are published in such a way that developers can quickly locate them and even reuse them to quickly assemble new applications. An SOA is illustrated in Figure 6-1.

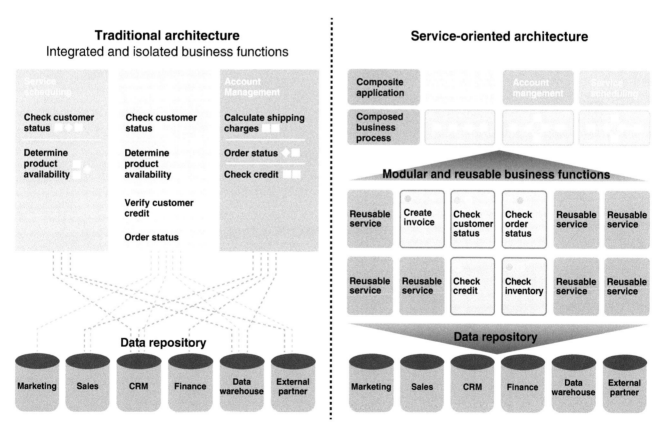

Figure 6-1   SOA

NOTE 2

Microservices, which are covered in Module 4, are a prime example of an SOA.

SOA has several advantages:

- *Improves business agility.* The speed and efficiency of assembling applications from reusable service interfaces instead of rewriting and reintegrating with each new business development project enables developers to build applications much more quickly in response to new business opportunities.
- *Leverages legacy functionality.* SOA enables developers to quickly take the functionality of one computing platform or environment and extend it to new environments and markets. For example, when first introduced, many companies used SOA to expose functionality from mainframe-based financial systems to web applications, thus enabling their customers to "serve themselves" to retrieve information that previously required direct personal contact with a company's employees.
- *Enhances collaboration.* A requested change or new application can be communicated by a business analyst to developers in general business terms (*calculate a monthly loan payment*) instead of working through the specific calculations needed. This can help both analysts and IT developers understand the data flow and even look for improvements.

Different standards and protocols can be used in an SOA.

Security Assertion Markup Language (SAML)

Security Assertion Markup Language (SAML) is an XML standard that allows secure web domains to exchange user authentication and authorization data in an SOA. A user's login credentials can be stored with a single identity provider instead of being stored on each web service provider's server. SAML is used extensively for online e-commerce business-to-business (B2B) and business-to-consumer (B2C) transactions. The following are the steps of a SAML transaction, which are also illustrated in Figure 6-2:

1. The user attempts to reach a website of a service provider that requires a username and password.
2. The service provider generates a SAML authentication request that is then encoded and embedded into a URL.
3. The service provider sends a redirect URL to the user's browser that includes the encoded SAML authentication request, which is then sent to the identity provider.
4. The identity provider decodes the SAML request and extracts the embedded URL. The identity provider then attempts to authenticate the user either by asking for login credentials or by checking for valid session cookies.
5. The identity provider generates a SAML response that contains the username of the authenticated user, which is then digitally signed using asymmetric cryptography.

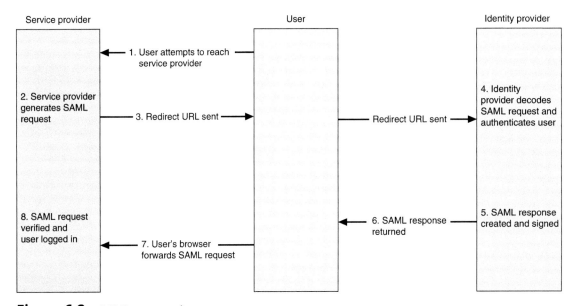

Figure 6-2 SAML transaction

6. The identity partner encodes the SAML response and returns that information to the user's browser.

7. The SAML response contains a mechanism so that the user's browser can forward the information to the service provider, either by displaying a form that requires the user to click a *Submit* button or by automatically sending it to the service provider.

8. The service provider verifies the SAML response by using the identity provider's public key. If the response is successfully verified, the user is logged in.

NOTE 3

SAML works with multiple protocols including Hypertext Transfer Protocol (HTTP), Simple Mail Transfer Protocol (SMTP), and File Transfer Protocol (FTP).

Simple Object Access Protocol (SOAP)

Simple Object Access Protocol (SOAP) is a message protocol that allows the distributed elements of an application to communicate in a web-services environment. SOAP's header structure identifies the actions that different SOAP nodes are expected to take on the message while its payload structure carries the information. These headers identify the tasks to be performed, routes the message to the microarchitecture, and then invokes the SOA feature. Developers can use SOAP to invoke processes running on different OSs (such as Windows, macOS, and Linux) to authenticate, authorize, and communicate using Extensible Markup Language (XML). This allows clients to invoke web services and receive responses independent of any language or OS platforms.

NOTE 4

SOAP can be carried over a variety of lower-level protocols, including HTTP, SMTP, TCP, and UDP.

The disadvantage of SOAP is that it can invoke different services, making it a "heavyweight" and complex protocol. Also, SOAP lacks a standardized interaction.

Representational State Transfer (REST)

Representational State Transfer (REST) is considered an improvement over SOAP as a means of communication between web-based systems. REST systems are considered both stateless (the server does not need to know the state the client is in and vice versa) and separate (code on the client can be changed without affecting the server and vice versa).

NOTE 5

Many applications rely upon a set of APIs known as *RESTful APIs*. These RESTful APIs use existing HTTP methods of GET, PUT, POST, and DELETE. RESTful APIs have become so foundational that they are sometimes called the "backbone of the Internet."

Application Development

It is no surprise that the strongest infrastructure management solutions and controls and the optimal configuration controls can easily be compromised by a vulnerable application. Application software that contains vulnerabilities is a leading contributor to attacks, making secure application software development critical. Developers must be aware of software vulnerabilities and how proper application development can serve as a counterweight.

Software Vulnerabilities

An unsecure application can open the door for attackers to exploit the application, the data that it uses, and even the underlying OS. Table 6-1 lists attacks that can be launched using vulnerabilities in applications.

Table 6-1 Attacks based on application vulnerabilities

Attack	Description	Defense
Executable files attack	Trick the vulnerable application into modifying or creating executable files on the system.	Prevent the application from creating or modifying executable files for its proper function.
System tampering	Use the vulnerable application to modify special sensitive areas of the operating system (Microsoft Windows registry keys, system startup files, etc.) and take advantage of those modifications.	Do not allow applications to modify special areas of the OS.
Process spawning control	Trick the vulnerable application into spawning executable files on the system.	Take away the process-spawning ability from the application.

The cause of unsecure applications is usually the result of how the application was designed and written. Some of the most dangerous weaknesses in an application due to poor coding can create vulnerabilities in computer memory or buffer areas that can be easily exploited. These vulnerabilities are summarized in Table 6-2.

Table 6-2 Memory vulnerabilities

Vulnerability	Description	How exploited
Buffer overflow	A process attempts to store data in RAM beyond the boundaries of a fixed-length storage buffer.	Attacker can overflow the buffer with a new address pointing to the attacker's malware code.
Integer overflow	The result of an arithmetic operation such as addition or multiplication exceeds the maximum size of the integer type used to store it.	Tallying the number of items sold could result in a negative value and a resulting negative total cost, indicating that a refund is due to the customer.
Memory leak	An application dynamically allocates memory but does not free that memory when finished using it.	Attacker can take advantage of unexpected program behavior resulting from a low memory condition.
Pointer deference	A pointer with a value of NULL is used as if it pointed to a valid memory area.	Launching the program by an attacker can cause the process to crash, resulting in loss of data.
DLL injection	Inserting code into a running process through a Dynamic Link Library (DLL).	Attacker can use DLL injection vulnerability to cause a program to function in a different way than intended.

However, addressing software vulnerabilities is difficult because of several factors:

- *Size and complexity.* As more features and functions are added to programs, they become very large (up to hundreds of millions of lines of code) and extremely complex.
- *Lack of formal specifications.* Specifications for a program may not always be in written form and formally communicated, so the work of one programmer may unintentionally open a security vulnerability that was closed by another programmer.
- *Ever-changing attacks.* As attackers continue to create new exploits, it is not possible to foresee all the ways that code written today could be vulnerable tomorrow.

Software Development Lifecycle

In recent years, major software developers have focused their attention on improving their software code to increase security. These improvements are aimed at reducing the number of design and coding errors in software. A **software development lifecycle (SDLC)** is a methodology that can be used to build a program or application from its inception to decommission. Although several SDLC models have been used over the years, all the various SDLC models include the basic steps of software planning, designing, testing, coding, and maintenance.

Until recently, it was common practice to perform security-related activities only as part of the SDLC testing phase. However, this "after-the-fact" technique often resulted in leaving many security issues undiscovered. Other vulnerabilities that were discovered late in the process would often be hurriedly corrected, but by doing so would introduce *another* vulnerability or cause the software to perform erratically.

Today it is recognized that integrating security activities across the entire process to form a secure SDLC can help discover and reduce vulnerabilities, often early in the software development process.
Here are the primary advantages of following a secure SDLC:

- Development of software that is more secure
- Earlier detection of security flaws
- Higher awareness of security by stakeholders
- Overall reduction of intrinsic business risks for the organization
- Reducing costs due to early detection and resolution of issues

> **NOTE 6**
>
> Implementing security throughout the SDLC process results in security being built in instead of only added on.

There are different sources of recommendations for secure SDLC best practices. Table 6-3 lists several of these sources.

Table 6-3   Secure SDLC sources

Source	Description	Materials available
OWASP (Open Web Application Security Project)	Group that monitors web attacks	Maturity models, development guides, testing guides, code review guides, and application security verification standards
SANS (SysAdmin, Audit, Network and Security Institute)	Company that specializes in cybersecurity and secure web application development	White papers, research reports, and best practices guidelines
CIS (Center for Internet Security)	Not-for-profit organization that compiles CIS security controls	Training, assessment tools, and consulting services

> **NOTE 7**
>
> In addition to these sources of information, entire secure SDLC frameworks are also available. The Microsoft Security Development Lifecycle (MS SDL) was one of the first of its kind, and the National Institute of Standards and Technology (NIST) 800-64 is a framework that U.S. federal agencies must observe.

Certain recognized secure SDLC principles practices should be used in software development. These include the following:

- *Security requirements definition.* The optimal time to define the security requirements of software is during the initial design and planning stages. This also gives the development teams the ability to integrate security requirements early in the process and minimize later disruption. Different factors that influence security requirements typically include regulatory compliance requirements, internal standards, and known threats.
- *User acceptance testing.* An application with a poor user interface (UI) may result in software that is underutilized. It may also encourage users to try to circumvent the security provisions of the software that the user finds as too cumbersome or restrictive. User acceptance testing can ensure that the UI is acceptable to users.
- *Application stress testing.* An application stress test determines if the software can withstand the workload placed on the software without crashing. This includes verifying that it can respond in a timely fashion to a high number of simultaneous users.

Coding Secure Applications

There are two levels of application development concepts. These are general concepts that apply to all application development and specific concepts that apply to a more rigorous security-based approach. There are also best practices for secure coding, software assessment methods, and code testing.

General Concepts   Developing an application requires several stages:

- *Development.* At the development stage, the requirements for the application are established, and it is confirmed that the application meets the intended business needs before the actual coding begins.
- *Testing.* The testing stage thoroughly tests the application for any errors that could result in a security vulnerability.
- *Staging.* The staging stage tests to verify that the code functions as intended.
- *Production.* In the production stage, the application is released to be used in its actual setting.

Often application development involves software diversity. Software diversity is a software development technique in which two or more functionally identical variants of a program are developed from the same specification but by different programmers or programming teams. The intent is to provide error detection, increased reliability, and additional documentation. It also can reduce the probability that errors created by different compilers, which are programs that create binary machine code from human source code, will influence the end results.

Another concept regarding application development involves how the completed application will be used in the context of the larger IT footprint of the enterprise. Provisioning is the enterprise-wide configuration, deployment, and management of multiple types of IT system resources, of which the new application would be viewed as a new resource. Deprovisioning in application development is removing a resource that is no longer needed.

Integrity measurement is an "attestation mechanism" designed to convince a remote party (external to the coding team) that an application is running only a set of known and approved executables. Whenever a file is called in an executable mode, such as when a program is invoked or a shareable library is mapped, the integrity measurement tool generates a unique digital value of that file. On request, the tool can produce a list of all programs run and their corresponding digital values. This list can then be examined to ensure that no unknown or known vulnerable applications have been run.

In recent years, mathematical models have been applied to software engineering. **Formal methods for verification of critical software** apply mathematically rigorous techniques (called *formal methods*) that use tools for the specification, design, and verification of software. These formal specifications are intended to be so precise that they have no risk of misinterpretation. By knowing that program implementation abides by the formal methods, assurance can be gained that the engineers have implemented what is described in the specification.

>  **CAUTION**   Despite its promise, formal methods for software engineering are not considered feasible for commercial applications. Few skilled software engineers are fluent in the elements of formal methods such as logic calculi, automata theory, and algebraic data types. In addition, significant expense and time are required when formal methodology is added to software development. Formal methods are generally used for government and military software development for critical systems.

DevSecOps   An *application development lifecycle model* is a conceptual model that describes the different stages involved in creating an application. There are two major application development lifecycle models.

The *waterfall model* uses a sequential design process: after each stage is fully completed, the developers move on to the next stage. This means that once a stage is finished, developers cannot go back to a previous stage without starting over again. For example, in the waterfall model, quality assurance (QA) (verification of quality) occurs only after the application has been tested and before it is finally placed in production. However, this makes any issues uncovered by QA difficult to address since they appear at the end of the process. The waterfall model demands extensive planning in the very beginning and requires that it be followed carefully.

The *agile model* was designed to overcome the disadvantages of the waterfall model. Instead of following a rigid sequential design process, the agile model follows an incremental approach. Developers might start with a simplistic project design and begin to work on small modules. The work on these modules is done in short (weekly or monthly) "sprints," and at the end of each sprint, the project's priorities are again evaluated as tests are being run. This approach allows for software issues to be incrementally discovered so that feedback and changes can be incorporated into the design before the next sprint is started.

One specific type of software methodology that follows the agile model and heavily incorporates secure coding practices and techniques to create secure software applications is called **DevSecOps**. Also known as *SecDevOps* and *DevOpsSec*, it is the process of integrating secure development best practices and methodologies into application software development and deployment processes using the agile model. DevSecOps is a set of best practices designed to help organizations implant secure coding deep in the heart of their applications.

DevSecOps is often promoted in terms of its elasticity (flexibility or resilience in code development) and its scalability (expandability from small projects to very large projects). However, the cornerstone of DevSecOps is automation. With standard application development, security teams often find themselves stuck with time-consuming manual tasks. DevSecOps, on the other hand, applies what is called automated courses of action to develop the code as quickly and securely as possible. This automation enables continuous monitoring (examining the processes in real-time instead of at the end of a stage), continuous validation (ongoing approvals of the code), continuous integration (ensuring that security features are incorporated at each stage), continuous delivery (moving the code to each stage as it is completed), and continuous deployment (continual code implementation).

Because DevSecOps is based on the agile method, it involves continuous modifications throughout the process. With these continual changes, it is important to use tools that support change management or to create a plan for documenting changes to the application. One tool for change management is version control software that allows changes to be automatically recorded and if necessary "rolled back" to a previous version of the software.

> **NOTE 8**
>
> The DevSecOps methodology also includes concepts such as *immutable systems* (once a value or configuration is employed as part of an application, it is not modified; if changes are necessary, a new system must be created), *infrastructure as code* (managing a hardware and software infrastructure using the same principles as developing computer code), and *baselining* (creating a starting point for comparison purposes in order to apply targets and goals to measure success).

Secure Coding Best Practices   Several coding techniques should be used to create secure applications and limit data exposure, or disclosing sensitive data to attackers. These best practices include the following:

- *Input validation.* All input from every source should go through **input validation**, or assuring that the data received is legitimate. This includes checking for the correct data type (such as date, string, integer, or floating point), range, size, and appropriateness (such as filtering for an invalid date like May 32).

> **⊘ CAUTION**   It is a mistake for the application to attempt to sanitize input data on behalf of the user to correct errors. Instead, an error message should be generated back to the user.

- *Output encoding.* When displaying dynamic information that was received from any data source (instead of being static information like a label), anything other than the text itself must be stripped away. This is called **output encoding**. For example, any HTML control characters (such as <, >, and /) should be purged.
- *Parameterized queries.* When giving input into a database, a **parameterized query** should be used instead of passing input. A parameterized query uses predefined variables or prepared statements as placeholders for parameters.
- *Session management.* A web session is a sequence of multiple network HTTP request and response transactions associated with the same user. Modern web applications are complex and require that the information or status of the user be retained for the duration of the interactions in that session. Once a user has presented his or her credentials and been authenticated, all subsequent requests must be able to apply appropriate security access controls as well. It is necessary to implement **session management** capabilities that link both the authentication and access control (or authorization) modules that are commonly available in web applications.
- *Data protection.* Different schemes for securing the integrity of any data that the application accesses (**data protection**) should be part of the application.

Additional secure coding best practices are summarized in Table 6-4.

Table 6-4   Secure coding techniques

Coding technique	Description	Security advantage
Normalization	Organizing data within a database to minimize redundancy	Reduces footprint of data exposed to attackers
Stored procedure	Making a subroutine available to applications that access a relational database	Eliminates the need to write a subroutine that could have vulnerabilities
Code signing	Digitally signing applications	Confirms the software author and guarantees the code has not been altered or corrupted
Obfuscation/ camouflaged code	Writing an application so that its inner functionality is difficult for an outsider to understand	Helps prevent an attacker from understanding a program's function
Dead code	Removing a section of an application that executes but performs no meaningful function	Provides an unnecessary attack vector for attackers
Server-side execution and validation or Client-side execution and validation	Requiring input validation generally uses the server to perform validation but can also have the client perform validation by the user's web browser	Adds another validation to the process
Code reuse of third-party libraries and SDKs	Using existing software in a new application; a software development kit (SDK) is a set of tools used to write applications	Existing libraries that have already been vetted as secure eliminate the need to write new code

Code Analysis

Analyzing code is one of the most important steps in application development. Code analysis involves static code analysis, which consists of analyzing the software from a security perspective before the source code is even compiled. Automated static code analysis may also be accompanied by manual peer reviews. In these reviews, software engineers and developers are paired together or in larger teams to laboriously examine each line of source code looking for vulnerabilities. Security testing should also be performed after the source code is compiled (a process called dynamic code analysis or run-time verification) and when all components are integrated and running. This testing typically uses a tool or suite of pre-built attacks or testing tools that specifically monitor the application's behavior for memory corruption, user privilege issues, and other critical security problems. A variety of tools can be used for static analysis and dynamic analysis.

NOTE 9

Static analysis and dynamic analysis are covered in Module 4.

Software Assessment Methods

There are different methods for assessing software after it has been developed. These methods include the following:

- *Code review*. Although a **code review** can be as simple as a colleague going through the code and suggesting tweaks to improve the performance, this has limited value. A comprehensive security code review, on the other hand, should involve running an automated tool followed by a manual analysis to uncover potential security vulnerabilities.

 **CAUTION**   Code reviews should not be conducted at the very end of the development lifecycle just prior to the release of the application. Rather, they should be incorporated into the development lifecycle at an early stage, thus reducing overhead costs and the time it takes developers to remediate security issues.

- *Security regression testing.* When an update is made to an existing application, it is obviously important to test the new functionality. However, it is also critical to again apply old tests that the application had previously passed. This is to ensure that new software does not reintroduce any old vulnerabilities that had been already corrected (that the software had not *regressed* back to a former insecure state). This type of testing is called security regression testing.
- *Stress testing.* Stress testing is a type of software testing that verifies stability and reliability of the software application when tested under extremely heavy load conditions. The goal of stress testing is measuring the software on its robustness and error handling capabilities when tested beyond normal operating points and then evaluating how software works under extreme conditions.
- *User acceptance testing.* User acceptance testing (UAT) is the final phase of the software assessment process. During this phase, those individuals who will use the software test it. At this phase, questions such as *Do they have trouble using it? Does it behave exactly as anticipated?* and *Is it really what they asked for?* are evaluated.

> **NOTE 10**
>
> Edsger W. Dijkstra, a famous software engineer, once said, "Program testing can be used to show the presence of bugs, but never to show their absence!"

TWO RIGHTS & A WRONG

1. A goal of software diversity is to reduce the probability that errors created by different compilers will influence the end results.
2. Provisioning is removing a resource that is no longer needed.
3. DevSecOps has elasticity and scalability.

See Appendix C for the answer.

HARDWARE BEST PRACTICES

✓ CERTIFICATION

2.3 Explain hardware assurance best practices.

3.2 Given a scenario, implement configuration changes to existing controls to improve security.

As with software, several hardware best practices should be followed. These include practices related to firmware, processors, hard drives, and other hardware.

Firmware

Protecting firmware involves understanding what firmware is and the role it plays in technology devices. It is important to protect firmware to confirm boot integrity.

What is Firmware?

Firmware is sometimes defined as "software in hardware." More precisely, firmware is a specific class of computer software that provides the low level control for a device's specific hardware. Firmware can be found not only in computers but also in embedded systems, consumer appliances, computer peripherals, and other devices.

> **NOTE 11**
>
> Other than very simple devices, virtually all modern electronic devices contain firmware.

NOTE 12

EPROM contents can be erased by exposing them to ultraviolet light while EEPROM and flash memory can be erased by using electric signals.

Firmware is held in nonvolatile memory (NVM) that is not affected by a loss of power as is computer random access memory (RAM). This memory is typically read-only memory (ROM), erasable programmable ROM (EPROM), electrically erasable programmable ROM (EEPROM), and flash memory. The original ROM firmware was not intended to be modified. However, because not being able to update firmware essentially rendered the device obsolete, later versions included the ability to modify its contents.

A special type of NVM programmable ROM uses eFuse technology. An eFuse is conceptually similar to a traditional electrical fuse that is used to prevent an electrical circuit overload. However, it is not used to protect from an electrical overload circuitry but to configure the contents of the chip so that it cannot be reversed. An eFuse is much smaller and is embedded into a NVM circuit chip. An eFuse link can be "blown" just like a conventional fuse, but it cannot be reset so that once written, it cannot be reversed. eFuse technology is used to store system parameters, security configuration, and sensitive data.

NOTE 13

An eFuse is a single bit of nonvolatile memory with the restriction that once an eFuse bit is programmed to 1, it can never be reverted to 0.

Due to the ability to change the contents of modern firmware, it is important that only approved and verified trusted firmware updates be used to edit the contents of firmware. Trusted firmware updates involve secure development, secure update digital signatures, robust distribution, and secure installation.

Confirm Boot Integrity

For personal computers, firmware is most often associated with the startup techniques used when an endpoint is powered on. Ensuring secure startup involves the Unified Extensible Firmware Interface (UEFI) and its boot security features.

Unified Extensible Firmware Interface (UEFI)   Early cowboys and workhands were known for wearing tight-fitting tall boots. These boots had a tab or loop at the top of the boot through which a tool called a boot hook could be inserted to assist in pulling on the boot. In the mid-1800s, the expression *pull yourself up by your own bootstraps* was used to describe the impossible task of lifting yourself off the ground by pulling on the bootstrap. The phrase later came to mean to improve your situation by your own efforts without any external help.

Computers adopted this language to describe the process of starting a computer when it has been powered off. Because a computer cannot rely on external assistance when powered on, this process of a computer starting up by itself is called *booting up* or just *booting*.

The booting process on early personal computers used firmware called the *BIOS (Basic Input/Output System)*. The BIOS was a chip integrated into the computer's motherboard. When the computer was powered on, the BIOS software would "awaken" and perform the following steps in a *legacy BIOS boot*:

1. The BIOS would first test the various components of the computer to ensure that they were functioning properly (called the *POST* or *power-on self-test*).
2. Next, the BIOS would reference the *Master Boot Record (MBR)* that specified the computer's *partition table*, which instructed the BIOS where the computer's operating system (OS) could be located.
3. Finally, the BIOS passed control over to the installed bootloader that launched the OS.

Originally, BIOS firmware was stored in a ROM chip on the motherboard, supplemented by a CMOS (Complementary Metal-Oxide-Semiconductor) chip that stored any changes to the BIOS. Later computer systems stored the BIOS contents in flash memory so it could be easily updated. This provided the ability to update the BIOS firmware so new features could be added.

NOTE 14

Although BIOS chips were nonvolatile (they retained the information even when the computer was turned off), CMOS needed its own dedicated power source, which was a lithium-ion battery about the size of a coin that could hold a charge for up to 10 years before needing to be replaced. If the CMOS battery died, the BIOS settings were not lost but instead were reset to their default settings.

To add functionality, an improved firmware interface was developed to replace the BIOS. Known as **UEFI (Unified Extensible Firmware Interface)**, it provides several enhancements over BIOS. This includes the ability to access hard drives that are larger than 2 terabytes (TB), support for an unlimited number of primary hard drive partitions, faster booting, and support for networking functionality in the UEFI firmware itself to aid in remote troubleshooting. UEFI also has a more advanced user interface for configurations and information, as seen in Figure 6-3.

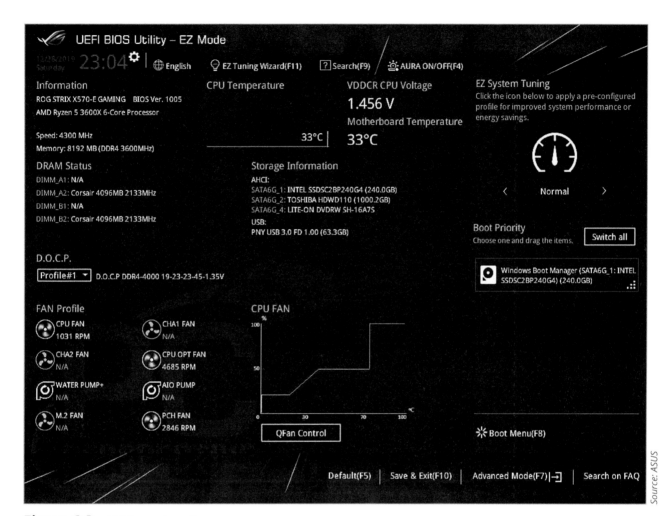

Figure 6-3   UEFI user interface

NOTE 15

Legacy BIOS boot support from motherboard manufacturers ended in 2020, and UEFI is now the standard.

Boot Security   Another significant improvement of UEFI over BIOS relates to boot security. The ability to update the BIOS in firmware also opened the door for a threat actor to create malware to infect the BIOS. Called a *BIOS attack*, it would exploit the update feature of the BIOS. Because the BIOS resides in firmware and an infected BIOS would then persistently reinfect the computer whenever it was powered on, BIOS attacks were difficult to uncover and hard to disinfect. UEFI, used along with other components, is designed to combat these BIOS vulnerabilities and provide improved boot security.

 **CAUTION**   UEFI by itself does not provide enhanced boot security. It must be paired with other boot security functions.

Boot security involves validating that each element used in each step of the boot process has not been modified. This process begins with the validation of the first element (boot software). Once the first element has been validated, it can validate the next item (such as software drivers) and so on until control has been handed over to the OS. This is called a *chain of trust*: each element relies on the confirmation of the previous element to know that the entire process is secure.

But how does the chain begin? What if a threat actor were to inject malware prior to start of the chain of trust? If the starting point is software, it can be replaced or modified. That would then compromise each element of the chain. To prevent this, a chain of trust requires a strong starting point.

The strongest starting point is hardware, which cannot be modified like software. This is known as the **hardware root of trust**. Security checks are "rooted" in (begin with) hardware checks. Because this chain of trust begins with a hardware verification, each subsequent check can rely upon it (called **boot attestation**).

Several techniques can be used to assure boot security, all of which rely on UEFI; some also rely on the hardware root of trust. Different boot security modes are listed in Table 6-5.

Table 6-5   Boot security modes

Name	Description	Advantages	Disadvantages
Legacy BIOS Boot	Uses BIOS for boot functions	Compatible with older systems	No security features
UEFI Native Mode	Uses UEFI standards for boot functions	Security boot modules can be patched or updated as needed.	No validation or protection of the boot process
Secure Boot	Each firmware and software executable at boot time must be verified as having prior approval	All system firmware, bootloaders, kernels, and other boot-time executables are validated	Custom hardware, firmware, and software may not pass without first being submitted to system vendors like Microsoft
Trusted Boot	Windows OS checks the integrity of every component of boot process before loading it	Takes over where Secure Boot leaves off by validating the Windows 10 software before loading it	Requires using Microsoft OS
Measured Boot	Computer's firmware logs the boot process so OS can send it to a trusted server to assess the security	Provides highest degree of security	Could slow down the boot process

 **CAUTION** The Secure Boot security standard is designed to ensure that a computer boots using only software that is trusted by the computer manufacturer. Manufacturers can update the list of trusted hardware, drivers, and OS for a computer, which are stored in the Secure Boot database on the computer. Although it is possible for the user to disable Secure Boot to install hardware or run software or OSs that have not been trusted by the manufacturer, this makes it difficult or impossible to reactivate Secure Boot without restoring the computer back to its original factory state.

Processor

Several enhancements to processors can provide a higher level of security. These include the following:

- *Processor security extensions*. Developers of processors—including Intel, ARM, and AMD—have added **processor security extensions** to their processors to provide additional enhancements and reduce the attack surface of the system. These extensions include defining portions of memory as secure memory, controlled entry into a secure processor state, and limited debugging.

- *Trusted execution.* Trusted execution is a secure area of the processor that guarantees code and data are loaded inside the special secure area. The execution of code is also isolated.
- *Secure enclave.* A secure enclave is a secure coprocessor that functions in addition to the regular processor. A secure enclave includes a hardware-based cryptographic key manager, which is isolated from the main processor to provide an extra layer of security. The data bus connection between the secure enclave and main processor is often protected by bus encryption that protects the transfer of data between the two processors.
- *Atomic execution.* Atomic execution, also called *atomic operation*, permits a processor to read from a memory location or write to a location during the same data operation. However, all other input and output mechanisms are suspended and cannot function at the same time. This reduces the risk of another thread of the operation manipulating a shared resource.

Hard Drive

The contents of a hard drive can be protected by cryptography. One method is implemented through software running on a device. However, software encryption suffers from the same fate as any application program: it can be subject to attacks to exploit its vulnerabilities.

As a more secure option, cryptography can be embedded in hardware. Hardware encryption cannot be exploited like software encryption. Hardware encryption can be applied to USB devices and standard hard drives. However, more sophisticated hardware encryption options include self-encrypting drives, the hardware security model, and the trusted platform module.

Self-Encrypting Drives (SED)

A self-encrypting drive (SED) automatically encrypts any data files stored on it. When the computer or other device with an SED is initially powered on, the drive and the host device perform an authentication process. If the authentication process fails, the drive can be configured to simply deny any access to the drive or even perform a cryptographic erase on specified blocks of data. (A cryptographic erase deletes the decryption keys so that no data can be recovered.) This also makes it impossible to install the drive on another computer to read its contents.

Hardware Security Module (HSM)

A hardware security module (HSM) is a removable external cryptographic device. An HSM can be a USB device, an expansion card, a device that connects directly to a computer through a port, or a secure network server. An HSM includes an onboard random number generator and key storage facility, as well as accelerated symmetric and asymmetric encryption, and can even back up sensitive material in encrypted form. Because all of this is done in hardware and not through software, malware cannot compromise it.

HSMs are popular consumer-level devices. Figure 6-4 shows a USB consumer HSM. Some financial banking software comes with a specialized HSM hardware key, also called a "security dongle." This device is paired with a specific financial account and cannot be cloned or compromised.

Trusted Platform Module (TPM)

The Trusted Platform Module (TPM) is a chip on the motherboard of the computer that provides cryptographic services. For example, TPM includes a true random number generator instead of a PRNG as well as full support for asymmetric encryption. (TPM can also

> **NOTE 16**
>
> A set of specifications for SEDs developed by the Trusted Computing Group (TCG) is Opal. SEDs that support Opal use hardware encryption technology to secure data stored in them. Opal also ensures the interoperability of SEDs between different vendors.

Figure 6-4   USB HSM

Source: Yubica

NOTE 17

An HSM is external while a TPM is internal.

generate public and private keys.) TPM can also measure and test key components as the computer is starting up. It prevents the computer from booting if system files or data have been altered. With TPM, if the hard drive is moved to a different computer, the user must enter a recovery password before gaining access to the system volume.

Other Hardware Best Practices

There are other hardware best practices for securing devices. These include endpoint detection and response tools, sandboxing, port security, malware signatures, antitampering, and trusted foundry.

Endpoint Detection and Response (EDR)

Endpoint detection and response (EDR) tools have a similar functionality to a host intrusion detection system (HIDS) of monitoring endpoint events and of a host intrusion prevention system (HIPS) of taking immediate action. However, EDR tools are considered more robust than HIDS and HIPS. First, an EDR can aggregate data from multiple endpoint computers to a centralized database so that security professionals can perform further investigation and gain a better picture of events that are occurring across multiple endpoints instead of on a single endpoint. This can help determine if an attack is more widespread across the enterprise and if more comprehensive and higher-level action needs to be taken. Second, EDR tools can perform more sophisticated analytics that identify patterns and detect anomalies. This can help detect unusual or unrecognized activities by performing baseline comparisons of normal behavior.

NOTE 18

Many EDRs also allow for a manual or user analysis of the data.

Sandboxing

A conceptual view of applications that interact with an OS is illustrated in Figure 6-5. A *sandbox* is a "container" in which an application can be run so that it does not impact the underlying OS, as illustrated in Figure 6-6. This process is called **sandboxing**. Anything that occurs within the sandbox is not visible to other applications or the OS outside

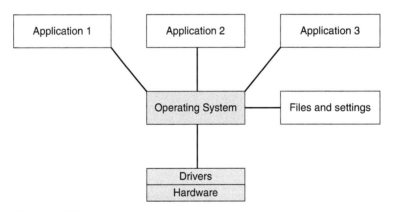

Figure 6-5 Applications interacting with an OS

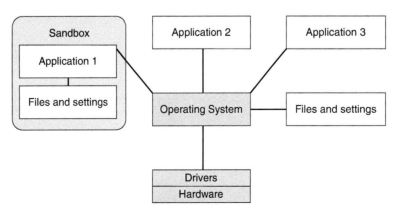

Figure 6-6 Sandboxing

the sandbox. Also, the contents of the sandbox are not saved when the sandbox is closed. Sandboxes are often used when downloading or running suspicious programs to ensure that the endpoint hardware will not be impacted.

Port Security

Securing the ports on a hardware device (**port security**) such as a network switch or router is essential to securing a network. A threat actor who can access a network device through an unprotected port can reconfigure the device to his or her own advantage. This could introduce a number of vulnerabilities, one of which is compromising route security or the trust of packets sent through a router. False route information can be injected or altered by weak port security that would enable the insertion of individual false route updates or the installation of bogus routers into the routing infrastructure. Port security steps to thwart an attack directed at network devices are summarized in Table 6-6.

NOTE 19

A sandbox is not the same as a virtual machine. A virtual machine is a "computer within a computer" in which an entire OS runs as an application on top of the regular OS. However, its contents can be saved for future use.

Table 6-6   Thwarting attacks through port security

Type of attack	Description	Port security defense
MAC flooding	An attacker can overflow the switch's address table with fake MAC addresses, forcing it to act like a hub, sending packets to all devices.	Use a switch that can close ports with too many MAC addresses.
MAC address spoofing	If two devices have the same MAC address, a switch may send frames to each device. An attacker can change the MAC address on her device to match the target device's MAC address.	Configure the switch so that only one port can be assigned per MAC address.
ARP poisoning	An attacker sends a forged ARP packet to the source device, substituting the attacker's computer MAC address.	Use an ARP detection appliance.
Unauthorized packet capturing	An attacker connects a device to the switch's port.	Secure the switch in a locked room.

Malware Signatures

Different methods can be used to identify and label malware code, known as creating **malware signatures**. One method is to use a one-way hash algorithm. A hash algorithm creates a unique "digital fingerprint" of a set of data. This process is called hashing, and the resulting fingerprint is a digest (sometimes called a message digest or hash) that represents the contents. Hashing is used primarily for comparison purposes, so that the digest of malware could be generated and distributed as evidence of malware.

Another method of creating a malware signature is to use the open source tool YARA. YARA provides a robust language compatible with Perl Compatible Regular Expressions based on **rule writing**, or generating signatures according to specific rules. These signatures are encoded as text files, which makes them easy to read and communicate with others. Figure 6-7 illustrates a YARA rule example that if a potential malware file contains any of the three strings ($a, $b, or $c), it will be reported as *malware_x0703*. YARA has several features for creating powerful rules.

```
rule malware_x0703 : exec
{
        meta:
                description = "Example 1"
                threat_level = 4
                in_the_wild = true
        strings:
                $a = { 6A 40 68 00 30 00 00 6A 13 8D 40}
                $b = {8D 4D B0 2B C1 83 40}
                $c = "UVODFRYSILHINEXCITEXNINOLINEWJON"
        condition:
                $a or $b or $c
}
```

Figure 6-7   YARA rule example

NOTE 20

YARA stands for either *Another Recursive Acronym* or *Yet Another Ridiculous Acronym*.

Antitampering

One of the challenges of protecting hardware is the fact that a threat actor who can gain physical access to the device can disassemble it to remove parts containing sensitive data. It is important that **antitampering** devices be installed on secure systems to prevent any physical actions by the threat actor on the device. The different levels and defenses of antitampering include the following:

- *Tamper prevention.* Tamper prevention involves making the housing difficult to open by drilling out the heads of screws, using high-strength adhesives to hold the housing together, or applying ultrasonic welding to make the shell difficult to open without noticeable damage.
- *Tamper detection.* Antitamper switches, sensors, or circuitry can be added to a hardware device to detect tampering.
- *Tamper response.* If tampering is detected, the device can be programmed to shut down, erase critical parts of memory, or physically destroy the entire device.

NOTE 21

In 2001, a U.S. Navy reconnaissance aircraft made an unauthorized emergency landing at a Chinese air base after a mid-air collision with a Chinese jet fighter that caused severe damage to the airplane. Despite the crew's attempts to destroy computers, hard disk drives, and other important equipment before landing, some sensitive and/or secret military information fell into the hands of the Chinese government as a result of the emergency landing. This incident started the U.S. military's efforts to include antitampering as a required feature on its sensitive equipment.

Trusted Foundry

The **trusted foundry** is a program by the U.S. Department of Defense that is designed to secure the manufacturing supply chain for vendors who supply technology to the military. The program provides a cost-effective means to assure the integrity and confidentiality of integrated circuits during design and manufacturing.

TWO RIGHTS & A WRONG

1. Firmware is a specific class of computer software that provides the low-level control for a device's specific hardware.
2. Measured Boot provides the highest degree of security and does not impact the boot process.
3. A secure enclave is a secure coprocessor that functions in addition to the regular processor.

See Appendix C for the answer.

VM LAB You're now ready to complete the live, virtual machine labs for this module. The labs can be found in the Apply It folder in each MindTap module.

MODULE SUMMARY

- Several software assurance best practices can be used to protect a variety of platforms including mobile and client/server platforms. A service-oriented architecture (SOA) combines both the code and necessary data integrations required to execute a complete and discrete business function. The services serve as "black boxes" that simply perform their tasks without requiring an understanding of how the functionality occurs. Different standards and protocols can be used in an SOA. Security Assertion Markup Language (SAML) is an XML standard that allows secure web domains to exchange user authentication and authorization data in an

SOA. A user's login credentials can be stored with a single identity provider instead of being stored on each web service provider's server. Simple Object Access Protocol (SOAP) is a message protocol that allows the distributed elements of an application to communicate in a web-services environment. SOAP's header structure identifies the actions that different SOAP nodes are expected to take on the message while its payload structure carries the information. Representational State Transfer (REST) is considered an improvement over SOAP as a means of communications between web-based systems.

- Application software that contains vulnerabilities is a leading contributor to attacks, making secure application software development critical. The cause of unsecure applications is usually the result of how the application was designed and written. In recent years, major software developers have focused their attention on improving their software code to provide increased security. These improvements are aimed at reducing the number of design and coding errors in software. A software development lifecycle (SDLC) is a methodology that can be used to build a program or application from its inception to decommission. Recognized secure SDLC principles practices should be used in software development.

- Some general concepts apply to all application development. Developing an application requires different stages, such as development, testing, staging, and production. Often application development involves software diversity. Software diversity is a software development technique in which two or more functionally identical variants of a program are developed from the same specification but by different programmers or programming teams. Provisioning is the enterprise-wide configuration, deployment, and management of multiple types of IT system resources, of which the new application would be viewed as a new resource. Integrity measurement is an "attestation mechanism" designed to convince a remote party (external to the coding team) that an application is running only a set of known and approved executables. In recent years, mathematical models have been applied to software engineering. Formal methods for verifying critical software apply mathematically rigorous techniques (called formal methods) that use tools for the specification, design, and verification of software.

- One specific type of software methodology that follows the agile model and heavily incorporates secure coding practices and techniques to create secure software applications is called DevSecOps (also known as SecDevOps and DevOpsSec). It is the process of integrating secure development best practices and methodologies into application software development and deployment processes. DevSecOps is often promoted in terms of its elasticity (flexibility or resilience in code development) and its scalability (expandability from small projects to very large projects). However, the cornerstone of DevSecOps is automation.

- Several coding techniques should be used to create secure applications and limit data exposure or disclosing sensitive data to attackers. These include input validation, output encoding, parameterized queries, session management, and data protection. Analyzing code is one of the most important steps in application development. Code analysis involves static code analysis, which consists of analyzing the software from a security perspective before the source code is even compiled. Security testing should also be performed after the source code is compiled (a process called dynamic code analysis or run-time verification) and when all components are integrated and running. A variety of tools can be used for static analysis and dynamic analysis. Once the software has been developed, software assessment methods should be applied, such as code review, security regression testing, stress testing, and user acceptance testing.

- As with software, several hardware best practices should be followed. Firmware is a specific class of computer software that provides the low-level control for a device's specific hardware. Firmware can be found not only in computers but also in embedded systems, consumer appliances, computer peripherals, and other devices. Firmware is held in nonvolatile memory that is not affected by a loss of power. Due to the ability to change the contents of modern firmware, it is important that only approved and verified trusted firmware updates be used to edit the contents of firmware. Trusted firmware updates involve secure development, secure update digital signatures, robust distribution, and secure installation.

- For personal computers, firmware is most often associated with the startup techniques used when an endpoint is powered on. The booting process on early personal computers used firmware called the BIOS (Basic Input/Output System). To add functionality, an improved firmware interface was developed to replace the BIOS. Known as UEFI (Unified Extensible Firmware Interface), it provides several enhancements over BIOS. One significant improvement of UEFI over BIOS relates to boot security. The strongest starting point is hardware, which cannot be modified like software. This is known as the hardware root of trust. Security checks are "rooted" in (begin with) hardware checks. Because this chain of trust begins with a hardware verification, each subsequent check can rely upon it (called boot attestation). Several techniques can be used to assure boot security, all of which rely on UEFI and some that rely on the hardware root of trust.

- Several enhancements to processors can provide a higher level of security. Developers of processors have added processor security extensions to their processors to provide additional enhancements and reduce the attack surface of the system. These extensions include defining portions of memory as secure memory, controlled entry into a secure processor state, and limited debugging. Trusted execution is a secure area of the processor that guarantees code and data are loaded inside a special secure area. The execution of code is also isolated. A secure enclave is a secure coprocessor that functions in addition to the regular processor. A secure enclave includes a hardware-based cryptographic key manager, which is isolated from the main processor to provide an extra layer of security. Atomic execution permits a processor to read from a memory location or write to a location during the same data operation.

- Cryptography can be embedded in hardware to protect data files. Hardware encryption cannot be exploited like software encryption. A self-encrypting drive (SED) automatically encrypts any data files stored on it. When the computer or other device with an SED is initially powered on, the drive and the host device perform an authentication process. A hardware security module (HSM) is a removable external cryptographic device and can be a USB device, an expansion card, a device that connects directly to a computer through a port, or a secure network server. An HSM includes an onboard random number generator and key storage facility, as well as accelerated symmetric and asymmetric encryption, and can even back up sensitive material in encrypted form. The Trusted Platform Module (TPM) is a chip on the motherboard of the computer that provides cryptographic services.

- There are other hardware best practices for securing devices. Endpoint detection and response (EDR) tools have a similar functionality to a host intrusion detection system (HIDS) of monitoring endpoint events and to a host intrusion prevention system (HIPS) of taking immediate action. However, EDR tools are considered more robust than HIDS and HIPS. A sandbox is a "container" in which an application can be run so that it does not impact the underlying OS. This process is called sandboxing and reduces any impact upon hardware from infections by malware. Securing the ports on a hardware device (port security) such as a network switch or router is essential to securing a network. Threat actors who can access a network device through an unprotected port can reconfigure the device to their own advantage.

- Different methods can be used to identify and label malware code, known as creating malware signatures. One method is to use a one-way hash algorithm. Another method of creating a malware signature is to use the open source tool YARA that is based on rule writing. It is important that antitampering devices be installed on secure systems to prevent any physical actions by the threat actor on the device. The trusted foundry is a program by the U.S. Department of Defense that is designed to secure the manufacturing supply chain for vendors who supply technology to the military.

Key Terms

antitampering
atomic execution
boot attestation
bus encryption
code review
data protection
DevSecOps
eFuse
endpoint detection and response
  (EDR)
firmware
formal methods for verification of
  critical software
hardware root of trust
hardware security module (HSM)

input validation
malware signatures
measured boot
output encoding
parameterized query
port security
processor security extensions
Representational State Transfer
  (REST)
rule writing
sandboxing
secure enclave
Security Assertion Markup
  Language (SAML)
security regression testing

self-encrypting drive (SED)
service-oriented architecture (SOA)
session management
Simple Object Access Protocol
  (SOAP)
software development lifecycle
  (SDLC)
stress testing
trusted execution
trusted firmware updates
trusted foundry
Trusted Platform Module (TPM)
UEFI (Unified Extensible Firmware
  Interface)
user acceptance testing (UAT)

Review Questions

1. Which boot security mode sends information on the boot process to a remote server?
   a. UEFI Native Mode
   b. Secure Boot
   c. Trusted Boot
   d. Measured Boot

2. Which stage conducts a test that will verify the code functions as intended?
   a. Production stage
   b. Testing stage
   c. Staging stage
   d. Development stage

3. Which model uses a sequential design process?
   a. Secure model
   b. Agile model
   c. Rigid model
   d. Waterfall model

4. Which of these provides cryptographic services and is external to the device?
   a. Trusted Platform Module (TPM)
   b. Hardware security module (HSM)
   c. Self-encrypting hard disk drives (SED)
   d. Encrypted hardware-based USB devices

5. Which of the following is NOT an advantage of a software-oriented architecture (SOA)?
   a. Improves business agility
   b. Leverages legacy functionality
   c. Eliminates the need for business analysts
   d. Enhances collaboration

6. What is an XML standard that allows secure web domains to exchange user authentication and authorization data in an SOA?
   a. REST-X
   b. SAML
   c. Macroservices
   d. SDLC

7. Which technology is REST replacing?
   a. SOAP
   b. XMLX
   c. SAM-X
   d. IPA-REST

8. Which of the following is NOT correct about the software development lifecycle (SDLC)?
   a. It is a methodology that can be used to build a program or application from its inception to decommission.
   b. There has been only one approved SDLC model.

   c. The SDLC includes the basic steps of software planning, designing, testing, coding, and maintenance.
   d. An advantage is that there is a higher awareness of security by stakeholders.

9. Which of the following is NOT a secure SDLC source?
   a. OWASP
   b. Nessus
   c. SANS
   d. CIS

10. Which of the following is NOT correct about the agile model?
    a. It follows a rigid sequential design process.
    b. Work is done in "sprints."
    c. The project's priorities are continually evaluated as tests are run.
    d. It was designed to overcome the disadvantages of the waterfall model.

11. Raul is removing HTML control characters from text that is to be displayed on the screen. What secure coding best practice is he following?
    a. Display sanitization
    b. Output encoding
    c. Screen scraping
    d. HTML cleaning

12. Simpson is using predefined variables as placeholders when querying a database. What secure best coding practice is he following?
    a. SQL injection
    b. Parameterized query
    c. SELECT Targeting
    d. Statement containerization

13. Which type of code analysis is conducted prior to the source code being compiled?
    a. Dynamic code analysis
    b. Precompiled code analysis
    c. Static code analysis
    d. DLDS code analysis

14. Ryker has added a new module to an application and now needs to test it to be sure that the new module does not reintroduce any old vulnerabilities. What testing is Ryker performing?
    a. Software coding analysis (SCA)
    b. Application SDLC verification
    c. Code reuse testing
    d. Security regression testing

15. Which of the following types of NVM that cannot be reset once code is written to it?
    a. EPROM
    b. EEPROM
    c. Flash
    d. eFuse

16. Where does a hardware root of trust security check begin?
    a. Software
    b. Firmware
    c. Hardware
    d. Appware

17. Which boot security mode provides the highest degree of security?
    a. Measured Boot
    b. Trusted Boot
    c. UEFI Native Boot
    d. ABAD Secure Boot

18. Which of the following is a secure area of the processor that guarantees that code and data are loaded inside a special secure area?
    a. Sandbox
    b. Container
    c. Trusted execution
    d. Restricted access processor (RAP)

19. Which of the following permits a processor to read from a memory location or write to a location during the same data operation?
    a. Atomic execution
    b. Data protection
    c. RAM confinement
    d. RAIA

20. Which of the following is NOT correct about YARA?
    a. It is method of creating a malware signature.
    b. It is a proprietary tool.
    c. Signatures are encoded as text files.
    d. It provides a robust language.

Case Projects

Case Project 6-1: Formal Methods

Research formal methods for verification of critical software. What is this approach? How is it being used? What mathematical principles apply? Write one to two paragraphs that summarize your research.

Case Project 6-2: YARA

Research YARA and developing malware signatures through rule writing. Read the different parameters that can be used with YARA rule writing. How extensive are these parameters and options? Then identify several examples of YARA rules. Are they easy or difficult to interpret? How is YARA being used today? Create a one-page paper of your research.

Case Project 6-3: eFuse

How is eFuse being used today? What are its advantages? What are its disadvantages? How does it differ from EPROM and EEPROM? Write a one-page paper on your research.

Case Project 6-4: REST vs. SOAP

Research REST and SOAP, and then compare the two technologies. How do they function? How are they being used? Why is REST so popular? What does the future hold for REST? Write a one-page paper on your research.

Case Project 6-5: On the Job

Suppose you work for a company that has been the frequent victim of cyberattacks. The chief information officer (CIO) has decided that all employees must be issued HSMs and that they will be used for both on-campus and off-campus work. However, several employees have resisted having "yet another" security hoop that they must "jump through" to get their work done. This has led to a showdown between IT and other levels of management. Where do you stand? Should the company force all employees to use HSMs? What are the advantages? What are the risks? What happens when an employee loses an HSM? Write a one-page memo about what you think should be done and why.

MONITORING AND SECURITY OPERATIONS

Cybersecurity defenses have continued to evolve as attacks become more widespread and damaging. There are two key areas in which this evolution can be seen. The first can be found in the use of sophisticated data analysis tools for monitoring. The second area is the new and enhanced functions that a security operations center conducts for an organization. The modules in this part examine these two key areas. Module 7 examines how data analysis can be used in security monitoring. Module 8 looks at the functions of a security operations center.

PART 3

MODULE 7
SECURITY MONITORING THROUGH DATA ANALYSIS

MODULE 8
SECURITY OPERATIONS

SECURITY MONITORING THROUGH DATA ANALYSIS

After completing this module, you should be able to do the following:

1 Describe how to monitor endpoints, networks, and email

2 Define data analytics

3 Explain how to conduct data analysis reviews

Cybersecurity Today

Despite the best spam filters on the market today, phishing emails invariably find their way into our inboxes. How do you determine if a given email is a phishing email or a legitimate message? A recent study by the security researcher Rick Wash uncovers some fascinating details about how IT experts determine if an email is a phishing attempt or legitimate communication. He makes a strong case that the current training for teaching users about phishing is only partially beneficial and should be changed.

Phishing emails are designed by threat actors to intentionally deceive users. Several elements of a phishing email can trick a user into thinking the message is legitimate. These elements include using similar domain names (like www.bankofamerican.com instead of the legitimate www.bankofamerican.com), displaying authentic logos in the email (which are easy to cut and paste from a legitimate website), and having an email layout that mimics an authentic email.

Research has shown that phishing emails use psychological tricks to help recipients to "fall" for the phishing email. More than 20 years ago, Robert Cialdini published research on the principles of influence, or how to get someone to do something. His principles are reciprocation (return a favor or kind gesture), commitment and consistency (honor a pledge), social proof (do things you see other people doing), authority (obey someone in command), liking (be persuaded by people you like), and scarcity (have limited quantity or time). While all six principles can increase the rates of victims clicking a link in a phishing email, "scarcity" and "authority" have a higher impact upon older users while "reciprocation" and "liking" have a higher impact upon younger email recipients.

Wash wanted to understand the cognitive process that IT experts go through to identify phishing messages. He interviewed IT experts about instances when they successfully identified emails as phishing. What he found was that IT experts follow a three-stage process for identifying phishing emails:

Phase 1: In this first stage, IT experts try to make general sense of the email message and understand how it relates to other parts of their lives. If it seems out of place, they may start to notice small discrepancies that indicate something does not look quite right. This triggers a reaction such as, "Hey, could this be a phishing email?"

Phase 2: In the second stage, IT experts look for technical details that could prove the email is indeed part of a phishing attack. They could look closely at the URL of the link that the user is asked to click or dig into the header data of the email.

Phase 3: The last stage involves what to do about the email message if it has been identified as phishing. Do you just delete it? Or should you report it so that others can be alerted? To whom should you give this information and how?

These three phases of how IT experts identify phishing emails are not reflected in how most organizations teach employees about phishing attacks. As part of a regular (sometimes just annual) "security awareness" training campaign, three methods are used most often for training: general-purpose training messages that communicate "best practices," fake phishing campaigns to see if the employee falls for the fake attack (and is then reprimanded or remediated to more training), or in-the-moment warning messages ("Watch out!"). Statements such as "Never click a link in an email message!" and "Never respond to an email that says it comes from your bank!" are also part of these training campaigns. Basically, the message of most current phishing training tells users to be suspicious of all emails and to spend time identifying every email to determine whether it is a phishing email.

However, is this training advice practical? Telling users to never click a link in an email message is rarely practiced, even by IT experts. Asking users to ignore all emails from their bank is likewise seldom practiced. And asking users to closely examine hundreds of daily emails (considering that some corporate users receive more than 300 emails each day) for evidence of phishing is simply not practical.

Current training regarding phishing attacks not only is unrealistic but also misses the three phases identified earlier. Training steps mostly relate only to Phase 2 of trying to determine by deep investigation if the suspicious email is indeed phishing. Training does not address Phase 1 as to first making sense of the email and then seeing discrepancies. Nor does it clearly address Phase 3 as to what to do with a phishing email.

This research may serve to prompt a move toward a more practical and realistic approach to training users about phishing. It may also help users to model these steps used by IT experts in identifying phishing email.

Security monitoring dates back to the earliest days of defending against attacks and continues to be a vital element in protection today. However, as attacks have become more sophisticated and "stealthy," monitoring has become increasingly difficult.

One security organization encourages security teams to strive to meet the *1-10-60 Rule*. This rule states that security defenders should detect threats within *1 minute*, be able to fully understand the threat within *10 minutes*, and then respond to the threat within *60 minutes*.[1] Yet most security professionals would throw their hands in the air over the 1-10-60 Rule. The actual time it takes security defenders to recognize that an intruder is in their network is not measured in minutes but instead in days; in fact, the average time to identify an intruder is 250 days.[2] In the infamous SolarWinds attack, threat actors infiltrated the SolarWinds network in September 2019 but were not discovered until December 2020.

Yet quickly identifying a breach is still an important goal. The solution to more proactive monitoring is to use sophisticated data analysis tools. These tools can help detect attacks more quickly and enable defenders to then respond promptly.

This module explores monitoring through data analysis. The module opens with a description of techniques for monitoring different types of systems. It then looks at data analytics and how to use them effectively in a cybersecurity defense.

MONITORING SYSTEMS

 **CERTIFICATION**

3.1 Given a scenario, analyze data as part of security monitoring activities.

To *monitor* means to observe, oversee, or keep an eye on. Cybersecurity monitoring is watching for evidence of threats and intrusions. Monitoring should be conducted on endpoints and networks. In addition, an often-overlooked area that also requires monitoring is the modern email system.

Endpoint Monitoring

Throughout the years, different terms have been used to describe network-connected hardware devices. Thirty years ago, when the TCP/IP protocol was becoming popular, the word *host* referred to any communicating device on the network (networks were made up of hosts). Twenty years ago, as servers became more popular, the word *client* was used (clients made requests to servers).

Today, a different word is commonly used when referring to network-connected hardware devices: *endpoints*. This change reflects the fact that devices connected to a network are far more than a computing device with a keyboard and monitor. Instead, devices ranging from mobile smartphones and tablets to wearable fitness trackers, industrial control system sensors, automotive telematics units, and even personal drones are all network-connected hardware devices. The word endpoint has become an accurate description of today's end-user technology devices.

This change in terminology also reflects the increased risks that have multiplied—exponentially—with the increase of these new devices. Instead of protecting hosts or clients located inside a network security perimeter, today each endpoint is a target for attackers to attempt to steal or manipulate their data. Because the endpoints are connected to the network, a vulnerability on an endpoint can result in an attack that penetrates the network and infects all other endpoints. In short, today *every endpoint is a potential entry point.*

Endpoint monitoring is typically performed by either monitoring hardware for evidence of a compromise or monitoring for irregular behavior. Ideally, both should be used together for endpoint monitoring.

Hardware Monitoring

It may be possible—but very challenging—to monitor all hardware elements of an endpoint manually and comprehensively (hard drive, memory, network interface, etc.) for evidence of a compromise. However, when the number of endpoints runs into the hundreds, thousands, or hundreds of thousands, monitoring becomes a virtually impossible task.

Two types of products can assist in monitoring endpoint hardware. An Endpoint Protection Platform (EPP) includes basic tools such as traditional antimalware scanning software. Endpoint Detection and Response (EDR) includes more advanced capabilities for detecting and investigating security incidents, along with the ability to intervene and even remediate endpoints back to a preinfection state. EDRs can scan an endpoint's memory and filesystem for evidence of a compromise, as well as monitor running processes and services (and the registry on Windows computers). An EDR dashboard is seen in Figure 7-1.

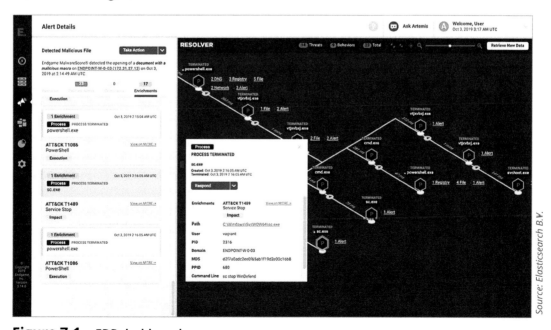

Source: Elasticsearch B.V.

Figure 7-1 EDR dashboard

NOTE 1

Reverse engineering is covered in Module 4.

Identifying software for the presence of malware so it can be identified by an EPP and EDR is typically done through reverse engineering malware. This is the process of disassembling and analyzing the malware to determine how it functions so that it can be recognized.

User and Entity Behavior Analytics (UEBA)

Suppose that Gia is a close friend of yours whom you have known for many years. Gia is outgoing and funny, always has a smile on her face, and wears clothes that reflect the latest fashion trends. You often meet Gia at a local coffee shop where she always orders a caramel macchiato.

After being gone for several weeks, you arrange to meet Gia at the coffee shop to catch up. However, when she walks in the door, you can barely recognize her. She looks frightened and nervous, and her clothes are old and rumpled. She orders a plain cup of coffee and sits across from you at your table. She barely looks at you but keeps turning around to see who has walked in the door, and she hardly has anything to say. You would immediately recognize that something is wrong with your friend, even though she has said nothing. Her change in behavior has revealed that something is wrong.

NOTE 2

UBA has been used for several years for protecting users, particularly by financial institutions. For example, if a bank customer normally accesses her bank's website from her home computer on evenings and weekends, then this information can be used to establish a profile pattern based on the Internet Protocol (IP) address of computer, the time of day, Internet service provider, and basic computer configuration. If a computer located in China suddenly attempts to access her online account at 2:00 AM, this might be an indication that an attacker is at work, and access is then immediately restricted.

Just as a change in Gia's behavior can indicate something is not right—or at least not the same as before—so, too, can a change in the normal behavior of a technology or user reveal that something is not right. An endpoint that starts crashing multiple times each day, an application that keeps locking up, or a user account that suddenly starts trying to access restricted files may indicate that something is wrong, or at least something has changed.

Behavior-based monitoring uses "normal" processes and actions as its standard (known-good behavior) instead of searching for abnormalities (anomalous behavior). Behavior-based monitoring continuously analyzes the behavior of processes and programs on a system and alerts the user if it detects any abnormal actions, at which point a decision can be made. Monitoring behavior is considered as adaptive and proactive instead of just reactive.

Originally, monitoring behavior only applied to user behavior. This includes gathering information such as the endpoints from which users normally log in, files and servers they often use, privileges they have, and the normal frequency and time of access. This information over time can build a profile for the users. When an activity significantly deviates from that profile—for example, if a user is attempting to run an application, open a file, access a resource, visit a website, or perform some behavior that the user has not done before—then this abnormal user behavior could indicate that the account has been compromised or the endpoint is under the remote control of a threat actor. This type of defense is known as user behavior analytics (UBA).

However, technology systems likewise have "normal" behaviors and can also be monitored for unusual activity as evidence of a compromise. User and entity behavior analytics (UEBA) encompass both users as well as "entities" such as networks, devices, applications, and servers (called system and application behavior).

NOTE 3

Some virtual machines (VMs) now offer "service-defined" protection over applications, data, and users by building a profile of known-good behavior both on the endpoint and network. This protection cannot be bypassed even if an attacker infects the guest OS because inspection can be made without having to install agents on the guest OS.

UEBA, however, has weaknesses that can be targeted by different exploit techniques, or methods for delivering malware. Building a complete understanding of every application is difficult to achieve. There are also challenges related to building a profile of users who access distributed applications. One exploit relates to how UEBA data is collected. Some UEBA systems rely on software agents installed on the endpoints to gather this data; however, threat actors often target these agents to disable them or bypass them so as not to raise an alarm.

Network Monitoring

Just as endpoints must be monitored, so too must networks: a single network compromise could potentially impact hundreds or thousands of devices connected to that network. But the very high volume of traffic crossing a network today as well as the fundamental structure of networks make networking monitoring a challenge. This can be seen by considering the reference model for networks.

The International Organization for Standardization (ISO) Open Systems Interconnection (OSI) reference model for networks is a set of specifications that was intended to describe how dissimilar computers could be connected together on a network. The key to the OSI reference model is *layers*. The model breaks networking steps down into a series of seven layers. Within each layer, different networking tasks are performed, and each layer cooperates with the layer immediately above and below it. Each layer in the sending device also corresponds to the same layer in the receiving device.

However, the OSI model was designed so that each layer is compartmentalized: one layer works without the knowledge and approval of the other layers. This means that if a layer is compromised, the other layers are unaware of any problem, which results in the entire communication being compromised.

Layer 2 of the OSI model is particularly weak in this regard and is a frequent target of threat actors. Layer 2, the Data Link Layer, is responsible for dividing data into packets along with error detection and correction, and performs physical addressing, data framing, error detection, and handling. A compromise at Layer 2 can impact the entire communication, as seen in Figure 7-2.

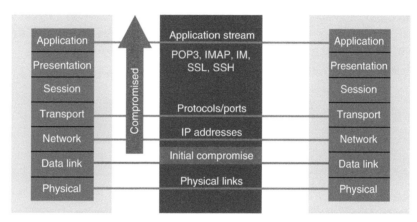

Figure 7-2   Layer 2 compromise

NOTE 4

Two of the common Layer 2 attacks are address solution protocol poisoning and media access control attacks.

Network monitoring involves packet and protocol analysis, flow analysis, and uniform resource location and domain name system analysis.

Packet and Protocol Analysis

Packet and protocol analysis, or analyzing packets and the protocols used on a network in search of malware, can provide valuable data for monitoring a network. This involves capturing packets, analyzing the packets, and analyzing the protocols used on the network.

Capturing Packets   Monitoring traffic to capture packets is often done through network switches and can generally be accomplished in one of two ways. One method is to install a separate port TAP (test access point). A port TAP transmits both the send and receive data streams simultaneously on separate dedicated channels so that all data arrives at the monitoring tool in real time. A port TAP, which is considered to be an out-of-band device (meaning it is not using the network itself as the media), is seen in Figure 7-3.

NOTE 5

A TAP device is completely passive: it has no power source and no IP or MAC address so that it cannot be attacked. Also, TAPs are "court approved" so that all data captured can be used as evidence in an investigation or trial.

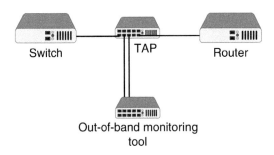

Figure 7-3   Port TAP

A network TAP is just one example of the types of devices that can be placed on a network to gather information. Typically, network sensors are used to monitor traffic (for network intrusion detection and prevention devices), collectors gather traffic (for network security appliances), and aggregators combine multiple network connections into a single link.

Another method takes advantage of a managed switch on an Ethernet network that supports port mirroring. Port mirroring is also called port spanning because it uses a Switched Port Analyzer (SPAN). Port mirroring allows the administrator to configure the switch to copy (mirror) traffic that occurs on some or all ports to a designated monitoring port on the switch. Port mirroring is illustrated in Figure 7-4, where the monitoring tool is connected to the mirror port and can view all network traffic moving through the switch.

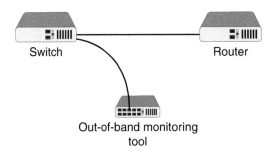

Figure 7-4   Port mirroring

NOTE 6

Port mirroring is designed for "spot checking" while a TAP is best for high-speed networks that have a large volume of traffic.

Packet Analysis   Once the packets are captured, analyzing the data packets can provide a wealth of valuable cybersecurity information. Packet analysis can detect unusual behavior (such as a high number of DNS responses) that could indicate the presence of malware, uncover unusual domains or IP address endpoints, and discover regular connections (beacons) to a threat actor's computer.

NOTE 7

Analyzing packets also provides excellent network information. Some of the common uses of packet analysis include troubleshooting network connectivity (determine packet loss, review TCP retransmission, and create graphs of high-latency packet responses), examining Application Layer sessions (captured packets can be used to view a full HTTP session for both requests and responses, view Telnet session commands and responses, and even read email traffic), and solving DHCP issues (examine DHCP client broadcasts, view DHCP offers with addresses and options, observe client requests for an address, and see the server's acknowledgment of the request).

Packet analysis typically examines the entire contents of the packet, which consists of both the header information and the payload. However, because all the information needed is rarely contained in a single packet, packet analysis involves the examination of multiple packets—often hundreds and even thousands of them—to "piece together" the information.

Several tools can be used for packet analysis. Wireshark is a popular GUI packet capture and analysis tool and is shown in Figure 7-5. EtherApe is an open source tool similar to Wireshark but is more focused on giving a virtual interpretation of the information, as shown in Figure 7-6. Tcpdump is a command-line packet analyzer. It displays TCP/IP packets and other packets being transmitted or received over a network and operates on UNIX and Linux operating systems; various forks are available for Windows computers. However, the output from tcpdump can be voluminous and difficult to parse. Tcpreplay is a tool for editing packets and then "replaying" the packets back onto the network to observe their behavior.

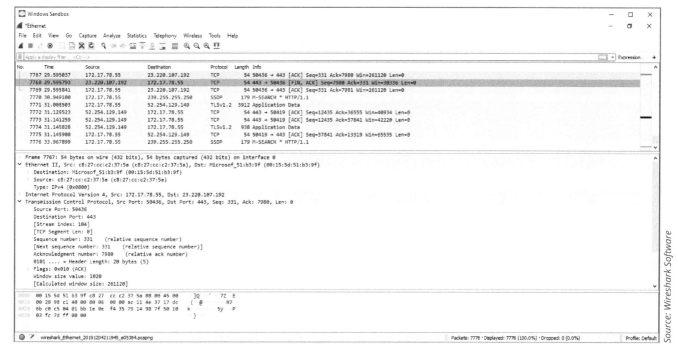

Figure 7-5   Wireshark packet capture and analysis tool

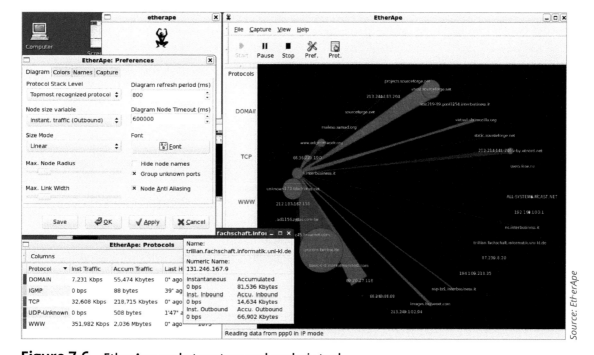

Figure 7-6   EtherApe packet capture and analysis tool

Another way to analyze packet captures is by saving the entire results of the packet capture session and then feeding them into a processing engine that will analyze the packets. That is, instead of a person viewing the packets in the

NOTE 8

Packet analysis tools are especially useful for filtering out normal network traffic to isolate unusual traffic.

NOTE 9

Some packet capture programs like Wireshark support two types of filters to support these two means of examining packet captures. A *display filter* limits what is shown to the user, while a *capture filter* limits what is saved via pcap for later processing.

NOTE 10

In a TCP/IP packet, the protocol is an 8-bit value that identifies the protocol being used. A packet analysis tool automatically decodes this value.

NOTE 11

Flow analysis is often used in identifying a ransomware attack. Flow analysis can detect when multiple filenames are being changed, which is a typical indicator of a ransomware attack, and an alert can be generated in real time.

Packet Bytes pane, a program analyzes the packets. Most packet capture programs support an export format known as *pcap* (packet *cap*ture). However, there are differences among pcap data based on the operating system being used.

Protocol Analysis Protocol analysis is used to verify which approved protocols are being used and to identify an unauthorized protocol used on the network, which may indicate that a successful attack has penetrated the network. Whereas packet analysis examines the entire contents of the packet, which consists of both the header information and the payload, protocol analysis is only concerned with the header information that contains the protocol information.

Flow Analysis

Although packet analysis is important, examining raw data packets is considered too slow to identify an attack. **Flow analysis** (also called *network traffic analysis*) is the evaluation of a collection of network data: instead of examining the individual performance of a device on the network by looking at raw data packets, network traffic analysis uses an aggregate or collection of data from the network's devices. One of the primary reasons that network traffic analysis is used in this way is because as the network itself becomes the connective link between local resources, virtual computing, and remote cloud servers, it also becomes the optimum means to view the security of the entire IT infrastructure as a whole.

Flow analysis has been performed for many years to troubleshoot network issues and identify performance bottlenecks by detecting which applications are "hogging" resources and bandwidth. The analysis usually looks at overall network usage and speed by generating statistics based on the flow of data through the network. However, flow analysis for cybersecurity is different from traditional network traffic flow for the following reasons:

- *Eliminates monitoring agents.* Threat actors often attempt to disable separate software monitoring agents installed on each network device. Some systems—such as database servers, application servers, DNS and DHCP servers, IoT devices, and embedded systems—cannot accept monitoring agents. However, by using network traffic analysis, network data can be collected passively and "quietly" so that threat actors cannot interfere with the data collection.
- *Uses deep packet inspection.* Unlike traditional network traffic analysis that only looks at the flow of data through the network, network traffic analysis for security extracts *metadata* (data about data) from the network packets and then converts it into a readable format using *deep packet inspection*. This can even facilitate decryption of application traffic and its contents so as to identify suspicious activities.
- *Provides richer information.* In addition to standard network analysis (such as identifying bottlenecks), deep packet inspection can indicate what devices are active on the network, what applications and protocols they are using, and what data they are accessing. Also, alerts can be set to advise security administrators of any unusual activity or network anomalies.

The output from a flow analysis network traffic analyst tool is shown in Figure 7-7.

Flow analysis data can be accumulated from different sources. NetFlow is a session sampling protocol feature on Cisco routers that collects IP network traffic as it enters or exits an interface and uses TCP/IP Internet Control Message Protocol (ICMP) Echo request packets. sFlow is a packet sampling protocol that gives a statistical sampling instead of the actual flow of packets. IPfix (IP Flow Information Export) is similar to NetFlow but adds capabilities such as integrating Simple Network Management Protocol (SNMP) information directly into the IPfix information so that all the information is available instead of needing to query the SNMP server separately.

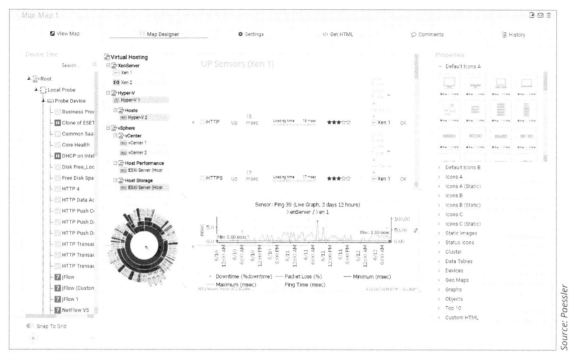

Figure 7-7   Network traffic analysis output

Source: Paessler

Uniform Resource Location and Domain Name System Analysis

It is important to filter requests to remote Internet sources to block users from accessing malicious websites and domains. Known as **Uniform Resource Location (URL) and Domain Name System (DNS) analysis**, networks must identify and block these requests. Repositories of blacklisted URLs and DNSs are available online, and firewalls are typically used for filtering requests to these malicious sites.

However, a growing challenge is blocking an infected endpoint from communicating back through the Internet to a site controlled by a threat actor to receive attack instructions. Infected endpoints receive instructions through a command and control (C&C) structure managed by attackers. This communication can occur in a variety of ways, including the following:

- An endpoint can receive its instructions by automatically signing in to a website that the threat actor operates and has placed information the endpoint knows how to interpret as commands.
- Endpoints can sign in to a third-party website; the advantage is that the attacker does not need to have a direct affiliation with that website.
- Commands can be sent via blogs, specially coded attack commands through posts on Twitter, or notes posted in Facebook.
- Threat actors are increasingly using a "dead drop" C&C mechanism by creating a Google Gmail account and then creating a draft email message that is never sent but contains commands the bot receives when it logs in to Gmail and reads the draft. Because the email message is never sent, there is no record of it. All Gmail transmissions are also protected so that outsiders cannot view them.

Threat actors have often "hard-coded" a static URL of the C&C into the malware itself. Yet once the URL is uncovered—often through reverse engineering the malware—it can be locally blocked to prevent any infected computers from communicating with the C&C. A global technique used to prevent C&C communication involves technology companies and law enforcement agencies petitioning a judge for permission to seize a known domain and then turn it into a sinkhole to stop all communication.

NOTE 12

Firewall filtering is covered in Module 5.

NOTE 13

Sinkholing is covered in Module 5.

Knowing that a static URL in malware could be uncovered and then used to stop all infected endpoints around the world from communicating with the C&C—and thus effectively ending the entire attack—threat actors have turned instead to adding code to malware to create dynamic URLs. This technique uses a domain generation algorithm (DGA) to create multiple random potential URLs. Although malware using DGA varies, the basic steps are illustrated in Figure 7-8 and include the following:

1. The threat actor embeds within the malware code a static value (such as a dictionary word or a predetermined string of numbers and letters), a link to a source that can generate a dynamic value (such as a trending Twitter hashtag, the insignificant digits of a foreign exchange rate, and/or the current weather temperature in a specific city), a pseudorandom string generator, and a list of top-level domains (TLDs).

2. At a predefined time, the DGA in the malware accesses the dynamic value and then uses it and the static value as input into the pseudorandom string generator to create a domain name. It also selects a TLD to create a random domain.

3. The threat actor, knowing the DGA and all the values, can generate a list of domains just like the malware can. The threat actor chooses one domain and registers it to serve as a link to the C&C. This registration occurs a short time (sometimes as little as one hour) before the malware generates its random domains.

4. The malware attempts to connect to the first domain generated. None of these domains can be resolved through DNS queries by the malware except for the one domain that the threat actor has previously registered. If the attempt succeeds, the malware has reached the C&C. If an attempt fails, the malware generates the next potential domain and attempts to reach it. This process continues until the malware is successful.

5. The malware receives its instructions from the C&C that apply for a specific period of time, such as 24 hours. Once that time is over, the process starts again for the malware to generate new potential domains to receive its next instructions for the next period of time.

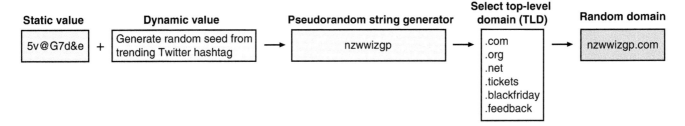

Figure 7-8   Generating domains using DGA

NOTE 14

Early uses of DGA generated as few as 250 domain names daily. More recent malware generates up to 50,000 domain names each day.

A listing of actual domains generated through a DGA is seen in Figure 7-9. This list contains the domain, the start time that the domain is valid, and the end time at which the domain is no longer available. Defending against DGA is very difficult due to the random generation of domain names.

kwciif.com	2021-01-10 00:00:00	2021-01-10 23:59:59
iinhherje.org	2021-01-10 00:00:00	2021-01-10 23:59:59
qytmidub.net	2021-01-10 00:00:00	2021-01-10 23:59:59
futswe.info	2021-01-10 00:00:00	2021-01-10 23:59:59
nzwwizgp.com	2021-01-10 00:00:00	2021-01-10 23:59:59
urmelbeg.com	2021-01-10 00:00:00	2021-01-10 23:59:59
jvpvtqv.biz	2021-01-10 00:00:00	2021-01-10 23:59:59
aarxlnz.biz	2021-01-10 00:00:00	2021-01-10 23:59:59
pjwmfqv.biz	2021-01-10 00:00:00	2021-01-10 23:59:59
hsvajyw.info	2021-01-10 00:00:00	2021-01-10 23:59:59
ksooubrnff.com	2021-01-10 00:00:00	2021-01-10 23:59:59

Figure 7-9   Domains generated using DGA

Email Analysis

A sometimes-overlooked system that requires monitoring is the email system. Monitoring email requires knowing the basics of how email works, the threats associated with email, and email defenses.

How Email Works

The basic components involved in sending and receiving email are the Mail User Agent (MUA) and Mail Transfer Agent (MTA). A MUA is what is used to read and send mail from an endpoint; this could be an app (like Thunderbird) or a webmail interface (like Gmail or Outlook). MTAs are programs that accept email messages from senders and route them toward their recipients.

Originally, email was sent to a mail server using the Simple Mail Transfer Protocol (SMTP). When it arrived at its destination, it was downloaded from the server using the Post Office Protocol (POP3). It was necessary for MUAs to use both SMTP and POP3 so that they could send user messages to the user's mail server (using SMTP) and could download messages intended for the user from the user's mail server (using POP3).

When Internet Access Message Protocol (IMAP) was introduced, it essentially replaced POP3. IMAP allows users to leave email on the mail server so that an email could be read from multiple endpoints. (For example, an email could be read on a smartphone when it was first received and then later referenced on a laptop.) IMAP also allowed messages to be organized into folders that could again be accessed consistently from any endpoint. Recently, webmail has become more popular and widespread. Users can use a website as their MUA (such as Gmail) and no longer need to configure endpoints with SMTP or IMAP server settings.

As email is transferred from MTA to MTA, information is added to the **email header**. The email header contains information about the sender, recipient, email's route through MTAs, and various authentication details. Each MTA along the path adds its own information to the top of the email header. This means that when reading an email header, the final destination MTA information will be at the top of the header, and reading down through each subsequent MTA will ultimately end at the sender MTA header information. Figure 7-10 shows a partial email header.

NOTE 15

DGA has been called "one of the most important 'innovations' in malware in the past decade."[3]

NOTE 16

Using email for political purposes helped introduce email to the general public. Former President Carter used a basic email system, which charged $4 per message, to coordinate strategies and send speeches during his 1976 presidential campaign.

```
Received: from BYAPR15MB3462.namprd15.prod.outlook.com (2603:10b6:a03:112::10)
by BN7PR15MB4081.namprd15.prod.outlook.com with HTTPS; Fri, 11 Dec 2020
12:42:27 +0000
Received: from BN6PR13CA0038.namprd13.prod.outlook.com (2603:10b6:404:13e::24)
by BYAPR15MB3462.namprd15.prod.outlook.com (2603:10b6:a03:112::10) with
Microsoft SMTP Server (version=TLS1_2,
cipher=TLS_ECDHE_RSA_WITH_AES_256_GCM_SHA384) id 15.20.3632.18; Fri, 11 Dec
2020 12:42:26 +0000
Received: from BN7NAM10FT025.eop-nam10.prod.protection.outlook.com
(2603:10b6:404:13e:cafe::a9) by BN6PR13CA0038.outlook.office365.com
(2603:10b6:404:13e::24) with Microsoft SMTP Server (version=TLS1_2,
cipher=TLS_ECDHE_RSA_WITH_AES_256_GCM_SHA384) id 15.20.3654.9 via Frontend
Transport; Fri, 11 Dec 2020 12:42:25 +0000
Authentication-Results: spf=softfail (sender IP is 161.6.94.39)
smtp.mailfrom=potomac1050.mktomail.com;
topperwkuedu94069.mail.onmicrosoft.com; dkim=fail (body hash did not verify)
header.d=raritan.com;topperwkuedu94069.mail.onmicrosoft.com; dmarc=none
action=none header.from=raritan.com;
Received-SPF: SoftFail (protection.outlook.com: domain of transitioning
potomac1050.mktomail.com discourages use of 161.6.94.39 as permitted sender)
Received: from email.wku.edu (161.6.94.39) by
BN7NAM10FT025.mail.protection.outlook.com (10.13.156.100) with Microsoft SMTP
Server (version=TLS1_2, cipher=TLS_ECDHE_RSA_WITH_AES_256_CBC_SHA384) id
15.20.3654.12 via Frontend Transport; Fri, 11 Dec 2020 12:42:25 +0000
Received: from e16-12.ad.wku.edu (161.6 94 62) by o16 05.ad.wku.edu
(101.6.94.39) with Microsoft SMTP Server (version=TLS1_2,
cipher=TLS_ECDHE_RSA_WITH_AES_256_CBC_SHA384_P256) id 15.1.1979.3; Fri, 11
```

— Sender policy framework (SPF) warning

— Domain keys identified mail (DKIM) rejection

— Domain-based message aunthetication, Reporting and conference (DMARC) not used

Figure 7-10   **Email header**

Email headers also contain an analysis of the email by the MTA. Table 7-1 shows the analysis categories and abbreviations used by Microsoft Office 365.

Table 7-1   Microsoft Office 365 email analysis

Abbreviation	Category
BULK	Bulk
DIMP	Domain impersonation
GIMP	Mailbox intelligence based impersonation
HPHISH	High confidence phishing
HSPM	High confidence spam
MALW	Malware
PHSH	Phishing
SPM	Spam
SPOOF	Spoofing
UIMP	User impersonation
AMP	Antimalware
SAP	Safe attachments
OSPM	Outbound spam

Email Threats

A variety of threats are related to email. These include the following:

- *Phishing.* One of the most common forms of social engineering is phishing. Phishing is sending an email or displaying a web announcement that falsely claims to be from a legitimate enterprise in an attempt to trick the user into surrendering private information or taking action. Phishing emails often contain valid logos and a realistic-looking signature block (an ending electronic "signature" containing the sender's name and contact information). Users are asked to respond to an email or are directed to a website where they are requested to update personal information, such as passwords, credit card numbers, Social Security numbers, bank account numbers, or other information. However, the email or website is actually an imposter and is set up to steal the information the user enters.

NOTE 17

The word *phishing* is a variation on the word "fishing," reflecting the idea that bait is thrown out knowing that while most will ignore it, some will "bite."

- *Malicious payload.* Often the email message itself contains an attack (malicious payload). This could include an attachment that, when opened, will launch an attack. Or users may receive a fictious overdue invoice that demands immediate payment and, in haste, make the payment (called an invoice scam).
- *Embedded links.* Links that are contained within email messages (embedded links) are particularly dangerous. Because email messages are typically formatted in HTML, the displayed link (*your-bank.com*) can be different from the underlying hyperlink (*steal-your-money.net*).
- *Impersonation.* A threat actor who gains access to the email account of a corporate executive could pretend to be that person (impersonation) and send malicious emails that contain embedded links to sites belonging to the attacker. An impersonation email could have a malicious attachment and include a subject line such as *This attachment requires your immediate attention!* to trick the user into opening the attachment.
- *Forwarding.* Several dangers are associated with forwarding emails to another account. While some users want to "auto-forward" (automatically forward) all corporate emails to their personal user accounts for different reasons (such as enhanced spam filter or ease of access), doing so involves many risks. For example, sensitive email messages could be distributed outside the corporate email environment, making it easier

for unauthorized individuals to read the messages. Also, if an email message forwarded from a corporate account is flagged as "spam" by a user's personal email account, it could damage the corporate email's "reputation score," which is used by email providers and spam filters. If legal action is initiated and all email evidence must be surrendered (eDiscovery), critical emails that may have been erased from a personal email account may not have backups available as with a corporate email system.

Email Defenses

Different defenses can be used to address email threats. Spam and phishing filters can help combat phishing attacks while strong endpoint antimalware can minimize malicious payloads. However, other email threats can only be addressed through improving user behavior, such as not clicking embedded links and not forwarding email to personal accounts. Some email threats—such as impersonation based on a compromised account—have virtually no defenses.

There are also technology defenses used to address weaknesses inherent in the email system. For example, the original SMTP protocol had no provisions for security: all MTAs were expected to accept all messages from all senders and send the message along to another MTA. Although modern email typically is encrypted from MTA to MTA as data in-transmit using Transmit Layer Protocol (TLS), the encryption only protects email as it is being relayed from one MTA to another MTA along the delivery path; it does not address protection at the MTAs. If an email travels from the sender through three MTAs before reaching its recipient, any MTA along the way can alter the content of the message or change the header information.

Several email defenses can be used to protect email. These include Sender Policy Framework (SPF), Domain Keys Identified Mail (DKIM), and Domain-based Message Authentication, Reporting, and Conformance (DMARC).

Sender Policy Framework (SPF)   It is important to protect against forged emails that pretend to come from one domain but actually come from another domain. Threat actors who can forge a domain can send fake messages that appear to come from an organization (called "spoofing"), and a recipient who trusts the domain would likewise trust the email. Spoofed messages can be used for malicious purposes to communicate false information, distribute malware, and trick users into giving out sensitive information. In addition, valid email messages must not be erroneously marked as spam, thus preventing their delivery to the recipient MTA.

Sender Policy Framework (SPF) is an email authentication method that identifies the MTA email servers that have been authorized to send email for a domain. SPF helps to protect a domain from spoofing and to prevent messages from a valid domain from being marked as unwanted spam. If a domain does not use SPF, the receiving MTA email servers cannot verify that messages appearing to be from a domain actually are from that domain. This could result in the receiving MTA servers forwarding valid emails into the recipients' spam folders or even rejecting valid messages.

The administrative owner of a domain can set a TXT record in its DNS that states which servers are allowed to send mail on behalf of that domain. For example, in Figure 7-11, the Cengage.com SPF record indicates that email from cengage.com should come only from the servers specified, namely *Microsoft Outlook* and *PPHosted. com*. Those coming from a different domain are met with a "SoftFail" warning that says to trust this message less than normal but do not completely invalidate it based on this alone.

However, SPF headers in an email message are not infallible. Once generated, there is no means of protecting the information. This makes SPF useful to the MTA servers themselves while transmitting the email, but the protection does not extend beyond that. However, SPF is still an excellent tool for quickly identifying and intercepting spam.

Domain Keys Identified Mail (DKIM)   Domain Keys Identified Mail (DKIM) is an authentication technique that validates the content of the email message itself. This validation is accomplished through a digital signature. The

NOTE 18

An analysis report by the U.S. Cybersecurity & Infrastructure Security Agency (CISA) titled "Strengthening Security Configurations to Defend Against Attackers Targeting Cloud Services" specifically mentions that threat actors are collecting sensitive information by taking advantage of email forwarding rules that users set up to forward work emails to their personal accounts. In one case, CISA determined that threat actors accessed a user-specified email rule on the user's account to forward emails sent from a certain sender to a personal account. The threat actors modified the rule to redirect all emails to an account that they controlled.

NOTE 19

The email header in Figure 7-10 indicates a SoftFail warning (*spf=softfail*).

Figure 7-11   Cengage SPF record

Source: MXToolbox

NOTE 20

The email header in Figure 7-10 indicates a DKIM rejection: *dkim=fail (body hash did not verify).*

administrative owner of the sending domain can generate an asymmetric public/private key pair and store the public key in a TXT record on the domain's DNS. Mail servers on the outer boundary of the domain's infrastructure then use the private DKIM key to generate a digital signature (which is an encrypted digest created with a hash algorithm) of the entire message body, including all headers accumulated by the different MTAs. Recipients can decrypt the DKIM signature using the public DKIM key retrieved from the DNS to ensure that the digests match.

Grow with Cengage Unlimited!

If you'd like more information about this topic, use your Cengage Unlimited subscription to go to the *CompTIA Security+ Guide to Network Security Fundamentals*, 7th edition, open Module 6, and read the section titled "Cryptographic Algorithms." If you don't have a Cengage Unlimited subscription, you can find more information at *cengage.com/unlimited*.

Domain-based Message Authentication, Reporting, and Conformance (DMARC)   Domain-based Message Authentication, Reporting, and Conformance (DMARC) extends SPF and DKIM. DMARC allows the administrative owners of a domain to publish a policy in their DNS records to specify which mechanism (DKIM, SPF, or both) is used when sending email from that domain. It also indicates how to check the *From:* field that is presented to users and a reporting mechanism for actions performed under those policies.

NOTE 21

The email header in Figure 7-10 indicates DMARC is not being used (*dmarc=none*).

TWO RIGHTS & A WRONG

1. UEBA includes networks, devices, applications, and users.
2. Flow analysis (also called network traffic analysis) is the evaluation of a collection of network data: instead of examining the individual performance of a device on the network by looking at raw data packets, network traffic analysis uses an aggregate or collection of data from the network's different devices.
3. DKIM is an email authentication method that identifies who the MTA email servers are that have been authorized to send email for a domain.

See Appendix C for the answer.

DATA ANALYTICS

☑ **CERTIFICATION**

3.1 Given a scenario, analyze data as part of security monitoring activities.

Figure 7-12 shows a typical log file of events from a single web server. Consider how difficult it would be for a person to scan this file looking for evidence of some type of specific activity. Then multiply this file from a single web server by *all* log files from web servers, email servers, firewalls, routers, and the other devices connected to the network that generate log files—and the overwhelming task of looking for evidence of an attack becomes clear.

Source: Notepad++

Figure 7-12   Typical log file

Because of the sheer volume of data accumulated in multiple log files, it would be virtually impossible for a person to identify an attack as it occurs. Instead, automated tools are used to look for patterns in the data that can indicate a security incident. This is known as data analytics. Data analytics seeks to find a relationship (called a data correlation) between different events.

Types of Analysis

Several techniques can be used to uncover a relationship. These include conditional analysis, signature analysis, anomaly analysis, behavioral analysis, availability analysis, trend analysis, heuristic analysis, and impact analysis.

Conditional Analysis

NOTE 22

Single condition analysis is also called "binary" analysis because it is a simple Yes or No proposition. The goal is simply to determine if an event did or did not occur.

Conditional analysis seeks to uncover one or more events that violate predefined rules. (These rules make up a *ruleset*.) The most basic analysis is called *single conditional analysis*, which tries to determine if a specific event (*Event X*) has occurred; if it has, then a response takes place. If this data correlation were indicated as a formula, it would then be *If X Then Respond*.

Although single conditional analysis can be useful, in reality it is very limited because more than one event is almost always needed by a threat actor to perform a nefarious action. This means not only that *multiple* events should be analyzed, but the *sequence* of those multiple events must likewise be considered. Both the connection and association between a specific sequence of events are considered important. Thus, data analytics seeks to find data correlations within many event sequences.

The answer is to use *multi-conditional analysis*, which looks at multiple conditions in a specific sequence. This analysis looks for a sequence of events (*X, Y, Z*) that, when coupled together in a specific sequence, violates one or more predefined rules in the ruleset. If this data correlation were indicated as a formula, it would be *If X and Y Then Respond* or *If X and (Y or Z) Then Respond*. Table 7-2 illustrates a multi-conditional analysis.

Table 7-2 Multi-conditional analysis

Event X	Event Y	Event Z	Explanation
Five failed login attempts using different usernames are attempted within 15 minutes from the same IP address.	A successful login was accomplished from the IP address within 30 minutes.		A threat actor who has stolen a valid password could be attempting to break into a system by guessing the corresponding username.
Outside connection is using UDP packets.	Packets have Port 67 as destination.	The destination IP address is not on the registered IP address list.	A threat actor may be attempting to establish a DHCP server to acquire access to the network.

However, conditional analysis—either single conditional or multi-conditional—is not considered robust or flexible enough to detect the wide variety of attacks that can occur. It also generates a high number of *false positives*, or warnings that do not indicate an attack.

Signature Analysis

For many years, a common method used for data correlation examined network traffic, activity, transactions, or behavior to look for well-known patterns of attack *signatures*. This method is known as *signature analysis* because it compares activities against a predefined signature. Signature-based monitoring requires access to an updated database of signatures along with a means of actively comparing and matching current behavior against a collection of signatures.

One of the weaknesses of signature analysis is that the signature databases must be constantly updated, and as the number of signatures grows, the behaviors must be compared against an increasingly large number of signatures. Also, if the signature definitions are too specific, signature-based monitoring can miss variations; if they are not specific enough, they may generate an abundance of false positives. Finally, signature analysis is useless to detect previously unknown attacks (*zero-day attacks*).

Anomaly Analysis

Anomaly analysis is designed for detecting statistical anomalies. First, a baseline of normal activities is compiled over time. (A *baseline* is a reference set of data against which operational data is compared.) Whenever there is a significant deviation from this baseline, an alarm is raised. An advantage of this approach is that it can detect anomalies quickly without first trying to understand the underlying cause.

However, normal behavior can change easily and even quickly, so anomaly-based monitoring is subject to a high number of false positives. In addition, anomaly-based monitoring can impose heavy processing loads on a system. Finally, because anomaly-based monitoring takes time to create statistical baselines, it can fail to detect events before the baseline is completed.

NOTE 23

The weakness of signature analysis can be seen in antivirus scanning products, which follow the same approach of having a database of known virus signatures for comparison. Based on the number of viruses unleashed, it is estimated that a virus signature database would have to be updated *every three seconds* to provide a current level of protection.

Behavioral Analysis

Behavioral analysis attempts to overcome the limitations of both anomaly analysis and signature-based monitoring by being adaptive and proactive instead of reactive. Rather than using statistics or signatures as the standard for making comparisons, behavior-based monitoring uses "normal" processes and actions as its standard. Behavior-based monitoring continuously analyzes the behavior of processes and programs on a system and alerts the user if it detects any abnormal actions, at which point the user can decide whether to allow or block the activity.

One advantage of behavior-based monitoring is that it is not necessary to update signature files or compile a baseline of statistical behavior before monitoring can take place. In addition, behavior-based monitoring can stop new attacks more quickly than other types of analysis.

Availability Analysis

Availability analysis examines whether a network device is properly functioning to provide resources to users. For example, an application server that is rejecting user login attempts would indicate an issue that needs attention.

Trend Analysis

As its name implies, trend analysis looks for a change or development over time to uncover a pattern. Trend analysis often looks at a change in the *frequency* of events, such as how often failed logins have occurred, which may indicate a threat actor is attempting to use a stolen password. Trend analysis can detect a sudden increase in the number of connection attempts to a publicly available service, which may signal a denial-of-service (DoS) attack. Trend analysis also looks at a change in the *volume* of events. A dramatic spike in the number of collected events in a log file can often be the first indication of an attack taking place.

 **CAUTION**   To circumvent trend analysis, threat agents may attempt to spread out a multipronged attack over time so that the second event takes place several hours or days after the first event. This approach helps make the attack less visible to trend analysis.

Heuristic Analysis

Another method takes a completely different approach and does not try to compare actions against previous behavior or trends, or against previously determined standards, such as with anomaly analysis and signature-based monitoring. Instead, the method is founded on *experience-based techniques*. Known as heuristic analysis (or just *heuristics*), it attempts to answer the question, *Will this do something harmful if it is allowed to execute?* Heuristic (from the Greek word for *find* or *discover*) monitoring uses an algorithm to determine if a vulnerability exists. Table 7-3 illustrates how heuristic analysis could trap a new port-scanning application that other methods might not catch.

Table 7-3   Analysis comparisons to trap port-scanning application

Analysis methodology	Will it trap the port-scanning application?	Comments
Multi-conditional	Unlikely	Port scanning usually does not involve looking for more than one condition.
Signature	No	The application is new, and no signature of scanning by the port-scanning application has been created.
Anomaly	No	Because the application is new, a baseline has not yet been established.
Behavioral	Depends	Behavioral scanning could trap the application but only if the action by the application is different from other applications.
Availability	No	Scanning would not prevent a network device from properly functioning.
Trend	Possibly	The volume of scan events could trigger a response.
Heuristic	Yes	A response is triggered if any application tries to scan multiple ports.

Impact Analysis

A final type of analysis is impact analysis. This type of analysis seeks to determine the implications of an event. Specifically, it tries to ascertain the timing of the event (is it immediate or gradual?) and its scope (is it a localized impact that only affects a limited number of users, or does it have an organization impact that will affect the entire corporation?).

Data Analysis

Data gathered from a variety of sources is critical in defending against today's attacks. It is important to collate, analyze, and review this data. This data analysis covers security information and event management tools and log files.

Security Information and Event Management (SIEM)

Virtually all types of network and cybersecurity appliances—such as resource monitors, NIDSs firewalls, and routers—generate continual security alerts because an enterprise is the target of daily attacks. How can these continual alerts, all from different sources and generated at different points of time, be monitored and managed while searching for correlations?

One answer is a Security Information and Event Management (SIEM) product (usually pronounced *seem* instead of *sim*). A SIEM consolidates real-time monitoring and management of security information with analysis and reporting of security events. A SIEM product can be a separate device, software that runs on a computer, or even a service provided by a third party. A SIEM dashboard is shown in Figure 7-13.

The starting point of a SIEM is the data inputs. Data feeds into a SIEM are the standard packet captures of network activity and log collections. Because of the numerous network devices producing logs, SIEMs also perform log aggregation.

A SIEM typically has the following features:

- *Aggregation. SIEM aggregation* combines data from multiple sources—such as network security devices, servers, and software applications—to build a comprehensive picture of attacks.
- *Correlation.* The *SIEM correlation* feature searches the data acquired through SIEM aggregation to look for common characteristics, such as multiple attacks coming from a specific source.
- *Automated alerting and triggers. SIEM automated alerting and triggers* can inform security personnel of critical issues that need immediate attention. A sample trigger may be *Alert when a firewall, router, or switch indicates 40 or more drop/reject packet events from the same IP source address occurring within 60 seconds.*

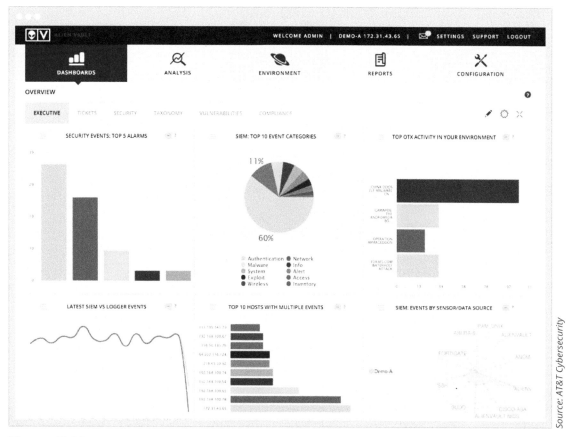

Figure 7-13   SIEM dashboard

- *Time synchronization.* Because alerts occur over a wide spectrum of time, *SIEM time synchronization* can show the order of the events.
- *Event duplication.* When the same event occurs that is detected by multiple devices, each device will generate an alert. The *SIEM event duplication* feature can help filter the multiple alerts into a single alarm.
- *Logs. SIEM logs* or records of events can be retained for future analysis and to show that the enterprise has complied with regulations.

SIEMs can even perform sentiment analysis. Sentiment analysis is the process of computationally identifying and categorizing opinions, usually expressed in response to textual data, to determine the writer's attitude toward a particular topic. In other words, sentiment analysis interprets and classifies emotions (positive, negative, and neutral) within text data using text analysis techniques. Sentiment analysis has been used when tracking postings threat actors make in discussion forums with other attackers to better determine the behavior and mindset of threat actors. This type of information can be valuable in determining their goals and actions and has even been used as a predictive power to alert against future attacks.

SIEMs are often paired today with *Unified Threat Management/Next-Generation Firewall (UTM/NGFW)* devices. Together, these devices can perform a wide range of operations, such as handling log correlations, offering intrusion prevention, performing web content filtering, and accepting threat feed inputs from third-party devices.

NOTE 24

A SIEM can also perform user behavior analysis.

NOTE 25

Sentiment analysis is often used by businesses while conducting online chats with customers or examining Twitter and social media posts to identify customer sentiment toward products, brands, or services.

NOTE 26

One of the latest features in UTM/NGFW and SIEM devices is a built-in template to support and record specific regulatory compliance. In addition, the actions that these devices perform are now often available as a cloud service, so the devices do not have to be installed on the corporate network.

Logs

Although SIEMs are frequently used to consolidate security information, log files generated from different sources can also be reviewed for specific data from that device. There are basic standards for recording logs, and different tools can be used for searching logs.

NOTE 27

Firewalls, intrusion detection systems, and intrusion prevention systems are covered in Module 3.

Log-Generating Devices Although almost any device can—and does—produce a log file, the devices that produce logs most important to cybersecurity include firewalls, intrusion detection systems, and intrusion prevention systems. Other valuable logs come from specialized firewall appliances and proxy servers.

Specialized Firewall Appliances Several specialized firewall appliances can generate valuable logs. These include the following:

- *Web application firewall.* One specialized firewall is a web application firewall (WAF), which looks at the applications using HTTP. A web application firewall, which can be a separate hardware appliance or a software plug-in, can block specific websites or attacks that attempt to exploit known vulnerabilities in specific client software and can even block cross-site scripting and SQL injection attacks.
- *Network address translation gateway.* Network address translation (NAT) is a technique that allows private IP addresses to be used on the public Internet. It does this by replacing a private IP address with a public IP address: as a packet leaves a network, NAT removes the private IP address from the sender's packet and replaces it with an alias IP public address, and then maintains a record of the substitution; when a packet is returned, the process is reversed. A *network address translation gateway* is a cloud-based technology that performs NAT translations for cloud services. It can also provide a degree of security: it can mask the IP addresses of internal devices.
- *Next-generation firewall.* A *next-generation firewall (NGFW)* has additional functionality beyond a traditional firewall. NGFWs can filter packets based on applications. NGFWs gain visibility of applications by using *deep packet inspection* and thus can examine the payloads of packets and determine if they are carrying malware. In addition to basic firewall protections, filtering by applications, and deep packet inspection, NGFWs can also perform URL filtering and intrusion prevention services.
- *Unified threat management.* Unified threat management (UTM) is a device that combines several security functions. These include packet filtering, antispam, antiphishing, antispyware, encryption, intrusion protection, and web filtering.

NOTE 28

Often a device that performs services beyond that of a NGFW is called a UTM.

Proxy Servers In the human world, a *proxy* is a person authorized to act as the substitute or agent on behalf of another person. For example, an individual who has been granted the power of attorney for a sick relative can make decisions and take actions on behalf of that person as her proxy.

Proxies are also used in computer networking. One device (proxy) acts as a substitute on behalf of the primary device. A *forward proxy* is a computer or an application program that intercepts user requests from the internal secure network and then processes that request on behalf of the user. When an internal endpoint requests a service such as a file or a webpage from an external web server, it normally would connect directly with that remote server. In a network using a forward proxy server, the endpoint first connects to the proxy server, which checks its memory to see if a previous request has already been fulfilled and whether a copy of that file or page is residing on the proxy server in its temporary storage area (*cache*). If it is not, the proxy server connects to the external web server using its own IP address (instead of the internal endpoint's address) and requests the service. When the proxy server receives the requested item from the web server, the item is then forwarded to the requester.

A *reverse proxy* routes requests coming from an external network to the correct internal server. To the outside user, the IP address of the reverse proxy is the final IP address for requesting services; however, only the reverse proxy can access the internal servers.

Acting as the intermediary, a proxy server can provide a degree of protection. First, it can look for malware by intercepting it before it reaches the internal endpoint. Second, a proxy server can hide the IP address of endpoints inside the secure network so that only the proxy server's IP address is used on the open Internet.

Standard Log Formats   Various log standards are used when recording log data. Microsoft provides a standard and centralized mechanism for both the OS and applications to record important software and hardware events. The Windows event logging service records events from various sources and stores them in a single collection called an event log.

NOTE 29

The Microsoft Event Viewer enables users to view logs. There is also a programming interface through which log data can be examined.

System Logging Protocol (Syslog) is a means by which network devices can use a standard message format to communicate with a logging server. It was designed to make it easy to monitor logs produced by network devices. Devices can use a Syslog agent to send notification messages under a wide range of specific conditions. Syslog works on all flavors of Unix and Linux, as well as macOS. Although Windows-based servers do not support Syslog natively, many third-party tools are available to allow Windows devices to communicate with a Syslog server.

Query Writing   Consider a common firewall log that displays the connections permitted or denied through the firewall. Although some of the information in a firewall log may be found in all types of firewall logs, there is no standard; vendors include their own choices of information. Figure 7-14 shows a Microsoft Windows firewall log. The #Fields: line is a key of the fields being displayed; a dash (-) is shown when there is no entry for a field. Selected fields are listed in Figure 7-14; these fields are explained in Table 7-4.

Table 7-4   Microsoft Windows firewall log fields

Field name	Explanation	Field contents
date	The date of the connection request	The date is in the format *YYYY-MM-DD*
time	The local time of the connection request	The time is in the format *HH:MM:SS*; all times are in 24-hour format
action	The action of the firewall as it processed the request	Possible actions are DROP (refuse the connection), OPEN (allow the connection), CLOSE (terminate the connection), OPEN-INBOUND (inbound session opened to the local computer), or INFO-EVENTS-LOST (processed by the firewall but not recorded in the log)
protocol	The protocol used	TCP, UDP, or ICMP
src-ip	The source IP address	The IP address of the computer attempting to establish communication
dst-ip	The destination IP address	The IP address of the computer to which a connection is attempted
src-port	The source port number	The port number on the sending computer from which the connection was attempted
dst-port	The destination port number	The port on the receiving computer to which the sending computer was trying to make a connection
size	The size of the packet	The packet size in bytes
tcpflags	TCP control flags	Information about TCP control flags in the TCP headers
tcpsyn	The TCP sequence number	The TCP sequence number in the packet
tcpack	The TCP acknowledgment number	The TCP acknowledgment number in the packet
tcpwin	The TCP window size	The TCP window size in bytes
icmptype	The ICMP type	Information about the ICMP message type
icmpcode	The ICMP code	Information about the ICMP code type
info	The information on the action	An entry that depends on the type of action that occurred
path	The direction of the communication	SEND, RECEIVE, FORWARD, or UNKNOWN

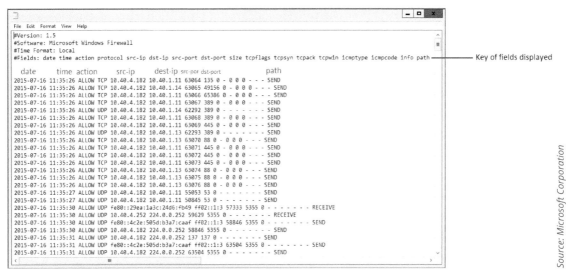

Figure 7-14 Microsoft Windows firewall log

Clearly, the volume of detail in logs can easily become overwhelming. While log analysis tools can "comb through" log files, other tools can be used for manually searching a log (called **query writing**). Query writing often involves generating a short "snippet" of code that can be run against the log file (a **script**) to produce output. Tools include those for looking for a specific item (**string search**) and redirecting the output from one command to function as the input to another command (**piping**).

TWO RIGHTS & A WRONG

1. Conditional analysis seeks to uncover one or more events that violate predefined rules.
2. Trend analysis seeks to answer the question, *Will this do something harmful if it is allowed to execute?*
3. A SIEM consolidates real-time monitoring and management of security information with analysis and reporting of security events.

See Appendix C for the answer.

⤢ VM LAB You're now ready to complete the live, virtual machine labs for this module. The labs can be found in the Apply It folder in each MindTap module.

MODULE SUMMARY

- Network-connected hardware devices are typically referred to as endpoints. This reflects the fact that devices connected to a network today are far more than a computing device with a keyboard and monitor. Instead, devices ranging from mobile smartphones and tablets to wearable fitness trackers, industrial control system sensors, automotive telematics units, and even personal drones are all network-connected hardware devices. There are likewise increased cybersecurity risks with these new devices.
- Endpoint monitoring can be performed by monitoring hardware for evidence of a compromise. An Endpoint Protection Platform (EPP) includes basic tools such as traditional antimalware scanning software. Endpoint Detection and Response (EDR) includes more advanced capabilities for detecting and investigating security incidents, along with the ability to intervene and even remediate endpoints back to a preinfection state. Another means of endpoint monitoring can be achieved through behavior-based monitoring, which uses

"normal" processes and actions as its standard (known-good behavior) instead of searching for abnormalities (anomalous behavior).

- Just as endpoints must be monitored, so too must networks. Packet and protocol analysis can provide valuable data for monitoring a network. Once the packets are captured, analyzing the data packets can provide a wealth of valuable cybersecurity information. Several tools can be used for packet analysis. Protocol analysis is used to verify which approved protocols are being used and to identify an unauthorized protocol used on the network, which may indicate that a successful attack has penetrated the network. Whereas packet analysis examines the entire contents of the packet, which consists of both the header information and the payload, protocol analysis is only concerned with the header information that contains the protocol information. Flow analysis (also called network traffic analysis) is the evaluation of a collection of network data: instead of examining the individual performance of a device on the network by looking at raw data packets, network traffic analysis uses an aggregate or collection of data from the network's devices.

- It is important to filter requests to remote Internet sources to block users from accessing malicious websites and domains. Known as Uniform Resource Location (URL) and Domain Name System (DNS) analysis, networks must identify and block these requests. A growing challenge is blocking an infected endpoint from communicating back through the Internet to a site controlled by a threat actor to receive attack instructions. Threat actors have turned to adding code to malware to create dynamic URLs. This technique uses a domain generation algorithm (DGA) to create multiple random potential URLs.

- A sometimes-overlooked system that requires monitoring is the email system. The basic components involved in sending and receiving email are the Mail User Agent (MUA) and Mail Transfer Agent (MTA). A MUA is what is used to read and send mail from an endpoint and could be an app or a webmail interface. MTAs are programs that accept email messages from senders and route them toward their recipients. As email is transferred from MTA to MTA, information is added to the email header. The email header contains information about the sender, recipient, email's route through MTAs, and various authentication details. A variety of threats are related to email. Different email defenses can be used to protect email. These include Sender Policy Framework (SPF), Domain Keys Identified Mail (DKIM), and Domain-based Message Authentication, Reporting, and Conformance (DMARC).

- Due to the volume of data accumulated in multiple log files, it would be almost impossible for a human to identify an attack as it occurs. Instead, automated tools are used to look for patterns in the data that can indicate a security incident. This data analysis is known as data analytics and seeks to find a data correlation relationship between different events. Several data correlation techniques can be used. Conditional analysis seeks to uncover one or more events that violate predefined rules. Single conditional analysis looks to determine if one specific event has occurred and, if so, generates a response. Multi-conditional analysis looks at more than one condition in a specific sequence. Signature analysis compares activities against a predefined known pattern or signature.

- Anomaly analysis detects statistical anomalies. After a baseline of normal activities is compiled over time, when there is a significant deviation from this baseline, an alarm is raised. Behavior-based monitoring uses the "normal" processes and actions as the standard by continuously analyzing the behavior of processes and programs on a system and generating alerts if it detects any abnormal actions. Availability analysis examines if a network device is properly functioning to provide resources to users. Trend analysis looks for a change or development over time to uncover a pattern. It looks at a change in the frequency of events or a change in the volume of events. Heuristic analysis attempts to answer the question, *Will this do something harmful if it can execute?* Heuristic analysis uses an algorithm to determine if a threat exists. Impact analysis seeks to determine the implications of an event.

- A Security and Information Event Management (SIEM) product consolidates real-time monitoring and management of security information with analysis and reporting of security events. Although SIEMs are frequently used to consolidate security information, log files generated from different sources can also be reviewed for specific data from that device. Although almost any device can produce a log file, the devices that produce logs most important to cybersecurity include firewalls, intrusion detection systems, and intrusion prevention systems. Other valuable logs come from specialized firewall appliances and proxy servers. Various log standards are used when recording log data. Various tools can also be used for manually searching a log, which is called query writing.

Key Terms

anomalous behavior	gradual	script
digital signature	heuristic analysis	Security Information and Event
domain generation algorithm	immediate	Management (SIEM)
(DGA)	impact analysis	Sender Policy Framework (SPF)
Domain Keys Identified Mail (DKIM)	impersonation	signature block
Domain-based Message	known-good behavior	string search
Authentication, Reporting, and	localized impact	system and application behavior
Conformance (DMARC)	malicious payload	System Logging Protocol (Syslog)
email header	organization impact	trend analysis
embedded links	packet and protocol analysis	Uniform Resource Location (URL)
event log	phishing	and Domain Name System (DNS)
exploit techniques	piping	analysis
firewall log	proxy	user and entity behavior analytics
flow analysis	query writing	(UEBA)
forwarding	reverse engineering malware	web application firewall (WAF)

Review Questions

1. Which data correlation analysis is designed for detecting statistical variations and identifying events that are a significant deviation from a baseline?
   a. Threat analysis
   b. Deviation analysis
   c. Data analysis
   d. Anomaly analysis

2. Which data correlation analysis examines if a network device is properly functioning to provide resources to users?
   a. Network analysis
   b. Availability analysis
   c. Uptime analysis
   d. SIEM analysis

3. Which data correlation analysis uses normal processes and actions as the standard?
   a. Process analysis
   b. User/network analysis
   c. Behavioral analysis
   d. Log analysis

4. Which data correlation analysis is founded on experience-based techniques and attempts to determine if an action will do something harmful if it is allowed to execute?
   a. Heuristic analysis
   b. Baseline analysis
   c. Experiential analysis
   d. Experimental analysis

5. Which data correlation analysis looks for a change or development over time to uncover a pattern?
   a. Time series analysis
   b. Trend analysis
   c. Pattern analysis
   d. Change analysis

6. Binnington was asked to recommend an analysis method to determine if an attack has successfully penetrated the network. He decided upon an analysis that only looked at the header information of captured packets. What analysis method did he select?
   a. Topology analysis
   b. Anomaly analysis
   c. Packet analysis
   d. Protocol analysis

7. Jade has been reviewing why three recent attacks were able to bypass the IDS system. He has discovered that these attacks were previously unknown attacks (zero-day attacks). What type of analysis was the IDS performing?
   a. Anomaly analysis
   b. Signature analysis
   c. Trend analysis
   d. Behavioral analysis

8. Aoibheann suspects that there may be infected devices on the network that are sending regular beacons to a threat actor's command and control (C&C) server. Which type of analysis would she use to determine if this is true?
   a. Traffic analysis
   b. Port analysis
   c. Packet analysis
   d. Probe analysis

9. Khawla has been asked to install a packet analysis tool on a Linux web server. Because this server does not do anything that is unnecessary in order to reduce the footprint that a threat actor could exploit, all applications on the server are command-line applications and there is no graphical user interface (GUI). Which tool would Khawla install?
   a. Ethereal
   b. Tcpdump
   c. Network General
   d. Sniffer

10. Zuhal needs to install a packet analyzer that allows her to easily look at the contents of each packet. She wants a tool that is open source and has many advanced features, including in-depth filtering. Which tool should Zuhal install?
    a. Wireshark
    b. NetworkPlumber
    c. NetDump
    d. GrepFinder

11. Feivish has been asked to recommend a new network hardware device. This device needs to support a universal standard for system messages. What standard should the new device support?
    a. NMAP
    b. Syslog
    c. NetFlow
    d. ALLAD

12. The CISO wants a single tool to consolidate real-time monitoring of security information and has asked Zelig to make a recommendation. What tool is he likely to recommend?
    a. SIEM
    b. Netflow analyzer
    c. Packet tracer
    d. Resource monitor

13. Uri needs to analyze a Microsoft Windows firewall log to determine if the firewall processed a request but did not record it in the log. Which field would Uri look at?
    a. Event
    b. Action
    c. INFO-EVENTS-LOST
    d. Task

14. What is deep packet inspection?
    a. A network traffic analysis for security that extracts metadata from the network packets and then converts it into a readable format
    b. The ability of Wireshark to drill down into the payload of a data packet

    c. An analysis by DUMP-TCP on a Linux computer
    d. A NetFlow analysis on a packet

15. Which of the following would be used to identify a DHCP issue?
    a. Packet analysis
    b. Protocol analysis
    c. Traffic analysis
    d. Wireless analysis

16. Which tool would a threat actor use in malware to generate random dynamic URLs?
    a. UIFE
    b. DGA
    c. SPIN
    d. TCTA

17. Which of the following is NOT correct about an email header?
    a. As email is transferred from MTA to MTA, information is added to the email header.
    b. Email headers are encrypted to prevent someone from altering the contents.
    c. The email header contains information about the sender, recipient, email's route through MTAs, and various authentication details.
    d. Each MTA along the path adds its own information to the top of the email header.

18. Which of the following is NOT correct about forwarding emails?
    a. Corporations can be fined for allowing employees to forward emails.
    b. Employees may "auto-forward" corporate emails to utilize enhanced spam filtering.
    c. Forwarded emails may not be available for eDiscovery.
    d. Unauthorized users could access forwarded emails.

19. Which of the following email defenses uses a digital signature?
    a. SPC
    b. DKIM
    c. DMARC
    d. It depends on whether or not the email payload has been encrypted.

20. Which of the following is a Microsoft Windows service that logs service records from various sources and stores them in a single collection?
    a. Syslog
    b. Event log
    c. Win-Log
    d. MS Log

Case Projects

Case Project 7-1: Identifying Data Correlations

Create a table of the eight different types of analysis, similar to Table 7-3. Select three recent attacks (you can search the Internet for some of the most recent attacks), and for each attack, explain if you think it could have been prevented by each of the data correlations.

Case Project 7-2: Flow Analysis

Research flow analysis for cybersecurity. How does it work? How does it collect data? How is the data analyzed? Then find three commercial flow analysis tools and compare them. Which would you recommend? Why? Write a one-page summary of your research.

Case Project 7-3: Domain Generation Algorithm (DGA)

Research DGA. Different malware families have used DGA, so find one particular instance of DGA and use information provided by security researchers to diagram how it functioned. What defenses could be used to combat DGA? Create a one-page paper of your research.

Case Project 7-4: Email Defenses

Create a table that lists the various email technology defenses of SPF, DKIM, and DMARC. Include a summary of how each works, its strengths and weaknesses, and how it is implemented.

Case Project 7-5: On the Job

Suppose you work for a company that has just hired a new chief information officer (CIO). The CIO has proposed a new approach to training employees about phishing. He wants to set up a fake phishing campaign in which weekly phishing emails are sent to all employees; any employee that falls for the attack immediately receives a warning message on the screen, and the identification of that employee is recorded. These employees who failed the test then are sent the next week at least two phishing emails that they must detect (employees who passed the test only receive one phishing email the next week). Any employee that again fails the test receives a detailed email of the dangers associated with phishing but little information about how to recognize an attack. These multiple tests continue to escalate until the point at which employees are required to take a four-hour mandatory security awareness session, after which they are again tested repeatedly. The CIO says that this campaign will continue until the rate of employees falling for fake phishing messages drops below 2 percent. What do you think? Is this a viable plan? What are the advantages? What are the disadvantages? What plan would you propose to be the most effective? Write a one-page memo about what you think should be done and why.

References

1. "2020 Global Threat Report," *Crowdstrike*, retrieved Nov. 25, 2020, https://go.crowdstrike.com/rs/281-OBQ-266/images/Report2020CrowdStrikeGlobalThreatReport.pdf.
2. Medairy, Brad, "The Future of Cybersecurity: The Best Defense Is a Good Offense," *Booz, Allen & Hamilton*, retrieved Jan. 7, 2021, www.boozallen.com/s/insight/blog/future-of-cybersecurity.html.
3. "Threat Brief: Understanding Domain Generation Algorithms (DGA)," *Paloalto*, Feb. 7, 2019, retrieved Jan. 9, 2021, https://unit42.paloaltonetworks.com/threat-brief-understanding-domain-generation-algorithms-dga/.

SECURITY OPERATIONS

After completing this module, you should be able to do the following:

1 Describe cybersecurity automation technologies

2 Define threat hunting

3 Explain different threat hunting tactics

Cybersecurity Today

Have you ever been to a carnival and played a game to win a prize? The game may be shooting a plastic ball at a star or spraying a stream of water into the mouth of a supervillain. Why is it so difficult to win at these games? The owners of the games apply an obvious principle that puts all the odds on their side: a small target is harder to hit than a larger target. By making the star or mouth small enough, most players lack the dexterity needed to squarely hit the target.

This same principle is also true for cybersecurity: a smaller hardware or software target is much harder for a threat actor to "hit" (exploit) than a larger target. An enterprise follows several well-known "attack surface reduction rules" to minimize its target "footprint" for attackers. These rules typically focus on certain software behaviors: restricting the behaviors minimizes the potential attack surface. Examples of attack surface reduction rules are restricting programs from launching executable files and scripts that then attempt to download or run files, stopping the execution of obfuscated or suspicious scripts, and preventing actions that programs and apps do not usually initiate during normal usage. Applying these rules, for example, may involve blocking executable code that has come from an email client or preventing all Microsoft Office applications from creating spawned "child" processes.

However, several security researchers have recently claimed that a particular type of software should not only have its behaviors restricted but should not even be installed on an endpoint. That is because this software provides a large and vulnerable attack surface for threat actors to exploit. But what is most surprising is that this software is actually intended to defend against attacks and is widely used on most computers today.

What is this widely used defensive software that nevertheless provides a large attack target? It's antivirus (AV) software.

In a scathing review of AV software, a former Firefox developer said from where he sits, AV software is, in a word, "terrible." At best, there is negligible evidence that AV products provide a net improvement in security; rather, he says, AV actually hurts security "significantly." He urges users to uninstall AV software immediately.

The reason is that in general, AV developers do not follow standard security practices, which causes three problems. First, AV products actually make it hard for browser vendors and other developers to improve their own security. They do this by "poisoning" the software ecosystem because AV software has invasive and poorly implemented code. The example the Firefox developer gives is when Firefox was trying to make sure that address space layout randomization (ASLR) was working for Firefox on Windows. (ASLR is a memory-protection process for operating systems that protects against buffer overflow attacks by randomizing the location where system executable files are loaded into memory.) Many AV products broke ASLR by injecting their own ASLR-disabled DLLs into the Firefox processes. Second, AV software often blocked web browser patches, making it impossible for users to receive important security fixes. This resulted in developers spending time and energy on dealing with "AV-induced breakage" instead of making security improvements to Firefox. Finally, the AV software itself presents a very large attack surface. Instead of trying to find a vulnerability in the browser or operating system, attackers can use vulnerabilities in AV software as yet another attack vector.

This security researcher is not alone in his observations on AV software. Google Chrome's security chief says that AV software is "my single biggest impediment to shipping a secure browser." AV software delayed Google sandboxing for more than a year and additional sandboxing efforts were placed on hold due to AV programs. In addition, AV software causes a stream of Transport Layer Security (TLS) errors that break some elements of HTTPS. Another developer working on a Firefox attempt to shrink its memory footprint said that AV software "is killing us" because it consumes a huge amount of RAM. In just one year, Google's Project Zero found 25 high-severity bugs in one vendor's AV security products. "These vulnerabilities are as bad as it gets," a Project Zero researcher claimed. He said that AV code affects the default configuration of software. And because AV runs at the highest privilege levels, any vulnerable AV code is loaded into the OS kernel, resulting in kernel memory corruption.

These statements have led many users to question the value of AV software. After all, if it blocks some malware but also gives a bigger target for threat actors to exploit, is the trade-off worth the risk?

The history of automation dates back not to recent times but hundreds and even thousands of years ago. This is when humans first developed primitive but useful Stone Age tools like hammerstones to crush the hulls of nuts. Later, simple mechanical devices such as the wheel, the lever, and the pulley, which were used to magnify the power of the human muscle, were introduced. The next era saw the development of powered machines that did not require human strength to operate, such as windmills and waterwheels. The steam engine, first developed in the 17th century, was a major advance and marked the beginning of the Industrial Revolution. Today electricity, chemical, nuclear, and green-powered sources are used to power an unlimited number of automated devices. These devices range from robots used in automated production lines to autonomous vehicles and voice-controlled appliances. They all provide the same benefit: relieving humans from manual labor.

However, this has not always been the case in the world of cybersecurity. Rather, security personnel have been forced to work manually to search for evidence of attacks, uncover the techniques used by the malware, and then configure devices for protection. Although these security *devices* are obviously automated, the *work* done by security personnel is highly manual. Defenders are essentially using labor-intensive Stone-Age tools to protect modern networks and endpoints.

In recent years, a shift has occurred in which more automation is becoming available to security personnel. Instead of relying on human power to battle attacks, automation is providing significant advancements. This helps to streamline and speed up security processes.

Cybersecurity automation has been augmented by a change in thinking about threat actors. Instead of believing the network is "clean" until hard evidence indicates that attackers have entered, the philosophy has now shifted 180 degrees. The approach today is realizing (and admitting) that the network is *already* infected; that is, attackers are not trying to enter from the outside but are currently inside. This change in thinking has significant impacts on how security is practiced.

In this module, you will explore these twin topics as part of security operations. First, you will look at automation concepts and technologies. Next, you will examine proactive security involved in seeking out and defending against attackers who have already infiltrated the network.

AUTOMATION AND ORCHESTRATION

✅ CERTIFICATION

3.4 Compare and contrast automation concepts and technologies.

Our lives today are governed by automation. *Automation* can be defined as an automatically controlled operation by a mechanical or electronic device that takes the place of human labor. A reminder on a computer screen of an upcoming meeting in 15 minutes is automatically generated because of an entry in a calendar app. A text message notification of a prescription waiting at the pharmacy is automatically sent because the pharmacist scanned the bar code of the just-filled bottle of medicine. An email message that the new tire installation on a car has been completed is automatically created because the tire service technician touched a button on her tablet indicating her assigned job is finished. The examples go on and on of how automation has affected virtually every part of our lives.

Home automation is one of the fastest-growing areas of automation. Voice assistants like Alexa and Siri have replaced the "human labor" of typing on a keyboard with speaking a command. Doorbell cameras that display a smartphone video of someone on the front porch have replaced the human labor of walking to the door. A "pet portal" in a door that slides open like an elevator whenever the home's dog approaches because of a sensor in its pet collar eliminates the human labor of letting the pet in and out.

Automation is increasingly finding its way into cybersecurity as well. To the surprise of many users, cybersecurity work has actually been more manual than automated for many years. Now a switch is starting to gather momentum. This automation includes cybersecurity automation, workflow orchestration, and the use of artificial intelligence.

Cybersecurity Automation

Cybersecurity defenders who operate in an organization's *security operations center (SOC)*—which houses the IT security team responsible for detecting, analyzing, and responding to cybersecurity incidents—typically use automated processes along with manual technology processes (most often more manual processes and less automated). However, using manual processes—*any* manual processes—topples the balance of the scale in favor of the threat actors. Modern cyberattacks are highly automated. Any organization forced to try to defend against these attacks manually spends precious time looking for evidence of an attack and how to counteract it while the attack spreads at network speed. This results in a losing fight between "man versus machine."

The solution is to "fight fire with fire" or, in this case, machine with machine. Known as *cybersecurity automation*, this solution uses automated processes instead of manual processes to better predict behaviors and execute protections much faster. If implemented appropriately and with the right tools, automation can aide in preventing successful cyberattacks.

One example of the necessity of cybersecurity automation is seen in correlating data. Organizations need to collect global threat intelligence outside of their infrastructure across all attack vectors and from security technologies within their own network. Finding the linkages (correlations) from these data sources can result in more accurate results and reduce the likelihood of false positives. Data correlation analysis must also be able to scale (increase) to meet ever-increasing threats (and ever-increasing data). Although SOCs collect voluminous amounts of threat data, it is of limited value unless it is organized into actionable next steps. Yet it is nearly impossible to perform the necessary correlations manually. However, applying cybersecurity automation to processes like data correlation can provide the needed insights in a timely fashion.

NOTE 1

Research has shown that computer users look to automate a manually oriented computer process if that process meets four criteria: it must be done frequently or on a set schedule, it involves moving information between apps, it does not require higher-level thinking, and it takes away from doing something that the user would rather do. An automatic computer process that saves just 15 minutes per day would add up saving more than 60 hours annually.

NOTE 2

Cybersecurity automation levels the playing field, reduces the volume of threats, and allows for faster prevention of zero-day attacks of new and previously unknown threats.

Cybersecurity automation provides these advantages:

- *Generate faster protections.* Once a threat is identified, protections must be created and distributed faster than the attack can spread to networks, endpoints, and the cloud. Because the newly discovered attack has already started, the focus is not on where it was discovered; instead, the defenses must be shored up at the attack's predicted next step. Manually correlating data from different sources to make accurate predictions, design a defense, and then distribute it faster than the attack is all but impossible. Cybersecurity automation, however, can expedite the process to keep pace with the attack.
- *Detect existing network infections.* To determine if the suspicious behaviors of an endpoint are evidence of an attack requires analyzing current data as well as looking backward for past behaviors and even forward to predict future behaviors. Manually, this takes a significant amount of time; cybersecurity automation can speed the process of finding existing network infections.

Cybersecurity automation can improve SOC operations to shorten incident response times by eliminating time-consuming, difficult, and even repetitive manual processes. Cybersecurity automation includes analyzing threat feeds, creating automated malware signatures, using automation protocols and standards, scripting, and enhancing software development.

Analyzing Threat Feeds

Sharing information among organizations about attacks on their networks and endpoints has been a significant aid in defending against attacks. Exchanging details about threats (threat data and intelligence) has helped organizations become aware of imminent attacks. Most organizations monitor their networking environment to determine what normally occurs, and this data is then used to create a database of key risk indicators (KRIs), which is a metric of the upper and lower bounds of specific indicators of normal network activity. These indicators may include the total network logs per second, the number of failed remote logins, network bandwidth, and outbound email traffic. Once a

NOTE 3

Using threat data and intelligence is covered in Module 2.

KRI exceeds its normal bounds, it could be (but is not always) evidence of an indicator of compromise (IoC). An IoC shows a malicious activity is occurring but is still in the early stages of an attack. Making IoC information available to others can prove to be of high value as it may indicate a common attack that other organizations may also be experiencing or will soon experience. This information aids others in their predictive analysis, or discovering an attack before it occurs.

As vital as these threat feeds are, however, it is critical that cybersecurity automation be used to analyze them. Two corresponding tools can enhance threat feeds by cybersecurity automation. These are data enrichment and threat feed combination.

Data Enrichment   As its name implies, data enrichment is enhancing data for cybersecurity analysis. This enhancement is both broad as well as deep. Expanding data sources from a single organization and then combining that with similar data from other organizations (breadth) as well as providing contextual data (depth) is the formal definition of data enrichment.

Consider a single organization that gathers IoC information from its security appliances. Although valuable, the IoC data still only reflects one organization and information from one type of security device. However, if this data were expanded to include other sources from that organization, such as log data from network routers and proxy servers or endpoint devices, the visibility from the broader set of data would help significantly to identify attacks. If all the IoC information from security appliances and log data were then combined with the same type of data from other organizations, it would create an even clearer picture by providing a broad scope of the data.

In addition to data being broader, it can also be deeper. This involves appending or otherwise enhancing collected data with relevant context obtained from additional sources. For example, if a username is found within an application log associated with a potential security event, that username information may be of some value. However, if the username can be referenced against a central identity and access management (IAM) system to obtain the user's actual name, departmental roles, and privileges, for example, the additional information enriches the original log data with context. As another example, if an IP address can be added to enrich a firewall log file, it could then be used to reference IP reputation servers for external addresses to see if known threat activity is associated with that IP address. By "drilling down" even further, that IP address could be referenced with geolocation services to determine the physical location of the IP address by country, state, or postal code.

Adding contextual data can occur in one of two ways. The first method is by performing a lookup at the time of collection and then appending the contextual information into the log data. Another method is to perform a lookup later, when the event is analyzed. Appending the data at the time of collection prevents errors that may occur as the network environment changes. (For example, if IP addresses are provided via the Dynamic Host Configuration Protocol (DHCP), the IP associated with a specific log could be different at the time of collection than at the time of analysis.) However, this method significantly increases the amount of stored information.

NOTE 4

Traditional log management platforms usually add data when it is analyzed, while Security Information and Event Management (SIEM) platforms add data at the time of collection.

Threat Feed Combination   Threat feed combination is an enhancement of data enrichment. It adds third-party threat feeds for the largest possible picture of both breadth and depth. Threat feed combination can significantly refine the data used by cybersecurity automation.

Automated Malware Signature Creation

One of the first antimalware software security applications was antivirus (AV) software. This software can examine a computer for infections, monitor computer activity, and scan new documents that might contain a virus. (Scanning is typically performed when files are opened, created, or closed.) Many AV software products contain a virus scanning engine and a database of "signatures" or identifiers of known viruses. There are two types of virus signatures:

- *Digests*. Using a hash algorithm, a digest of the virus file is taken and then used for identifying the malware. For example, the digest of *5cac917b4903266524e-de6512f800cf5* is taken and then a digest of the file in question is also taken and compared; a match indicates that malware has been detected.
- *Byte detection*. A sequence of bytes in the malware file (such as *B1 52 90 4E 54 46 53 EB*) is compared against a byte sequence of the file in question. A strict matching is called *string scanning*. Other variations include *wildcard scanning* (a wildcard is allowed to skip bytes or ranges of bytes instead of looking for an exact match) and *mismatch scanning* (mismatches allow a set number of bytes in the string to be any value regardless of their position in the string).

NOTE 5

The weakness of signature-based monitoring is that the AV vendor must constantly be searching for new viruses, extracting virus signatures, and distributing those updated databases to all users. An out-of-date signature database could result in an infection.

However, there are several disadvantages with digest and byte detection signatures. Digest signatures are used to identify a single malware file and not an entire malware "cluster" consisting of multiple files. Generating signatures can also be very time intensive, especially given the high number of new and evolving malware instances that are released daily. Finally, malware for which a signature has been generated can be detected by virus scanners relatively easily. Most viruses today go to great lengths to avoid detection; this type of virus is called an *armored virus*. Some of the armored virus infection techniques include the following:

- *Swiss cheese infection*. Instead of having a single "jump" instruction to the "plain" virus code, some armored viruses perform two actions to make detection more difficult. First they "scramble" (encrypt) the virus code to make it more difficult to detect. Then they divide the engine to "unscramble" (decrypt) the virus code into different pieces and inject these pieces throughout the infected program code. When the program is launched, the pieces are tied together to unscramble the virus code. A Swiss cheese infection is shown in Figure 8-1.
- *Split infection*. Instead of inserting pieces of the decryption engine throughout the program code, some viruses split the malicious code itself into several parts (along with one main body of code), and then these parts are placed at random positions throughout the program code. To make detection even more difficult, the parts may contain unnecessary "garbage" code to mask their true purpose. A split infection virus is shown in Figure 8-2.
- *Mutation*. Instead of just hiding within a file, some viruses can "mutate" or change. Oligomorphic viruses change their internal code to one of a set number of predefined mutations whenever they are executed, while polymorphic viruses completely change from their original form when they are executed. A metamorphic virus can actually rewrite its own code and thus appears different each time it is executed by creating a logical equivalent of its code whenever it is run.

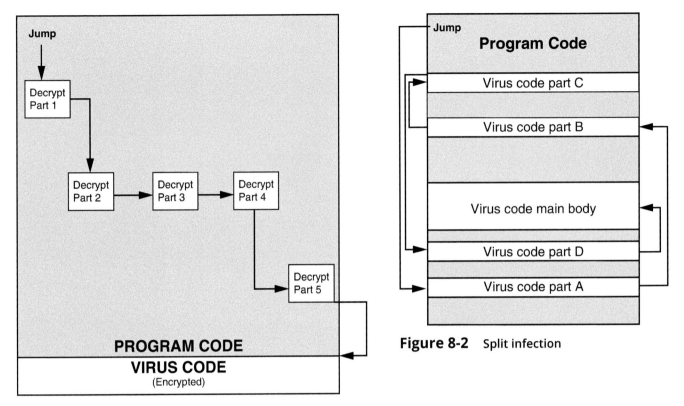

Figure 8-1 Swiss cheese infection

Figure 8-2 Split infection

To overcome these obfuscation techniques, automated malware signature creation technologies can be used. These technologies closely monitor the action of the virus, including any variations generated, to create a signature more quickly and accurately.

NOTE 6

A newer approach to AV is heuristic monitoring (called *dynamic analysis*), which uses a variety of techniques to spot the characteristics of a virus instead of attempting to make matches. The difference between static analysis and dynamic analysis detection is similar to how airport security personnel in some nations screen for terrorists. A known terrorist attempting to go through security can be identified by comparing his face against photographs of known terrorists (static analysis). But what about a new terrorist for whom there is no photograph? Security personnel can look at the person's characteristics—holding a one-way ticket, not checking any luggage, showing extreme nervousness—as possible indicators that the individual may need to be questioned (dynamic analysis).

Using Automation Protocols and Standards

It has become increasingly important for different security appliances, ranging from vulnerability scanners to intrusion detection products, to identify vulnerabilities by using automation protocols and standards. This eliminates the need for managing a range of formats from different devices. One standard has evolved to facilitate products accessing and sharing common information. The Security Content Automation Protocol (SCAP), pronounced *S-Cap*, is an open standard that enables an automated vulnerability management, measurement, and policy compliance evaluation. SCAP is a suite of selected open standards that perform the following functions:

- Enumerate software flaws, security-related configuration issues, and product names.
- Measure systems to determine the presence of vulnerabilities.
- Provide mechanisms to rank (score) the results of these measurements in order to evaluate the impact of the discovered security issues.

SCAP defines how these standards are combined. Table 8-1 lists the standards that make up SCAP.

Table 8-1 SCAP standards

Standard	Description
Common Vulnerabilities and Exposures (CVE)	Vulnerabilities in operating systems and application software
Common Configuration Enumeration (CCE)	Configuration best-practice statements
Common Platform Enumeration (CPE)	Vulnerabilities in operating systems, applications, and hardware devices
Common Weakness Enumeration (CWE)	Software design flaws that could result in a vulnerability

Scripting

By its very nature, a script, which is a short "snippet" of code, is ideal for automation. In fact, it is often argued that scripting languages were specifically developed for automation tasks. This is because they often have features not found in formal programming languages. These features include simple mechanisms for invoking other programs, less strict language requirements such as no specified type system (a type system comprises rules that assign a property to variables and expressions), and no requirement to declare variables. In addition, the language runtime of a scripting language is usually included in the installation of the OS on the target systems. For example, Shell, Perl, and Python are widely available on most UNIX and Linux OSs, making development and deployment of automation scripts a fast and easy process. Common scripting languages include JavaScript, PHP, Python, and Ruby.

NOTE 7

Scripts are covered in Module 7.

Enhancing Software Development

Cybersecurity automation can also be used to enhance software development to create more secure code. This includes using continuous integration, delivery, and deployment as well as using application programming interface integration.

Continuous Integration, Delivery, and Deployment   Software development has long been considered a highly manual process. As such, it has always been ripe for the introduction of security vulnerabilities due to human errors. However, implementing an automated process can not only produce code more quickly but also deliver code that is more secure. Table 8-2 lists the basic processes found in enhancing software development by automation.

Table 8-2 Automated software development processes

Process name	Description	Advantage	Explanation
Continuous integration (CI)	Developers merge their changes back to the main branch of code as often as possible, even several times each day.	Changes are validated by creating a build and running automated tests against it so that any problems can easily be identified as coming from a smaller segment of code.	Continuously integrating changes from different developers prevents surprises on release day at the end of the project when all changes are merged.
Continuous delivery (CD or CDE)	Developers automatically deploy all code changes to a testing and/or production environment after the source code has been compiled (build stage).	An extension of continuous integration, it allows application deployment more quickly and easily while making troubleshooting easier as small batches of code are released.	Software can be released daily or weekly based on business requirements.
Continuous deployment (CD)	Every change that passes all stages of the production pipeline is immediately released to customers.	No human intervention is needed, and only a failed test will prevent a new change to be deployed to production.	An excellent way to accelerate feedback loop with customers and take pressure off developers because there is not a single release day.

Figure 8-3 illustrates continuous integration, continuous deployment, and continuous development.

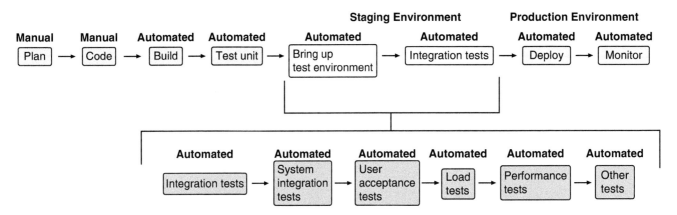

Figure 8-3 Continuous integration, continuous deployment, and continuous development

Application Programming Interface (API) Integration Uber, Airbnb, Instagram, and WhatsApp exemplify the modern business environment. These tech corporations are forerunners of the sharing economy and digital disruption with valuations exceeding $1 billion. The companies are seen as more agile and able to adapt faster and adjust better to changing market conditions than large enterprises. In fact, they are often held up as models for today's business environment.

One driving factor that helped these companies succeed was how they created their customer and internal platforms. Instead of writing all software code from scratch, they relied heavily on application program interfaces (APIs). An API is a link provided by an OS, web browser, or other platform that allows a developer access to resources at a high level. An example of an API is when a user visits a website and the message *This site wants to know your location* appears. The website is attempting to the use the geolocation API available in the web browser. APIs relieve the developer from having to write code for specific hardware and software. Because APIs provide direct access to data and an entry point to an application's functions, they can be used to create code rapidly.

This use of APIs has led to application program interface (API) integration, also called *integration platform as a service (iPaaS)*. This is a set of automated tools for connecting software applications deployed in different environments. API integration is used to integrate on-premises applications and data with cloud applications and data. It provides pre-built connectors and business technologies that ease the development of integration flows and API management. It also offers custom development kits for linking legacy applications with mobile and social applications.

NOTE 8

As attractive as API integration is, it is also a target for attackers looking to exploit vulnerabilities in the API, called an API attack. API vulnerabilities are particularly attractive because they can have a broad impact and may take a long time to discover. In 2018, Facebook found a vulnerability in its API code that allowed attackers to steal access tokens and take over the accounts of 30 million users. It took Facebook 14 months before it discovered the API vulnerability. It is predicted that by 2022, API abuses will become the most common type of web application attack resulting in a data breach.[1]

Workflow Orchestration

An orchestra is a large instrumental ensemble (group) that plays a variety of types of music. Composed of four families of instruments (strings, brass, woodwinds, and percussion), a full symphony orchestra can have more than 100 members, while a smaller chamber orchestra may have up to 40 members, depending upon the music being played. While leading rehearsals, the conductor is responsible for bringing the orchestra to a specific interpretation of the piece being played. The conductor "takes apart" the piece of music during rehearsals to practice with the different families and groups of instruments before bringing everything together in the performance. A symphony orchestra is seen in Figure 8-4.

Figure 8-4   Symphony orchestra

NOTE 9

A symphony orchestra is defined by its string family; without the strings, it would be classified as a band.

In recent years, the concept of a musical orchestra in which many varied instruments all work together, called orchestration, has made its way into cybersecurity. Often called workflow orchestration, it involves automating and combining many individual tasks and processes. In contrast to cybersecurity automation, which automates only one task, workflow orchestration involves organizing many tasks into a functional process (workflow) that is automated. In other words, workflow orchestration is automation used for entire processes instead of for a single task.

 **CAUTION**   Although cybersecurity literature occasionally uses cybersecurity automation and workflow orchestration synonymously, this is incorrect. Security automation is setting a single security operations-related task to run on its own without needing human intervention, whereas workflow orchestration is automating multiple tasks that make up an entire process.

The various tasks that make up workflow orchestration are large and complex scenarios, and these tasks often cross multiple platforms. This automated coordination involves hardware, software, middleware, and services. It uses multiple automated (and sometimes semiautomated) tasks to automatically execute a complex process or workflow.

NOTE 10

The purpose of workflow orchestration is to streamline and optimize repeatable processes and ensure the correct execution of tasks. Whenever a process becomes repeatable and its tasks can be automated, workflow orchestration can be used to optimize the process and eliminate redundancies, speed up completion time, and reduce errors.

Workflow orchestration has given rise to a new type of cybersecurity platform known as a security orchestration, automation, and response (SOAR) platform. SOAR is a combination of software programs and tools that allow organizations to synthesize and automate a range of security operations, threat intelligence, and incident response in a single platform. Consider a threat actor who is attempting to use a brute force attack against a login prompt. Normally, this would result in a human security administrator receiving an alert. The administrator would then have to open the firewall app and manually block the IP address of the attacker. However, when using a SOAR platform, the SOAR can automatically and immediately block the IP address of a computer attempting to brute-force a login. Figure 8-5 illustrates a SOAR dashboard.

Figure 8-5   SOAR dashboard

Source: Metron Labs

NOTE 11

In Figure 8-5, the SOAR dashboard displays a "dollars saved" amount, which is a common feature in SOAR dashboards.

The function of a SOAR platform can most clearly be seen when compared to a SIEM product. A SIEM consolidates real-time monitoring and management of security information with analysis and reporting of security events. It can perform automated alerts and triggers to inform security personnel of critical issues that need immediate attention. A SOAR, on the other hand, can go farther and automatically take immediate action against the threat.

NOTE 12

SIEM devices, which are covered in Module 7, and SOARs are not competitive and alternative technologies (either/or) but are complementary tools (both/and) that help organizations respond to security threats. Whereas a SIEM helps SOC teams detect threats based on data collected from applications and the infrastructure, a SOAR responds to threats more efficiently.

Artificial Intelligence

Artificial intelligence is being used worldwide in a variety of applications, ranging from the mundane to the very sophisticated. Cybersecurity is likewise using these innovative technologies to enhance the detection of malicious behavior and advanced threats. However, there are significant vulnerabilities and risks with using these new tools.

Understanding artificial intelligence includes knowing what it is, what the tools are and what they can do in cybersecurity, and their potential risks.

What Is Artificial Intelligence (AI)?

What do each of the following have in common?

- Raising salmon in a fish farm
- Identifying patients with early-stage dementia
- Determining who voters will elect for office
- Combating wildfires
- Catching chess cheaters
- Monitoring short-term rental activity
- Deciding on which script to fund for a motion picture
- Creating the perfect crunchy cheese puff

The answer is that each of them uses *artificial intelligence (AI)*. Although definitions of AI vary, at its core, AI may be defined as technology that imitates human abilities. Although the practical use of AI has only appeared recently, it has a long history dating back to the first large-scale computers.

A recognized subset of AI is **machine learning (ML)**. Consider how humans learn. One way is by direct commands of someone older and wiser, though this means the other person must always be present. Rather, humans also learn through experiences (such as touching a hot stove results in a painful burn). ML is defined as "teaching" a technology device to "learn" by itself without the continual instructions of a computer programmer. ML also involves learning through repeated experience: that is, if something attempted does not work, then determine how it could be changed to make it work.

A *neural network* is a form of machine learning that attempts to mimic the human brain through a set of algorithms. It has four main components: inputs, weights, a bias or threshold, and output. *Deep learning* refers to the depth of layers in a neural network: a neural network that consists of more than three layers is considered a deep learning algorithm.

NOTE 13

The original goal of AI was to make computers more useful and more capable of independent reasoning. Most historians trace the birth of AI to a Dartmouth research project in 1956 that explored problem solving and symbolic methods. In the 1960s, the U.S. Department of Defense (DoD) became interested in this research and worked on training computers to imitate human reasoning. Some projects that came from the DoD were a street mapping project in the 1970s and intelligent personal assistants in the early 2000s.

NOTE 14

The relationship between AI and ML is AI applies ML to solve problems without being explicitly programmed about what to do.

NOTE 15

A U.S. defense bill passed in early 2021 dedicated more than $6.3 billion for AI research and development efforts to bolster the nation's position in this technology amid increasing competition from other countries. It calls for creating a government office to coordinate a national effort to advance AI and establishing a task force to begin laying the groundwork for a national research cloud to grant AI researchers across the country access to advanced computing power and government data.

Uses in Cybersecurity

Cybersecurity AI allows organizations to detect, predict, and respond to cyberthreats in real time using ML. The prime advantages of using AI to combat threats are continual learning and greater speed in response. By relying on data and knowledge gained from previous similar attacks, AI can predict and prevent future attacks. ML learning algorithms can apply complex pattern recognition techniques to spot and thwart attacks much faster than humans can.

To the surprise of many users, AI is already being used in cybersecurity defenses. Virtually all email systems use some type of AI to block phishing attacks by examining obvious clues (such as the URL of the link that the victim is being tempted to click) but also subtle clues (such as the tense and voice of words in the email). AI using ML can analyze these factors to continually learn to distinguish and block phishing emails while allowing genuine emails to reach the user's inbox.

The use of AI in cybersecurity is spreading rapidly. About one in five organizations used cybersecurity AI before 2019, increasing to two out of three organizations deploying it just one year later. Telecommunications providers use cybersecurity AI more than any other sector: 80 percent of telecom companies said that they would not be able to respond to cyberattacks without using AI.[2] Figure 8-6 illustrates where AI cybersecurity is used in specific areas within an enterprise.

NOTE 16

In a survey of 500 IT directors, managers, chief information officers, and chief technology officers, almost one out of every three predicted that AI would replace humans in cybersecurity by 2030.[3]

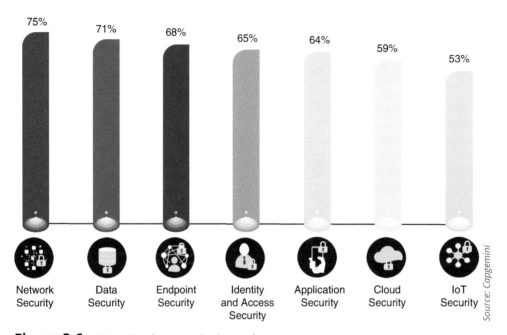

Figure 8-6 How AI cybersecurity is used

Risks of AI in Cybersecurity

Although the use of AI in cybersecurity is growing, risks are associated with using AI and ML in cybersecurity. This is called adversarial artificial intelligence. The first risk is the security of the ML algorithms. Just as all hardware and software is subject to being infiltrated by threat actors, AI-powered cybersecurity applications and their devices likewise have vulnerabilities. Threat actors could attack and compromise these vulnerabilities and then alter the algorithms to ignore attacks, much like a rootkit can instruct an OS to ignore malicious actions.

Another risk is tainted training data for machine learning. Attackers can cloak themselves by attempting to alter the training data used by ML to produce false negatives. A final risk is that threat actors themselves will turn to using AI for attacks to circumvent defenses.

TWO RIGHTS & A WRONG

1. An SOC houses the IT security team responsible for detecting, analyzing, and responding to cybersecurity incidents and typically uses a combination of automated and manual technology processes.
2. Data enrichment is an enhancement upon threat feed combination.
3. SCAP is an open standard that enables an automated vulnerability management, measurement, and policy compliance evaluation.

See Appendix C for the answer.

THREAT HUNTING

3.3 Explain the importance of proactive threat hunting.

Cybersecurity threat hunting has become an important process for protecting networks and endpoints. Threat hunting involves understanding what it is and the processes and tactics it uses.

What Is Threat Hunting?

Understanding threat hunting involves knowing its definition and comparing it with other security roles. As exciting as it may seem, significant challenges are associated with threat hunting.

Definition of Threat Hunting

Reactive is defined as responding to an event that has already occurred. It is action based on something that happened in the past. *Proactive* is taking steps in anticipation of a future event that has not yet occurred. In a reactive mode, problems are solved as they arise, which can even spark creativity while focusing on a solution. A proactive mode, on the other hand, attempts to address problems before they become an issue; however, being proactive may result in lost time if the event never occurs or if it has a much smaller impact than anticipated.

While both reactive and proactive actions are necessary, cybersecurity has for many years been considered solely reactive: following a successful infiltration by the threat actors, steps are taken to fix the problem. This obviously is too late to prevent damages from occurring.

However, that posture is now changing: cybersecurity is becoming more proactive than reactive. This can most clearly be seen in **threat hunting**. Threat hunting is an emergent activity that combines a proactive, repetitive (iterative), and predominately human (instead of automated) identification of a cyber invasion to an IT network or endpoints. This invasion has thus far evaded detection by existing security controls. Threat hunting assumes that the network is already infected, and attackers are not trying to enter from the outside but are currently inside.

Although the roles of a threat hunter and other security roles may have similarities and may sometimes overlap, they actually are quite different. The differences in roles are listed in Table 8-3.

Table 8-3 Security roles

Title	Role	Goal	Task	Driving force	Time frame
Incident responder	Reactive	Secure environment after alarm has been raised.	Minimize impact of attack on the organization through formal process.	Business continuity	Immediate
Penetration tester	Proactive	Secure environment through controlled offensive exercises.	Mimic actions of threat actors to test and validate security posture.	Uncover vulnerabilities	Soon
Threat hunter	Proactive	Identify suspicious activity before alarm has been raised.	Seek evidence of malicious behavior.	Prevent infection from spreading	Longer

NOTE 17

Threat hunting has been described as "incident response—but without the incident!"

The result of successful work performed by a threat hunter can be to reduce the attack surface area, which minimizes the "footprint" that threat actors can use for their malware. It can also provide the motivation to group or cluster important resources together to produce a higher level of protection for the resources (bundling critical assets). Finally, threat hunting can pinpoint gaps in security defenses that could not detect an infection and increase the competence of identifying infections (improve detection capabilities).

Challenges of Threat Hunting

Despite the allure of seeking hidden attackers, threat hunting is associated with several significant challenges. Threat hunters must be able to differentiate and identify two key elements. Historical evidence of an infection (artefact) is an IoC. When detected by threat hunting, it suggests malicious activity is occurring. The descriptions of adversary behavior that IoCs indicate are called tactics, techniques, and procedures (TTPs). IoCs are known knowns, while TTPs are known unknowns.

NOTE 18

This way of classifying threats as known knowns and known unknowns is covered in Module 2.

Most automated network and endpoint security controls use signature and rule-based alerting for IoCs such as malware hashes. However, targeting TTPs is significantly more difficult and labor intensive. This can be illustrated through the "Pyramid of Pain" developed by David Bianco in 2013. This simple diagram shows the increasing difficulty of the types of indicators used to detect an adversary's activities. For defenders, calculating hash values is a trivial indicator (and can be easily automated), while determining TTPs is very difficult and labor intensive. However, a threat hunter must operate at this top level. The Pyramid of Pain is shown in Figure 8-7.

NOTE 19

The pyramid also describes the pain it will cause attackers when security defenders are able to deny the attacks at the different levels!

Figure 8-7   Pyramid of Pain

Finally, not all threat hunting occurs at the same threat-hunting level, so an organization that practices threat hunting may not be doing so effectively or efficiently. Table 8-4 lists the levels of "maturity" of threat hunting along with the people, processes, and tools needed.

Table 8-4 Levels of threat hunting

Threat hunting level	People	Processes	Tools
Initial (Level 1)	Existing SOC personnel	Ad hoc hunts with little data collected	Standard SOC reactive tools with little automation
Managed (Level 2)	Threat hunting performed by volunteer	Uses basic threat feeds with IoC, hunts only occasionally	Searching for text strings and automatic matching of IoCs
Defined (Level 3)	Dedicated threat hunter	Formal hunting process that occurs regularly with data collection from key areas	Uses statistical analysis techniques
Quantitatively Managed (Level 4)	SOC analysts rotated into threat hunting team	Hunts occur frequently with moderate data collection	Use of dashboards and visualization tools
Optimized (Level 5)	Threat hunting teams integrated across SOC with proper resources integration into process	Hunts occur continuously and data shared across security community	Takes advantage of machine learning

NOTE 20

Threat hunters should continue to strive for the highest level and, once there, maintain that level, which can be challenging.

Threat Hunting Process and Tactics

Although threat hunting varies from one organization to the next, the fundamental steps and the tactics used are to select the attack model, identify the most concerning threats, create a calendar, generate a hypothesis, investigate the hypothesis, and then act on the results.

Select the Attack Model

Although often not considered, an organization must decide how it envisions the process the threat actors used to compromise the organization's assets. This is important because it defines the philosophy of how threat hunting will occur and helps to identify who the threat actors are and how they function (**profiling threat actors and activities**).

The process used by the attackers is very likely not a "white paper" that the threat actors developed prior to initiating their attack. However, the general progression of how most attacks are carried out tends to share many common elements. It is important for an organization to select an attack model and use that as a foundation for its threat hunting. This can help identify the TTPs and attacker behaviors that should be hunted. Common attack models include the Lockheed Martin Cyber Kill Chain®, the Gartner cyber attack model, the FireEye attack lifecycle, and MITRE's ATT&CK Life Cycle.

NOTE 21

Models are covered in Module 2.

Identify the Most Concerning Threats

Not all potential threats are of the same importance. A variety of factors should be considered when identifying the threats that are the highest concern. Depending upon the threat model chosen, this step involves going through each phase in the model to identify the most concerning attacker activities.

Each phase in a model can include multiple categories of higher-level tactics. Figure 8-8 shows a small sample of the MITRE ATT&CK matrix. These categories can be subdivided into a number of actual **attack vectors** (a path by which threat actors can gain access) such as "DLL Injection," "Pass the Hash," and "Malware Beaconing." These are the activities that the hunt will search for.

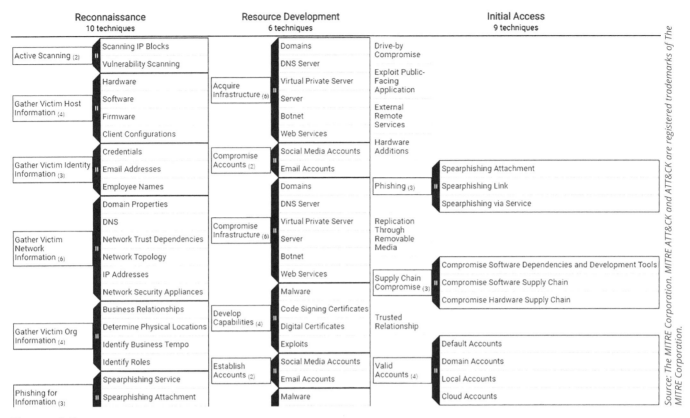

Figure 8-8 MITRE ATT&CK matrix

Create a Calendar

The next step is to create a calendar of how frequently to hunt for specific threats. Activities found near the end of the selected threat model are those of the highest importance, because these are the activities the attacker is about to implement to achieve the desired result, and, thus, they need to be identified and stopped immediately. The various activities can be organized as having a low impact, medium impact, or high impact. High-impact activities should be hunted more frequently than those with a lower impact.

Generate a Hypothesis

A **hypothesis** is a tentative assumption that is made and will then be tested to determine if it is valid. Threat hunting begins with a threat hunter asking basic questions such as "How would a threat actor infiltrate our network?" These questions are then divided into specific and measurable hypotheses that state what threats may be present in the network and how they can be identified. For example, a hypothesis of looking for an instance of ransomware may be, *We hypothesize that if our network is infected with WannaCry ransomware, we will see an increase in the rate of file renaming.*

NOTE 22

Hypotheses cannot be generated by automated tools but instead must be derived from the threat hunter's observations and experiences.

Investigate the Hypothesis

Once the hypothesis is developed, the threat hunter "follows up" on it by investigating through different tools and techniques. Threat hunting techniques include the following:

- *Searching.* Searching is the most basic method of querying a set of collected data such as a log file. The search criteria should be specific enough so that the results returned are not unmanageable but general enough so that no adversary activities are missed. When possible, wildcard (*) characters should be used.

- *Clustering.* Clustering is a form of statistical analysis that separates groups (clusters) of similar data points from a larger set based on specific characteristics.
- *Grouping.* Grouping identifies when multiple unique data points appear together based on specific criteria, such as multiple events occurring in a specific window of time. Unlike clustering, grouping requires an explicit set of data points as input.
- *Stack counting.* Stack counting (stacking) is the application of frequency analysis (how often something occurs) to large sets of data to identify outliers.
- *Machine learning.* Machine learning uses algorithms and statistical models to progressively improve performance of a specific task. This could be identifying anomalous data that might indicate adversary activities. In supervised machine learning, a set of training data is fed into the algorithm with each data point (normal and anomalous) labeled with the desired output. Unsupervised machine learning is provided with "unlabeled" data, so the algorithm uses techniques like clustering and grouping to categorize the outputs instead.

A variety of tools are used within these processes. These include using threat intelligence feeds, selecting sources through which manual lookups can be performed, accessing threat intelligence platforms, and tracking of developing standards. These various types of sources should be combined for integrated intelligence. In addition, these tools allow for an investigation of how the malware functions (executable process analysis).

Act on Results

After the hypothesis has been examined, it will be found to be either true or false. If the hypothesis is found to be false—for example, there is no increase in the rate of file renaming—it may be concluded that the ransomware has not infected the system. However, this is not an indication of failure; rather, it simply means that there is no indication of an infiltration based on the specifics of the hypothesis. Moreover, it *only* indicates that there is no indication based on the specific hypothesis under investigation. There could be evidence elsewhere that must be uncovered.

NOTE 23

A hypothesis found to be invalid is not an indication of failure. After experimenting with more than 10,000 types of filaments for his light bulb before finding the correct substance, Thomas Edison was asked about his long string of "failures." Edison replied that they were not failures; rather, they were eliminations of what did not work to find what did work.

What happens if a hypothesis is proven correct? First, this information should be turned over to the SOC so that the infiltration can be "rooted out" and more secure defensive barriers erected. Second, when possible, successful hunts should be automated to maximize the efficient use of the threat hunting team's time. This can also limit the need to continuously repeat the same hunts. This automation can be done in different ways:

- Schedule a saved search.
- Develop a new analytic within existing tools.
- Provide feedback to a supervised machine learning algorithm.
- Provide a new IoC for matching.
- Write a new SIEM rule for reactive detection.

NOTE 24

The sooner a hunt can be automated, the less repetition is required of the threat hunters so their curiosity and skills can be put toward testing new hypotheses.

However, when processes are automated, care should be taken to ensure that the automated hunts are reliable and will continue to add value. Each analytic should be tested for its accuracy and precision. This can be done by a penetration testing "red team" performing the new technique and checking that the analytic reliably detects its activity. Once the processes based on the new analytics have been launched, they should be monitored for any issues for a period of time. The analytics should be assessed periodically to ensure they still add value and are relevant.

TWO RIGHTS & A WRONG

1. Threat hunting is both reactive and proactive.
2. Reducing the attack surface area is a goal of a successful threat hunt.
3. A hypothesis is a tentative assumption that is made and will then be tested to determine if it is valid.

See Appendix C for the answer.

VM LAB   You're now ready to complete the live, virtual machine labs for this module. The labs can be found in the Apply It folder in each MindTap module.

MODULE SUMMARY

- Cybersecurity defenders who operate in an organization's security operations center (SOC)—which houses the IT security team responsible for detecting, analyzing, and respond to cybersecurity incidents—typically use automated processes along with manual technology processes. However, using manual processes favors the threat actors who use highly automated processes. It is important for SOCs to use more automated processes, known as cybersecurity automation. Cybersecurity automation provides the advantages of generating faster protections and detecting existing network infections.

- One cybersecurity automation process is known as data enrichment, which is enhancing data for cybersecurity analysis. This enhancement is broad as well as deep. Threat feed combination enhances data enrichment. It adds third-party threat feeds for the largest possible picture of both breadth and depth. Automated malware signature-creation technologies can closely monitor the action of the virus, including any variations generated, to create a signature more quickly and accurately. It has become increasingly important for security appliances to use automation protocols and standards. This eliminates the need for managing a range of formats from different devices. One standard has evolved to facilitate products accessing and sharing common information and is known as Security Content Automation Protocol (SCAP).

- By its very nature, a script, which is a short "snippet" of code, is ideal for automation. It is often stated that scripting languages were specifically developed for automation tasks. Common scripting languages include JavaScript, PHP, Python, and Ruby. Software development has long been considered a highly manual process, which results in the introduction of security vulnerabilities due to human errors. Implementing an automated process can produce secure code more quickly. This process involves continuous integration, continuous deployment, and continuous development. The use of application program interfaces (APIs) has led to API integration, also called integration platform as a service (iPaaS). This is a set of automated tools for connecting software applications deployed in different environments. API integration is used to integrate on-premises applications and data with cloud applications and data.

- Workflow orchestration involves automating and combining many individual tasks and processes. In contrast to cybersecurity automation, which only automates one task, workflow orchestration involves organizing many tasks into a functional process (workflow) that is automated. Workflow orchestration has given rise to a new type of cybersecurity platform known as a security orchestration, automation, and response (SOAR) platform. SOAR is a combination of software programs and tools that allow organizations to synthesize and automate a range of security operations, threat intelligence, and incident response in a single platform.

- Artificial intelligence (AI) is defined as technology that imitates human abilities. A recognized subset of AI is machine learning (ML). ML is defined as "teaching" a technology device to "learn" by itself without the continual instructions of a computer programmer. ML also involves learning through repeated experience. A neural network is a form of machine learning that attempts to mimic the human brain through a set of algorithms. It has four main components: inputs, weights, a bias or threshold, and output. Deep learning refers to the depth of layers in a neural network. Cybersecurity AI allows organizations to detect, predict, and respond to cyberthreats in real time using ML. The prime advantages of using AI to combat threats are continual learning and greater speed in response. By relying on data and knowledge from previous similar attacks, AI can predict and prevent future attacks. ML learning algorithms can apply complex pattern recognition techniques to spot and thwart attacks much faster than humans. Although the use of AI in cybersecurity is growing, there are risks associated with using AI and ML in cybersecurity.
- Threat hunting is an emergent activity that combines a proactive, repetitive (iterative), and predominately human (instead of automated) identification of a cyber invasion to an IT network or endpoints. This invasion has thus far evaded detection by existing security controls. Threat hunting assumes that the network is already infected, and attackers are not trying to enter from the outside but are currently inside. The result of successful work performed by a threat hunter can be to reduce the attack surface area, provide the motivation to group or cluster important resources together to produce a higher level of protection, and identify gaps in security defenses that were unable to identify that an infection occurred.
- Despite the attraction and thrill of seeking hidden attackers, threat hunting is associated with several significant challenges. Threat hunters must be able to differentiate and identify key elements. Targeting TTPs is difficult and labor intensive. Not all threat hunting occurs at the same threat hunting level, so an organization that practices threat hunting may not be doing so effectively or efficiently.
- Although threat hunting varies from one organization to the next, there are common basic steps in the process of threat hunting and the tactics used. An organization needs to decide how it envisions the process the threat actors used to compromise their assets. This is important because it defines the philosophy of how threat hunting will occur and helps to identify who the threat actors are and how they function. Another step involves going through each phase in the model to identify the attacker activities that are most concerning. It is also important to create a calendar regarding how often to hunt for specific threats.
- A hypothesis is a tentative assumption that is made and will then be tested to determine if it is valid. Threat hunting involves manually creating specific and measurable hypotheses that state what threats may be present in the network and how they can be identified. Once the hypothesis is developed, the threat hunter investigates the hypothesis through different tools and techniques. The investigation will reveal if the hypothesis is true (valid) and the information must be turned over to the SOC so that the infiltration can be "rooted out" and more secure defensive barriers erected, or if it is false and there is no evidence of an infiltration based on the hypothesis.

Key Terms

application program interface (API) integration
attack vector
automated malware signature creation
bundling critical assets
continuous delivery (CD or CDE)
continuous deployment (CD)
continuous integration (CI)

data enrichment
executable process analysis
hypothesis
improve detection capabilities
integrated intelligence
machine learning (ML)
profiling threat actors and activities

reduce the attack surface area
Security Content Automation Protocol (SCAP)
security orchestration, automation, and response (SOAR)
threat feed combination
threat hunting
workflow orchestration

Review Questions

1. Which of the following is correct about cybersecurity automation?
   a. Cybersecurity operations have been more manual than automated for many years.
   b. Cybersecurity automation requires both AI and ML.
   c. Cybersecurity automation has been used since the very beginning of cybersecurity.
   d. Threat hunting relies heavily upon cybersecurity automation.

2. Which of the following is NOT true about an SOC?
   a. It houses the IT security team.
   b. It is responsible for detecting and analyzing cybersecurity incidents.
   c. It uses strictly automatic processes.
   d. It responds to cybersecurity incidents.

3. Which of the following is NOT correct regarding cybersecurity automation?
   a. Using manual cybersecurity processes by an SOC will tip the balance in favor of attackers.
   b. Modern cyberattacks are highly automated so defenses need to be automated.
   c. Cybersecurity automation is now required by most certification bodies.
   d. Time spent on manual processes allows threat actors time to spread their malware.

4. What is data correlation?
   a. Finding linkages from multiple data sources
   b. A requirement for using ML
   c. A dated technology no longer used due to the introduction of SIEMs
   d. Using a minimum of three external and three internal data sources to understand a zero-day attack

5. Which of the following is NOT correct about data enrichment?
   a. It is the enhancement of data for cybersecurity analysis.
   b. It includes expanding data sources from a single organization and then combining that with similar data from other organizations.
   c. It is both broad and deep.
   d. It is identical to threat feed combination.

6. What is a strict matching of bytes in an AV signature called?
   a. Heuristic scanning
   b. Skip scanning
   c. String scanning
   d. Match scanning

7. Which of the following is NOT a disadvantage with digest and byte signature detection?
   a. They are considered inaccurate.
   b. They cannot always detect a cluster of malware files.
   c. They are time intensive.
   d. Threat actors can circumvent them by creating an armored virus.

8. Which is an open standard that enables an automated vulnerability management, measurement, and policy compliance evaluation?
   a. SORA
   b. SCAP
   c. SRSR
   d. SARC

9. Which of the following are configuration best practice statements?
   a. CVE
   b. CCE
   c. CPE
   d. CWE

10. Which of the following is NOT correct about scripting?
    a. JavaScript, PHP, Python, and Ruby are common scripting languages.
    b. The language runtime of a scripting language is usually included in the installation of the OS.
    c. Scripting has features not found in formal programming language.
    d. Scripting should not be used for automation.

11. In which of the following processes do developers merge their changes back to the main branch of code as often as possible, even several times each day?
    a. CI
    b. CDE
    c. CD
    d. CX

12. What is another name for application program interface (API) integration?
    a. APIaaS
    b. PaaS
    c. SaaS
    d. iPaaS

13. Which of the following involves automating and combining many tasks and processes?
    a. Multitask combination (MTC)
    b. Cybersecurity automation
    c. Workflow orchestration
    d. Autoflow

14. Which of the following platforms can take immediate action when it detects a malicious action?
    a. SIEM
    b. SOAR
    c. RSOC
    d. SAII

15. Which of the following technologies can learn by itself without the continual instructions of a computer programmer?
    a. AI
    b. RA
    c. ML
    d. XI

16. Which of the following is NOT a risk associated with using AI in cybersecurity?
    a. Attackers can cloak themselves by attempting to alter the training data that is used by ML to produce false negatives.
    b. The time needed for AI to provide indicators of attacks is considered too slow to be useful today.
    c. Threat actors may turn to using AI for attacks to circumvent defenses.
    d. AI-powered cybersecurity applications and their devices likewise have vulnerabilities that could be attacked and compromised so that the algorithms could be altered by threat actors to ignore attacks.

17. Which of the following is NOT a characteristic of threat hunting?
    a. Recursive
    b. Predominately human
    c. Iterative
    d. Proactive

18. Which of the following security roles has the goal of securing the environment after an alarm has been raised?
    a. Incident responder
    b. Penetration tester
    c. SOC analyst
    d. Threat hunter

19. Which of the following is NOT the result of successful work performed by a threat hunter?
    a. Bundling critical assets
    b. Creating a new data enrichment threat feed
    c. Reduction of the attack surface area
    d. Improvement in detection capabilities

20. Which level of threat hunting uses a threat hunting team integrated across the SOC?
    a. Managed
    b. Quantitatively managed
    c. Optimized
    d. Defined

Case Projects

Case Project 8-1: Threat Hunting Hypothesis

Use the Internet to locate four different threat hunting hypotheses. Next, determine the tools and techniques that you would use to determine if these hypotheses are valid. Finally, address the actions that you would take if each of the hypotheses were determined to be valid. Create a table of your findings.

Case Project 8-2: Security Content Automation Protocol (SCAP)

Research SCAP. How is it used? How popular is it among security vendors? What are its advantages? What are its disadvantages? Write a one-page summary of your research.

Case Project 8-3: Security Orchestration, Automation, and Response (SOAR)

Research SOAR platforms. Identify three products and list the features of each. Also describe the advantages and disadvantages of each product. Explain how a SOAR can be used with at least three other security appliances. Create a one-page paper of your research.

Case Project 8-4: Cybersecurity Artificial Intelligence (AI)

Use the Internet to identify six ways AI is used in cybersecurity. Next, identify three areas in your school or place of business in which cybersecurity AI could make a difference. Write a one-page paper on your research.

Case Project 8-5: On the Job

Suppose you work for a company in which the chief technology officer (CTO) appears before the executive staff and proposes that three new positions be funded to start a threat hunting team. When asked to define threat hunting, the CTO starts to explain it and its advantages. However, he is immediately cut off by a new senior vice president who is incensed to hear that attackers have already infiltrated the network. This senior vice president demands that the CTO and the entire security team be fired since they "have not done their job." How would you address the concerns of the senior vice president? How can you explain to a general manager who lacks a cybersecurity background the successes of attackers today and how they need to be addressed? Write a one-page memo that contains your explanation.

References

1. Zumerle, Dioisio; D'Hoinne, Jeremy; O'Neill, Mark, "How to Build an Effective API Security Strategy," Gartner Research, Dec. 8, 2017, accessed May 12, 2020, www.gartner.com/en/documents/3834704.
2. "Reinventing Cybersecurity with Artificial Intelligence: The New Frontier in Digital Security," Capgemini Research Institute, accessed May 13, 2020, www.capgemini.com/wp-content/uploads/2019/07/AI-in-Cybersecurity_Report_20190711_V06.pdf.
3. Brown, Eileen, "AI Set to Replace Humans in Cybersecurity by 2030, Says Trend Micro," *ZDNet*, Jan. 15, 2021, retrieved Jan. 17, 2021, www.zdnet.com/article/ai-set-to-replace-humans-in-cybersecurity-by-2030-says-trend-micro/#:~:text=AI%20set%20to%20replace%20humans%20in%20cybersecurity%20by%20 2030%2C%20says%20Trend%20Micro,In%202021%20Trend&text=Dallas%2C%20TX%2Dbased%20cloud%20 security,replace%20their%20role%20by%202030.

INCIDENT RESPONSE

The goal of threat management is to look at the cybersecurity threats an organization faces, while vulnerability management seeks to uncover how exposed the organization may be to these threats and how to mitigate the vulnerabilities. However, despite the best efforts at building a defense, attacks will be successful. Cyber incident response addresses how to react to a successful attack in order to contain the attack, minimize its impact, restore the systems to their pre-attack state, and make the necessary changes to stop future attacks. The modules in this part examine incident response. Module 9 examines the planning and the procedures used for incident response. Module 10 looks at the how organizations respond to a cyber incident.

PART 4

MODULE 9
INCIDENT RESPONSE PLANNING AND PROCEDURES

MODULE 10
RESPONDING TO A CYBER INCIDENT

INCIDENT RESPONSE PLANNING AND PROCEDURES

After completing this module, you should be able to do the following:

1 Define incident response

2 Explain how to prepare for a cyber incident

3 Describe how to apply appropriate incident response procedures

Cybersecurity Today

At 6:30 AM on Christmas Day 2020, a bomb blast shook a large part of downtown Nashville, Tennessee. A recreational vehicle (RV) parked in the midst of the historic district on 2nd Avenue North exploded and damaged 41 businesses. One building completely collapsed, and others were so damaged they will eventually have to be torn down. The perpetrator behind the bombing was the only person killed. There were several reasons an explosion of this magnitude did not claim more victims. First, it occurred early on Christmas morning, when traffic was at an absolute minimum. Second, a recorded warning broadcast from the RV counted down the last 15 minutes before the RV exploded, warning residents to flee. Third, heroic law enforcement personnel went door to door to awaken those in the area and told them to leave immediately. Only three individuals, all police officers, were slightly injured in the blast.

While the motive still remains a mystery—and may never be fully known—it appears that the perpetrator was working alone and was not part of a larger conspiracy group. He evidently was targeting an AT&T building in front of which the RV was parked. This building was one of hundreds located in urban centers around the country. These buildings are generally brick and concrete multistory buildings that have a key feature: no windows. Originally, the buildings housed telephone operators. As telephony migrated away from human operators to more fully electronic systems over the past 60 years, these buildings became "switching centers" or "central offices."

Typically, these central offices house the electronics for completing wireline telephone calls. When smartphones were introduced in the early 1990s, these switching centers added support for cellular telephony. The cell towers that send and receive signals to and from users' mobile phones are connected to a mobile telecommunications switching office (MTSO) that controls all of the transmitters in the cellular network and serves as the link between the cellular network and the wired telephone world. The central offices can also serve as MTSOs and support the Internet point of presence (PoP). A PoP is a collection of telecommunications technologies and equipment that allows users to access the Internet.

With everything contained in these central offices, taking just one of them offline could have a significant impact on multiple telecommunications services over a wide geographic area. That is exactly what happened in the Nashville bombing. The impacts on services and areas included the following:

- Citizens and businesses lost cellular telephone service as well as Internet access in large areas of Tennessee, Kentucky, Alabama, and Georgia.
- Many cities outside of Nashville lost emergency 911 capabilities.
- The emergency communications system that AT&T provides to the state of Tennessee was no longer available.
- The Metro Nashville Police Department communication was impacted, as were Tennessee state employees who temporarily lost data access.
- Multiple hospitals reported problems following the blast because many of their computer and phone systems relied on AT&T networks, forcing the frontline hospital staff to switch to paper records, which resulted in long waits for lab results, issues in recording prescriptions, and problems handling medical records.
- Major corporations and small businesses lost access to credit card processing equipment that relied on AT&T.
- Federal Aviation Administration (FAA) communications at the Nashville airport were also affected, temporarily delaying flights leaving from Nashville and prompting air traffic control to use different air routes for other flights.

Shouldn't these central offices have increased security since they house services that are vital to a large part of the economy and to citizens? Yes, though that is much easier said than done. Many of the central offices are located in the heart of downtown areas, like the one in Nashville. They are a stone's throw away from the street and immediately adjacent to buildings on each side, so it is not possible to erect perimeter fencing around the building. Moving these central offices to another location that can be surrounded by layers of security is also not an easy option: fiber optic lines that shuttle the data to and from these central offices cannot always be easily moved to a more remote location.

One key takeaway for AT&T from this incident was a new set of "lessons learned." It is unlikely that AT&T ever envisioned this central office being bombed. This can be seen in how AT&T had to work to restore the interrupted services. In the aftermath of the explosion, the biggest issue, according to AT&T, was the interruption of electricity because the building's power source was entirely knocked out. For about eight hours following the explosion, wireline AT&T Internet service continued to be available before it ceased to function. It is likely that AT&T had backup generators and battery systems that were designed to last about eight hours; after all, the thinking was likely that if a problem lasted longer, AT&T engineers could enter the building and work on a solution. But because the building was an active crime scene, AT&T could not access the central office to immediately start work on restoring power. When it was eventually granted access, AT&T was forced to burrow through walls to connected gas-powered generators to pump out more than three feet of water that had accumulated in the central office as it had been sprayed on the building to put out numerous fires.

It may be unlikely that AT&T had a chapter in their incident response plan with the title "What to Do When the Building Is Bombed." Yet if they did not have such a chapter, it is a sure bet they are working on one now.

Organizations use reconnaissance for gathering information about users and the organization's network to uncover patterns or correlations in the data to mitigate uncovered vulnerabilities. Penetration testing, the next step, attempts to exploit vulnerabilities just as a threat actor would. Vulnerability management is an ongoing examination of the organization's security posture instead of a single pen test event. This requires analyzing vulnerability scans and identifying common vulnerabilities.

However, despite these well-established processes for protection, significant gaps in cybersecurity still exist. Only 30 percent of U.S. organizations are considered as "cyber-ready" to ward off attacks, and less than half (45 percent) have a formal cybersecurity strategy in place, while only two-thirds consistently deploy antimalware technologies.[1] As a result, attacks will invariably be successful. That is where incident response comes into play.

How can an organization prepare for a cyber incident? What type of planning is required to support meaningful communication? How can the critical nature of data be determined to protect it or respond if it is compromised? What incident response procedures should be used for detection, analysis, containment, eradication, and recovery? This module explores incident response planning and procedures.

INCIDENT RESPONSE PREPARATION

✓ CERTIFICATION

4.1 Explain the importance of the incident response process.

As with virtually all meaningful activities in life, the most important part lies in preparation. The same is particularly true of incident response: preparing for an incident is absolutely critical. Without advance preparation, the time to recover from a cyber incident will triple or even quadruple, inflating from days to weeks and even months. The importance of preparation for a cyber incident should never be underestimated.

Preparing for a cyber incident requires knowing what cyber incident response is. It also involves the four "Cs" of incident response preparation: communication, coordination with stakeholders, criticality of data, and classification of threats.

Defining Cyber Incident Response

Which sounds worse: a *breach, attack,* or *incident*?

Most users would probably say that breach or attack sounds worse than an incident. That is because "incident" is often used to refer to an event or occurrence and thus could be either positive (*That was as wonderful an incident as you could imagine.*) or negative (*As small as that incident was, it marked a change in her behavior.*).

However, in cybersecurity, an incident carries a different definition. A *cyber incident* is the act of violating an explicit or implied security policy.[2] A cyber incident does not necessarily have to be successful; a failed attempt likewise qualifies as a cyber incident. Any of the following may be considered as a cyber incident, whether failed or successful:

- Gaining unauthorized access to a system or its data
- Causing unwanted disruption or denial of service
- Accessing a system for the processing or storage of data
- Making changes to system hardware, firmware, or software characteristics without the owner's knowledge, instruction, or consent

NOTE 1

Sometimes a further distinction is made between a *security event* (any occurrence in a system, network, or application that may have security implications, but is not necessarily malicious or dangerous), an *adverse security event* (a security event that has negative consequences), and a *security incident* (an adverse security event that caused or threatened to cause a violation of the organization's security policies).

As the term implies, a cyber incident response is the actions an organization takes in reaction to a cyber incident. Cyber incident response includes creating and following a cyber incident response plan and building a cyber incident response team.

What Is a Cyber Incident Response Plan?

A cyber incident response plan is a detailed document that clearly outlines the roles, responsibilities, and processes for responding to a cyber incident. While the number may vary as they are combined or separated, a cyber incident response plan generally has seven actionable goals, as seen in Figure 9-1. The actionable goals are detailed in Table 9-1.

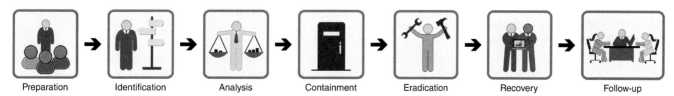

| Preparation | Identification | Analysis | Containment | Eradication | Recovery | Follow-up |

Figure 9-1   Cyber incident actionable goals

Table 9-1   Goals of cyber incident response plan

Plan item	Goal
Preparation	Equip users and systems to handle incidents as they occur.
Identification	Decide if the action is a cybersecurity incident that requires an immediate response.
Analysis	Determine how the incident functions, identify the affected systems, and gauge the overall impact.
Containment	Isolate the affected systems to prevent further damage.
Eradication	Remove affected systems from production to eliminate the root cause.
Recovery	Permit affected systems back into the production environment.
Follow-up	Review and analyze results to improve future efforts.

Building a Cyber Incident Response Team

A cyber incident response plan should be facilitated by a cyber incident response team. A cyber incident response team is the "engine" behind the plan that analyzes information, takes appropriate actions, and shares important communications across all stakeholders. The incident response team's primary objective is to coordinate and align the key resources during a cyber security incident to minimize its impact and to restore operations as quickly as possible. This includes tasks such as investigation and analysis, communications, documentation, and timeline development.

At a minimum, a cyber incident response team should have the members outlined in Table 9-2.

Table 9-2   Members of a cyber incident response team

Role	Responsibility
Team leader	Leads and coordinates all incident response team activity and helps the team to focus on minimizing damage and recovering quickly from an incident
Lead investigator	Collects and analyzes evidence to determine the root cause and then directs other security analysts to implement recovery
Communications coordination	Actively informs all stakeholders both inside and outside of the organization
Documenter	Records all team activities—including investigation, discovery, and recovery tasks—and creates a workable timeline for each stage
Legal council	Keeps the team informed of any legal issues that may impact the incident and recovery

NOTE 2

Because an incident may occur at any time, team members must be on call 24/7 during their tenure on the team. It is recommended that each team member be provided a *go bag* that contains all the important tools needed for an immediate response. These tools include a journal, the incident response team contact list, USB flash drives, antimalware utilities, laptop computer, and various computer and network tool kits.

Communication

The first "C" of incident response preparation is communication. One of the most important elements of a cyber incident response plan is determining a communication plan as to how, when, and what type of information about the incident will be distributed and to whom. There are reasons for communicating information about the incident and communication best practices that should be considered.

Reasons for Communications

Why should an organization communicate that a cyberattack against them has been successful? Wouldn't revealing the news just bring bad publicity? Why not then keep the news hidden in the hopes that over time it will simply fade away? The importance of communicating can be illustrated in the infamous Yahoo! data breach. The facts of this case are clear, although the motivations are not entirely known.

In December 2014, Yahoo's security team discovered that threat actors had circumvented its security and obtained the usernames and passwords, email addresses, phone numbers, birthdates, and security questions and answers for at least 500 million Yahoo! accounts. Within days of the discovery, members of Yahoo's senior management and legal teams received internal reports from Yahoo's chief information security officer (CISO) that these thefts had occurred. However, Yahoo! chose not to make this information known to the general public or its investors for the next *two years*.

In the summer of 2016, Yahoo! was negotiating to sell its operating business to Verizon. As Verizon conducted its due diligence (a comprehensive appraisal of a business undertaken by a prospective buyer), it formally asked Yahoo! about its history of data breaches. Yahoo! chose to not report the December 2014 data breach and instead responded that it was aware of only *four minor breaches* involving users' personal information. In June 2016, a new Yahoo! CISO concluded that Yahoo's entire database, including the personal data of its users, had likely been stolen. This finding was reported to Yahoo's senior management, but again, Yahoo! chose not to disclose this information to Verizon or the public.

However, on September 22, 2016, Yahoo! finally revealed the 2014 data breach to Verizon in a press release that was part of a filing with the Securities and Exchange Commission (SEC). The result of hiding the data breach for two years was immediate and dramatic. The following day, Yahoo's stock price dropped, resulting in a loss of $1.3 billion in market capitalization. After Verizon declared the disclosure and data breach a "material adverse event" under the stock purchase agreement, Yahoo! agreed to reduce its purchase price to Verizon by $350 million (a 7.25 percent reduction) and to share any future liabilities and expenses relating to the breaches.

In December 2016, Yahoo! revised its figures and disclosed that threat actors had stolen data from one billion Yahoo! users in August 2013 and had forged cookies that would allow an intruder to access user accounts *without supplying a valid password in 2015 and 2016*. In October 2017, Yahoo! revised its figures once again and disclosed that *all* its users—*three billion accounts*—had likely been affected by the hacking activity that traces back to August 2013.

Since that time, Yahoo!, which was later known as Altaba, became the first public company to be fined ($35 million) by the SEC for filing false statements that failed to disclose known data breaches. It also paid $80 million in a federal securities class action settlement, the first of its kind based on a cyberattack. Numerous shareholder actions against Yahoo! were filed, and a consumer data breach class action lawsuit resulted in a $117 million settlement. In late 2020, Altaba liquidated its assets.

> **NOTE 3**
>
> Yahoo's internal security team continued to monitor attacks against Yahoo's user database throughout 2015 and early 2016 and received information that stolen Yahoo! user credentials were for sale.

> **NOTE 4**
>
> Security breaches of this magnitude continue to plague businesses. In late 2018, Marriott announced that half a billion potential victims had their names, addresses, credit card numbers, phone numbers, passport numbers, travel locations, and arrival/departure dates stolen. The security firm Risk Based Security, Inc., estimates that more than 24 billion credentials have been stolen or exposed.

This cautionary tale illustrates the danger of trying to hide a cyber incident. Yahoo's attempt to hide the cyber incident from the public and investors by not providing timely and accurate communications resulted in a devastating financial impact and generated a large amount of ill will toward Yahoo! that significantly contributed to its downfall. It proves that proper communication during a cyber incident is not negotiable but is essential.

Reasons for communicating information about the incident include limiting adverse reactions, preventing inadvertent release of information, satisfying state legislative mandates, and meeting federal regulatory requirements.

Limit Adverse Reactions   One reason for communicating during a cyber incident is so that the organization can limit adverse reactions. This is done by "controlling the conversation" surrounding the incident. Controlling the conversation means that the organization works to be "out in front" of the discussion instead of on the defensive by always responding to adverse reactions to the cyber incident.

Considering the Yahoo! incident in hindsight, had Yahoo! been forthcoming and timely with the information about the incident, it could have controlled the conversation. Yahoo! could have set the tone by communicating information while finding ways to include its own messages of vision, safety, and quality by emphasizing timelines, the expertise of its security team, a description of specific events, and how they were being addressed.

 **CAUTION**   Media consultants often coach organizations about how to interact with the news media regarding a cyber incident. For example, consultants stress the difference between *answering* a question and *responding* to a question from the media. Answering a question only provides data. Responding to a question provides data but in a context so that the response contains information, intent, direction, and management. Such responses to questions can infuse power and meaning into information rather than simply giving an answer.

Prevent Inadvertent Release of Information   Another reason for communicating during a cyber event is to prevent the inadvertent release of information (providing information unintentionally). The Yahoo! incident also illustrates this principle. Whereas Yahoo! was able to keep the incident quiet for almost two years, it ultimately was forced to release the information as part of a required filing with the SEC. This unintentional and unplanned release of information immediately put Yahoo! on the defensive with no means to explain or exonerate itself.

NOTE 5

Had Yahoo! communicated in a timely and open fashion, it would have been in control of releasing information about the incident. As unpleasant as it would have been to admit to a breach, nevertheless, by releasing the information on its own terms, Yahoo! would have prevented an unplanned release of information.

Satisfy State Legislative Mandates   The United States currently does not have a federal law that requires notification of a specific type of cyber incident. However, state legislative mandates regarding communication must be satisfied (disclosing based on legislative requirements). Since the initial passage of California's Database Security Breach Notification Act in 2003, by 2018, all other states had passed similar notification laws mandating that users be promptly notified (reporting requirements). Initially, these laws all used the same definitions:

- *Personal information.* Personal information is defined as an individual's first name or first initial and last name plus one or more of the following data elements: Social Security number; driver's license number or state-issued ID card number; or account number, credit card number or debit card number combined with any security code, access code, PIN or password needed to access an account.

NOTE 6

Personal Information does not include publicly available information that is lawfully made available to the general public from federal, state, or local government records or widely distributed media.

- *Breach of security.* This is defined as the unlawful and unauthorized acquisition of personal information that compromises the security, confidentiality, or integrity of personal information.

NOTE 7

The California Consumer Privacy Act (CCPA) of 2018 allows users to know what personal data is being collected about them, to know whether their personal data is sold or disclosed and to whom, to say no to the sale of personal data, to access their personal data, and to request a business delete any personal information that has been collected from them. It does not address notification in the event of a data breach.

However, due to a lack of a comprehensive federal regulation regarding data breach notification, many states have amended their breach notification laws from these basic definitions. As a result, no two state laws are the same.

 **CAUTION** The differences among state laws vary widely. For example, in Arkansas, notification is not required if, after a reasonable investigation, the business determines that there is no reasonable likelihood of harm to customers. Colorado requires additional notice to be provided to the State Attorney General. The Hawaiian statute applies to personal information in any form, whether computerized, paper, or otherwise.

Meet Federal Regulatory Requirements   Several federal regulatory requirements mandate communication from an organization if a specific cyber event occurs (disclosing based on regulatory requirements). Those companies that perform business in the European Union (EU) are legally obligated under the General Data Protection Regulation (GDPR) to inform the EU's Information Commissioner's Office (ICO) if they suffer a breach involving personal information of customers or employees. The Personal Information Protection and Electronic Documents Act (PIPEDA) in Canada likewise protects user data. An amendment passed in late 2018 also requires organizations subject to PIPEDA to report to the Privacy Commissioner of Canada breaches of security safeguards involving personal information that pose a real risk of significant harm to individuals and to notify affected individuals about those breaches.

NOTE 8

The GDPR not only applies to organizations that are located within the EU but also to organizations located outside of the EU if they offer goods or services to or monitor the behavior of EU data that pertains to its subjects. GDPR also applies to all companies processing and holding the personal data of subjects residing in the EU regardless of the company's location.

Several U.S. federal laws require communication if a cyber incident involves the disclosure of specific information. These include the Health Insurance Portability and Accountability Act of 1996 (HIPAA), the Sarbanes–Oxley Act of 2002 (Sarbox), and the Gramm–Leach–Bliley Act (GLBA).

NOTE 9

Sarbox requires that in the event of a data breach, customers should be provided a general description of the incident and the information that was the subject of unauthorized access, a telephone number for further information and assistance, a recommendation that incidents of suspected identity theft be reported promptly, and a general description of the steps taken by the financial institution to protect the information from further unauthorized access or use. It should also contain a reminder for customers "to remain vigilant" over the next 12 to 24 months.

Communications Best Practices

Best practices for communications regarding a cyber incident include the following:

- *Limit communication to trusted parties.* Unless necessary, a cyber incident should not immediately be broadcast to the general public. Instead, communication should be restricted to trusted parties who are stakeholders (called limiting communication to trusted parties).
- *Use a secure method of communication.* To avoid any inadvertent release of information, it is important to use a secure communication method. When sending emails, the contents of the messages should be encrypted, as seen in Figure 9-2. Likewise, when using short message service (SMS) text messages, an app should be used that provides end-to-end encryption.

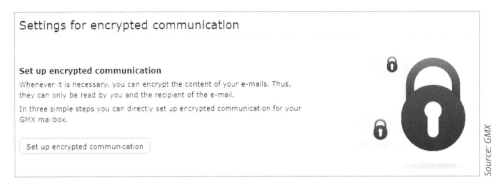

Figure 9-2 Encrypted email

- *Be transparent but be careful.* Transparent communication builds trust; however, in a cyber incident, often few facts are certain initially. It is important to avoid providing any details that may change as the investigation progresses or to speculate on who was behind the incident. All public comments should demonstrate that the issue is being taken seriously.
- *Focus on what is being done.* Communicating the steps that are being taken and what is being done to protect information is important.
- *Provide a context.* In a cyber incident, there may be a temptation for public speculation. Businesses should counter this speculation with facts and a context to reduce the risk of undermining public trust. Where possible, they should include investigation timelines.
- *Respond quickly.* Waiting too long can allow misinformation to spread rapidly. As soon as possible—but not too soon, before any facts are known—the communication should begin.
- *Use social media appropriately.* Organizations should assess whether it would be helpful to suspend planned social media campaigns in light of a cyber incident. Because social media can take unpredictable turns, it should direct the public back to the official statement on the issue, which should be posted on the organization's website. The tone of social media communications is usually casual, but in a cyber incident, communications should use a more formal, just-the-facts approach while maintaining the organization's voice. It is important to promote posts as necessary. A counter-message should be ready for dissemination if necessary and as soon as possible.

Coordination with Stakeholders

The second "C" of incident response preparation is coordination with stakeholders. Different individuals or groups of individuals should be involved in the coordination and even receive different communications. These include internal and external entities, or those stakeholders (those with an interest or concern) who are part of the organization and those who are outside of it.

Internal Stakeholders

There are two categories of internal stakeholders with whom to coordinate efforts and information. These can be divided by their roles:

- *Technical.* The responsibilities of the technical staff are to identify and then react to the cyber incident. This involves determining the impact of the cyber incident and using forensics to investigate the incident. The technical staff must coordinate and communicate clearly with the cyber incident response team and keep that team continually informed of the impact, the vulnerability that was exposed, the type of threat, and the severity of the threat.
- *Management.* As the cyber incident response team receives information from the technical staff, it is responsible for coordination with the organization's managerial teams. The management teams can then provide input and make the appropriate business-level decisions based on the cyber incident. Management stakeholders include public relations (those charged with addressing the public to minimize negative publicity), human resources (because a cyber incident may impact employee contracts and employment laws,

those who handle the human assets may need to be involved), legal (the department that handles legal matters for ensuring compliance with laws and regulations), and senior leadership (the executive-level managers).

External Stakeholders

External stakeholders also need to be included in coordination and communications. As noted previously, those entities responsible for providing regulatory oversight (regulatory bodies) must be informed in the event of a cyber incident. Two other external stakeholders are law enforcement and incident response providers.

Law Enforcement Agencies   While a data breach may require an organization to contact the affected parties, the question is often raised regarding the need to contact law enforcement agencies after a cyber incident has occurred. In one study, it was revealed that only 28 percent of businesses in the United Kingdom (UK) reported a cybercrime to law enforcement agencies.[3] In the United States, the FBI estimates that only 15 percent of victims report their cybercrimes.[4] The following reasons are often cited for the reluctance to report cyber incidents to law enforcement agencies:

- Identifying threat actors, especially when attacks come from abroad, is notoriously difficult for domestic law enforcement agencies and often leads to no arrests or convictions.
- While the interest of the organization is to resume operations as quickly as possible, the interest of law enforcement is to identify and track down and prosecute the perpetrator. This may result in competing interests and may impede the organization from resuming normal operations as law enforcement seeks to retain evidence and launch an investigation.
- Reporting an incident may lead to it becoming public knowledge and could harm the organization's reputation unnecessarily.

However, advantages to reporting a cyber incident include the following:

- Law enforcement agencies can work with foreign counterparts to stop organized cybercrime gangs, which can help reduce the number of overall attacks on a business.
- Large federal law enforcement agencies have many resources and experience and can even make the company's internal investigation easier by having these experts at hand.
- Companies reporting to law enforcement can help provide information toward intelligence-sharing efforts.
- Many law enforcement agencies stress that a business might have the missing piece of the jigsaw puzzle that can be used to help capture repeat cyber criminals.

> **NOTE 10**
>
> The primary federal law enforcement agencies that investigate domestic crime on the Internet include the Federal Bureau of Investigation (FBI), the United States Secret Service, the United States Immigration and Customs Enforcement (ICE), the United States Postal Inspection Service, and the Bureau of Alcohol, Tobacco, and Firearms (ATF).

Different law enforcement agencies have responsibilities to investigate different types of cybercrime. These agencies are listed in Table 9-3.

Table 9-3   Law enforcement agencies' responsibilities

Type of cybercrime	Law enforcement agency responsible
Computer intrusion, password trafficking	FBI local office, Secret Service, Internet Crime Complaint Center
Child pornography or exploitation	FBI local office, Immigration and Customs Enforcement (if material originated overseas), Internet Crime Complaint Center
Internet fraud	FBI local office, Secret Service, Federal Trade Commission, Securities and Exchange Commission (if cybercrime involves investment-related fraud), Internet Crime Complaint Center
Harassment	FBI local office

Incident Response Providers   Due to the complexities of a cyber incident response, some businesses turn to a third-party organization to provide assistance. These organizations are called *incident response providers*. Although the providers may not initiate the communication themselves, they can help facilitate communication between the parties. The providers can assist any or all parts of cyber incident investigation, including preparation, incident response management, data identification, evidence collection, and data recovery.

NOTE 11

Some incident response providers even offer expert witness training by law professors and attorneys to assist employees who must testify in court.

One area of specialization for incident response providers is litigation support to help their clients be successful if a cyber incident results in legal actions against the organization. Incident response providers can author expert reporting declarations and affidavits to support cases based on the collected evidence and key findings of the investigations. Independent assessments of compliance with consent decrees, agreements, court orders, contractual obligations, and other requirements can also be provided.

Criticality of Data

The third "C" of incident response preparation is criticality of data. This part of cyber incident response planning is to identify the organization's critical data. These "crown jewels" are the assets that require special vigilance and a high degree of protection. Table 9-4 lists critical data types.

Table 9-4   Critical data types

Data type	Description	Examples	Reason for high value
Personally identifiable information (PII)	Data that could identify a specific individual	Full name, Social Security number, driver's license number, bank account number, and passport number	Can be used by threat actors to steal the identity of a user or conduct financial transactions in the user's name
Sensitive Personal Information (SPI)	Information that does not directly identify an individual but is related to an individual and communicates information that is private or could potentially harm an individual should it be made public	Biometric data, genetic information, sex, political party affiliation, and union membership	Inferences can be made about the data and applied to the individual to place the individual in a specific "category" that may or may not be accurate
Personal health information (PHI)	Also called protected health information, it is information as it relates to a person's health data, transactions, and history	Mental health history, healthcare services used, and payments for healthcare services	Federal HIPAA laws require many of the key persons and organizations that handle PHI to have policies and security safeguards in place or face fines
Financial information	The storage, processing and transmission of information related to a financial transaction; for an individual, it could be transactions initiated with a credit/debit card, while for an enterprise, it may be detailed accounting data in electronic or paper format that supports a financial statement	Name, card number, expiration date, card verification value (CVV) for individuals, and ledgers, journals, and spreadsheets for enterprises	Loss of data could result in fraudulent purchases by a threat actor in the card holder's name, while loss of accounting data prevents an organization from providing stakeholders an accurate picture of its financial health
Intellectual property	Creations of the mind, such as inventions, literary and artistic works, and designs; and symbols, names, and images used in commerce	Trademarks, copyrights, and patents	These serve to uniquely identify the organization to the public, so any compromise would seriously impact brand recognition and revenue

Data type	Description	Examples	Reason for high value
High value asset (HVA) information	Information that is so critical to an organization that the loss or corruption of this information or loss of access to the system would have serious impact to the organization's ability to perform its mission or conduct business	Assets, systems, and datasets that contain sensitive controls, instructions, or data used in critical operations, or that may house unique collections of data	The direct exploitation of the data can cause a loss of confidence by the public in the organization
Corporate information	Data that is confidential to the organization, such as that used to support the consolidation of companies or assets through various types of financial transactions (mergers, acquisitions, consolidations, tender offers, purchase of assets, and management acquisitions)	Discounted Cash Flow (DCF), Replacement Cost, Enterprise-Value-to-Sales Ratio (EV/Sales), and Price-Earnings Ratio (P/E Ratio)	The unauthorized premature disclosure of this information could have a severe impact on an organization, such as preventing a merger or acquisition from occurring

NOTE 12

In the European Union, even the IP address of an Internet subscriber may be classified as PII.

Classification of Threats

The final "C" of incident response preparation is classification of threats. Because not all threats have the same impact, it is important in the planning phase to classify them. This helps identify the "high-value" threats that must be immediately dealt with, while setting aside lesser-value threats until the high-value threats have been mitigated.

One effective means of classifying threats is to use the Johari window to classify cybersecurity threats, particularly known threats vs. unknown threats, or classifying threats by comparing the knowledge of the threat actor to security personnel.

NOTE 13

The Johari window is covered in Module 2.

TWO RIGHTS & A WRONG

1. A cyber incident is the act of violating an explicit or implied security policy, whether or not it is successful.
2. Most but not all states have notification laws requiring that users be promptly notified in the event of a data breach.
3. SPI is information that does not directly identify an individual.

See Appendix C for the answer.

INCIDENT RESPONSE PROCEDURES

 **CERTIFICATION**

4.2 Given a scenario, apply the appropriate incident response procedure.

Source: Toa55/Shutterstock.com

Figure 9-3   Firefighter

Consider a firefighter, as illustrated in Figure 9-3. Before she is certified, she must go through extensive preparation and testing. Once on the job, a firefighter must be able to handle a variety of tasks. Because an emergency call may be due to different events—structure fires, brush fires, automobile accidents, life-threatening medical emergencies, and even false alarms—upon arrival, she must first quickly analyze the situation and then prioritize what must be done immediately. She will then notify those in charge and other firefighters of the situation. When battling a structure fire, the firefighter must work to contain the fire so that it does not spread. Once contained, firefighters may carry furniture, clothing, and appliances from the building to reduce fire and smoke damage, and they may tear down or shore up weakened floors, roofs, and overhangs.

Before leaving the scene, firefighters will examine the structure once again to ensure that the fire will not reignite from smoldering embers. Finally, a detailed report is filed, and a debriefing is held to determine if any changes need to be made for the future.

The response procedures that a firefighter follows are in some ways similar to cybersecurity incident response procedures. These procedures include the five steps of incident response: preparation, detection and analysis, containment, eradication and recovery, and post-incident activities.

NOTE 14

Although there are slight variations in these steps provided by different organizations, they are remarkably similar. The National Institute of Standards and Technology (NIST) combines containment, eradication, and recovery into a single step and thus has four steps, while the SANS (SysAdmin, Audit, Network, and Security) organization splits them out and has six steps. Nevertheless, they all cover the same activities.

Preparation

A fundamental principle of incident response can never be overlooked: *Preparation is the key to a rapid and thorough response*. Without adequate preparation, responding to an incident will be haphazard, tedious, and error prone.

In addition to the specific preparations discussed previously as incident response relates to cybersecurity (building a cyber incident response team, determining how communications will occur, examining how coordination with internal and external stakeholders should take place, determine the criticality of data, and create a classification of threats), there are also general preparation activities. These activities include the following:

- *Documentation of procedures*. It is important that all phases of the incident response procedures be clearly recorded (documentation of procedures). These procedures should explain the roles and responsibilities and be accessible to all personnel who play a role in the response. The procedures should also be reviewed and revised as necessary on a regular basis.
- *Training*. All personnel involved in responding should receive adequate instruction and coaching (training) on how to react to an incident.
- *Testing*. Testing is an important step in incident response preparation. This serves as an assessment of all parts of the incident response preparation phase that can uncover weaknesses to be addressed. Incident response "drill" scenarios and "mock" data breaches are critical to evaluating an incident response plan and procedures. The more prepared employees are through testing, the less likely they will make critical mistakes when an event occurs.

 **CAUTION**   Another element of the preparation phase is to ensure that all parts of the incident response plan (training, execution, hardware and software resources, etc.) are approved and funded in advance.

Detection and Analysis

The next step in incident response is the detection of an incident followed by an analysis of that incident. The detection and analysis phase answers three questions: Did an incident occur? How severe is it? What is its priority for being addressed?

Did an Incident Occur?

One of the most difficult steps in an incident response and recovery process is the initial analysis: *Did a cyber incident just occur?* Although it may seem that this is a basic and simple question, in reality, it can be difficult to answer. The reasons for the difficulty include the following:

- *Inaccurate security indicators.* Security Event and Information Management (SIEM) devices often report false positives, so every alarm may not be the result of a cyber incident.
- *Multiple indicators.* Depending upon the size and scope of the network, the total number of indicators may reach the hundreds of thousands each day. Sorting through these to identify any related to a cyber incident can be overwhelming.
- *Lack of multiple clear symptoms.* The goal of threat actors is to hide any evidence of their actions so that they can remain undetected. A seemingly innocent and insignificant small symptom, such as a change in a single configuration file, may be the only indicator of a cyber incident.
- *Faulty human statements.* Employees often attribute reports of a device acting erratically to a "computer virus," while in reality, erratic behavior may be the result of any number of reasons.

How can security professionals properly analyze events and then decide what to do? First, the professionals should rely on their experience and training: if an indicator *seems* important, then it should not be ignored. Second, collaborating with other security personnel is very helpful. Third, every situation should be handled in a similar fashion whether or not it is a security incident. Finally, determining if it is an incident may simply be a matter of educated judgment.

 **CAUTION** Not all successful attacks result in a detectable irregular activity and thus do not produce a steady stream of clear and valid indicators. A security professional needs to be thorough and even flexible when analyzing incidents to determine if they are malicious.

How Severe Is It?

Suppose you are a member of the cyber incident response team, and you received a communication from the team leader that the following three events have just occurred in rapid succession:

- A senior vice president opened an email attachment containing malware that has now infected his computer and established connections with an external host.
- A distributed denial of service (DDoS) attack appears to be directed at a web server.
- A firewall has blocked a remote connection attempt.

Determining the severity of an incident is a critical step. That is because attending to an incident that is not critical can give a different critical incident sufficient time to cause widespread damage.

When faced with determining the severity of an event, it is important to consider its impact in the context of security as a whole. In the previous example, a security "novice" might be drawn to the firewall incident as the most severe. However, a firewall that has blocked a remote connection attempt is a normal security action: the firewall properly functioned, and as a result, no data was threatened (although a continued effort by a threat actor may need to be investigated). Once these low-level security "non-incidents" have been eliminated, the severity of the remaining incidents can be determined. This can be done based on the value of the data being compromised, the extent of the threat, and even organizational priorities.

What Is Its Priority?

Which is more important: a distributed denial of service (DDoS) attack that has brought down the company's public web server so that customers cannot make any purchases? Or is an unauthorized root-level access to a device that is allowing the theft of PII a higher priority? If determining whether an incident occurred is one of the most *difficult* steps, then prioritizing is perhaps the most *critical* step. A security professional must be able to quickly prioritize events to respond to the most damaging event first. Or, if two events have an almost equal priority, a decision must be made as to the order of addressing them.

 **CAUTION** Cyber incidents must always be prioritized; they should never be handled simply as they occur on a first-come, first-served basis.

One approach to determining the priority of incidents is to perform a two-step process. The first step is to eliminate (or postpone) those incidents that have lesser consequences. Sometimes called a *triage*, this step identifies incidents that should be immediately addressed with the available resources. Table 9-5 lists general principles to consider when performing a first-level triage of cybersecurity incidents.

Table 9-5 General principles for first-level triage

Principle	Explanation
Consider both current and future consequences	Limiting a prioritization to incidents that only have an immediate consequence on the functionality of a business system could inadvertently ignore the more serious long-term impact.
Consider who will be affected	Often a cyber incident has a much wider impact on one or more other organizations or the wider public at large.
Consider the ability to recover	Some incidents cannot be fully recovered from (such as the theft and release of PII information cannot be undone), so consideration should be given as to the level of recoverability.

NOTE 15

Triage comes from a French word meaning to sift or sort. In the medical community, the word is used for sorting patients—especially battlefield wounded soldiers, disaster victims, and even COVID-19 patients—according to a system of priorities designed to maximize the number of survivors. In a general sense, triage is used for assigning priority to incidents on the basis of where funds and other resources can be best used, are most needed, or are most likely to achieve success.

Each of these general principles can also be further subdivided. For example, when considering the ability to recover, the amount of effort needed should also be considered. The amount of effort can be subdivided into the following categories:

- *Normal.* The time to recover can be accomplished with a reasonable estimate of time by using current resources.
- *Supplementary.* The time to recover can be accomplished with a reasonable estimate of time but additional resources are necessary.
- *Expanded.* The time to recover is unknown and additional resources are necessary.
- *Unrecoverable.* It is not possible to fully recover to the state prior to the incident (such as securing PII that has been stolen and then posted online).

Once the list has been reduced to only cybersecurity incidents that should be quickly addressed, there is a second stage of evaluation. This is used to sort the incidents so that the most critical receive the highest level and must be addressed immediately. These are called characteristics contributing to severity level classification (also called scope of impact). These characteristics can help identify the incident (or incidents) that are the most serious. These characteristics include the following:

- *Downtime.* The length of time that the incident interrupts the normal business processes, or downtime, is a major criterion to consider when identifying the most serious incidents. Downtime ranges from incidents that limit some of the normal activities to a complete interruption of all services.

- *Recovery time.* Recovery time is not the same as downtime. Recovery time is the length of time needed for the IT systems to be disinfected and returned to their normal functions.
- *Data integrity.* A cybersecurity incident that compromises the "soundness" (correctness and completeness) of the data, called the data integrity, is perhaps the most important characteristic. An incident that impacts the organization's data should be considered as having a very high level of priority. This is because data that is corrupted may be difficult to clearly and completely identify and using suspicious data in normal business processes can have a widespread and serious impact on the organization.
- *System process criticality.* The degree to which the impacted systems affect the overall functionality of the entire system, called system process criticality, can also play a role in prioritization. Those systems that are essential to the organization, such as a web application server, may escalate the priority over auxiliary systems of lessor importance.
- *Economic impact.* The financial effect of an incident (economic impact) is also an important criterion to consider when prioritizing incidents. The economic impact can be either short term or long term and can be the result of any or all of the previous criteria.

These characteristics may not always be easy to determine given the attack. For example, it may be necessary to perform reverse engineering on malware to determine its characteristics. It may also be necessary to collect global threat intelligence outside of the organization's infrastructure across all attack vectors and from security technologies within its network to find the linkages (data correlations) so that these multiple data sources can result in more accurate results and reduce the likelihood of false positives.

NOTE 16

Reverse engineering is covered in Module 4 while data correlations are covered in Module 8.

Because every organization is different, no two lists of characteristics will or should look the same. However, organizations that are part of a larger entity often use a common scope of impact. This common scope can assist in compiling similar data from a range of sources. For example, the US-CERT (United States Computer Emergency Readiness Team) requires that all federal government departments and agencies along with state, local, tribal, and territorial government entities and others must submit incident notifications within one hour of being identified by the US-CERT cybersecurity incident response team. Part of the requirements when reporting to US-CERT are for impacted organizations to identify the current level of impact on agency functions or services (*functional impact*); identify the type of information lost, compromised, or corrupted (*information impact*); and estimate the scope of time and resources needed to recover from the incident (*recoverability*). Table 9-6 lists the information impact severity levels.

Table 9-6   US-CERT information impact severity levels

Impact severity level	Description
No Impact	No data impact is known.
Suspected but Not Identified	A data loss or impact to availability is suspected, but no direct confirmation exists.
Privacy Data Breach	The confidentiality of PII or PHI was compromised.
Proprietary Information Breach	The confidentiality of unclassified proprietary information, such as intellectual property or trade secrets, was compromised.
Destruction of Noncritical Systems	Destructive techniques, such as master boot record (MBR) overwrite, have been used against a noncritical system.
Critical Systems Data Breach	Data pertaining to a critical system has been copied and transferred to an unauthorized remote system (*exfiltrated*).
Core Credential Compromise	Core system credentials (such as domain or enterprise administrative credentials) or credentials for critical systems have been exfiltrated.
Destruction of Critical System	Destructive techniques, such as MBR overwrite, have been used against a critical system.

 **CAUTION**   A common error is for an organization to replicate another organization's scope of impact without considering its own uniqueness. Each organization should develop its own scope of impact priority rating system based upon the functions it provides to its stakeholders.

Containment

Containment is designed to keep a cyber incident under control by limiting its impact. Without containment, an incident not only will increase the degree of damage but also may result in other types of damage; in fact, without containment, the effects could even overwhelm resources to the point that a response may no longer be possible.

There are different containment techniques or strategies for containing a cyber incident. How these are implemented depends upon the situation and type of attack. The most common containment techniques include the following:

- *Removal.* The *removal containment technique* is the simplest: the affected system is removed from the network by disabling the switch port or disconnecting it from the network connection. However, removal by "pulling the plug" on the affected system may not always be the best action for several reasons. First, the incident may be multifaceted and impact many systems; removing multiple systems from the network without proper planning can have widespread consequences and in some instances do more harm than the cyber incident itself. Second, removing one system that is not the primary target may not actually contain the attack. Finally, efforts need to be taken to preserve as much evidence as possible for a forensic investigation or for law enforcement, and immediately containing a system by removal may limit the preservation of evidence.
- *Isolation.* Instead of disconnecting the system from the network, the isolation containment technique permits the device to continue to function. All network communication is redirected to a sinkhole so that evidence may continue to be gathered and the malware analyzed. However, this isolation technique may alert the threat actors that the attack has been uncovered.

NOTE 17

Sinkholing is covered in Module 5.

- *Segmentation.* Similar to isolation, the segmentation containment technique continues to allow the affected device to talk to the command and control (C&C) system, but the communication is filtered.
- *Reverse engineering.* The *reverse engineering containment technique* is similar to the segmentation containment technique: it allows the device to talk to the C&C with filtered communication. However, at the same time, the malware is closely examined through reverse engineering. This helps to determine how the malware functions and if additional systems are infected. It also allows for evidence to be gathered and determines what communications with the C&C should be blocked or altered.

Eradication and Recovery

After the incident has been contained, then eradication, which is the elimination of the infection, should be performed. In addition, at this step, the procedures for recovering the systems back to their necessary performance (restoration of capabilities and services) is also begun. Of course, recovery does not mean restoring the systems back to their original state, for this would also reintroduce the vulnerability. Instead, vulnerability mitigation, which includes the steps to reduce or eliminate the vulnerabilities, is also implemented.

Different eradication techniques can clean malware that has infected the hard disk drive of a system. The first step is to physically erase the data from the hard drive. The following methods should *not* be used for eradicating malware:

- *Delete.* Using the operating system's *Delete* utility is not considered safe, since the data itself is not removed. Instead, what is deleted are the "pointers" to the data and not the data itself.
- *Format.* Reformatting a drive is likewise not considered safe. When using Microsoft Windows, for example, a Quick Format only deletes the organizational structure of the files on the drive without removing the data files themselves. The Quick Format option is shown in Figure 9-4.

Figure 9-4 Quick Format option

A more secure approach is data *sanitization* (also called *data wipe*). This method performs a complete data destruction of all contents of the drive by "overwriting" the entire drive, which is replacing data on the drive by writing other data over it. The new data could be *1s*, *0s*, or random characters.

>  **CAUTION** There is disagreement as to how many passes should be made over the existing data. Some researchers maintain that a single pass is sufficient, while others claim that multiple passes should be made. Most data sanitation programs can be customized as to the characters used and the number of passes. For example, a program could be configured to overwrite the data with a 0 on the first pass, a 1 on the second pass, and then random characters on subsequent passes.

Table 9-7 lists some of the common data sanitization methods and software based on these methods. Figure 9-5 lists the configuration options of CBL Data Shredder, a popular data sanitizer.

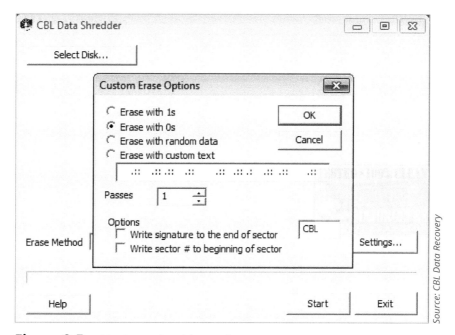

Figure 9-5   CBL Data Shredder options

Table 9-7   Sanitation methods and software

Sanitation method	Description	Characters and passes	Software
Secure Erase	Uses the commands embedded in the firmware of hard drives	Writes a *1* or *0* on one pass	N/A
DoD 5220-22-M	Department of Defense standard and one of most commonly used	Writes a *1* on first pass, a *0* on second pass, and a random character on the third pass	DBAN, CBL Data Shredder, Eraser, Freeraser
Schneier	Considered the most secure method	Writes a *1* on first pass, a *0* on second pass, and a random character on passes 3–7	CyberShredder, EASUS

NOTE 18

Several methods also perform a verification after writing a character over the data to ensure that the contents were destroyed. Because verifying the entire drive after each pass takes a significant amount of time, several software packages contain the option to configure verification, such as verifying only once at the end of the last pass.

Shearing

Crushing

Figure 9-6 Shearing and crushing hard drives

Source: Shred-it

Once the hard drive has been sanitized, it can be restored (recon-struction) by installing the operating system, application programs, and data files. Due to the amount of time needed to reconstruct a hard drive "from scratch," most organizations maintain a digital "snapshot" (*image*) of the drive. Applying a saved image to a sanitized hard drive is called reimaging.

If the hard drive cannot be sanitized and reconstructed or reimaged, the drive should be completely destroyed. This is known as secure dis-posal. Third-party secure disposal services can destroy hard drives through *shearing* (slicing the entire drive into small pieces using 40,000 pounds of force) or *crushing* (punching a hole through the drive). Shear-ing and crushing are illustrated in Figure 9-6.

After the malware has been eradicated and before it is fully integrated back into the system (reconstitution of resources), it is important to take actions to ensure that the repaired systems will not be susceptible to the same incident again. This is known as validation, or the action of making something officially acceptable. Steps in the validation process include the following:

- *Patching*. All patches to the operating system and application software should be applied. If the cyber incident was the result of a missing patch, an investigation as to why this patch was overlooked should be conducted and necessary changes to procedures should be implemented. If the cyber incident was the result of a zero-day attack, then other controls should be implemented to prevent another incident.

NOTE 19

Patching is covered in Module 3.

- *Permissions*. Before reapplying permissions (restoration of permissions), it is important to first review the permissions that were on the compromised system to determine if any changes need to be made. Also, a common technique of threat actors is, after compromising one system, they attempt to change the per-missions on other systems as well. A more extensive review of permissions on other systems should be conducted as well.
- *Scanning*. Once the system is functioning, a vulnerability scanner should be used for scanning the system to identify any issues.
- *Security monitoring*. As a final step, a check should be made to ensure that the system is being monitored cor-rectly (verification of logging/communication to security monitoring). This includes reviewing the collec-tion of log data using Syslog, intrusion detection system (IDS) data, and SIEM information.

Post-Incident Activities

Once the impacted system has been restored, the final step is to perform various post-incident activities. These are designed to lessen the chance of a reoccurrence by taking corrective actions and to document the event. The most obvious activity is to persist in watching for attacks (continue monitoring) and not "let your guard down." The post-incident activities are to generate IoCs from retained evidence, update plans and processes, and create reports.

Generate IoCs from Retained Evidence

Post-incident activities cannot be accurately performed unless the evidence of the attack has been retained (evi-dence retention). Preserving critical electronic evidence during a cybersecurity incident is essential to use after the incident to fully understand all the parts of the attack. Evidence retention is also vital to establish a basis for further investigation.

NOTE 20

Incident responders must be properly trained to be fully prepared to contain and remediate the incident as quickly as possible. However, responders must be careful not to rush the collection of evidence because this could destroy or compromise items of evidentiary value, which could identify attacker's methodology and how the system was compromised. Items of evidence must also be appropriately collected in accordance with established regulations so that evidence can assist law enforcement in successful prosecution of the crime.

One of the primary uses of retained evidence is to generate Indicators of Compromise (IoCs). IoCs can be used to clean up and identify the compromised endpoints within the organization, create custom signatures for future detections, and share them with the broader security community. Evidence and artifacts left by attackers such as running malware process, dropped malware in the system, and logs that show adversary lateral movement can all be used to generate IoCs.

 **CAUTION** Although sometimes used interchangeably, IoCs (which are covered in Module 2) are not the same as Indicators of Attacks (IoAs). IOAs describe the active attack occurring in real time and found through monitoring and detection devices such as security sensors that can identify malicious IPs probing network, repetitive malware infection on a high-value endpoint, and inbound/outbound connections to an IP from a remote country for which there should be no connection.

A variety of artifacts can be used to generate IoCs. These include hashes of executable malware, identification of C&C IPs, domains and subdomains used by threat actors, and changes to network traffic levels.

NOTE 21

The difficulty levels of creating the IoCs from artifacts can be illustrated through the "Pyramid of Pain" introduced in Module 8.

Sharing IoCs with the security community at large is also important. To share IoCs, different platforms can be used, such as the Security Content Automation Protocol (SCAP), Structured Threat Information Expression (STIX), Trusted Automated Exchange of Intelligence Information (TAXII), and YARA.

NOTE 22

STIX and TAXII are covered in Module 2, YARA is covered in Module 6, and SCAP is covered in Module 8.

Update Plans and Processes

Another important post-incident activity is to update plans and processes based on the attack. The success of an attack is often due to a faulty process, so it is important for these processes to be strengthened.

Often, vulnerabilities are introduced into systems due to a faulty change control process. For example, changes to network or system configurations might have been made haphazardly to alleviate a security problem but did not include proper documentation. A vulnerability could also be the result of a lack of coordination with the change management team (CMT) or even an incorrect composition of the CMT (such as the lack of a qualified network security technician serving on the team). As a corrective follow-up action, a review of the change control process may be necessary.

NOTE 23

Change management is covered in Module 5.

While it may be difficult to see any "silver lining" to a cyber incident, in one respect, a cyber incident can serve to thoroughly test and expose any weaknesses in the cyber incident response plan. Each of the actionable goals of the incident response plan should be analyzed in light of the cyber incident to determine if updates need to be made (incident response plan update). Table 9-8 lists cyber incident response plan goals and the type of questions that should be asked of each when reviewing the plan.

Table 9-8 Cyber incident response plan goal review questions

Plan item	Question
Preparation	Did we equip our users and systems to handle the incident as it happened?
Identification	Were we able to promptly decide if the action was a cybersecurity incident that required an immediate response?
Analysis	Could we determine how the incident functioned? Did we identify the affected systems? How accurate was our assessment of the overall impact?
Containment	Did we isolate the affected systems promptly to prevent further damage?
Eradication	Did we make the correct determination as to how to remove the affected system from production?
Recovery	Were our recovery efforts timely?
Follow-up	Was our review clear and detailed?

Create Reports

Different reports should be created following an incident. A review of the change control process and update to the incident response plan should result in a formal written document known as a lessons learned report. This report should include all of weaknesses that were uncovered and detail the changes that were made to address them.

NOTE 24

Depending upon the severity of the cyber incident, other areas in addition to the change control process and incident response plan may call for review and corrections. These should also become part of the lessons learned report.

Another document known as the incident summary report should provide the details of the entire cyber incident from initial detection to final correction and follow-up. This report should answer the following questions:

- When was the incident first detected?
- How was the incident detected?
- How was the incident analyzed?
- Was the prioritization timely and accurate?
- Did proper notification occur?
- Which containment technique was used and why? Was this the correct technique?
- How was the infection eradicated?
- What validations were used?
- What changes were implemented as a result of the follow-up activities?

TWO RIGHTS & A WRONG

1. The first step in incident response is to determine if an actual attack did occur.
2. If the initial analysis is one of the most difficult steps in an incident response and recovery process, prioritizing is perhaps the most critical step.
3. Recovery time is the length of time needed for the IT systems to be disinfected and to return to their normal functions.

See Appendix C for the answer.

> **⌐ VM LAB**   You're now ready to complete the live, virtual machine labs for this module. The labs can be found in the Apply It folder in each MindTap module.

MODULE SUMMARY

- A cyber incident response includes the actions that an organization takes in reaction to a cyber incident. A cyber incident response plan is a detailed document that clearly outlines the roles, responsibilities, and processes for responding to a cyber incident. A cyber incident response plan should be facilitated by a cyber incident response team. A cyber incident response team is the "engine" behind the plan and analyzes information, takes appropriate actions, and shares important communications with all stakeholders. The incident response team's primary objective is to coordinate and align the key resources during a cyber security incident to minimize its impact and to restore operations as quickly as possible.

- One of the most important elements of a cyber incident response plan is determining a communication plan as to how, when, and what type of information about the incident will be distributed and to whom. Reasons for communicating information about the incident include limiting adverse reactions, preventing the inadvertent release of information, satisfying state legislative mandates, and meeting federal regulatory requirements.

- Incident response preparation also involves coordination with stakeholders. Different individuals or groups should be involved in the coordination and even receive different communications. There are two categories of internal stakeholders with whom to coordinate efforts and information: technical and management. Management stakeholders include public relations, human resources, legal, and senior leadership. External stakeholders include law enforcement and incident response providers.

- Another part of cyber incident response planning is identifying the organization's critical data. This data includes personally identifiable information (PII), personal health information (PHI), Sensitive Personal Information (SPI), high-value asset data, financial information, intellectual property, and corporate information. The final "C" of incident response preparation is classification of threats. Because not all threats have the same impact, it is important in the planning phase to classify them. This helps identify the "high-value" threats that must be immediately dealt with, while setting aside lesser-value threats until the high-value threats have been mitigated.

- Cybersecurity incident response procedures include five steps of incident response: preparation, detection and analysis, containment, eradication and recovery, and post-incident activities. Without adequate preparation, responding to an incident will be haphazard, tedious, and error prone. General preparation activities include documentation of procedures, training, and testing. Detection of an incident is followed by an analysis of that incident. The detection and analysis phase addresses three questions: Did an incident occur? How severe is it? What is its priority for being addressed?

- Containment is designed to keep the incident under control by limiting its impact. Without containment, an incident will not only increase the degree of damage but also may result in other types of damage; in fact, without containment, the effects could even overwhelm resources to the point that a response may no longer be possible. There are different containment techniques or strategies for containing a cyber incident, and how these are implemented depends upon the situation and type of attack. The most common are the removal containment technique, isolation containment technique, segmentation containment technique, and reverse engineering containment technique.

- After the incident has been contained, then eradication, which is the elimination of the infection, should be performed. In addition, at this step, the necessary procedures for recovery of the systems back to their necessary performance (restoration of capabilities and services) is also begun. Recovery does not mean restoring the systems back to their original state, for this would also reintroduce the vulnerability again.

Instead, vulnerability mitigation, which involves the steps to reduce or eliminate the vulnerabilities, is also implemented.

- There are different eradication techniques to clean malware that has infected the hard disk drive of a system. The first step is to physically erase the data from the hard drive. The most secure approach is data sanitization. This method performs a complete data destruction of all contents of the drive by "overwriting" the entire drive, which is replacing data on the drive by writing other data over it. If the hard drive cannot be sanitized and reconstructed or reimaged, the drive should be completely destroyed. After the malware has been eradicated and before it is fully integrated back into the system (reconstitution of resources), it is important to take actions to ensure that the repaired systems will not be susceptible to the same incident again.

- Once the impacted system has been restored, the final step includes various post-incident activities. These are designed to lessen the chance of a reoccurrence by taking corrective actions and documenting the event. Post-incident activities cannot be accurately performed unless the evidence of the attack has been retained (evidence retention). One of the primary uses of retained evidence is to generate Indicators of Compromise (IoCs). IoCs can be used to clean up and identify the compromised endpoints within the organization, create custom signatures for future detections, and share them with the broader security community. Another important post-incident activity is to update plans and processes based on the attack. The success of an attack is often due to a faulty process, so it is important for these processes to be strengthened. Different reports should be created following an incident. A review of the change control process and update to the incident response plan should result in a formal written document known as a lessons learned report. Another document known as the incident summary report should provide the details of the entire cyber incident from initial detection to final correction and follow-up.

Key Terms

change control process
characteristics contributing to
  severity level classification
containment
continue monitoring
corporate information
data integrity
disclosing based on legislative
  requirements
disclosing based on regulatory
  requirements
documentation of procedures
downtime
economic impact
eradication
evidence retention
financial information
high value asset (HVA) information
human resources
incident response plan update

incident summary report
intellectual property
internal and external entities
isolation containment technique
legal
lessons learned report
limiting communication to trusted
  parties
personal health information
  (PHI)
personally identifiable information
  (PII)
prevent the inadvertent release of
  information
public relations
reconstitution of resources
reconstruction
recovery time
regulatory bodies
reimaging

reporting requirements
restoration of capabilities and
  services
restoration of permissions
sanitization
secure disposal
segmentation containment
  technique
senior leadership
Sensitive Personal Information
  (SPI)
system process criticality
testing
training
use a secure communication
  method
verification of logging/
  communication to security
  monitoring
vulnerability mitigation

Review Questions

1. What is the act of violating an explicit or implied security policy that may or may not be successful?
   a. Cyber breach
   b. Cyber incident
   c. Security event
   d. Adverse security event

2. Adamo has been asked to create a new cyber incident response plan. What will be the final phase in the plan?
   a. Reporting
   b. Eradication
   c. Recovery
   d. Post-incident

3. Rico is developing a list of personnel who may be asked to serve on a cyber incident response team. Who will have the responsibility of helping the team to focus on minimizing damage and recovering quickly from a cyber incident?
   a. Associate director
   b. Coordinator
   c. Lead investigator
   d. Team leader

4. Viola is examining data that was compromised during a recent attack. Into which category would a password number be classified?
   a. PII
   b. PHI
   c. SPI
   d. PUI

5. Which of the following is NOT an example of intellectual property?
   a. Trademark
   b. Brand image
   c. Copyright
   d. Patent

6. Why is financial information data considered to have a high value?
   a. The loss of accounting data prevents an organization from providing stakeholders an accurate picture of its financial health.
   b. Federal laws prohibit backing up corporate accounting data, so the loss cannot be replaced.
   c. Corporate accounting data only has a high value if it is part of a merger and acquisition.
   d. Accounting data is very detailed and would require a significant effort to restore it.

7. What is the first step in determining the detection and analysis phase of incident response?
   a. Deciding how many systems were impacted
   b. Determining who launched the attack
   c. Deciding if what occurred was a cybersecurity incident
   d. Examining the type of data that was compromised

8. Which of the following scopes of impact describes the length of time needed for IT systems to return to their normal functions?
   a. Downtime
   b. Recovery time
   c. Response time
   d. Recapture time

9. Kristin is reviewing the impact of a recent attack and found that it only caused a seldom-used test server to be taken offline for short period of time. She has decided that this incident does not deserve a high priority ranking. What scope of impact has she used in making this determination?
   a. Network importance measure (NIM)
   b. System evaluation
   c. System process criticality
   d. Structural impact

10. What is the best way for an organization to limit adverse public reactions to a cyber incident?
    a. By keeping the news of a cyber incident secret
    b. By controlling the conversation
    c. By communicating only with stakeholders
    d. By responding defensively

11. Which of the following is NOT a reason for communications in a cyber incident?
    a. To limit adverse reactions
    b. To allow for unplanned release of information
    c. To satisfy state legislative mandates
    d. To meet federal regulatory requirements.

12. Which of the following is false regarding state legislative mandates about communication in a cyber incident?
    a. Only California has a state security breach notification law.
    b. No two state laws are identical.
    c. Some states have a broader definition of personal information.
    d. Providing notice to the State Attorney General is required in some states.

13. Pat is researching requirements for communicating with affected parties in a cyber incident. What requirement would Pat find that is in place in the European Union (EU)?
    a. PIPEDA
    b. GDPR
    c. PI
    d. ICO

14. Isabella has been asked to research HIPAA requirements for her employer. Which of the following is false regarding HIPAA?
    a. Healthcare enterprises must guard protected healthcare information.
    b. HIPAA only applies to information in electronic format.
    c. HIPAA includes any third-party business associate that handles protected healthcare information.
    d. Healthcare enterprises must implement policies and procedures to safeguard information.

15. For internal communications. which two categories are often used?
    a. Senior-level and junior-level
    b. Technical and management
    c. Security and networking
    d. Communication and cyber

16. Kaitlyn is creating an incident response plan. Who should first be notified in the event of a cyber incident?
    a. Cyber incident response team
    b. CEO
    c. Law enforcement
    d. Local media

17. Which of the following is a reason for contacting law enforcement agencies in the event of a cyber incident?
    a. They can work with foreign counterparts to stop organized cybercrime.
    b. They have many resources and experience.
    c. Identifying threat actors often leads to no arrests or convictions.
    d. Companies providing information can assist in intelligence-sharing efforts.

18. Eva is researching which law enforcement agency to contact in the event of different types of cyber incidents. Which law enforcement agency should be contacted no matter the type of incident?
    a. CIA
    b. NSA
    c. FBI
    d. Secret Service

19. Which of the following is NOT a communications best practice strategy?
    a. Contact local news media before the word leaks out.
    b. Use a secure method of communication.
    c. Be transparent but be careful.
    d. Provide a context.

20. Anabelle needs to eradicate malware from a hard drive. Which should she NOT do?
    a. Delete the files from the hard drive by using the Quick Format option.
    b. Overwrite the data using sanitization.
    c. Use secure disposal as a last resort.
    d. Use the Schneier sanitation method.

Case Projects

Case Project 9-1: Comparing Cyber Incident Response Plans

Use the Internet to locate four cyber incident response plans. Compare each plan for its strengths and weaknesses. Finally, from the strengths of each plan, create your own plan. Explain why you chose the specific items to include.

Case Project 9-2: State Data Breach Requirement

Identify three state legislative data breach requirements and compare them, one of which is the from the state in which you currently reside. What is the strength of each requirement? What is the weakness? What changes would you suggest to your state's requirements? Why? Write a one-page summary of your research.

Case Project 9-3: Sensitive Personal Information (SPI)

Use the Internet to research SPI. What type of information is covered by SPI? Why is it necessary to protect this type of data that cannot directly identify an individual? What are three additional data elements that SPI should cover? Create a one-page paper of your research.

Case Project 9-4: Generating IoCs

Select a recent security incident, and research its background. Then identify the IoCs that have been made available based on this incident. Finally, place each of the IoCs in the different categories from the "Pyramid of Pain." Are these IoCs sufficient for the incident? What additional IoCs would be helpful? Write a one-page paper on your research.

Case Project 9-5: On the Job

Suppose you work for a company that has suffered a cybersecurity incident in which PII customer data was stolen. The new chief technology officer (CTO) has stated that because no evidence indicates that the data has been used against customers, the company does not need to report the cyber incident publicly or to law enforcement agencies. Doing so, she argues, would only generate bad publicity. Despite a state law requiring disclosure, the CTO thinks a loophole in the law could allow the company to avoid disclosure. The Legal Department is currently understaffed with no director, and the junior-level employees are concerned about repercussions if they object to the CTO. What do you think? Write a one-page memo to the CTO that outlines your stance on contacting law enforcement and making a public statement.

References

1. "Hiscox Cyber Readiness Report 2018," *Hiscox*, retrieved Jul. 29, 2019, www.hiscox.com/sites/default/files/content/2018-Hiscox-Cyber-Readiness-Report.pdf.
2. "Computer Security Incident Handling Guide," *National Institute of Standards and Technology Special Publication 800-61*, retrieved Jul. 29, 2019, www.csirt.org/publications/sp800-61.pdf.
3. "Cyber Security Underpinning the Digital Economy," *IoD*, Mar. 3, 2016, retrieved Aug. 16, 2019, www.iod.com/cyber-security-for-your-business/articles/cyber-security-underpinning-the-digital-economy.
4. "2016 Internet Crime Report," *IC3*, retrieved Aug. 16, 2019, https://pdf.ic3.gov/2016_IC3Report.pdf.

RESPONDING TO A CYBER INCIDENT

After completing this module, you should be able to do the following:

1 List and explain indicators of compromise for networks, endpoints, and applications

2 Explain the procedures for a digital forensics investigation

3 Describe specialized digital forensics techniques used for different platforms

Cybersecurity Today

In late 2020, an analysis report was released by the U.S. Cybersecurity and Infrastructure Security Agency (CISA) on a recent successful attack against a federal agency's enterprise network. The report (AR20-268A) is a detailed analysis on the threat actor's "tactics, techniques, and procedures as well as indicators of compromise (IoCs)." But perhaps what is most surprising in this report is the list of recommended solutions to prevent future attacks. This has some security professionals wondering why such a list of basic preventative steps was included. Is it because this agency was not already following these fundamental cybersecurity procedures?

The federal agency that is the victim is not named, the time frame when the attack occurred is not given, and there is no indication of what information was stolen or compromised in the analysis report. The CISA became aware of the attack through its own intrusion detection system (IDS) known as EINSTEIN and not that of the compromised agency.

First, how did the threat actors enter this enterprise network? The attackers had "valid access credentials for multiple users' Microsoft Office 365 (O365) accounts and domain administrator accounts." There is no indication in the analysis report of how they secured these usernames and passwords. The attackers then logged in to a user's O365 account and browsed through pages on the agency's Microsoft SharePoint site before they downloaded a file with critical information. The type of information that can be gathered from SharePoint includes links to network shares and other internal resources; physical and logical network diagrams; policies, procedures, and standards; system architecture diagrams; and technical system documentation.

Next, the threat actors connected to the agency's virtual private network (VPN) server. The CISA researchers say that although they could not determine how the attackers gained the credentials to access the VPN server, they suspect that the VPN server had not been patched to address a known vulnerability for which a patch had been released almost 18 months prior. This vulnerability in the VPN server allows "remote, unauthenticated retrieval of files, including passwords." The CISA notes that it has observed wide exploitation of this vulnerability across the federal government because VPN servers were left unpatched.

The threat actors then logged in to an agency O365 email account and downloaded Help Desk email attachments that had "Intranet access" and "VPN passwords" in the email subject line. The attackers also logged in to the same email account using the Remote Desktop Protocol (RDP) before extracting information from Active Directory and Group Policy. They also changed a registry key for the Group Policy to allow them to access and search (using basic Microsoft Windows utilities such as ipconfig, netstat, ping, and whoami) the now-compromised system and network.

Using a Windows Server Message Block (SMB) client, they next used an aliased secure identifier account they had previously created to log in to a virtual private server. After creating a persistent Secure Socket Shell (SSH) tunnel and a reverse proxy, they started dropping their malware for distribution through the network. To cover their tracks, they set up their own hard drive as a locally mounted remote share. Their actions were then recorded on their hard drive so that there would be little evidence for a future forensic investigation. This essentially gave the threat actors free reign on the network to exfiltrate any data they wanted.

The CISA analysis report concludes with a "Solution" section and a "Prevention" section. However, in both of these sections, the cybersecurity recommendations are so fundamental that it causes the reader to wonder if they are included because this victim agency was not practicing them. As one cybersecurity professional said, "You mean they don't do this already?" For example, in the "Solutions" section, the recommendations are that organizations should monitor network traffic for unusual activity, such as unusual open ports (e.g., port 8100), large outbound files, and the use of unexpected and unapproved protocols, especially outbound to the Internet (e.g., SSH, SMB, RDP). In the "Prevention" section, the CISA says organizations should do the following:

- Block unused ports. ("Organizations should conduct a survey of the traffic in and out of their enterprise to determine the ports needed for organizational functions. They should then configure their firewall to block unnecessary ports. Organization should develop a change control process to make control changes to those rules. Of special note, unused SMB, SSH, and FTP ports should be blocked.")
- Deploy an enterprise firewall. ("Organizations should deploy an enterprise firewall to control what is allowed in and out of their network. If the organization chooses not to deploy an enterprise firewall, they should work with their Internet Service Provider to ensure the firewall is configured properly.")
- Deploy and maintain endpoint defense tools on all endpoints.
- Implement multifactor authentication, especially for privileged accounts.
- Implement the principle of least privilege on data access.
- Keep software up to date.
- Secure RDP and other remote access solutions using multifactor authentication.
- Use separate administrative accounts on separate administration workstations.

Although the details of this attack may never be fully revealed, it is hoped that this agency read this analysis report and implemented these most fundamental cybersecurity measures.

After examining in Module 9 incident response planning and the procedures taken when an incident occurs, now Module 10 looks at the steps that are taken in the aftermath of a cyber incident. These steps include identifying indicators of compromise (IoCs) on networks, endpoints, and applications as well as performing digital forensics.

INDICATORS OF COMPROMISE

 **CERTIFICATION**

4.3 Given an incident, analyze potential indicators of compromise.

In the aftermath of a cyber incident, it is important that evidence of the attack be retained (called evidence retention). One of the primary uses of retained evidence is to generate Indicators of Compromise (IoCs). IoCs can be used to identify and disinfect compromised systems, create custom signatures for future detections, and to share these with the broader security community. IoCs can be created from networks, endpoints, and applications.

Network IoCs

One of the first indicators of an attack is often found in the network. The network evidence of an attack includes abnormal network traffic volume, stealth transmissions, scan sweeps, and unauthorized network devices.

Abnormal Network Traffic Volume

Bandwidth monitoring on a network is an important activity for an organization of virtually any size. Following are several reasons that general (non-cybersecurity-related) bandwidth monitoring should be practiced:

- *Monitor bandwidth agreements.* Internet bandwidth purchased from an Internet Service Provider (ISP) typically guarantees that the speed will be at a specific level. By monitoring network bandwidth, it can be determined if the ISP is providing the agreed upon bandwidth as specified in the Service Level Agreement (SLA).
- *Troubleshoot network performance.* Network bandwidth monitoring can help identify performance issues on a network that otherwise may be difficult to isolate. In one example, an organization had contracted with their ISP for what was considered an acceptable volume of bandwidth, but users constantly complained of slow Internet access. A consultant was hired to investigate the problem. After several days of analysis, the consultant discovered that a faulty router interface was dropping packets that made up more than *half* the entire bandwidth purchased from the ISP.
- *Identify network abuse.* With the proliferation of wireless connections, it is not uncommon for a handful of employees to monopolize wireless bandwidth to the detriment of other users. Slow wireless network traffic may also be the result of unauthorized users who are accessing the wireless network. A network bandwidth monitoring tool can analyze wireless access points (APs) and connected wireless clients to determine who is potentially abusing the network.
- *Plan for future network capacity.* By monitoring network bandwidth, organizations are better able to plan ahead for future bandwidth capacity. Table 10-1 lists typical traffic estimates and required bandwidth requirements for selected activities and numbers of users.

NOTE 1

IoCs are introduced in Module 2, and the generation of IoCs resulting from a cyber incident are covered in Module 9.

Table 10-1   Traffic estimates and bandwidth requirements

Activity	Traffic estimate	Number of users	Bandwidth requirement
Using email with attachments	1.15 Mbps	5	5.75 Mbps
Cloud services	1.5 Mbps	20	30 Mbps
Online training webinar	1.5 Mbps	50	75 Mbps
Web browsing	0.33 Mbps	75	25 Mbps
Backing up	2 Mbps	100	200 Mbps

A variety of tools can be used for bandwidth monitoring. Figure 10-1 shows the dashboard of a basic bandwidth monitoring tool. However, more sophisticated bandwidth monitoring tools can provide enhanced data. Figure 10-2 shows a bandwidth monitoring tool that has been configured to examine only Simple Management Network Protocol (SNMP) traffic but in much greater detail.

Another use of network bandwidth monitoring is to look for evidence of a cybersecurity incident. These incidents of abnormal network traffic volume may appear as either traffic spikes or overall bandwidth consumption.

Traffic Spikes   A sudden unusual surge in network bandwidth utilization is called a traffic spike. Figure 10-3 illustrates a traffic spike.

The following are several normal reasons why a network traffic spike may occur:

- *Scheduled internal backups.* Because backups contain large amounts of data, they likewise consume a large amount of bandwidth to complete the backups in a reasonable amount of time.

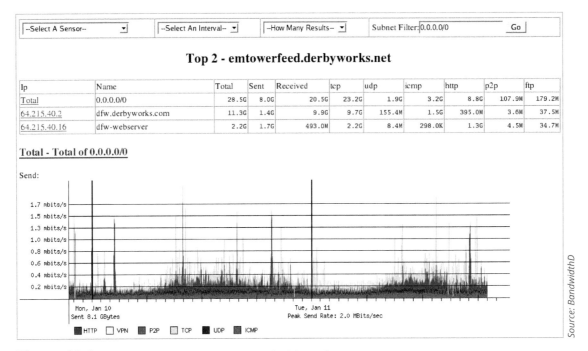

Figure 10-1 Basic bandwidth monitoring dashboard

Figure 10-2 Enhanced bandwidth monitoring dashboard

- *Remote external backups*. Most organizations also perform remote backups to the cloud, which likewise may cause a traffic spike.
- *Software updates*. Operating system patches, application software updates, and other software updates can temporarily cause a spike.
- *Mail server problems*. When operating properly, an email server rarely has an impact on bandwidth. However, if a problem occurs in the delivery of email, a mail server may persistently try to send out the messages over a set period of time (usually 24 hours). If the emails contain large file attachments such as high-resolution photos or video clips, this can cause a spike.

Source: Paessler

Figure 10-3   Traffic spike

Traffic spikes may also be evidence of a cyber incident. To determine the cause of a traffic spike and know if it is normal or a cyber incident, a series of questions can be considered. These questions are listed in Table 10-2.

Table 10-2   Questions when determining the cause of a traffic spike

Question	Explanation
Do the spikes appear at the same time on the same day?	Identifying a pattern in the spikes may help indicate if this is a normal activity or a cyber incident.
Do the spikes occur during business hours or at other times?	A spike that occurs during business hours may indicate a user is causing the spike, while a spike in off hours could be due to a scheduling issue, so further investigation is needed.
Do other monitoring points on the network match these patterns?	A CPU load spike on a server may be creating a corresponding network traffic spike.
Can the traffic be analyzed with a packet analyzer?	A packet analyzer can identify the data and underlying cause of the network spike.

> **⊘ CAUTION**   Even if the cause of a traffic spike is determined to be from a normal event, spikes can still be damaging to the enterprise. One study revealed that for an e-commerce web service, just a one-second delay in the time it takes to load a webpage can result in a 12 percent loss in conversions (sales), while a two-second delay during transactions leads to shopping cart abandonment rates of up to 87 percent.[1]

However, using traffic spikes as evidence of a cyber incident is considered to be difficult for several reasons. First, because normal spikes are not uncommon, it is easy for the malware's spike to become camouflaged. In addition, malware can also be programmed to perform an event that causes a traffic spike on a regular interval, such as a large data exfiltration that occurs at 6:00 PM each Wednesday, so that it looks like a normal event.

Bandwidth Consumption   Whereas a sudden traffic spike may indicate a cyber incident, so can an overall increase in the amount of bandwidth being used (**bandwidth consumption**). Most network bandwidth monitoring tools can be set to sound an alert when bandwidth consumption exceeds a certain threshold, as shown in Figure 10-4.

Figure 10-4 Bandwidth consumption alert

Source: SolarWinds Worldwide, LLC

NOTE 2

To set a bandwidth consumption alert, it is first important to know the normal amount of bandwidth that is being consumed. This requires that a baseline of normal bandwidth utilization be determined. Samples of bandwidth consumption should be taken over a period of time to establish the baseline.

Stealth Transmissions

Stealth is defined as *something done so as not to be seen or heard—something that is secretive, clandestine, or covert.* Often secretive and unexpected network transmissions may be a symptom of a cyber incident. These stealth transmissions can be irregular internal peer-to-peer communication or external beaconing. Because threat actors go to great lengths to hide their stealth transmissions, security professionals should be vigilant in detecting them.

Irregular Peer-to-Peer Communication   Under normal network conditions, most communications will occur between multiple lower-level clients to fewer higher-level servers. However, if the clients unexpectedly begin irregular internal communication with other peers on the network (irregular peer-to-peer communication), this unusual symptom could be an indication of a cyber incident. An infected endpoint could be targeting another endpoint to spread malware or to pivot to other devices and services. This is especially true if the communications occur sporadically and at odd hours.

Beaconing   Beaconing occurs when infected devices attempt to contact the threat actor's external command and control (C&C) server. The purpose of communicating with the C&C server is usually two-way: to receive updated or new instructions from the C&C server and to upload stolen data to the C&C server.

Receive Instructions   Not all compromised endpoints access the C&C server to receive updated or new instructions with the same frequency: some endpoints communicate more frequently than other endpoints, depending upon the type of attack. One particular type of attack by its very nature receives many instructions from a C&C server. This is an attack that places the infected device under the remote control of an attacker for the purpose of launching attacks on other remote devices. The infected robot computer is known as a bot or zombie. When hundreds, thousands, or even millions of bot computers are gathered into a logical computer network, they create a botnet under the control of a bot herder. Table 10-3 lists some of the attacks that can be generated through botnets.

Table 10-3 Uses of botnets

Type of attack	Description
Spamming	Botnets are widely recognized as the primary source of spam email. A botnet consisting of thousands of bots enables an attacker to send massive amounts of spam.
Spreading malware	Botnets can be used to spread malware and create new bots and botnets. Bots have the ability to download and execute a file sent by the attacker.
Manipulating online polls	Because each bot has a unique Internet Protocol (IP) address, each "vote" by a bot will have the same credibility as a vote cast by a real person. Online games can be manipulated in a similar way.
Denying services	Botnets can flood a web server with thousands of requests and overwhelm it to the point that it cannot respond to legitimate requests.

NOTE 3

In early 2021, one of the most notorious botnets known as Emotet was taken down by law enforcement agencies seizing its C&C servers. The takedown required the participation and cooperation of law enforcement agencies from eight different countries. In existence since 2014, Emotet, which infected more than one million endpoints, was used to spread a wide array of malware, most notably ransomware, and may be responsible for losses by victims exceeding $2.5 billion. In an interesting twist, because the C&C servers are now under the control of law enforcement, an update will be sent to all infected endpoints from the C&C servers that will disable the malware on them.

Steal Data   Attacks that are designed to steal information communicate with the C&C server as the means to transport the data back to the threat actors. A variety of techniques can be used, often depending upon the cunning and ingenuity of the threat actors. This can be illustrated by the infamous attack on the point of sale (PoS) terminals at Target Corporation that lasted only three weeks but resulted in more than 40 million credit and debit cards stolen along with 70 million records of personally identifiable information (PII) including the name, address, email address, and phone number of Target customers. As credit and debit card data was captured whenever customers swiped their cards at PoS terminals, the card numbers were encrypted and uploaded back to the Target network to be deposited on Target internal servers that were under the control of the threat actors, who had also installed back doors on three Target FTP (File Transfer Protocol) servers. These back doors were created using carefully chosen usernames to blend in with network management software. At set intervals, the stolen information was sent to the closest Target FTP server and then transferred to C&C servers in Miami and Brazil.

NOTE 4

The impact of the attack on Target was substantial. Not only was the Target CEO forced to resign due to the incident, but Target registered a 46 percent decline in profits compared to the prior year, much of it attributed to consumer backlash to the attack. Target was also forced to spend more than $100 million upgrading its PoS devices.

Hiding Stealth Transmissions   To mask or hide stealth transmissions to hinder or prevent detection, malware typically does not use a distinctive protocol that can be easily identified. For example, BitTorrent is a popular file sharing protocol used to distribute data and files over the Internet and has been used for external beaconing. However, this protocol can easily be detected using a packet analyzer, as seen in Figure 10-5. Many packet analyzers have these protocols built in so that identifying transmissions based on these protocols becomes a simple task. Figure 10-6 illustrates the Gnutella protocol, another similar file sharing protocol, as part of a packet analyzer.

Instead of distinctive protocols, threat actors may use standard network protocols that do not attract attention. For example, when sending stolen data, the malware may use the HTTP or FTP protocol, which can easily blend into

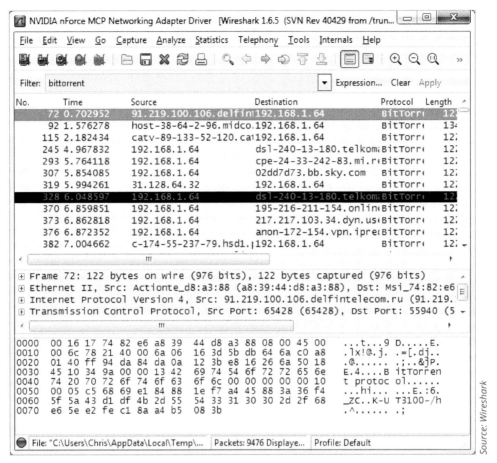

Figure 10-5   BitTorrent packets identified by packet analyzer

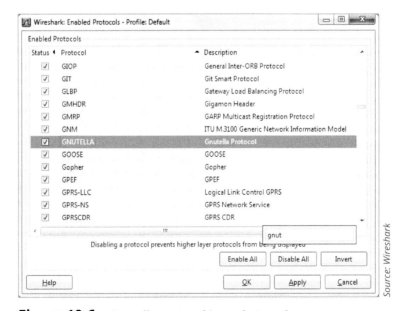

Figure 10-6   Gnutella protocol in packet analyzer

normal traffic. However, the volume of traffic may make the beaconing detectable: HTTP traffic generally has more volume incoming from external sources than outgoing so that threat actors exporting large amounts of stolen data could be identified.

NOTE 5

In the Target attack, stolen data was sent internally to the Target FTP servers only during peak times of the day to hide evidence of communications. Because FTP was a common protocol used by Target, the protocol did not raise suspicion.

Another attempt to avoid detection is to use **common protocols over nonstandard ports**. (A nonstandard port is one used for a purpose other than its default assignment.) For example, the infected endpoint could beacon to the C&C by using the common HTTP protocol over Port 143, which is normally used for Internet Message Access Protocol (IMAP) email communication. However, tools are available that can detect traffic on Port 143 that is different from normal IMAP traffic.

One technique used to mask both types of stealth transmissions—irregular peer-to-peer communications and data exfiltration through beaconing—is to combine standard protocols with an internal mesh network of infected devices so that the devices can communicate with each other easily. This allows for a single compromised endpoint to act as an internal C&C device. This one device receives instructions from the threat actor's main C&C server and then distributes these commands to other compromised endpoints while also acting as the single exit point for sending stolen data back to the threat actor's main external C&C server. This is called a peer-to-peer command and control (P2P C&C) configuration and is illustrated in Figure 10-7.

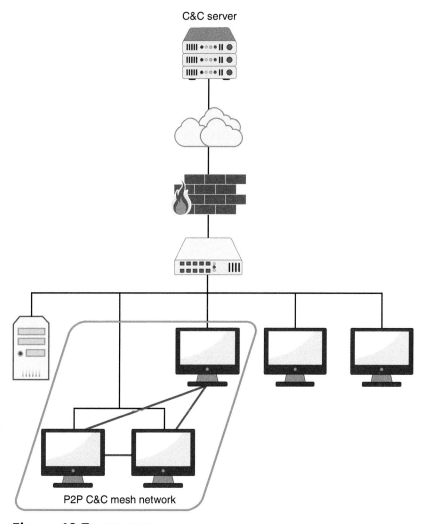

Figure 10-7   P2P C&C

A P2P C&C configuration has several advantages for a threat actor:

- *Reduced number of external beacons.* A P2P C&C has only a single device that performs beaconing with the C&C server instead of each device. This results in less traffic beyond the edge of the network that likely would not raise suspicion.
- *Aligns with traffic inspection prioritizations.* Most security technicians tend to maximize the priority of inspecting external traffic on the edge of the network while minimizing inspection on the internal network. The assumption is that there is more risk from external traffic than internal traffic. Because a P2P C&C has only one device communicating externally, it better aligns with this tendency.
- *Does not use restricted protocols.* Most networks treat certain classes of traffic differently depending upon if it is used internally within the network or at the edge of the network for external communications. A P2P C&C does not have to rely on restricted protocols that draw attention.

One means of how a P2P C&C can circumvent restricted protocols can be illustrated in the following example. HTTP traffic (Port 80) is routinely allowed as outbound over the edge of the network so that employees may browse the Internet; however, HTTP traffic is restricted if that traffic originates from internal servers or a high-value network subnet. A standard C&C approach that requires each infected device to maintain contact with restricted servers or high-value subnets using restricted protocols such as HTTP will raise red flags.

NOTE 6

SMB is not the only protocol that can be used internally for P2P C&C. Essentially any protocol that supports reading and writing data between two devices could be used. Other interprocess communication options on a Windows network include Windows Management Instrumentation (WMI), Windows Mailslots, and even Active Directory (AD).

In a P2P C&C configuration, external beaconing typically uses HTTP because this protocol is so common. For an internal network that uses Microsoft Windows devices, a common protocol is Server Message Block (SMB). A named pipe is a logical connection (such as a TCP session) between a client and server that uses SMB. The name of the pipe serves as the endpoint for communication in the same way that a port number serves as the endpoint for TCP sessions. Thus, named pipes, a native Windows technology that allows for interprocess communication across remote systems over the SMB access protocol, can be used for internal P2P C&C communication. This allows for the internal devices to communicate through the mesh network using common protocols without raising any alarms.

Detecting Stealth Transmissions It is generally recognized that detecting P2P C&C can be difficult since the traffic uses standard protocols to blend in with normal internal and external network traffic. However, some symptoms can be helpful in detecting a P2P C&C. These include the following:

- *Abnormal processes to named pipes.* After collecting and creating a baseline process to named pipe relationships, security professionals can watch for new events compared to the baseline.
- *Known malicious named pipe names.* If the threat actor does not change the default name of the named pipes that now generate large amounts of traffic, this could be a symptom of a cyber incident.
- *Abnormal named pipe security descriptors.* P2P C&C often applies a single security descriptor to a named pipe that allows full control to an *Everyone* group. Monitoring named pipe security descriptors can also be a symptom.

When examining networks for stealth transmissions, the following may serve as symptoms:

- *Remote connections to named pipes.* Using a network tap or collector, SMB network traffic can be inspected to look for a remote connection to named pipes.
- *Abnormal host-to-host traffic.* If certain high-value servers rarely if ever create network connections with certain network subnets that contain user workstations but suddenly a large number of network connections is identified from one of these high-value servers to a workstation subnet, this could be identified as abnormal.

NOTE 7

Detection of a P2P C&C is considered difficult because it uses normal protocols and features. Generally speaking, it may be easier to detect malicious behaviors of the infected device itself.

Scan Sweeps

In preparation for unleashing a cyber incident, threat actors attempt to perform scan sweeps on a network to uncover any vulnerabilities. These scan sweeps include ping sweeps (determining if a host is "awake") and port scans (looking for available services on open ports). Any scan sweeps originating from unknown IP addresses should serve as symptoms to be investigated.

Rogue Devices

A final symptom of a cyber incident are unauthorized devices (rogue detection on a network). On a wired network, a rogue device may attempt to monitor network traffic. For example, a managed switch on an Ethernet network that supports port mirroring allows the network administrator to configure the switch to copy traffic that occurs on some or all ports to a designated monitoring port on the switch. A threat actor (or more likely an insider who is performing work for the threat actor) can connect a rogue monitoring computer to the mirror port and then view all network traffic moving through the switch. (The monitoring computer can be a standalone device or a computer that runs protocol analyzer software.)

On a wireless network, a rogue mobile device can connect to the network if it is weakly protected. These are particularly dangerous since they can provide unfettered access to the entire network, bypassing network security protections or tricking users into connecting with a sinister AP.

> **NOTE 8**
>
> Wireless networks are covered in Module 4.

Several methods can be used to detect a rogue AP by continuously monitoring the radio frequency (RF) airspace. This requires a special sensor called a wireless probe, a device that can monitor the airwaves for traffic. Following are the four types of wireless probes:

- *Wireless device probe*. A standard wireless device, such as a portable laptop computer, can be configured to act as a wireless probe. At regular intervals during the normal course of operation, the device can scan and record wireless signals within its range and report this information to a centralized database. This scanning is performed when the device is idle and not receiving any transmissions. When a many mobile devices are used as wireless device probes, they can provide a high degree of accuracy in identifying rogue access points.
- *Desktop probe*. Instead of using a mobile wireless device as a probe, a desktop probe uses a standard desktop computer. A universal serial bus (USB) wireless adapter is plugged into the desktop computer to monitor the RF frequency in the area for transmissions.
- *Access point probe*. Some AP vendors have included in their APs the functionality of detecting neighboring APs, friendly as well as rogue. However, this approach is not widely used. The range for a single AP to recognize other APs is limited because APs are typically located so that their signals overlap only to provide roaming to wireless users.
- *Dedicated probe*. A dedicated probe is designed to exclusively monitor the RF frequency for transmissions. Unlike access point probes that serve as both an AP and a probe, dedicated probes only monitor the airwaves. Dedicated probes look similar to standard access points.

> **NOTE 9**
>
> Once a suspicious wireless signal is detected by a wireless probe, the information is sent to a centralized database where wireless LAN (WLAN) management system software compares it to a list of approved APs. Any device not on the list is considered a rogue AP. The WLAN management system can instruct the switch to disable the port to which the rogue AP is connected, thus severing its connection to the wired network.

Any unknown network device that is discovered connected to the network should be treated as an unauthorized device and immediately disconnected from the network. Further investigation should reveal if the device is being used by threat actors or is the result of a faulty change control process.

Endpoint IoCs

IoCs can also be found on endpoints. The evidence includes a high-volume consumption of resources, evidence that is OS and software related, and data exfiltration.

High-Volume Consumption of Resources

Consider a homeowner who receives a monthly electric bill. The bill lists the amount due based on the current usage of electricity and includes a comparison of that month against the same month over the last five years. Suppose one month, the bill unexpectedly shows the amount due is *triple* what it has been over the last five years. The homeowner would certainly investigate the sudden increase in electrical usage. Was it an unusually hot month that required the air conditioner to run around the clock? Was a window left open in an unoccupied room? Did an unscrupulous neighbor tap into the electrical connection to siphon off electricity? The unexpectedly high amount of electricity used would serve as an indication that something unusual had occurred.

Likewise, with an endpoint system, an abnormally high volume of resource consumption is often an IoC. The categories of consumption of resources include processor, memory, and hard drive.

NOTE 10

Some software programs are better able to take advantage of multiple threads than others. Games are considered "lightly threaded" and do not benefit as much from multiple cores, while video editing programs can run much faster with extra threads.

Processor   Unlike previous generations of central processing units (CPUs) containing only one core that received instructions and performed actions, modern processors contain multiple cores (usually 2 to 18). In addition, today's processors use simultaneous multithreading or hyperthreading that can split each core into multiple threads or virtual cores. Thus, a single physical CPU chip has the capacity of multiple CPUs all working together.

Threat actors take advantage of processors with multiple cores. Malware that infects an endpoint computer can run using multiple cores and threads without any appreciable impact upon the normal tasks that the user is performing. This shows no effect on the processor's performance, and thus, the user is unaware of the presence of malware. However, if the malware performs a significantly complicated or lengthy task, then the processor may begin to slow down to the point that the malware becomes apparent.

Several tools can be used to determine if the reason the processor's resources are being taxed is a result of a cyber incident (called **processor consumption**). A resource monitor can audit and display the CPU along with other endpoint resources. Figure 10-8 shows the Microsoft Windows Resource Monitor.

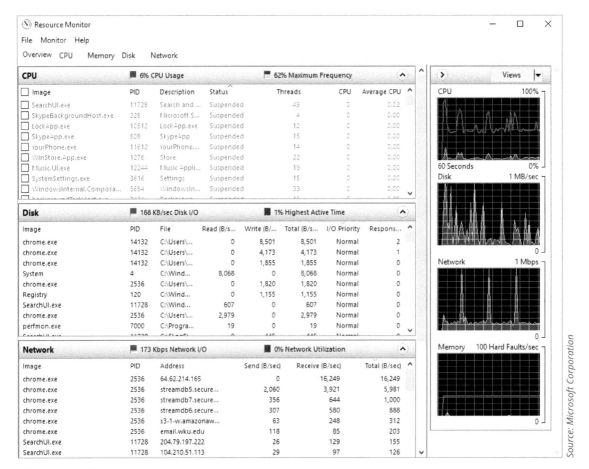

Figure 10-8   Microsoft Windows Resource Monitor

Memory Abnormal memory consumption could likewise be a symptom of a cyber incident. As malware loads into RAM, it may consume large parts of memory, causing the endpoint to slow down or become unstable. Memory consumption can be identified by resource monitor tools.

Hard Drive Drive capacity consumption refers to the unexpected loss of available hard drive space as a result of malware. This may be due to malware gathering files from several different endpoints or servers prior to data exfiltration, or it can be because of continual scan sweeps performed by malware that result in the rapid increase in the size and number of log files. Resource monitor tools can help provide clues to determine if drive capacity consumption is a symptom of a cyber incident.

Operating System Evidence

Evidence of a compromise can most often be found in the OS running on the endpoint, as this is a frequent target of threat actors. Evidence from the OS includes the following:

- *Malicious process*. A process is the instance of a computer program being executed by one or more threads; that is, it is an application in execution. Threat actors often create an unauthorized malicious process that the OS runs. These can be difficult to detect and trap. A single malicious process may launch ("spawn") multiple interdependent processes. These can easily hide among the normal processes from user programs along with the normal OS processes. This makes it easy for a malicious process to remain hidden.
- *Abnormal process behavior*. Threat actors also attempt to change a normal process into performing a malicious action, known as abnormal OS process behavior.
- *File system changes*. Changes to files (file system change or anomaly) may serve as an IoC as threat actors infect or modify a file. However, on a normal day, a system may see hundreds of file system changes on a single endpoint, making it difficult to identify abnormal file changes.
- *Changes to registry*. The Windows registry is a database that stores low-level settings for the Windows OS and applications. Device drivers, services, the OS kernel, and some security applications use the registry. Unexpected modifications or an abnormal registry setting (registry change or anomaly) can serve as an IoC.
- *Unauthorized scheduled task*. Modern OSs run specific operations (tasks) at a certain time or when an event occurs (such as when a user logs in). In addition, users can create their own tasks with "triggers" that launch the task but are modified by "conditions," as seen in the Microsoft Windows Task Manager in Figure 10-9. An unauthorized scheduled task that was not approved and initiated by an administrator can often be an IoC.

NOTE 11

With multicore CPUs, large RAM capacity, and hard drives that measure in the billions of bytes of storage, it is easy for malware to hide in these resources and not be detected. Establishing baselines can be helpful in identifying if high-volume consumption is a result of malware.

NOTE 12

It is not uncommon for Microsoft Windows to run more than 50 background processes and more than 100 Windows processes in its normal operation.

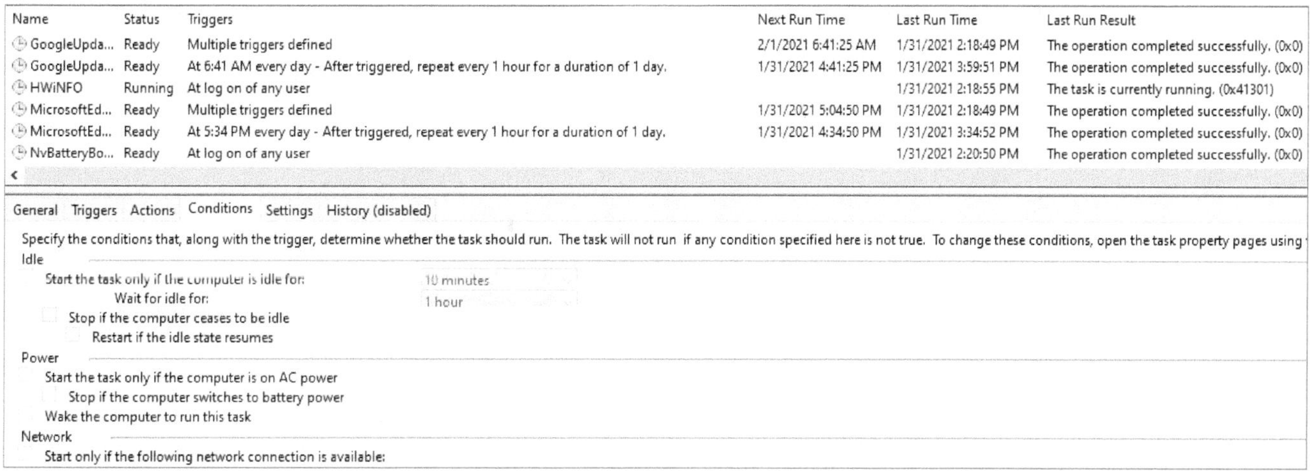

Name	Status	Triggers	Next Run Time	Last Run Time	Last Run Result
GoogleUpda...	Ready	Multiple triggers defined	2/1/2021 6:41:25 AM	1/31/2021 2:18:49 PM	The operation completed successfully. (0x0)
GoogleUpda...	Ready	At 6:41 AM every day - After triggered, repeat every 1 hour for a duration of 1 day.	1/31/2021 4:41:25 PM	1/31/2021 3:59:51 PM	The operation completed successfully. (0x0)
HWiNFO	Running	At log on of any user		1/31/2021 2:18:55 PM	The task is currently running. (0x41301)
MicrosoftEd...	Ready	Multiple triggers defined	1/31/2021 5:04:50 PM	1/31/2021 2:18:49 PM	The operation completed successfully. (0x0)
MicrosoftEd...	Ready	At 5:34 PM every day - After triggered, repeat every 1 hour for a duration of 1 day.	1/31/2021 4:34:50 PM	1/31/2021 3:34:52 PM	The operation completed successfully. (0x0)
NvBatteryBo...	Ready	At log on of any user		1/31/2021 2:20:50 PM	The operation completed successfully. (0x0)

General Triggers Actions Conditions Settings History (disabled)

Specify the conditions that, along with the trigger, determine whether the task should run. The task will not run if any condition specified here is not true. To change these conditions, open the task property pages using

Idle

    Start the task only if the computer is idle for: 10 minutes

        Wait for idle for: 1 hour

      Stop if the computer ceases to be idle

        Restart if the idle state resumes

Power

    Start the task only if the computer is on AC power

      Stop if the computer switches to battery power

    Wake the computer to run this task

Network

    Start only if the following network connection is available:

Source: Microsoft Corporation

Figure 10-9 Microsoft Windows Task Manager

- *Unauthorized changes.* Often threat actors attempt to make changes to OS system settings, particularly as they relate to security. These unauthorized changes to system security policies are common. If the threat actor can manipulate the security settings, such as disabling antimalware software, then their malicious software has a better chance of running undetected.
- *Unauthorized privileges.* Another change is unauthorized privilege. Access rights are privileges to access hardware and software resources that are granted to users or devices. OSs and many applications have the ability to restrict a user's privileges in accessing its specific functions. Creating unauthorized privileges is changing OS settings or exploiting a vulnerability in software to gain access to resources that the user normally would be restricted from accessing.

Software-Related Evidence

Evidence of a cyber incident can also be found in software. The most obvious evidence is unauthorized software (applications that are not approved) that is silently installed by threat actors on the endpoint.

Most organizations simply restrict users from installing unauthorized software by configuring their user account to "standard" instead of "administrator" and thus not provide them with privileges to install software. However, restricting unauthorized software from running on a computer in which the user has administrative privileges can be much more difficult. Some OS configurations allow an administrator to create a preapproved whitelist of software permitted to run. Figure 10-10 illustrates creating a whitelist for a Microsoft Windows host using Group Policy; other Windows options include using Windows AppLocker or restricting through the Windows registry.

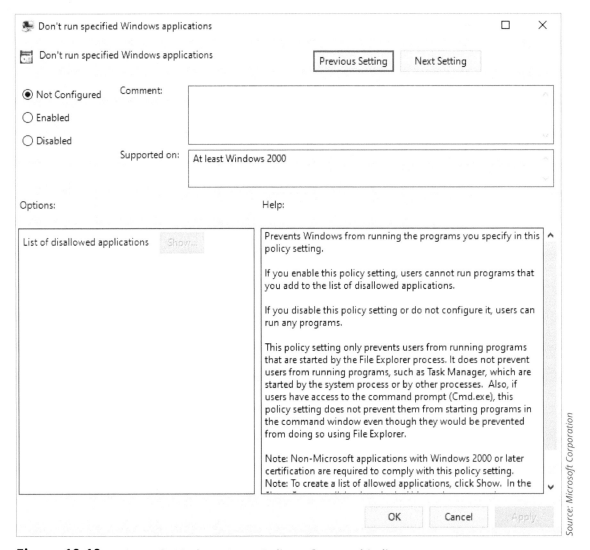

Figure 10-10 Microsoft Windows Group Policy software whitelist

 **CAUTION** Creating and constantly updating a whitelist of approved software can be a time-consuming task.

Data Exfiltration

Another symptom is the attempts by threat actors to steal data and transfer it to an external source (**data exfiltration**). Symptoms often include hard drive consumption on select servers that serve as "staging areas" for accumulating the data into a single location before it is exported.

NOTE 13

Data exfiltration can in many instances be mitigated by data loss prevention (DLP), which is covered in Module 5.

Application IoCs

Several indicators of a cyber incident relate to applications. These include unusual activity, new account creation, and unfamiliar outbound communications.

Unusual Activity

An application that suddenly exhibits unusual activity compared to its normal activity may be the result of a cyber incident. These activities include the following:

- *Anomalous activity.* An application that has been functioning normally and suddenly exhibits unusual or strange behavior (**anomalous activity**) could indicate that the application simply needs to be reinstalled. However, it may also indicate that malware has altered an application in some way, such as a virus infecting an application and causing it to function erratically.
- *Unexpected output.* An application that suddenly produces unanticipated output, such as an error message that is poorly formatted or a request for unusual user input, may be an indication of a malware infection. This is called **unexpected output**.
- *Service interruptions.* Some applications link to other applications for data exchange or communication. For example, object linking and embedding (OLE) is a Microsoft technology that facilitates the sharing of application data and objects written in different formats from multiple sources and applications. When a **service interruption** occurs in this feature, it may be a symptom of a cyber incident.
- *Modified application log.* As a means of "covering their tracks," threat actors may attempt to edit the application log that shows what applications were launched, when, and by whom. A changed log file (**modified application log**) can serve as an IoC.

New Account Creation

For a higher level of security, some applications require that a separate user account be created and stored in a database linked to the application. This means that a user must log in to the application separately from logging in to the OS.

Malware can often attempt to compromise the user application database by creating a new account (**introduction of new accounts**). This could allow the threat actor to log in to the application or a malicious running process to connect to the application itself. In either case, unexpected new account creation should be immediately investigated.

 **CAUTION** For enhanced security, some Windows applications can make the user application database dependent on the current Windows user account. This means that you can only log in to the application (open the application database) when you are logged in as the same Windows user when creating the database. However, caution should be used with this option. If the Windows user account is deleted or the operating system must be reinstalled, you will no longer be able to open the application database. And creating a new Windows account on the new installation with the old username and password still does not allow you access to the application database.

Unexpected Outbound Communication

An application that has the capacity for external communication, such as through an internal FTP feature, and unexpectedly begins performing outbound communication should be considered as compromised. Any unfamiliar and unanticipated outbound communication (unexpected outbound communication) is likely an indicator of an application compromise.

TWO RIGHTS & A WRONG

1. Traffic spikes are always an indication of data exfiltration by threat actors.
2. Beaconing occurs when infected devices attempt to contact the threat actor's external command and control (C&C) server.
3. Threat actors attempt to avoid detection by using common protocols over nonstandard ports.

See Appendix C for the answer.

DIGITAL FORENSICS

 **CERTIFICATION**

4.4 Given a scenario, utilize basic digital forensics techniques.

Digital forensics, also known as *forensic science*, is the application of science to questions that are of interest to the legal profession. Forensics is not limited to analyzing evidence from a murder scene; it also can be applied to technology. As computers are the foundation for communicating and recording information, computer forensics uses technology to search for computer evidence of a crime and can attempt to retrieve information—even if it has been altered or erased—that can be used in the pursuit of the cyber attacker or criminal who has used technology for their criminal activity.

NOTE 14

Digital evidence can be retrieved from computers, mobile devices, cell phones, digital cameras, and virtually any device that has memory or storage.

The importance of computer forensics is due in part to the following:

- *Amount of digital evidence.* Just as technology is widely used in all areas of life today, criminals use technology in the preparation and often the execution of their crimes. This leaves behind large volumes of digital evidence that can be retrieved through computer forensics.
- *Increased scrutiny by the legal profession.* No longer do attorneys and judges freely accept computer evidence. The procedures used in retrieving, transporting, and storing digital evidence are now held to the same standards as those used with physical evidence.
- *Higher level of computer skill by criminals.* As criminals become increasingly sophisticated in their knowledge of computers and techniques such as encryption, a computer forensics expert is often needed to retrieve the evidence.

Using forensics to investigate a cyber incident involves knowing the elements of a forensics kit and the procedures and tools that are used. There are also specialized forensics for platforms such as mobile devices, virtualization, and the cloud.

Elements of a Forensics Kit

A forensics kit is a tool bag that contains the necessary instruments for carrying out a forensics investigation. These instruments can include a digital forensics workstation, write blocker, cables and drive adapters, and other tools.

Digital Forensics Workstation

The primary tool in a forensics kit is a computer specially configured to perform forensics activities, called a digital forensics workstation. Digital forensics workstations are typically configured with the latest computer hardware, such as multiple gigabit network ports and USB ports, along with up to 10 drive "hot swap" bays to hold up to eight drives. This allows for two additional empty bays that can be used for backups or additional processing such as copying data directly to a network attached storage (NAS) device. The workstations also are configured with eight or more 6 TB hard drives configured in RAID 5 for redundancy and have 1000-watt power supply units and multiple fans for cooling along with the latest high-end CPUs.

NOTE 15

Digital forensics workstations are expensive, costing more than $20,000 depending on the options.

Write Blockers

A hard drive in an endpoint to be analyzed should first be removed from that system and inserted into another system for analysis. However, once a drive is inserted into another system, the OS will immediately attempt to write data to the drive, thus contaminating it so that it can no longer be used as evidence.

A write blocker is a device or special software on a digital forensics workstation that allows a hard drive to be examined without the possibility of accidentally writing to the drive. A hardware write blocker is shown in Figure 10-11.

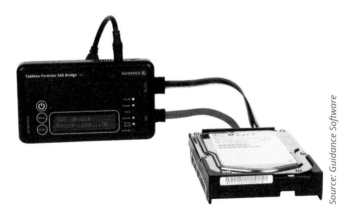

Figure 10-11 Write blocker

There are two types of hardware write blockers: native and tailgate. A native write blocker uses the same type of interface for both connections, such as IDE to IDE. A tailgate device uses one interface for a connection and a different interface for the other, such as a Firewire to SATA write block. A write blocker can either allow all commands to pass from the computer to the drive except for those that are on a particular list, or it can specifically block all write commands and let everything else pass through.

NOTE 16

The two individuals who first invented write blocking hold a U.S. patent on the technology.

Cables and Drive Adapters

Other items that should be included in a forensics kit are different types of cables to connect a wide range of devices to the digital forensic workstation. Since most forensic workstations have only USB connection ports, these cables should have a USB connection on one end with connectors for SATA, Firewire, and other connection types. A multiport "hub" device can also be used to connect multiple cables or storage devices, as shown in Figure 10-12.

NOTE 17

In addition to carrying multiple cables to connect external devices, it is necessary to have a variety of hard drive adapters for connecting different types of hard drives to a forensics workstation.

Figure 10-12   Multiport hub

Other Tools

Several other tools should also be included in a forensics kit. These include the following:

- *Cameras*. Both video and still (records one picture at a time) cameras are important tools. The physical surroundings of the computer in question should be clearly documented, and many forensics experts use a video camera to capture video of the entire process. Photographs of the area should be taken before anything is touched to help document that the computer was working prior to the attack. (Some defense attorneys have argued that a computer was not functioning properly and thus the suspect could not be held responsible for any damages.) The computer should be photographed from several angles, including those showing the images displayed on the screen. Because digital pictures can be easily altered, some security professionals recommend that photographs be taken with a camera using film.
- *Wiped removable media*. Various types of removable media that have been wiped clean should also be included. This may include USB flash drives, portable external hard drives, Secure Digital (SD) cards, and Compact Flash (CF) cards.
- *Crime scene tape*. Also called barricade tape, this is brightly colored tape used to warn others that the area is restricted, and they should not enter without permission.
- *Seals*. Evidence from a suspected device should be placed in bags that are then sealed. This serves as protection to prevent the evidence from being altered. Two types of seals are commonly used. A tamper-evident seal is a seal or tape that cannot be removed and reapplied without leaving obvious visual evidence. If the seal or tape is lifted or removed, a clearly visible *OPENED* message appears on the packaging. For additional traceability and security, tape is usually sequentially numbered every 9 inches (22 centimeters). A tamper-resistant seal is designed to deter tampering with the bag. However, the seal does not necessarily produce visual evidence if tampering has occurred: if the sticker is removed carefully, it can be reapplied with no visual evidence of tampering.
- *Documents and forms*. Several different forms should be included in a forensics kit. A chain of custody form helps to document that the evidence was under strict control at all times and no unauthorized person was given the opportunity to corrupt the evidence. A chain of custody includes documenting the serial numbers of the systems involved, who handled and had custody of the systems and for what length of time, and the final disposal of the evidence. Other forms include an incident form that contains detailed information about the event (date, time, location, official in charge, type of incident, etc.) and assigns a case number to the incident. An incident response plan outlines the steps to be taken during the forensic investigation. Finally, a call/escalation list provides contact information for each of the individuals who should be notified.

Forensics Procedures

When responding to an incident that requires an examination using computer forensics, five basic steps (forensics procedures) are followed, which are similar to those of standard forensics. The steps are to secure the crime scene, preserve the evidence, document the chain of custody, examine the evidence, and enable recovery.

Secure the Scene

When an illegal or unauthorized incident occurs that involves technology, action must be taken immediately. A delay of even a few minutes can allow digital evidence to be overwritten in the normal function of the device, become contaminated by other users, or give the perpetrator time to destroy the evidence.

Individuals in the immediate vicinity should perform "damage control," which is the effort to minimize any loss of evidence. The steps in damage control include contacting the incident response team, securing and then quarantining the electronic equipment involved, and, if necessary, reporting the incident to the appropriate external authorities.

Once the incident response team arrives, their first job is to secure the scene, which includes the following activities:

- The physical surroundings of the device computer should be clearly documented. Many forensics experts use a video camera to capture video of all the work performed by the incident response team to demonstrate that proper procedures were followed.
- Photographs of the area should be taken before anything is touched to help document that the computer was working prior to the attack.
- Any cables connected to a device should be labeled to document the hardware components and how they are connected.
- The team should take custody of the device along with any peripherals so that data evidence is secured (data acquisition). In addition, USB flash drives and any other media must be secured.
- The team must speak with those present to perform interviews with witnesses and everyone who had access to the system and then document their findings, including what those people were doing with the system, what its intended functions were, and how it has been affected by the unauthorized actions.

Preserve the Evidence

The next task is preservation of the evidence or ensuring that important proof is not corrupted or even destroyed. Preserving evidence can also help mitigate non-repudiation, or a denial by perpetrators that they were involved or did anything wrong.

Depending upon the type and severity of the incident, it may be necessary to immediately involve the judicial system to help collect and preserve the digital evidence. This ensures that the integrity of the evidence is maintained and can hold up in a court of law (admissibility). One of the first steps is eDiscovery, which is identifying, collecting, and producing electronically stored information (ESI) in response to a request in an investigation or lawsuit. Once data has been identified, it can be placed under a legal hold, meaning that it cannot be modified, deleted, erased, or otherwise destroyed.

 **CAUTION** There is a tendency to issue legal holds that are too broad in scope. For example, to place a legal hold on all email correspondence may result in retaining thousands or millions of unneeded messages and associated attachments, while placing a legal hold on all portable devices requiring them to be locked away makes them useless to the organization. Instead, appropriate filters should be used to capture only data that is relevant.

It is important to validate that what is being analyzed is what was on the original device and has not been altered (changing the binaries). Documenting the contents can be accomplished by using a one-way hash cryptographic algorithm. A hash algorithm creates a unique "digital fingerprint" of a set of data. This process is called hashing, and the resulting fingerprint is a digest (sometimes called a message digest or hash).

NOTE 18

A hashing algorithm is ideal for validating the contents because of its characteristics: fixed size (a digest of a short set of data will produce the same size as a digest of a long set of data), uniqueness (two different sets of data cannot produce the same digest), and original (it should not be possible to produce a data set that has a desired or predefined hash). Hashing is often used as a check to verify that the original contents of an item has not been changed.

Two common hash algorithms are used in forensic investigations. One of the earliest hash algorithms is actually a "family" of algorithms known as Message Digest (MD). The most well-known of these algorithms is Message Digest 5 (MD5). Another family of hashes is the Secure Hash Algorithm (SHA).

 **CAUTION**   Despite their popularity, serious weaknesses have been identified in MD5 and SHA-1. Other hash algorithms such as RipeMD160 and SHA-256, SHA-512, or SHA3-512 should be considered instead.

Document Chain of Custody

As soon as the team begins its work, it must start and maintain a strict chain of custody. Documenting the evidence from the very beginning is called provenance. The chain of custody documents that the evidence was always under strict control and no unauthorized person was given the opportunity to corrupt the evidence. A chain of custody includes documenting all the serial numbers of the systems involved, who handled and had custody of the systems and for what length of time, how the computer was shipped, and any other steps in the process. In short, a chain of custody is a detailed document describing where the evidence was at all times from the beginning of the investigation.

 **CAUTION**   Gaps in a chain of custody can result in severe legal consequences. Courts have dismissed cases involving computer forensics because a secure chain of custody could not be verified.

Examine for Evidence

When examining technology devices that may contain evidence, called artifacts, it is critical to follow a specific order. This is because different data sources have different degrees of preservation. An order of volatility must be followed to preserve the most fragile data first. Table 10-4 lists the order of volatility.

Table 10-4   Order of volatility

Order	Examples	Description
1	Registers and CPU cache	Registers and the CPU cache are extremely volatile and change constantly.
2	Routing tables, ARP cache, process table, kernel statistics, RAM	The network routing and process tables have data located on network devices that can change quickly while the system is in operation, and kernel statistics are moving between cache and main memory, which make them highly volatile. RAM information can be lost if power is lost.
3	Temporary file systems	Temporary file systems are not subject to the degree of rapid changes as the preceding elements.
4	Hard drive	Hard drive data is relatively stable.
5	Remote logging and monitoring data	Although remote logging and monitoring is more volatile than hard drive data, the data on a hard drive is considered more valuable and should be preserved first.
6	Physical configuration and network topology	These items are not considered volatile and do not have a significant impact on an investigation.
7	Archival media	Data that has been preserved in archival form is not volatile.

Often clues are not obvious and must be mined and exposed. One source of hidden data is called slack. Windows computers use two types of slack. The first is RAM slack. Windows stores files on a hard drive in 512-byte blocks called sectors, and multiple sectors are used to form a cluster. Clusters are made up of blocks of sectors. When a file that is being saved is not long enough to fill up the last sector on a disk (a common occurrence because a file size only rarely matches the sector size), Windows pads the remaining cluster space with data currently stored in RAM. This padding creates RAM slack, which can contain any information that has been created, viewed, modified, downloaded, or copied since the computer was last booted. Thus, if the computer has not been shut down for several days, the data stored in RAM slack can come from activity that occurred during that time. Data stored in RAM such as RAM slack can be viewed by using endpoint memory forensic tools.

RAM slack pertains only to the last sector of a file. If additional sectors are needed to round out the block size for the last cluster assigned to the file, then a different type of slack is created. This is known as drive file slack (sometimes called drive slack) because the padded data that Windows uses comes from data stored on the hard drive. Such data could contain remnants of previously deleted files or data from the format pattern associated with disk storage space that has yet to be used by the computer. Both RAM slack and drive slack can hold valuable evidence.

When examining hard drives for evidence (endpoint disk forensic tools), it is important to not rely on an application running under a standard OS in an attempt to view the underly data. This is because most modern OSs are not designed to retrieve all data on a drive. A process known as carving should be used instead. Carving extracts raw data blocks of the hard drive so that the full contents of the drive can be examined.

Enable Recovery

A final analysis looks at recovering the data from the security event and considers lessons that can be learned from it. The forensics procedures have gathered strategic intelligence—or the collection, processing, analysis, and dissemination of intelligence for forming policy changes. A more in-depth application of strategic intelligence is strategic counterintelligence, which involves gaining information about the attacker's intelligence collection capabilities.

Forensics Tools

Different software and hardware forensics tools are available for analysis. For an endpoint, one important set of tools is imaging utilities used for generating a physical copy of a disk. A utility named *dd*, sometimes called GNU dd, is the oldest imaging tool still in use, primarily because it requires only minimal resources to run and generates raw image files that can be read by many other programs. However, dd is a command-line program and lacks some of the useful features found in more modern imagers, such as metadata gathering, error correction, and a user-friendly interface. Other popular forensics software tools are memdump, a Linux utility that "dumps" system memory, WinHex, a hexadecimal editor that can be used for forensics, and Autopsy, a digital forensics platform.

>  **CAUTION**   Because dd is a command-line program, it requires several ambiguous command-line arguments (*switches* or *flags*) to tailor the imaging command. Some of these arguments are similar and easily confused and can even result in destroying the source media being duplicated. Users should exercise extreme caution when using the dd utility.

Products are available that package multiple tools into a single suite with a common user interface and can more easily exchange information among the different tools. Two of the most common forensic suites are EnCase (shown in Figure 10-13) and FTK Imager.

For capturing network traffic to be used in a forensics investigation, the packet capture utility Wireshark is often used. Another tool is tcpdump, which is a command-line packet analyzer. It displays TCP/IP packets and other packets being transmitted or received over a network. Tcpdump operates on UNIX and Linux OSs, and various forks are available for Windows computers.

Specialized Forensics

There are also specialized forensics for platforms other than standard computers. These include mobile devices, cloud repositories, and virtualized images.

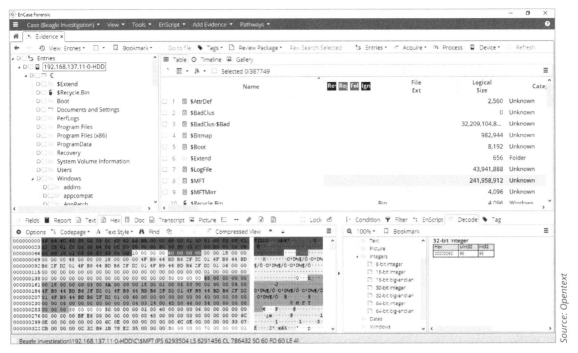

Figure 10-13 EnCase software

Mobile Device

Due to their very nature, **mobile device forensics** is different from performing forensics on an endpoint computer. Although mobile devices are sometimes characterized merely as "portable computers," they actually contain a broader wealth of information than a desktop or laptop computer. Mobile devices are almost constantly in a user's possession, unlike a standard computer, and thus can more accurately reveal the user's actions. Forensic information that can be uniquely extracted from a mobile device includes the following:

- *Call detail records*. This information can reveal the date and time a telephone call was started and ended, the terminating and originating cell phone towers that were used, whether the call was outgoing or incoming, the call's duration, who was called, and who made the call.
- *Global Positioning System (GPS) data*. GPS data can accurately pinpoint the location of users and what activities they were performing in a specific location.
- *App data*. Many apps store and access data such as media files, contact lists, and a gallery of all the photos on the device.
- *Short Message Service (SMS) texts*. Text messaging is a popular means of communication. It leaves electronic records of dialogue that can be used as evidence.
- *Photos and videos*. Media recorded as photos and videos on a mobile device can often contain incriminating evidence.

Virtualization

Performing a forensics investigation on a standard endpoint computer can be a delicate operation. Preserving elements in volatile memory before they change or disappear is especially important. However, what if the entire device has been virtualized and resides only in memory? This is the challenge when performing forensics in a virtualized environment (**virtualization forensics**).

NOTE 19

Virtualization is covered in Module 5.

Analyzing a virtual device is different from investigating an endpoint computer. For example, after capturing the contents of registers, the CPU and ARP cache, process table, kernel statistics, RAM, and temporary file systems on a standard computer, an endpoint computer can then be powered down to transport it to another location for more in-depth analysis. However, powering down a virtual machine (VM), which is a simulated software-based emulation of a computer, and then resuming it later will change the volatile evidence. Attempting to perform a "live" analysis on a running VM may change information that resides in memory or cause open network connections to be terminated.

NOTE 20

Research has shown that how a VM is powered down can impact the amount of data available for analysis.

When performing virtualization forensics, there are two basic options. When using the first option, the VM is suspended and resumed later under forensic analysis so that the forensics investigator can use normal procedures to analyze the VM. However, when resuming, the VM files that are stored could change, destroying critical evidence.

The second option is to create a snapshot of the VM and then work directly with the VM files that are stored on the host system. By taking a snapshot, the state of the hard disk is preserved and any changes to the disk are stored in a separate file, while the virtual memory of the VM is stored in a file and any state changes are written to another virtual memory file. This can ensure that evidence is preserved and can be presented to court as forensically sound evidence.

NOTE 21

Both EnCase and FTK support conversion of VMware .vmdk files to raw (dd) format. However, FTK also converts the snapshot along with any previous snapshots and the base .vmdk files.

Cloud

If the incident is the result of a breach of cloud-based resources, it is not possible to secure the scene to perform a forensics investigation on the cloud (**cloud forensics**) as in an on-prem incident. When dealing with a cloud incident, the following should be considered:

- A primary concern is to ensure that the digital evidence has not been tampered with by third parties so it can be admissible in a court of law. In Software as a Service (SaaS) and Platform as a Service (PaaS) models, because customers do not have control of the hardware, they must depend on the cloud service providers for accumulating log data. A right-to-audit clause in a cloud contract gives the customer the legal right to review the logs, and these should be negotiated in advance.
- When a cloud customer is notified by its cloud service provider that an incident occurred, the immediate response from the customer's in-house legal and IT teams will be to ask for details about the scope of the impact. However, unless they are contractually obligated, the cloud provider may take weeks or even months to provide its client with details as they perform an investigation. However, once the cloud customer has been notified, the "clock has started ticking" regarding data breach notification law deadlines. This can place the cloud customer in an awkward situation.
- The legal regulatory/jurisdiction laws that govern the site in which the cloud data resides may present difficulties. For example, a court order issued in a jurisdiction where the cloud data center is located will likely not be applicable to another jurisdiction in another country.

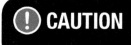 **CAUTION**   When creating a cloud platform, the customer can often choose the region in which the data will reside. It is at this time that issues regarding jurisdiction should be considered and the region should be chosen carefully.

TWO RIGHTS & A WRONG

1. The amount of digital evidence, increased scrutiny by the legal profession, and the higher level of computer skill by criminals are all reasons why computer forensics is increasingly important.
2. There are two types of hardware write blockers: native and tailgate.
3. A Legal Stop Order (LSO) is a judicial requirement that once data has been identified, it cannot be modified or deleted.

See Appendix C for the answer.

VM LAB   You're now ready to complete the live, virtual machine labs for this module. The labs can be found in the Apply It folder in each MindTap module.

MODULE SUMMARY

- In the aftermath of a cyber incident, it is important to retain evidence of the attack. One of the primary uses of retained evidence is to generate Indicators of Compromise (IoCs). One of the first indicators of an attack is often found in the network. Bandwidth monitoring on a network is an important activity for normal network operations. Another use of network bandwidth monitoring is to look for evidence of a cybersecurity incident. A sudden unusual surge in network bandwidth utilization is called a traffic spike. Traffic spikes may also be evidence of a cyber incident. Whereas a sudden traffic spike may indicate a cyber incident, so can an overall increase in the amount of bandwidth being used, known as bandwidth consumption.

- Secretive and unexpected network transmissions are often symptoms of a cyber incident. Under normal network conditions, most communications occur between multiple lower-level clients to fewer higher-level servers. However, if the clients unexpectedly begin irregular internal communication with other peers on the network (irregular peer-to-peer communication), this unusual symptom could be an indication of a cyber incident. An infected endpoint could be targeting another endpoint to spread malware or to pivot to other devices and services. Beaconing occurs when infected devices attempt to contact the threat actor's external command and control (C&C) server. The purpose of communicating with the C&C server is usually two-way: to receive updated or new instructions from the C&C server and to upload stolen data to the C&C server.

- To mask or hide stealth transmissions to hinder or prevent detection, malware typically does not use a distinctive protocol that can be easily identified. Instead of distinctive protocols, threat actors may use standard network protocols that do not attract attention. For example, when sending stolen data, the malware may use the HTTP or FTP protocol, which can easily blend into normal traffic. However, the volume of traffic may make the beaconing detectable. Another attempt to avoid detection is to use common protocols over nonstandard ports. One technique used to mask stealth transmissions is to combine standard protocols with an internal mesh network of infected devices so that the devices can communicate with each other easily. This allows for a single compromised endpoint to act as an internal C&C device. It is generally recognized that detecting P2P C&C can be difficult since the traffic uses standard protocols to blend in with normal internal and external network traffic.

- In preparation for unleashing a cyber incident, threat actors attempt to perform scan sweeps on a network to uncover any vulnerabilities. These scan sweeps include ping sweeps and port scans. Another symptom of a cyber incident is the presence of unauthorized devices, called rogue detection on a network. On a wireless network, a rogue mobile device can connect to the network if it is weakly protected. These are particularly dangerous since they can provide unfettered access to the entire network, bypassing network security protections or tricking users into connecting with a sinister AP.

- IoCs can also be found on endpoints. On an endpoint system, an abnormally high volume of resource consumption is often an IoC. Malware that infects an endpoint computer can run using multiple cores and threads without any appreciable impact upon the normal tasks that the user is performing. This shows no effect on the processor's performance, and thus, the user is unaware of the presence of malware. However, if the malware performs a significantly complicated or lengthy task, then the processor may begin to slow down to the point that the malware becomes apparent. Abnormal memory consumption could likewise be a symptom of a cyber incident. Drive capacity consumption refers to the unexpected loss of available hard drive space as a result of malware. This may be due to malware gathering files from several different hosts or servers prior to data exfiltration, or it can be because of continual scan sweeps performed by malware that result in the rapid increase in the size and number of log files.

- Evidence of a compromise can most often be found in the OS running on the endpoint. Indicators include a malicious process, abnormal process behavior, file system changes, changes to the registry, an unauthorized scheduled task, unauthorized changes, and unauthorized privileges. Another symptom is the attempt by threat actors to steal data and transfer it to an external source (data exfiltration). Symptoms often include hard drive consumption on select servers that serve as "staging areas" for accumulating the data into a single location before it is exported.

- Several indicators of a cyber incident relate to applications. An application that suddenly exhibits unusual activity compared to its normal activity may be the result of a cyber incident. These activities include an anomalous activity, unexpected output, service interruptions, and a modified application log. Malware can often attempt to compromise a user application database by creating a new account. This could allow the threat actor to log in to the application or a malicious running process to connect to the application itself. An application that has the capacity for external communication, such as through an internal FTP feature, and unexpectedly begins performing outbound communication should be considered as compromised. Any unfamiliar and unanticipated outbound communication (unexpected outbound communication) is likely an indicator of an application compromise.

- Digital forensics, also known as forensic science, is the application of science to questions that are of interest to the legal profession. Forensics is not limited to analyzing evidence from a murder scene; it also can be applied to technology. As computers are the foundation for communicating and recording information, computer forensics uses technology to search for computer evidence of a crime and can attempt to retrieve information—even if it has been altered or erased—that can be used in the pursuit of the cyber attackers or criminals who used technology for their criminal activity. A forensics kit is a tool bag that contains the necessary instruments for carrying out a forensics investigation. These instruments can include a digital forensics workstation, write blockers, cables and drive adapters, and other tools.

- When responding to an incident that requires an examination using computer forensics, five basic forensics procedures are followed. When an illegal or unauthorized incident occurs that involves technology, then action must be taken immediately to secure the scene. The next task is preservation of the evidence or ensuring that important proof is not corrupted or even destroyed. It is important to validate that what is being analyzed is what was on the original device and has not been altered. Documenting the contents can be accomplished by using a one-way hash cryptographic algorithm. A hash algorithm creates a unique "digital fingerprint" of a set of data.

- As soon as the forensics team begins its work, it must start and maintain a strict chain of custody. The chain of custody documents that the evidence was always under strict control and no unauthorized person was given the opportunity to corrupt the evidence. When examining technology devices that may contain evidence, it is critical to follow a specific order because different data sources have different degrees of preservation. A final analysis looks at recovering the data from the security event and considers lessons that can be learned from it. The forensics procedures have gathered strategic intelligence, or the collection, processing, analysis, and dissemination of intelligence for forming policy changes.

- Different software and hardware forensics tools are available for analysis. For an endpoint, one important set of tools is imaging utilities used for generating a physical copy of a disk. Products are available that package multiple tools into a single suite with a common user interface and can more easily exchange information among the different tools. For capturing network traffic to be used in a forensics investigation, the packet capture utility Wireshark is often used. Another tool is tcpdump, which is a command-line packet analyzer.

- There are also specialized forensics for platforms other than standard computers. Due to their very nature, mobile device forensics is different from forensics on an endpoint computer. Mobile devices are almost constantly in a user's possession, unlike a standard computer, and thus can more accurately reveal the user's actions. Analyzing a virtual device is different from investigating an endpoint computer. One option is to create a snapshot of the VM and then work directly with the VM files stored on the host system. By taking a snapshot, the state of the hard disk is preserved and any changes to the disk are stored in a separate file, while the virtual memory of the VM is stored in a file and any state changes are written to another virtual memory file. If the incident is the result of a breach of cloud-based resources, it is not possible to secure the scene to perform a forensics investigation as in an on-prem incident. Often this involves creating an agreement with the cloud provider when the service is first initiated.

Key Terms

abnormal OS process behavior	endpoint memory forensic tools	rogue detection on a network
anomalous activity	file system change or anomaly	scan sweeps
bandwidth consumption	forensics procedures	service interruption
beaconing	hashing	tcpdump
carving	introduction of new accounts	traffic spike
changing the binaries	irregular peer-to-peer	unauthorized changes
cloud forensics	communication	unauthorized privilege
common protocols over	legal hold	unauthorized scheduled task
nonstandard ports	malicious process	unauthorized software
data acquisition	memory consumption	unexpected outbound
data exfiltration	mobile device forensics	communication
digital forensics	modified application log	unexpected output
drive capacity consumption	processor consumption	virtualization forensics
endpoint disk forensic tools	registry change or anomaly	Wireshark

Review Questions

1. Which of the following is NOT a reason why computer forensics is important?
   a. Amount of digital evidence
   b. Increased scrutiny by the legal profession
   c. Higher level of computer skill by criminals
   d. Federal laws that mandate all attacks be examined using forensics

2. What is the name of a device that prevents writing to a hard drive?
   a. Drive blocker
   b. Write blocker
   c. Sector restrictor
   d. Device blocker

3. What type of cameras should NOT be used in a forensics investigation?
   a. Digital still camera
   b. Video camera
   c. Still camera
   d. HD camera

4. Alvaro has been asked to acquire tape to secure evidence bags that cannot be removed and reapplied without leaving visual evidence. What type of tape should he use?
   a. Tamper-evident
   b. Tamper-resistant
   c. Tamper-impervious
   d. Tamper-controlled

5. Which of the following is NOT a name for a unique digital fingerprint of a set of data?
   a. Hash
   b. Digest
   c. Message digest
   d. Certificate

6. Which imaging utility can generate a physical image copy?
   a. dd
   b. dr
   c. dt
   d. de

7. Which of the following is NOT a reason for bandwidth monitoring?
   a. To identify cyber incident
   b. To troubleshoot network performance
   c. To monitor bandwidth agreements
   d. To find application buffer overflows

8. Which of the following is NOT a reason for a traffic spike?
   a. Mail server problems
   b. Software updates
   c. Remote external backups
   d. Processor consumption

9. Which of the following is NOT a helpful question in determining the cause of a traffic spike?
   a. Do the spikes appear at the same time on the same day?
   b. Do other monitoring points on the network match these patterns?
   c. Do the spikes occur during business hours or at other times?
   d. Is the traffic using all common protocols?

10. Which of the following is false about traffic spikes?
    a. Using traffic spikes as a symptom of a cyber incident is considered to be easy and straightforward.
    b. A malware's spike can become camouflaged among normal spikes.
    c. Malware can be programmed to perform an event that causes a traffic spike on a regular interval.
    d. Normal traffic spikes are not uncommon.

11. Aika wants to monitor bandwidth consumption to determine if there has been a cyber incident. What will be her first step?
    a. Identify an open port on the router.
    b. Install a packet tracker on the network.
    c. Receive permission from her Internet Service Provider (ISP).
    d. Establish a baseline of normal bandwidth utilization.

12. Which of the following is false about beaconing?
    a. Beaconing occurs when infected devices attempt to contact the threat actor's external C&C server.
    b. Beaconing is a three-way communication process.
    c. Beaconing is used to receive updated or new instructions from a C&C server.
    d. Data exfiltration is accomplished through beaconing.

13. Which of the following is NOT a type of attack that can be generated through a botnet?
    a. Spamming
    b. Spreading malware

    c. Buffer overflows
    d. Manipulating online polls

14. Etsu is reviewing log files and discovers that data has been stolen and sent out from the network. In her report, what does she call this?
    a. Exfiltration
    b. Infiltration
    c. Gathering
    d. Sweeping

15. Why would a threat actor NOT use BitTorrent for data exfiltration?
    a. BitTorrent has never been used for data exfiltration and thus is untested.
    b. BitTorrent is not popular and would be difficult for the threat actors to find clients.
    c. BitTorrent is considered too slow for file transfers.
    d. The BitTorrent protocol can be easily identified.

16. Which of the following is NOT true about a P2P C&C?
    a. It can mask irregular peer-to-peer communications but not data exfiltration through beaconing.
    b. A single compromised computer acts as an internal C&C device.
    c. It uses an internal mesh network.
    d. A P2P C&C uses common protocols.

17. If an attacker wants to learn which services are running on a server, which of the following would he use?
    a. Port scan
    b. Sweep scan
    c. Ping sweep
    d. IP sweep

18. Which of the following about new account creation is false?
    a. Malware can often attempt to compromise a user application database by creating a new account.
    b. New account creation can only be used for a threat actor to log in to the application.
    c. New account creation should be immediately investigated.
    d. Some applications allow logging in to an application to only be performed by the same Windows user who created the database.

19. Which of the following is NOT correct about tcpdump?
    a. Various forks are available for Windows computers.
    b. It operates on UNIX and Linux OS.
    c. It only displays TCP/IP packets being transmitted.
    d. It is a command-line packet analyzer.

20. Which of the following is the best way to perform forensics on a VM?

   a. Suspend the VM and resume it later under forensic analysis so that the forensics investigator can use normal procedures to analyze the VM.

   b. Take a snapshot of the state of the hard disk so that it is preserved and any changes to the disk are stored in a separate file.

   c. Load the VM into a virtual container box (VCB) and use regular forensic tools.

   d. It is not recommended that forensics be performed on a VM due to its volatile nature.

Case Projects

Case Project 10-1: Comparing Forensic Suites

Use the Internet to compare the forensic suites EnCase and FTK. Create a table listing the features of each suite. Based on your analysis, which would you recommend? Why? Create a one-page paper on your research and analysis.

Case Project 10-2: Mitigating Beaconing

How can beaconing be mitigated? Use the Internet to research five different methods for preventing beaconing. Which is the most effective? Why? Write a one-page summary of your research.

Case Project 10-3: Virtualization Forensics

Use the Internet to research the latest tools and techniques for performing virtualization forensics. Which of these would you recommend? Why? Create a one-page paper of your research.

Case Project 10-4: Uncovering OS Evidence

Create a table of each of the bulleted items in the section "Operating System Evidence" (such as "malicious process," and "abnormal OS process behavior"), and create two to three ways to detect each. Draw a table of each item and the ways to detect if it has occurred.

Case Project 10-5: On the Job

Suppose you work for a company that has suffered a cybersecurity incident. An intern was one of the first personnel on the scene but failed to follow organizational policies for preserving the evidence. A senior vice president is now pressuring this intern to state that he "probably" followed the preservation of evidence procedures, but his reluctance may be due to this being his first incident. The intern has come to you in private and asked you for advice. He is anxious that he might lose his internship if he does not follow what the senior vice president has "suggested" that he do. Write a one-page memo to the intern stating what you would do and why.

Reference

1. "What Are Peak Traffic Spikes?" *Netacea*, retrieved Aug. 28, 2019, www.netacea.com/peak-traffic-spikes.

COMPLIANCE

Cybersecurity compliance is defined as establishing risk-based controls to protect assets and the integrity, confidentiality, and accessibility of the information that they contain. In this final part, the modules will examine cybersecurity compliance. Module 11 looks at mitigating risk, particularly through policies, procedures, and established frameworks. Module 12 explores technical and nontechnical countermeasures for data protection and privacy.

MODULE 11
RISK MITIGATION

MODULE 12
DATA PROTECTION AND PRIVACY

PART 5

RISK MITIGATION

After completing this module, you should be able to do the following:

1 Define risk

2 Explain how to identify and mitigate risks

3 List and describe policies, procedures, and frameworks that are used as controls

Cybersecurity Today

While the year 2020 will long be remembered as the start of the worldwide COVID-19 pandemic, for cybersecurity professionals, the date will also be remembered as the year of the massive SolarWinds incident. And "massive" is a good way to describe it. The number of the victims is massive, with perhaps as many as 400 of the top Fortune 500 companies being compromised. The scope of the victims is massive, ranging from enterprises to government agencies like the Department of Homeland Security, the Treasury and Commerce Departments, national security agencies, and defense contractors. The ingenuity of the threat actors is likewise massive. Although the fallout, with one U.S. senator saying the attack is "virtually a declaration of war," is yet to be known, by all indications it, too, will be massive.

SolarWinds is a company in Austin, Texas, that sells network and computer management tools. The SolarWinds suite of tools includes monitoring capabilities (so that administrators immediately know when a critical computer goes down) and the ability to remotely restart services. One tool in this suite is SolarWinds Orion. At its peak, SolarWinds had more than 300,000 clients, and about 33,000 were using the Orion product, which generated slightly less than half of SolarWinds' $1 billion in annual revenue.

In early December 2020, the security firm FireEye discovered that it had been the victim of an attack. As FireEye set out to determine how attackers got past its defenses, it found that a back door had been planted through an unlikely place: SolarWinds Orion, the software that they used internally on their network. FireEye immediately contacted SolarWinds and law enforcement agencies.

It appears that as early as September 2019—and likely even earlier—threat actors were able to access the software development or software distribution pipeline on the SolarWinds servers. Malicious code was injected into a software update that SolarWinds was developing for distribution to all its clients. Because this update was given a digital certificate by Solar-Winds, this would ensure that the update was trusted by its clients as being secure.

The attackers had targeted the dynamic link library (DLL) in Orion called SolarWinds.Orion.Core.BusinessLayer.dll for their malware. Why they chose this DLL and how they implemented their code illustrates the very high level of sophistication of the attackers. This can be seen in five different ways.

First, the location within the DLL is the ideal spot for the malware, because that code is part of a larger sequence that initializes other components and schedules the execution of other tasks, and thus, it is always running. Second, the threat actors made the code very small and compact so that it would be easily overlooked. Third, unlike some threat actors, they did not use words like "back door" to raise suspicion if anyone did stumble upon the code. Fourth, the attackers hid the filenames that the DLL invoked to launch the different parts of the malware. They did this by using BASE64 to name the files, which is a binary-to-text encoding scheme, so the code to unzip the malware files was not noticeable.

Finally, their malware included a series of checks that the code made prior to its execution. The threat actors did not want the infected code to launch automatically, but to run only under certain conditions. Here are just a few of the checks the code made that had to be passed before it executed:

- There are no running processes related to security software.
- There are no drivers loaded from security-related software.
- The host "api.solarwinds.com" (the attacker's command and control server) resolves to an expected IP address.
- The current domain must not contain "solarwinds" and not look like a test domain.

Why all the checks? They were to prevent security professionals or SolarWinds from analyzing the code. Several of these checks prevented the malware from launching in a test network or on any computers belonging to SolarWinds.

It will take years to know the full impact of the SolarWinds Orion supply chain attack. Cybersecurity professionals are concerned that, given its high level of sophistication and the lengthy period of time that it went undetected, this attack could be an ominous precursor of things to come.

It would be difficult to scan the Internet on almost any cybersecurity topic without coming across the word *risk*. Risk is a key element in any conversation about protection, and organizations are (or should be) constantly on the lookout for ways to reduce risk.

One way to mitigate risk is through creating and then implementing various policies and procedures that address cybersecurity. But not all of these must be created from scratch: existing frameworks can be used as well. However, it is vital to perform audits and assessments to ensure that the cybersecurity controls are in compliance.

In this module, mitigating risks—especially through using policies, procedures, and frameworks—will be analyzed. First, you learn about risk and study strategies for mitigating risks. Next, you explore various policies and procedures that can help to minimize risk.

MINIMIZING RISK

 CERTIFICATION

5.2 Given a scenario, apply security concepts in support of organizational risk mitigation.

Minimizing risk is an important task for enterprises. This task involves three key steps: defining risk, identifying risk, and mitigating risk.

Defining Risk

Defining risk involves understanding what risk encompasses for an organization. It also involves knowing different types of risks.

What Is Risk?

An asset is any item that has a positive economic value. In an enterprise, assets have the following qualities: they provide value to the enterprise; they cannot easily be replaced without a significant investment in expense, time, worker skill, and/or resources; and they can form part of the enterprise's corporate identity. Examples of enterprise assets range from people (employees, customers, business partners, contractors, and vendors) to physical assets (buildings, automobiles, and plant equipment).

Obviously, not all assets have the same value or worth. The asset value is the relative worth of an asset. Consider the assets in an enterprise's information technology (IT) infrastructure. Some assets have a very high value while others do not. For example, a faulty desktop computer that can easily be replaced would not be considered an asset with a high value, yet the information contained on that computer can be an asset. Table 11-1 lists descriptions of the elements of an enterprise's IT infrastructure and whether these assets would normally be considered as having a high value.

Table 11-1   Typical IT assets

Asset	Description	Example	High value?
Information	Data that has been collected, classified, organized, and stored in various forms	Customer, personnel, production, sales, marketing, and finance databases	Yes: Extremely difficult to replace
Customized business software	Software that supports the business processes of the enterprise	Customized order transaction application	Yes: Unique and customized for the enterprise
System software	Software that provides the foundation for application software	Operating system	No: Can be easily replaced
Physical items	Computers equipment, communications equipment, storage media, furniture, and fixtures	Servers, routers, and power supplies	No: Can be easily replaced
Services	Outsourced computing services	Voice and data communications	No: Can be easily replaced

Assets are continually under threat, or a type of action that has the potential to cause harm. Several threat classifications are listed in Table 11-2.

Table 11-2   Threat classifications

Threat category	Description	Example
Strategic	Action that affects the long-term goals of the organization	Theft of intellectual property, not pursuing a new opportunity, loss of a major account, competitor entering the market
Compliance	Following (or not following) a regulation or standard	Breach of contract, not responding to the introduction of new laws
Financial	Impact of financial decisions or market factors	Increase in interest rates, global financial crisis
Operational	Events that impact the daily business of the organization	Fire, hazardous chemical spill, power blackout
Technical	Events that affect information technology systems	Denial of service attack, SQL injection attack, virus
Managerial	Actions related to the management of the organization	Long-term illness of company president, key employee resigning

Organizations must determine how realistic is the chance that a given threat will compromise an asset, called the likelihood of occurrence. This is stated in terms of risk. At a basic level, risk may be defined as a situation that involves exposure to some type of danger. At a more advanced level, risk can be described as a function of threats, consequences of those threats, and the resulting vulnerabilities.

Risk Types

There are many different types of risk. Risk types can be grouped into these broad categories:

- *Internal and external.* An internal risk comes from within an organization (such as employee theft), while an external risk is from the outside (like the actions of a hactivist).
- *Legacy systems.* One type of platform that is well known for its risks is a legacy system. A legacy system is no longer in widespread use, often because it has been replaced by an updated version of the earlier technology. Although legacy hardware introduces some risks, more often risks result from legacy software, such as an OS or program.
- *Multiparty.* Often overlooked in identifying risk types is the impact that vulnerabilities of one organization will have on other organizations that are connected to it. These are called multiparty risks that impact multiple "downstream" organizations.

NOTE 1

The results from the vulnerability of one organization rippling downstream are staggering. One study that examined more than 90,000 cyber events found that multiparty risks that were exploited resulted in financial losses 13 times larger than single-party incidents. The number of organizations impacted by multiparty incidents outnumber primary victims by 850 percent, and these multiparty incidents will continue to increase at an average rate of 20 percent annually.

- *Intellectual property (IP) theft.* Intellectual property (IP) is an invention or a work that is the result of creativity. The owner of IP can apply for protection from others who attempt to duplicate it; these protections over IP or its expression are patent, trademark, copyright, and trade secret. Threat actors attempt to steal IP (intellectual property (IP) theft) that may include research on a new product from an enterprise so that they can sell it to an unscrupulous foreign supplier who will then build an imitation model of the product to sell worldwide. This deprives the legitimate business of profits after investing hundreds of millions of dollars in product development, and because these foreign suppliers are in a different country, they are beyond the reach of domestic enforcement agencies and courts.
- *Software compliance and licensing.* Specialized software that is used by an enterprise is subject to licensing restrictions to protect the rights of the developer. An obvious violation would be for an organization to license software for a single manufacturing plant but then distribute that software to five other plants without paying for its usage. Software compliance and licensing risks are today considered a serious problem for organizations. It is recognized that most organizations unknowingly violate one or more licensing agreements. Several of the reasons for this are listed in Table 11-3.

Table 11-3   Reasons for software non-compliance

Reason	Example	Explanation
Software licensed for one reason but now used for a different reason	Limited use license purchased only to be used in non-production development environment used in a production environment.	Organizations may purchase limited use licenses rather than full use licenses to obtain a pricing discount; a newly hired technician was not aware of the restriction and copied software into the production facility.
Product use rights changed	A third party accesses software purchased by the organization and uses it in violation of new product use rights.	Although developers initially allowed third parties approved by the organization to use their software, now this "indirect access" is changed so a new license requires all users to have a purchased license.
Software installed on a virtual machine	Software migrated to a virtual machine and moved to multiple other machines in violation of license.	Some developers restrict software from being installed and then moved among multiple virtual machines without purchasing a new license.

Identifying Risk

It is important to properly identify risks. This is because not all threats may be risks. The procedures for identifying risk (risk identification process) involves performing a cyber systems assessment and a business impact analysis, considering the risks associated with a supply chain, and determining risk calculations.

Cyber Systems Assessment

As its name implies, a cyber systems assessment is a process for evaluating the cybersecurity protections of a system. The following are several methods to assess cyber systems:

- Penetration testing can determine how current configurations of security system controls can be defeated.
- Vulnerability assessment can examine attack paths and system weaknesses according to the severity of the results.
- Security auditing can determine if computers and networks are consistent with security policies and best practices.
- Analytical testing using formal mathematical methods can be used to verify software.

NOTE 2

Formal methods for verification of critical software is covered in Module 6.

While many metrics can be used in a cyber systems assessment to evaluate the protections, the measurements commonly used include the following:

- How long it takes to detect an attack
- The response time until the attack can be neutralized
- The time to recover from a successful attack by using redundant systems and compensatory measures
- The extent of the damage that limits the ability of the system to perform its standard processes
- The total time to recover from an attack

Business Impact Analysis (BIA)

A business impact analysis (BIA) identifies business processes and functions and then quantifies the impact a loss of these functions may have on business operations. These impacts include the impact on property (tangible assets), impact on finance (monetary funding), impact on safety (physical protection), impact on reputation (status), and even the impact on life (well-being). When identifying the critical processes and functions through a site risk assessment (a detailed evaluation of the processes performed at a site and how they can be impacted), a BIA has an important role in determining risks.

NOTE 3

A BIA can also be the foundation for a functional recovery plan that addresses the steps to be taken to restore those processes if necessary.

A BIA is designed to identify those processes that are critically important to an enterprise. A BIA will help determine the mission-essential function or the activity that serves as the core purpose of the enterprise. For example, a mission-essential function for a hospital could be to *Deliver healthcare services to individuals and their families*, while a nonessential function is to *Generate and distribute a monthly online newsletter*. In addition, a BIA can also help identify critical systems that in turn support the mission-essential function. In a hospital setting, a critical system could be *Maintain an emergency room facility for the community*. Although this is a critical system, it is not the core purpose of the hospital.

Identifying the single point of failure—which is a component or entity in a system that, if it no longer functions, will disable the entire system—is also a goal of a BIA. A patient information database in a hospital could be considered a single point of failure. Minimizing these single failure points results in a system that can function for an extended period with little downtime. This availability is often expressed as a percentage of uptime in a year. Table 11-4 lists the percentage availability and the corresponding downtimes.

Table 11-4 Percentage availability and downtimes

Percentage availability	Name	Weekly downtime	Monthly downtime	Yearly downtime
90%	One Nine	16.8 hours	72 hours	36.5 days
99%	Two Nines	1.68 hours	7.20 hours	3.65 days
99.9%	Three Nines	10.1 minutes	43.2 minutes	8.76 hours
99.99%	Four Nines	1.01 minutes	4.32 minutes	52.56 minutes
99.999%	Five Nines	6.05 seconds	25.9 seconds	5.26 minutes
99.9999%	Six Nines	0.605 second	2.59 seconds	31.5 seconds

NOTE 4

Because privacy of data is of high importance today, many BIAs also contain a privacy impact assessment, which is used to identify and mitigate privacy risks. This includes an examination of what personally identifiable information (PII) is being collected, the reasons it is collected, and the safeguards regarding how the data will be accessed, shared, and stored. A privacy threshold assessment can determine if a system contains PII, whether a privacy impact assessment is required, and if any other privacy requirements apply to the IT system.

Supply Chain Assessment

Suppose you purchased a fireproof safe for storing your important papers that could only be opened with a key. You would naturally assume that only you had the key to open the safe. But how do you know that for certain? Could a nefarious employee of the store have made a duplicate key before he delivered the safe to your house? Or could someone at the warehouse where the safe was first stored have made a copy of the key? Or could the driver of the truck that brought the safe to the warehouse have made a duplicate key? Or could the foreman in the plant that manufactured the safe have made a copy of the key?

When we purchase an item, especially one that has a security protection component, we generally assume that the item has been protected all the way from manufacturing to final delivery. However, because we are unable to watch the entire process, we cannot know for certain that no compromises have been made. This inability to monitor the entire process for security is behind a growing number of cybersecurity attacks.

A *supply chain* is a network that moves a product from the supplier to the customer. It is made up of vendors that supply raw material, manufacturers who convert the material into products, warehouses that store products, distribution centers that deliver them to the retailers, and retailers who bring the product to the consumer. Today supply chains are global in scope: manufacturers are usually thousands of miles away overseas and not under the direct supervision of the enterprise that is selling the product. The fact that products move through many different steps in the supply chain—and that many of these steps are not closely supervised—has opened the door for malware to be injected into products during their manufacturing or storage (called *supply chain infections*).

Supply chain infections can occur with either hardware or software. For example, an employee at an overseas plant might be bribed into installing malware on hard drives of new computers. Or nation-state actors could force the owners of a plant that manufactures security appliances to install a component into the firmware of each device that opens a "window" to allow for remote monitoring. Software supply chain infections, like the SolarWinds Orion attack, occur because of a lack of protection over a software update that is eventually distributed to all customers.

NOTE 5

The SolarWinds Orion attack is covered in the "Cybersecurity Today" feature at the beginning of this module.

Reducing the risk of supply chain infections can be done by evaluating the steps in the chain (supply chain assessment). Vendor due diligence (VDD) is the steps that the purchasers take to vet the supplier from which they are purchasing the hardware or software. VDD often includes requiring the supplier to complete annual questionnaires about its supply chain and the security protections in force, and even provide documentation of the oversight of the supply chain. However, VDD does not entirely rest on the supplier; it also includes additional steps that the purchaser should perform, such as researching the supplier and viewing any history of vulnerabilities in the product that could have been introduced through a supply chain infection. This can help verify that hardware components have been purchased from a reputable supplier (hardware source authenticity).

 **CAUTION**   Supply chain assessment is difficult. Ultimately, the purchaser has to trust somebody—the supplier, the manufacturer, the DevSecOps team, or others—but it is increasingly complicated to know who can be trusted.

Risk Calculation

An organization that can accurately calculate risk is better prepared to address the risk. For example, if a customer database is determined to be of high value and to have a high risk, the necessary resources can be directed to strengthen the defenses surrounding that database.

There are two approaches to risk calculation. The first approach is qualitative risk assessment. This approach uses an "educated guess" based on observation. For example, if it is observed that the customer database contains important information, the database would be assigned a high asset value. Also, if it is observed that this database has frequently been the target of attacks, it would be assigned a high risk value as well. Qualitative risk typically assigns a numeric value (*1–10*) or label (*High, Medium,* or *Low*) that represents the risk.

The second approach, quantitative risk assessment, is considered more scientific. Instead of arbitrarily assigning a number or label based on observation, the quantitative risk calculation attempts to create "hard" numbers associated with the risk of an element in a system by using historical data. In the example, if the customer database has a higher risk calculation than a product database, more resources would be allocated to protecting it.

Quantitative risk calculations can be divided into the likelihood of a risk and the impact of a risk being successful. Different tools can be used for representing the likelihood and impact of risks.

Risk Probability   The likelihood that a risk will be exploited within a specific period of time (risk probability) uses historical data for calculating the risk. This historical data can be acquired through a variety of sources. Some of these sources are summarized in Table 11-5.

Table 11-5   Historical data sources

Source	Explanation
Law enforcement agencies	Crime statistics on the area of facilities to determine the probability of vandalism, break-ins, or dangers potentially encountered by personnel
Insurance companies	Risks faced by other companies and the amounts paid out when these risks became reality
Computer incident monitoring organizations	Data regarding a variety of technology-related risks, failures, and attacks

Once historical data is compiled, it can be used to determine the likelihood of a risk occurring within a year. This is known as the annualized rate of occurrence (ARO).

Risk Magnitude   Once historical data is gathered so that the ARO can be calculated, the next step is to determine the impact of that risk (risk magnitude). This can be done by comparing it to the monetary loss associated with an asset to determine the cost that represents how much money would be lost if the risk occurred.

 **CAUTION** When calculating the loss, it is important to consider all costs. For example, if a network firewall failed, the costs would include the amount needed to purchase a replacement, the hourly wage of the person replacing the equipment, and the pay for employees who could not perform their job functions because they could not use the network while the firewall was not functioning.

Two risk calculation formulas are commonly used to calculate expected losses. The single loss expectancy (SLE) is the expected monetary loss every time a risk occurs. The annualized loss expectancy (ALE) is the expected monetary loss that can be expected for an asset due to a risk over a one-year period.

Grow with Cengage Unlimited!

If you'd like more information about this topic, use your Cengage Unlimited subscription to go to the CompTIA Security+ Guide to Network Security Fundamentals, 7th edition; open Module 15; and read the section titled "Managing Risk."

If you don't have a Cengage Unlimited subscription, you can find more information at cengage.com/unlimited.

Representing Risks   Different tools can be used to visually represent risks. A risk register is a list of potential threats and associated risks along with the likelihood, impact, and severity of the risk. Often shown as a table, a risk register can help provide a clear snapshot of vulnerabilities and risks. A sample risk register is shown in Figure 11-1.

Risk Register											
Risk Id	Risks	Current risk			Status	Owner	Raised	Mitigation Strategies	Residual risk		
		Likelihood	Impact	Severity					Likelihood	Impact	Severity
Category 1: Projecty selection and project finance											
RP-01	Financial attraction of project to investors	4	4	15	Open		01-march	• Data collection • Information of financial capability of investor • Giving them assurance of tremendous future return.	4	3	12
RP-02	Availability of finance	3	4	12	Open		03-march	• Own resources • Commitment with financial institution • Exclusive management of investor.	3	3	9
RP-03	Level of demand for project	3	3	9	Open		08-march	• Making possibility and identification of low cost and best quality material • Eradication of extra expenses from petty balance.	2	3	6
RP-04	Land acquisition (site availability)	3	3	9	Open		13-march	• Making feasibilites • Analysis and interpretation of feasibilities • Possession and legal obligation of land.	2	2	4
RP-05	_High finance costs	2	2	4	Open		15-march	• Lowering operational expenses and transportation expenses • Proper management of current expenses.	1	2	2

Figure 11-1   Risk register

Another tool is called a risk matrix/heatmap. This is a visual, color-coded tool that lists the impact and likelihood of risks. Figure 11-2 illustrates a risk matrix/heatmap.

Risk Matrix

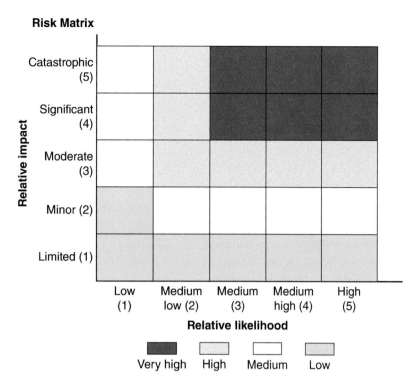

Figure 11-2 Risk matrix/heatmap

Mitigating Risk

The objective of minimizing risk is to create a level of protection that mitigates the vulnerabilities to the threats and reduces the potential consequences—that is, to reduce or mitigate risk to a level that is considered acceptable for the organization (called a risk appetite). Mitigating risk involves prioritizing risk factors so that the proper security controls can be applied. In addition to the application of these technical controls, nontechnical controls such as training and exercises can also mitigate risks.

Risk Prioritization

Risk prioritization involves ranking risks so that the most critical risks are addressed first. Risk prioritization includes making decisions about which risks will be addressed, how they should be controlled, and how this information should be communicated. It also involves determining which strategies should be applied to which risks. Risk prioritization deals with engineering trade-offs, security controls, and communication of risk factors.

Risk Strategies   There are four different strategies for dealing with risks. These can be illustrated through the following scenario. Suppose that Ellie wants to purchase a new motorized Italian scooter to ride from her apartment to school and work. However, because several scooters have been stolen near her apartment, she is concerned about protecting the scooter. Although she parks the scooter in the gated parking lot in front of her apartment, a hole in the fence surrounding the apartment complex makes it possible for someone to access the parking lot without restriction.

The following different options are available to Ellie when dealing with the risk of her scooter being stolen, which are the same as those that can be used by an organization:

- *Acceptance.* Risk acceptance simply means that the risk is acknowledged, but no steps are taken to address it. In Ellie's case, she could accept the risk and buy the new scooter, knowing there is the chance of it being stolen by a thief entering through a hole in the fence. In a similar fashion, an organization may decide to accept the risk that a flood will engulf its manufacturing plant if that flood is estimated to occur only once every 50 years.
- *Transference.* Ellie could transfer the risk to a third party. She can do this by purchasing insurance so that the insurance company absorbs the loss and pays if the scooter is stolen. This is known as risk transference. An organization may elect to purchase cybersecurity insurance as an example of transference so that in exchange for paying premiums to the insurance company, the organization is compensated in the event of a successful attack.

- *Avoidance.* Risk avoidance involves identifying the risk but making the decision to not engage in the activity. Ellie could decide based on the risk of the scooter being stolen that she will not purchase the new scooter. Likewise, an organization may decide after analysis that building a new plant in another location is not feasible.
- *Mitigation.* Risk mitigation is the attempt to address risk by making the risk less serious. Ellie could complain to the apartment manager about the hole in the fence to have it repaired, and an organization could erect a fence around a plant to deter thieves.

Engineering Trade-Offs   When making decisions about which strategy to apply to a risk, there are always compromises to consider: Which risks should be addressed? Of these risks to address, which is the most important? How should the time and energy needed to address risks be distributed?

These compromises can be addressed through a process known as system security engineering (SSE) and are called engineering trade-offs. SSE activities are used for the identification and incorporation of security design and process requirements into risk identification and management. SSE applies scientific and engineering principles to identify security vulnerabilities and minimize or contain risks associated with these vulnerabilities.

Security Controls   Risk prioritization also involves determining which compensating security controls can be applied to the risks. (A cybersecurity control is the countermeasures that companies implement to detect, prevent, reduce, or counteract security risks.) Numerous technical controls and nontechnical controls can be applied. It is important that these be properly recorded (documenting compensating controls). Without proper documentation, a risk that is not eliminated but only compensated could easily be overlooked and not reviewed in a future analysis. This could result in the risk's danger escalating but not being elevated by the organization.

Communication of Risk Factors   Once risks have been prioritized, it is critical that they are properly communicated to all parties (communication of risk factors). However, the language used should vary based on the audience. For example, when communicating risk factors to upper management, language relating to costs, reputation, and other business impacts should be included. Yet when communicating risk factors to users, the emphasis should be on what actions to avoid and how insecure behavior will affect their workload, reputation, and even the future of the organization.

Training and Exercises

Too often, controlling risk is viewed as that which is accomplished through technical security controls. However, nontechnical controls are equally important. An often-overlooked nontechnical control for reducing risk is to provide training and exercises to constituents. This can be divided into end-user training and cyberteam exercises.

End-User Training   End-user training results in risk awareness, which is raising the understanding of what risks exist, their potential impacts, and how they are managed. Training helps make users aware of common risks and how they can become a "human firewall" to help mitigate these risks.

All computer users in an organization have a shared responsibility to protect the assets of the organization. It cannot be assumed that all users have the knowledge and skill to protect these assets. Instead, users need training in the importance of securing information, the roles they play in security, and the steps they need to take to prevent attacks. Because new attacks appear regularly, and new security vulnerabilities are continuously being exposed, user awareness and training must be ongoing. User training is an essential element of security.

NOTE 6

Education in an enterprise is not limited to the average employee. Human resource personnel also need to keep abreast of security issues because in many organizations, it is their role to train new employees on all aspects of the organization, including security. Even upper management needs to be aware of the security threats and attacks that the organization faces, if only to acknowledge the necessity of security in planning, staffing, and budgeting.

The following techniques can be for user training:

- *Computer-based training (CBT).* Computer-based training (CBT) uses a computer to deliver the instruction. It is frequently used for user training due its flexibility (training can be done from any location and at any time) and ability to provide feedback about the progress of the learner. However, CBT is not always considered the best means for training. Instead, a variety of other modalities, such as specialized face-to-face instruction or informal "lunch-and-learn" sessions may provide better overall learning results.
- *Role-based awareness training.* Many organizations use role-based awareness training. Role-based training involves specialized training customized to the specific role that an employee holds in the organization. An office associate, for example, should be provided security training that is different from training provided to an upper-level manager, because the duties and tasks of these two employees are significantly different.
- *Gamification.* The fast-growing field of digital gaming is generally divided into two distinct markets: recreational gaming for entertainment and instructional gaming for training and education. Gamification is using game-based scenarios for instruction. User training can often include gamification in an attempt to heighten the interest and retention of the learner.

Cyberteam Exercises   In addition to end-user training, specific exercises for cyberteams can also reduce risk by preparing these teams to identify and react to cybersecurity events. One valuable exercise is an "in-house pen test." An organization will divide security employees into opposing teams to conduct a "war game" scenario. Table 11-6 lists the composition and duties of the teams in a pen test war game.

Table 11-6   Penetration testing war game teams

Team name	Role	Duties	Explanation
Red Team	Attackers	Scans for vulnerabilities and then exploits them	Has prior and in-depth knowledge of existing security, which may provide an unfair advantage
Blue Team	Defenders	Monitors for Red Team attacks and shores up defenses as necessary	Scans log files, traffic analysis, and other data to look for signs of an attack
White Team	Referees	Enforces the rules of the penetration testing	Makes notes of the Blue Team's responses and the Red Team's attacks
Purple Team	Bridge	Provides real-time feedback between the Red and Blue Teams to enhance the testing	The Blue Team receives information that can be used to prioritize and improve their ability to detect attacks while the Red Team learns more about technologies and mechanisms used in the defense

NOTE 7

Sometimes organizations add an incentive called a *capture the flag (CTF)* exercise. A series of challenges with varying degrees of difficulty are outlined in advance. When one challenge is solved, a "flag" is given to the pen tester, and the points are totaled once time has expired. The winning player or team is the one that earns the highest score. CTF events are often hosted at information security conferences or by schools.

It is likewise important to conduct simulated exercises. This helps to identify overlooked risks or change the priority of a risk. The different types of simulated exercises are summarized in Table 11-7.

Table 11-7   Incident response exercises

Exercise name	Description	Example
Tabletop	A monthly 30-minute discussion of a scenario conducted in an informal and stress-free environment	This scenario is presented: An employee casually remarks about how generous it is of a vendor to provide the box of USB drives on the conference room table, embossed with the company logo. After making some inquiries, you find the vendor did not provide USB drives to employees. What do we now do?
Walkthrough	A review by IT personnel of the steps of the plan by paying particular attention to the IT systems and services that may be targeted in an attack	A technician with knowledge of the current system will walk through the proposed recovery procedures to determine if there are omissions, gaps, errors, or false assumptions.
Simulation	A hands-on simulation exercise using a realistic scenario to thoroughly test each step of the plan	A simulation of a senior vice president who opens a malicious attachment and introduces malware into the network is presented.

NOTE 8

During the first few months of the COVID-19 pandemic, many medical professionals around the world who were active in combating the disease participated online in a tabletop game called Pandemic. The players collaborated (not competed) to contain outbreaks around the world and search for cures. Each player chose a role such as scientist, researcher, or medic, each with unique abilities, and had to work together to develop cures before the diseases overwhelmed them. Many medical professions reported that playing the game was therapeutic and a boost to morale.

TWO RIGHTS & A WRONG

1. At a basic level, risk may be defined as a situation that involves exposure to some type of danger, while at a more advanced level, risk can be described as a function of threats, consequences of those threats, and the resulting vulnerabilities.
2. The Annualized Loss Expectancy (ALE) is the expected monetary loss that can be expected for an asset due to a risk over a one-year period.
3. Risk avoidance utilizes cybersecurity insurance.

See Appendix C for the answer.

RISK-BASED CONTROLS

 **CERTIFICATION**

5.3 Explain the importance of frameworks, policies, procedures, and controls.

Although there is a wide array of cybersecurity controls, some controls are more tuned for risk management than other controls. There are different control classifications and types. Typical controls include policies, procedures, and frameworks. In addition, audits and assessments should be used to monitor these controls.

Classifying Controls

A security control is a safeguard or countermeasure employed within an organizational information system to protect the confidentiality, integrity, and availability of a technology system and its data. It attempts to limit exposure to a danger. There are three broad categories of controls. These are listed in Table 11-8, using phishing as an example.

Table 11-8 Categories of controls

Control category	Description	Phishing example
Managerial	Controls that use administrative methods	Acceptable use policy that specifies users should not visit malicious websites.
Operational	Controls implemented and executed by people	Conducting workshops to help train users to identify and delete phishing messages.
Technical	Controls incorporated as part of hardware, software, or firmware	Unified threat management (UTM) device that performs packet filtering, antiphishing, and web filtering.

The following are specific types of controls found within the three broad categories of controls:

- *Deterrent controls*. A **deterrent control** attempts to discourage security violations before they occur.
- *Preventative controls*. A **preventative control** works to prevent the threat from coming in contact with the vulnerability.
- *Physical controls*. A **physical control** implements security in a defined structure and location.
- *Detective controls*. A **detective control** is designed to identify any threat that has reached the system.
- *Compensating controls*. A **compensating control** is a control that provides an alternative to normal controls that for some reason cannot be used.
- *Corrective controls*. A control that is intended to mitigate or lessen the damage caused by the incident is called a **corrective control**.

These control types are summarized along with examples in Table 11-9.

Table 11-9 Control types

Control type	Description	When it occurs	Example
Deterrent control	Discourage attack	Before attack	Signs indicating that the area is under video surveillance
Preventative control	Prevent attack	Before attack	Security awareness training for all users
Physical control	Prevent attack	Before attack	Fences that surround the perimeter
Detective control	Identify attack	During attack	Installing motion detection sensors
Compensating control	Alternative to normal control	During attack	An infected computer is isolated on a different network
Corrective control	Lessen damage from attack	After attack	A virus is cleaned from an infected server

 **CAUTION** Security professionals do not universally agree on the nomenclature and classification of control types. Some researchers divide control types into administrative, logical, and physical. Other security researchers specify up to18 different control types.

Policies and Procedures

Several terms are used to describe the "rules" for an organization. A *standard* is a collection of requirements specific to the system or procedure that must be met by everyone. For example, a standard might describe how to secure a computer at home that remotely connects to the organization's network. Users must follow this standard if they want to be able to connect. A *guideline* is a collection of suggestions that should be implemented. These are not require- ments to be met but are strongly recommended. A policy is a document that outlines specific requirements or rules that must be met. A procedure is the step-by-step implementation of a policy.

NOTE 9

A policy says "why" while a procedure says "how."

A policy generally has the following characteristics:

- Communicates a consensus of judgment
- Defines appropriate behavior for users
- Identifies what tools and procedures are needed
- Provides directives for human resources action in response to inappropriate behavior
- May be helpful if it is necessary to prosecute violators

At its core, a cybersecurity policy is a recorded document that states how an organization plans to protect the company's information technology assets. The policy outlines the protections that should be enacted to ensure that the organization's assets face minimal risks. A cybersecurity policy, along with the accompanying procedures, is key to implementing information security in an organization. Having a written cybersecurity policy empowers an organization to take appropriate action to safeguard its data.

NOTE 10

A policy is considered the correct tool for an organization to use when establishing security because a policy applies to a wide range of hardware or software (it is not a standard) and is required (it is not just a guideline).

An organization's cybersecurity policy can serve the following functions:

- It can be an overall intention and direction, formally expressed by the organization's management. A security policy is a vehicle for communicating an organization's information security culture and acceptable informa- tion security behavior.
- It details specific risks and how to address them, and so provides controls that executives can use to direct employee behavior.
- It can help to create a security-aware organizational culture.
- It can help to ensure that employee behavior is directed and monitored in compliance with security requirements.

Typical cybersecurity policies include the following:

- *Password policy.* Although passwords often form the weakest link in information security, they are still the most widely used form of authentication. A password policy can address how passwords are created and managed. (Many organizations call their password policy a *password management and complexity policy.*) In addition to controls that can be implemented through technology (such as setting passwords to expire after 60 days and not allowing them to be recycled), users should be reminded through a password policy of how to select and use passwords. Often password policies contain information regarding weak passwords, as shown in Figure 11-3.

Weak Passwords Have the Following Characteristics

- *The password contains fewer than 12 characters.*
- *The password is a word found in a dictionary (English or foreign).*
- *The password is a common usage word such as names of family, pets, friends, coworkers, fantasy characters, and so on, or computer terms and names, commands, sites, companies, hardware, and software.*
- *Birthdays and other personal information such as addresses and phone numbers.*
- *Word or number patterns like qwerty, 123321, and so on.*
- *Any of the preceding spelled backward or preceded or followed by a digit (e.g., secret1, 1secret).*

Figure 11-3   Weak password characteristics

- *Account management policy.* Whereas a password policy involves users, an **account management policy** is intended for those personnel who are responsible for the management of user accounts, access to shared information or network devices, or to information held within a database, application, or shared file space. The purpose of an account management policy is to create a standard for the administration of computing accounts. Figure 11-4 shows elements of a typical account management policy.

Accounts that access electronic computing and information resources require appropriate oversight, and the following security precautions should be taken:

- *All accounts must have a password that adheres to the practices outlined in the Password Policy document.*
- *Any account that is not used for interactive login or authentication must be "locked" or "disabled."*
- *Prior to creating a user account, that user's affiliation with the organization must be verified by the sponsoring unit or division. Accounts for individuals not affiliated with the organization must have prior approval from the Office of Information Technology.*
- *There may be only one user associated with an account. Users may NOT share an account.*
- *Accounts should not be granted any more privileges than those that are necessary for the functions the user will be performing. When establishing accounts, standard security principles of "least required access" to perform a function must always be used, where administratively feasible. For example, a root or administrative privileged account must not be used when a non-privileged account will suffice.*
- *Directory and file permissions should be set correctly to prevent users from listing directory contents or reading, modifying, or deleting files that they are not authorized to access.*
- *Account setup and modification shall require the signature of the account requestor, the requestor's immediate supervisor, the data owner and the Office of Information Technology.*

Figure 11-4   Account management policy elements

- *Acceptable use policy.* An **acceptable use policy (AUP)** is a policy that defines the actions users may perform while accessing devices and networks belonging to the organization. The *users* in "AUP" are not limited to employees; the term can also include vendors, contractors, or visitors, each with different privileges. The AUP usually provides explicit prohibitions regarding unacceptable use, as shown in Figure 11-5.

The following actions are not acceptable ways to use the system:

- *Introduction of malicious programs into the network or server*
- *Revealing your account password to others or allowing use of your account by others, including family and other household members when work is being done at home*
- *Using the Company's computing asset to actively engage in procuring or transmitting material that is in violation of sexual harassment or hostile workplace laws in the user's local jurisdiction*
- *Any form of harassment via email, telephone, or paging, whether through language, frequency, or size of messages*
- *Unauthorized use, or forging, of email header information*

Figure 11-5   AUP explicit prohibitions

- *Data retention policy.* A data retention policy outlines how to maintain information in the user's possession for a predetermined length of time. Different types of data may require different lengths of retention. In addition to describing how long various types of information must be maintained in the user's possession, retention policies usually describe the procedures for archiving the information and special mechanisms for handling the information when under litigation.
- *Data ownership policy.* A data ownership policy defines the duties of a *data custodian* (the employee who is responsible for day-to-day maintenance of a set of data) and a *data owner*, who is the manager responsible for the business function supported by the data. For example, the data ownership policy may state that the data owner shall perform a security risk assessment on an annual basis and identify, recommend, and document acceptable risk levels for data under their authority.
- *Code of conduct/ethics policy.* A code of conduct/ethics policy outlines the expectations regarding employees' behavior toward their colleagues, supervisors, customers, and other constituents. These policies often indicate that while the organization promotes freedom of expression and open communication, it nevertheless expects all employees to follow the code of conduct and avoid offending it, participating in serious disputes, and disrupting the workplace. The overall goal is to foster a well-organized, respectful, and collaborative work environment.
- *Continuous monitoring policy.* A continuous monitoring policy defines how the organization may monitor its employees. For example, a policy may state that *A regular monitoring program is key to managing risk in an organization* and that security monitoring *occurs on both physical areas as well as logical components in many different information system areas*. It usually lists the benefits of security monitoring (*the early identification of wrongdoing or new security vulnerabilities* and *it can help block wrongdoing or vulnerabilities before harm can be done*). Other benefits listed may include audit compliance, service level monitoring, performance measuring, limiting liability, and capacity planning.
- *Work product retention policy.* A work product retention policy outlines who owns the material produced by an employee in the course of his or her work. Generally, these policies state that the employee acknowledges that during the term of employment he or she *may conceive of, discover, invent, or create inventions, improvements, new contributions, literary property, material, ideas, and discoveries, whether patentable or copyrightable or not*. However, the policy indicates that *all of the foregoing shall be owned by and belong exclusively to the Company and that you shall have no personal interest therein*.

Frameworks

A cybersecurity framework is a series of documented processes used to define policies and procedures for implementation and management of security controls in an enterprise environment. About 84 percent of U.S. organizations use a security framework, and 44 percent use multiple frameworks.[1]

Frameworks can be one of two types. Prescriptive frameworks (also called compliance-based frameworks) describe specific cybersecurity issues, such as security controls, which must be addressed. Risk-based frameworks instead focus on the management and measurement of risk. Risk-based frameworks give organizations more flexibility to identify their own specific risk profiles and craft the necessary controls based on these risks.

Some of the most common frameworks are from the National Institute of Standards and Technology (NIST), International Organization for Standardization (ISO), American Institute of Certified Public Accountants (AICPA), and the Center for Internet Security (CIS).

National Institute of Standards and Technology (NIST)

The National Institute of Standards and Technology (NIST), operating under the U.S. Commerce Department, created the NIST cybersecurity frameworks as a set of guidelines for helping private companies identify, detect, and respond to cyberattacks. These frameworks also include guidelines for how to prevent and recover from an attack.

The NIST cybersecurity frameworks are divided into three basic parts. The first part is the *framework core*, which defines the activities needed to attain different cybersecurity results. The framework core is further subdivided into four different elements, which are listed in Table 11-10.

Table 11-10   Cybersecurity framework core elements

Element name	Description	Example
Functions	The most basic cybersecurity tasks	Identify, protect, detect, respond, and recover
Categories	Tasks to be carried out for each of the five functions	To protect a function, organizations must implement software updates, install antivirus and antimalware programs, and have access control policies in place
Subcategories	Tasks or challenges associated with each category	To implement software updates (a category), organizations must be sure that Windows computers have auto-updates turned on
Information Sources	The documents or manuals that detail specific tasks for users and explain how to accomplish the tasks	A document is required that details how auto-updates are enabled on Windows computers

The second part of the NIST cybersecurity frameworks is the *implementation tiers*. The NIST framework specifies four implementation tiers that help organizations identify their level of compliance; the higher the tier, the more compliant the organization is.

The third and final part is *profiles*. Profiles relate both to the current status of the organization's cybersecurity measures and the "roadmaps" toward compliance with the NIST cybersecurity framework. Profiles are like an executive summary of everything an organization has done for the NIST cybersecurity framework and can help demonstrate how each function, category, or subcategory can increase security. These profiles allow organizations to see their vulnerabilities at each step; once the vulnerabilities are mitigated, the organization can move up to higher implementation tiers.

The following are the two widely used NIST frameworks:

- *Risk Management Framework (RMF)*. The NIST Risk Management Framework (RMF) is considered a guidance document designed to help organizations assess and manage risks to their information and systems. It is viewed as comprehensive roadmap that organizations can use to seamlessly integrate their cybersecurity, privacy, and supply chain risk management processes.
- *Cybersecurity Framework (CSF)*. The NIST Cybersecurity Framework (CSF) is used as a measuring stick against which companies can compare their cybersecurity practices relative to the threats they face.

International Organization for Standardization (ISO)

The International Organization for Standardization (ISO) has created a wide array of cybersecurity standards. The ISO 27000 is a "family" of 72 different standards designed to help organizations keep information assets secure. ISO 27001 is a standard that provides requirements for an information security management system (ISMS). An ISMS is a systematic approach to managing sensitive assets so that they remain secure. These assets include the people, processes, and IT systems used to apply a risk management process. ISO 27002 is a "code of practice" for information security management within an organization and contains 114 different control recommendations. ISO 27701 is an extension to ISO 27001 and is a framework for managing privacy controls to reduce the risk of privacy breach to the privacy of individuals. ISO 31000 contains controls for managing and controlling risk.

American Institute of Certified Public Accountants (AICPA)

The American Institute of Certified Public Accountants (AICPA) is the national professional organization for Certified Public Accountants (CPAs) in the United States. The AICPA has created a series of Statements on Standards for Attestation Engagements (SSAE) (an "attestation engagement" is technically "an arrangement with a client where an independent third party investigates and reports on subject matter created by a client" but is better known as an "internal controls report" or "audit"). One of the AICPA's SSAE is a suite of services called the System and Organization Controls (SOC), which are service offerings that Certified Public Accountants (CPAs) may provide in connection with system-level controls of a service organization or entity-level controls of other organizations.

Center for Internet Security (CIS)

The Center for Internet Security (CIS) is a nonprofit community-driven organization. It has created two recognized frameworks. The *CIS Controls* are controls for securing an organization and consists of more than 20 basic and advanced cybersecurity recommendations. The *CIS Benchmarks* are frameworks for protecting 48 different operating systems and application software.

Audits and Assessments

It is important to periodically monitor cybersecurity controls to ensure that they have been implemented and are functioning properly. An assessment is an internal review of security controls that are compared against stated security objectives. An audit is a more systematic evaluation of the effectiveness of the controls when compared against a state of established criteria. These audits can be compliance audits to determine if the controls are being properly implemented or regulatory audits to ensure the controls are aligning to regulations established by outside agencies.

> **⊘ CAUTION** There is no universal agreement on the definition of these terms. Sometimes the phrase "compliance audit" is used for determining if an organization is meeting regulatory requirements, while a "system audit" looks for conformance to an industry standard. To add to the confusion, "compliance" is sometimes defined as meeting legal and regulatory obligations, while "audit" is an impartial view of the organization to be sure it is in line with what they said that they did.

TWO RIGHTS & A WRONG

1. An operational control is implemented and executed by people.
2. A preventative control is designed to identify any threat that has reached the system.
3. An assessment is an internal review of security controls that are compared against stated security objectives.

See Appendix C for the answer.

 **VM LAB** You're now ready to complete the live, virtual machine labs for this module. The labs can be found in the Apply It folder in each MindTap module.

MODULE SUMMARY

- A risk is a situation that involves exposure to some type of danger. There are many types of risk. An internal risk comes from within an organization (such as employee theft), while an external risk is from the outside (like the actions of a hactivist). One type of platform that is well known for its risks is a legacy system. Although legacy hardware introduces some risks, risks more often result from legacy software, such as an OS or program. Often overlooked in identifying risk types is the impact that vulnerabilities of one organization have on other organizations connected to it. Intellectual property (IP) theft involves threat actors who attempt to steal IP and profit from it. Specialized software used by an enterprise is subject to licensing restrictions to protect the rights of the developer. Software compliance and licensing risks are considered a serious problem for organizations today. It is recognized that most organizations unknowingly violate one or more licensing agreements.

- It is important to properly identify risks. As its name implies, a cyber systems assessment is a process for evaluating the cybersecurity protections of a system. Several methods to assess cyber systems and metrics can be used to assess the protections. A business impact analysis (BIA) identifies business processes and functions and then quantifies the impact a loss of these functions may have on business operations. The inability to monitor the entire supply chain process for security is behind a growing number of cybersecurity attacks. Reducing the risk of supply chain infections can be done by evaluating the steps in the chain (supply chain assessment) and performing vendor due diligence (VDD).

- An organization that can accurately calculate risk is better prepared to address the risk. There are two approaches to risk calculation. The first approach is qualitative risk assessment, and the second is quantitative risk assessment, which is considered more scientific. Quantitative risk calculations can be divided into the likelihood of a risk and the impact of a risk being successful. Different tools can be used to visually represent risks.

- The objective of minimizing risk is to create a level of protection that mitigates the vulnerabilities to the threats and reduces the potential consequences—that is, to reduce or mitigate risk to a level that is considered acceptable for the organization (called a risk appetite). Risk prioritization involves ranking risks so that the most critical risks are addressed first. Risk prioritization includes making decisions about which risks will be addressed, how they should be controlled, and how this information should be communicated. Compromises associated with addressing different risks can be addressed through a process known as system security engineering (SSE) and are called engineering trade-offs. SSE applies scientific and engineering principles to identify security vulnerabilities and minimize or contain risks associated with vulnerabilities.

- Risk prioritization also involves determining which compensating security controls can be applied to the risks. (A cybersecurity control is the countermeasures that companies implement to detect, prevent, reduce, or counteract security risks.) Numerous technical controls and nontechnical controls can be applied. It is important that these be properly recorded, a process called documenting compensating controls. Once risks have been prioritized, it is critical that these be properly communicated to all parties, which is known as communication of risk factors. The language used should vary based on the audience.

- An often-overlooked nontechnical control for reducing risk is to provide training and exercises to constituents. End-user training results in risk awareness, which is raising understanding of what risks exist, their potential impacts, and how they are managed. In addition to end-user training, specific exercises for cyberteams can also reduce risk by preparing these teams to identify and react to cybersecurity events. One valuable exercise is an "in-house pen test." An organization will divide security employees into opposing teams to conduct a "war game" scenario.

- Although there is a wide array of cybersecurity controls, some controls are more tuned for risk management than other controls. There are three broad categories of controls: managerial, operational, and technical. Specific types of controls are found within the three broad categories of controls. A policy is a document that outlines specific requirements or rules that must be met. A procedure is the step-by-step implementation of a policy. At its core, a cybersecurity policy is a recorded document that states how an organization plans to protect the company's information technology assets. The policy outlines the protections that should be enacted to ensure that the organization's assets face minimal risks. Typical cybersecurity policies include a code of conduct/ethics, acceptable use policy (AUP), password policy, data ownership, data retention, account management, continuous monitoring, and work product retention.

- It is important for an organization to regularly perform a risk analysis, or a process to identify and assess the factors that may place in jeopardy the success of a project or reaching a stated goal. Identifying risks can be difficult due to the elusive nature of risks, unconscious human biases, and prejudices toward certain types of risks. Risk Control Self-Assessment (RCSA) is an "empowering" methodology by which management and staff at all levels collectively work to identify and evaluate risks. The goal of RCSA is to not only minimize biases and prejudices but also to integrate risk management practices into the culture of the organization.

- A cybersecurity framework is a series of documented processes used to define policies and procedures for implementation and management of security controls in an enterprise environment. Prescriptive frameworks describe specific cybersecurity issues, such as security controls, which must be addressed, while risk-based frameworks instead focus on the management and measurement of risk. Some of the most common frameworks are from the National Institute of Standards and Technology (NIST), International Organization for Standardization (ISO), American Institute of Certified Public Accountants (AICPA), and the Center for Internet Security (CIS).

- It is important to periodically monitor cybersecurity controls to ensure that they have been implemented and are functioning properly. An assessment is an internal review of security controls that are compared against stated security objectives. An audit is a more systematic evaluation of the effectiveness of the controls when compared against a state of established criteria. These audits can be compliance audits to determine if the controls are being properly implemented or regulatory audits to ensure the controls are aligning to regulations established by outside agencies.

Key Terms

acceptable use policy (AUP)
account management policy
assessment
audit
Blue Team
business impact analysis (BIA)
code of conduct/ethics policy
communication of risk factors
compensating control
compliance audit
continuous monitoring policy
corrective control
data ownership policy
data retention policy
detective control
deterrent control

documenting compensating
 controls
engineering trade-offs
exercise
framework
hardware source authenticity
managerial
operational
password policy
physical control
policy
prescriptive framework
preventative control
procedure
Red Team
regulatory audit

risk
risk-based framework
risk identification process
risk magnitude
risk prioritization
risk probability
security controls
supply chain assessment
systems assessment
tabletop
technical
training
vendor due diligence (VDD)
White Team
work product retention policy

Review Questions

1. Which of the following threats would be classified as the actions of a hactivist?
   a. Compliance threat
   b. Internal threat
   c. Environmental threat
   d. External threat

2. Which of these is NOT a documented and formal response to risk?
   a. Mitigation
   b. Transference
   c. Resistance
   d. Avoidance

3. Which of the following is NOT a threat classification category?
   a. Compliance
   b. Financial
   c. Tactical
   d. Strategic

4. In which of the following threat classifications would a power blackout be classified?
   a. Operational
   b. Managerial
   c. Technical
   d. Strategic

5. Which of the following is a systematic evaluation of the effectiveness of the controls as compared to a state of established criteria?
   a. Comparison
   b. Evaluation
   c. Assessment
   d. Audit

6. Which of the following frameworks focuses on the management and measurement of risk?
   a. Prescriptive frameworks
   b. Descriptive frameworks
   c. Risk-based frameworks
   d. Assessment frameworks

7. What does a work product retention policy address?
   a. How long a document of work must be retained before it can be destroyed
   b. What the approved methods are for storing a document
   c. Who owns material produced by an employee
   d. Where a document can be stored

8. Which of the following is NOT covered by an AUP?
   a. Vendors
   b. Competitors
   c. Visitors
   d. Contractors

9. Which of the following is a step-by-step implementation of a policy?
   a. Standard
   b. Procedure
   c. Guideline
   d. Rule

10. Which of the following approaches to risk calculation typically assigns a numeric value (*1–10*) or label (*High, Medium,* or *Low*) to represent a risk?
    a. Quantitative risk calculation
    b. Qualitative risk calculation
    c. Rule-based risk calculation
    d. Policy-based risk calculation

11. Which of the following is a list of potential threats and associated risks?
    a. Risk assessment
    b. Risk matrix
    c. Risk register
    d. Risk portfolio

12. Giovanni is completing a report on risks. Which risk option would he use to classify the action that the organization has decided not to construct a new a data center because it would be located in an earthquake zone?
    a. Transference
    b. Avoidance
    c. Rejection
    d. Prevention

13. Which of the following control categories includes conducting workshops to help users resist phishing attacks?
    a. Managerial
    b. Operational
    c. Technical
    d. Administrative

14. Emiliano needs to determine the expected monetary loss every time a risk occurs. Which formula will he use?
    a. AV
    b. SLE
    c. ARO
    d. ALE

15. Simona needs to research a control that attempts to discourage security violations before they occur. Which control will she research?
    a. Deterrent control
    b. Preventative control
    c. Detective control
    d. Corrective control

16. Which of the following is NOT correct about supply chain infections?
    a. They can be mitigated by VDD.
    b. Supply chain assessment can reduce the risk.
    c. They only involve software.
    d. A supply chain is often global and more difficult to monitor.

17. What identifies business processes and functions and then quantifies the impact a loss of these functions may have on business operations?
    a. BIA
    b. VDR
    c. RBP
    d. AUP

18. Which of the following is NOT a category of risk?
    a. Internal and external
    b. Legacy systems
    c. Public
    d. Multiparty

19. Which threat classification affects the long-term goals of the organization?
    a. Managerial
    b. Financial
    c. Compliance
    d. Strategic

20. Which of the following is NOT used in a cyber systems assessment?
    a. SOAR analysis
    b. Analytical testing
    c. Vulnerability assessment
    d. Penetration testing

Case Projects

Case Project 11-1: Supply Chain Attacks and Assessment

Use the Internet to research supply chain attacks. Give three examples of security incidents that were the result of a vulnerability in one organization affecting multiple other organizations. What were the outcomes of each of these? Should an organization that allows other organizations to be compromised through a multiparty risk be held liable? What should be the penalty? How can these be mitigated? Write a one-page paper on your findings.

Case Project 11-2: Intellectual Property (IP) Theft

Use the Internet to find details on four recent incidents of intellectual property (IP) theft from an organization. What was stolen? What vulnerability did the threat actors exploit? How valuable was the IP? What did the threat actors do with it? What loss did it create for the organization? How could it have been prevented? Write a one-page paper on your findings.

Case Project 11-3: End-User Training

Create an outline for end-user training. List at least eight topics that you think end-users should know regarding cybersecurity. Write a brief paragraph for each that lists a summary of the topic, why it is important, and how end-users could benefit from this knowledge. Finally, briefly describe how you would recommend each of these topics be presented.

Case Project 11-4: Communication of Risk Factors

Select three current cybersecurity risks. For each risk, write a one-paragraph explanation of this risk that would go to senior management, to cybersecurity technical professionals, and finally to users (for a total of nine paragraphs). How does the approach, language, vocabulary, and emphasis differ for each group?

Case Project 11-5: On the Job

Suppose you work for a company that has just suffered a cybersecurity incident due to a supply chain attack. The president of the company is outraged that the attack was due to, as he said, the "vendor's incompetence." He has grilled the chief technology officer (CTO) as to why his cybersecurity employees did not catch this vulnerability. He is now demanding that vendor due diligence be performed on all future hardware and software purchases, and he is holding the CTO and his staff responsible for any future breaches due to a supply chain attack. The CTO has asked several staff members to create a document outlining what the organization could do to mitigate supply chain attacks and how effective these would be. Write a one-page memo to the CTO stating what you would do and why to mitigate supply chain attacks.

Reference

1. Watson, Melanie, "Top 4 Cybersecurity Frameworks," *IT Governance*, Jan. 17, 2019, accessed Sep. 13, 2019, *www.itgovernanceusa.com/blog/top-4-cybersecurity-frameworks*.

DATA PROTECTION AND PRIVACY

After completing this module, you should be able to do the following:

1 List technical controls for protecting data

2 Explain nontechnical controls used for data protection

3 Describe issues surrounding data privacy

Cybersecurity Today

Data privacy is a major concern among users today. Recently, two tech giants, Google and Apple, have made headlines by announcing new steps that they claim will help users protect their personal data. However, these steps do not necessarily mean that users will have more data privacy.

Third-party cookies (also known as tracking cookies or trackers) are created by entities ("parties") other than the website the user is currently visiting. These cookies can allow other parties such as marketers to track user behavior, location, and device type to serve relevant ads to users. In 2020, Google announced that its Chrome web browser would soon join other web browsers such as Safari and Firefox in blocking third-party cookies.

However, Google's efforts are not a complete end to tracking users through their web browser behavior. One reason is that Google generates a sizeable amount of revenue from digital advertising by selling ads that are displayed to users in their browser. By some estimates, Google's total digital advertising revenue was $146.92 billion in 2020. By completely turning off the ability to track users, Google would seriously cripple its ad revenue.

Google is replacing third-party cookies with a "Privacy Sandbox." In short, data on users will be aggregated together through each user's Privacy Sandbox so that marketers can observe and serve up ads to large groups of people who exhibit similar browsing habits. The Privacy Sandbox has five application programming interfaces (APIs) that advertisers will use to receive aggregated data about conversion (how well their ads performed) and attribution (which entity is credited for a purchase). The Privacy Sandbox Federated Learning of Cohorts API will rely on machine learning to study the browsing habits of groups of similar users. Another component is PIGIN (Private Interest Groups Including Noise), which lets the Chrome browser track a set of interest groups a user may belong to.

Google ultimately wants to turn the Privacy Sandbox APIs into open web standards that could then be adopted by other web browsers like Safari and Mozilla. Because the standards organization World Wide Web Consortium has been involved in the development of the Privacy Sandbox, some industry analysts believe it could pave the way in the future for the Privacy Sandbox APIs to be used across all major browsers.

However, the Privacy Sandbox may not solve the problem of user privacy. It appears that users will not be able to "opt out" of the Privacy Sandbox. Unlike third-party cookies, users cannot clear their data from the Privacy Sandbox. And because there are numerous ways for marketers to determine a user's identity in a web browser besides third-party cookies, it is likely that web browser vendors who do not adopt the Privacy Sandbox will simply use other means to gather user information from the browser.

Apple, long a vocal supporter of user privacy, announced in 2020 that the iOS operating system will require app developers to add an opt-in permission option from users. Users who agree to opt in will allow advertisers to access the Apple Identifier for Advertisers (IDFA), which is an advertising cookie that enables advertisers to track user actions on their mobile devices. Apple says that it will strictly police any attempt to circumvent the opt-in requirement. App developers cannot disable an app function if users decline to opt in, nor can an app attempt to incentivize users with in-app "perks" or giveaways in return for an opt-in. Any app that tries to replace the IDFA with another identifying piece of information, such as an email address, will also be in violation.

Advertising companies and publishers have filed a complaint against Apple for giving users the choice of whether to be tracked through the IDFA. This complaint has been filed with France's competition authority and claims it is based on antitrust grounds. These advertisers and publishers give several arguments against the Apple user opt-in for the IDFA. First, they say that most users will not opt-in from being tracked; one survey indicated that 85 percent of those polled said that if given the choice, they would decline to opt-in. If users could not be tracked, then it would be harder for the companies to sell personalized ads. Second, they expressed concern that they will not be able to charge as much to show ads to iPhone users. Finally, it would be harder for the advertising firms that broker ad sales to make money.

However, refusing to opt in to IDFA will still not fully protect user privacy. Users who opt in are not only giving their approval for an app to collect their data but are also giving permission for that data to be shared with other apps. The apps for which users decline to opt in to IDFA can still access other information provided through the app for targeting advertising (though that information cannot be shared with another company).

Apple says the rules will also apply to its own apps. However, unlike the opt-in for IDFA, which requires a message to appear prominently on the app screen, Apple apps will not do this. Apple does have an iOS setting in which users can decline Apple tracking, but it is buried deep in the phone's settings. Apple also says that because it is not sharing the data with other companies but is only using it internally by Apple, it does not count as tracking.

Despite Apple's outspokenness on user privacy, the company is often criticized for an agreement with Google that nets Apple billions of dollars annually. This agreement makes Google search the default search engine on the Apple Safari browser. The user data-gathering techniques that richly benefits Apple through the agreement with Google are the same data-gathering techniques for which Apple criticizes other tech giants—including Google. Apple has also been criticized for agreeing to store the data of Chinese users on servers that are located in China because it opens the possibility of a foreign government using that private user data against its own people.

The bottom line is that safeguarding user privacy has a long, long way to go.

Suppose that users were asked to take steps to protect the *security* of their data. Understandably, almost all users would respond with a blank stare. Whereas SIEMs, SOCs, and SOARs are commonplace to a security professional, average users would hardly know where to start if they were tasked with protecting a network or server that stored their data.

Now suppose that users were asked to take steps to protect the *privacy* of their data on their personal devices. While still challenging, many users would likely be able to find the configuration settings that would give them at least a degree of control on protecting the privacy of their information. One reason that users can handle this task is because most users have taken a keen interest in their privacy and have increasingly shown a willingness to be personally involved in protecting their private data on their endpoint devices. Users have grown to understand that web browsers and smartphones collect a vast array of their personal information—from online purchases to the websites they visit to text messages they receive—and this can then be used by nameless entities performing who-knows-what with what they consider as "their" data.

In recent years, this has become a growing global concern by citizens in many different nations. The result has been various laws passed—in both large collections of nations and small local municipalities—that mandate how private data can be collected and used. Many of these laws also require that users be able to view the data that has been collected from them and even demand that it be purged. This growing universal concern over personal data privacy has significantly increased the responsibilities of organizations to protect user data to achieve user data privacy.

In this final module, we will explore data protection and privacy. First, we will look at controls organizations can use to protect data. Then we will examine data privacy.

CONTROLS FOR PROTECTING DATA

5.1 Understand the importance of data privacy and protection.

Two categories of controls should be used by organizations to protect user data in order to achieve user data privacy. These categories are technical controls and nontechnical controls.

Technical Controls

The different technical controls for protecting data can be grouped into four classifications. There are controls for preventing access to data, controls for limiting access to data, controls for hiding data, and controls for destroying data.

Preventing Access to Data

One obvious but nevertheless very important classification of technical controls is to prevent access to data so that a threat actor cannot reach it. These controls include access controls, data loss prevention, geographic access requirements, and encryption.

Access Controls   As its name implies, access control is granting or denying approval to use specific resources; it is limiting or controlling access to assets. While physical access control consists of fencing, hardware door locks, and mantraps to limit contact with devices, technical access control consists of technology restrictions that limit users on digital devices from accessing resources and data. Access control has a set of associated concepts and terminology used to describe its actions. There are also standard access control schemes and access control lists that are used to help enforce access control.

> ### NOTE 1
> Physical access control is covered in Module 1.

Access Control Concepts   Suppose that Rowan is babysitting his cousin Cora one afternoon. Before leaving the house, Rowan's mother tells him that a package delivery service is coming to pick up a box, which is inside the front door. Soon there is a knock at the door, and as Rowan looks out, he sees the delivery person standing on the porch. Rowan asks her to display her employee credentials, which the delivery person is pleased to do, and then he opens the door and allows her inside, but only to the area by the front door, to pick up the box. Rowan then signs the delivery person's tablet device so there is a confirmation record that the package was picked up.

This scenario illustrates the basic steps in limiting access. The package delivery person first presents her ID to Rowan to review. A user accessing a computer system would likewise present credentials or *identification*, such as a username, when logging in to the system. Identification is the process of recognizing and distinguishing the user from any other user. Checking the delivery person's credentials to be sure they are authentic and not fabricated is *authentication*. Computer users, likewise, must have their credentials authenticated to ensure that they are who they claim to be, often by entering a password, fingerprint scan, or other means of authentication. *Authorization*, granting permission to take an action, is the next step. Rowan allowed the package delivery person to enter the house because she had been preapproved by Rowan's mother and her credentials were authentic. Likewise, once users have presented their identification and been authenticated, they can be authorized to log in to the system and access resources.

Rowan only allowed the package delivery person access to the area by the front door to retrieve the box; he did not allow her to go upstairs or into the kitchen. Likewise, computer users are granted access only to the specific services, devices, applications, and files needed to perform their job duties. Rowan signing on the tablet is akin to *accounting*, which is making and preserving a record of who accessed the network, what resources they accessed, and when they disconnected from the network. Accounting data can be used to provide an audit trail and for billing, determining trends, identifying resource utilization, and future capacity planning. The basic steps in this access control process are summarized in Table 12-1.

NOTE 2

Authentication, authorization, and accounting are sometimes called AAA ("triple-A"), providing a framework for controlling access to computer resources.

Table 12-1 Basic steps in access control

Action	Description	Scenario example	Computer process
Identification	Review of credentials	Delivery person shows employee badge	User enters username
Authentication	Validation of credentials as genuine	Rowan reads badge to determine whether it is real	User provides password
Authorization	Permission granted for admittance	Rowan opens door to allow delivery person in	User authorized to log in
Access	Right given to access specific resources	Delivery person can only retrieve box by door	User allowed to access only specific data
Accounting	Record of user actions	Rowan signs to confirm the package was picked up	Information recorded in log file

Other terminology is used to describe how computer systems impose this technical access control:

- *Object*. An object is a specific resource, such as a file or a hardware device.
- *Subject*. A subject is a user or a process functioning on behalf of the user that attempts to access an object.
- *Operation*. The action that is taken by the subject over the object is called an operation. For example, a user (subject) may attempt to delete (operation) a file (object).

Individuals are given different roles in relationship to access control objects or resources. These roles are summarized in Table 12-2.

Table 12-2 Roles in access control

Role	Description	Duties	Example
Data privacy officer (DPO)	Manager who oversees data privacy compliance and manages data risk	Ensures the enterprise complies with data privacy laws and its own privacy policies	Decides that users can have permission to access SALARY.XLSX
Data custodian/ steward	Individual to whom day-to-day actions have been assigned by the owner	Periodically reviews security settings and maintains records of access by end users	Sets and reviews security settings on SALARY.XLSX
Data owner	Person responsible for the information	Determines the level of security needed for the data and delegates security duties as required	Determines that the file SALARY.XLSX can be read only by department managers
Data controller	Principal party for collecting the data	Acquires user's consent, stores the data, and manages consent or revokes access	Gathers data for SALARY. XLSX and identifies where it is stored
Data processor	Proxy who acts on behalf of data controller	Person or agency that holds and processes personal data for a third party but does not make decisions about using the data and is not responsible for the data	Manages SALARY.XLSX file on behalf of data controller

Figure 12-1 illustrates selected technical access control roles and terminology.

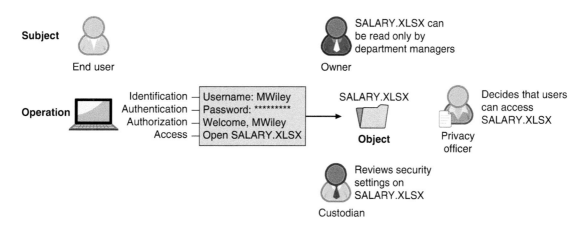

Figure 12-1   Technical access control roles and terminology

Access Control Schemes   The task of a system administrator who needs to act as an access control data custodian/steward for multiple employees using hundreds of thousands of files scattered across a multitude of servers can be made easier by using the predefined framework hardware and software have for controlling access. This framework, called an access control scheme, is embedded in the software and hardware. The custodian/steward can use the appropriate scheme to configure the necessary level of control. Using these schemes is part of privileged access management, which is the technologies and strategies for controlling elevated (privileged) access and permissions.

NOTE 3

The access control schemes of Mandatory Access Control (MAC), Role-Based Access Control (RBAC), and Attribute-Based Access Control Access (ABAC) are covered in Module 5.

There are five major access control schemes. Besides MAC, RBAC, and ABAC, the *Discretionary Access Control (DAC)* scheme is the least restrictive. With the DAC scheme, every object has an owner, who has total control over that object. Most importantly, owners have discretion (the choice) as to who can access their objects and can grant permissions to other subjects over these objects. DAC is used on all major operating systems (OSs). Figure 12-2 illustrates the DAC that a Microsoft Windows owner has over an object. These controls can be configured so that another user can have full or limited access over a file, printer, or other object.

DAC has two significant weaknesses. First, although it gives a degree of freedom to the subject, DAC poses risks in that it relies on decisions by the user to set the proper level of security. As a result, incorrect permissions might be granted to a subject or permissions might be given to an unauthorized subject. A second weakness is that a subject's permissions will be "inherited" by any programs that the subject executes. Threat actors often take advantage of this inheritance because users frequently have a high level of privileges. Malware downloaded onto a user's computer that uses the DAC scheme would then run at the same high level as the user's privileges.

The *Rule-Based Access Control* scheme, also called the *Rule-Based Role-Based Access Control (RB-RBAC)* scheme or *automated provisioning*, can dynamically assign roles to subjects based on a set of rules defined by a custodian (called conditional access). Each resource object contains a set of access properties based on the rules. When a user attempts to access that resource, the system checks the rules contained in that object to determine if the access is permissible.

Rule-Based Access Control is often used for managing user access to one or more systems, where business changes may trigger the application of the rules that specify access changes. For example, a subject on Network A wants to access objects on Network B, which is located on the other side of a router. This router contains the set of access control rules and can assign a certain role to the user, based on her network address or protocol, which will then determine whether she will be granted access. Similar to MAC, Rule Based Access Control cannot be changed by users. All access permissions are controlled based on rules established by the custodian or system administrator.

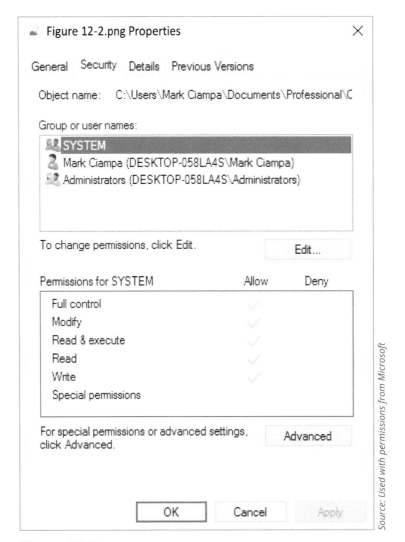

Source: Used with permissions from Microsoft

Figure 12-2 Windows Discretionary Access Control (DAC)

Access Control Lists (ACLs) An access control list (ACL) contains rules that administer the availability of digital assets by granting or denying access to the assets. There are two types of ACLs. The first type is a filesystem ACL that filters access to files and directories on an endpoint. (A filesystem is a method for storing and organizing computer files to facilitate access.) Filesystem ACLs provide filesystem permissions for protecting files managed by the OS by telling the OS who can access the device and what privileges they are allowed. The second type is networking ACLs that filter access to a network. Network ACLs are often found on routers.

NOTE 4

ACLs are the oldest and most basic form of access control. They became popular in the 1970s with the growth of multiuser systems, particularly UNIX systems, when it became necessary to limit access to files and data on shared systems. Later, as multiuser operating systems for personal use became popular, the concept of ACLs was added to them. Today all major OSs make use of ACLs at some level.

It is important to take advantage of access control schemes and ACLs to prevent access to data. They can help secure data protection and user data privacy.

Data Loss Prevention (DLP) Another means of preventing access to data is to implement data loss prevention (DLP). DLP allows the owner of the data to impose restrictions on its use. DLP is a system of security tools used to recognize and identify data that is critical to the organization and ensure it is protected. This protection involves monitoring who is using the data and how it is being accessed. Data that is considered critical to the organization or is confidential can be tagged as such. A user who then attempts to access the data to disclose it to an unauthorized user will be prevented from doing so.

NOTE 5

DLP is covered in Module 5.

Geographic Access Requirements   Whereas DLP restricts data based on the *content* of the data, another control technology can be used to restrict data based on the *location* of the user. This requires the user to be in a specific location to access the data. This is known as geographic access requirements, or more commonly as geofencing.

NOTE 6

Geofencing is often used by the court system. As a condition of release until trial, accused individuals are put under house arrest and are fitted with an ankle bracelet that will alert authorities if they leave the house.

Geofencing begins by taking advantage of the Global Positioning System (GPS), which is a satellite-based navigation system that provides information to a GPS receiver anywhere on (or near) the Earth where there is an unobstructed line of sight to four or more GPS satellites. Mobile devices with GPS capabilities typically support geolocation, or the process of identifying the geographical location of the device. By identifying the location of the device (and hence the person carrying it), geolocation can tell the location of a close friend or the address of the nearest coffee shop. Location services are used extensively by social media, navigation systems, weather systems, and other mobile-aware applications.

NOTE 7

Banks are expanding the use of geolocation to help reduce bank card fraud. When a user makes a purchase at a specific store, the bank can immediately check the location of the cell phone. If the cell phone and the bank card are in the same place, then the purchase may be considered legitimate. But if the cell phone is in Nashville and someone is trying to make a purchase in a store in Tampa, then the payment may be rejected. Geolocation can also help prevent rejecting valid purchases. One credit card issuer says that this can reduce these unnecessary declines by as much as 30 percent.[1]

By using the GPS, geofencing can define the geographical boundaries within which an app can be used to access specific data. For example, a tablet containing patient information that leaves the hospital grounds or an employee who attempts to enter a restricted area with a device can result in blocking data access as well as sending an alert to an administrator.

NOTE 8

There are also risks of geolocation. Mobile device users using geolocation are at increased risk of targeted physical attacks since an attacker can determine where the user with the mobile device is currently located and then use that information to follow the user to steal the mobile device or inflict harm upon the person. A related risk is geotagging, which is adding geographical identification data to media such as digital photos taken on a mobile device. A user who, for example, posts a photo on a social networking site may inadvertently be identifying a specific private location to anyone who can access the photo.

Encryption   A final means of preventing access to data is to make the data impossible to read through cryptography, a term from Greek words meaning *hidden writing*. Cryptography is the practice of transforming information so that it cannot be understood by unauthorized parties and thus is protected. This is usually accomplished through "scrambling" the information in such a way that only approved recipients (either human or machine) can understand it. When using cryptography, the process of changing the original text into a scrambled message is known as encryption (the reverse process is decryption, or changing the message back to its original form).

NOTE 9

The European Union's (EU) 2018 General Data Protection Regulation (GDPR) does not consider encryption or replacing identifying information as strong enough measures that can fully anonymize data to remove all personally identifiable information.

Grow with Cengage Unlimited!

If you'd like more information about this topic, use your Cengage Unlimited subscription to go to the CompTIA Security+ Guide to Network Security Fundamentals, 7th edition; open Module 6; and read the section titled "What Is Cryptography?" If you don't have a Cengage Unlimited subscription, you can find more information at cengage.com/unlimited.

Several common use cases (situations) for cryptography can provide a range of security protections. These protections include the following:

- *Confidentiality.* Cryptography can protect the **confidentiality** of information by ensuring that only authorized parties can view it. When private information, such as a list of employees to be laid off, is transmitted across the network or stored on a file server, its contents can be encrypted, which allows only authorized individuals who have the key to read it.
- *Integrity.* Cryptography can protect the integrity of information. Integrity ensures that the information is correct and no unauthorized person or malicious software has altered that data. Because ciphertext requires that a key must be used to open the data before it can be changed, cryptography can ensure its integrity. The list of employees to be laid off, for example, can be protected so that no names can be added or deleted by unauthorized personnel.
- *Authentication.* The authentication of the sender can be verified through cryptography. Specific types of cryptography, for example, can prevent a situation such as the circulation of a list of employees to be laid off that appears to come from a manager but, in reality, was sent by an imposter.
- *Nonrepudiation.* Cryptography can enforce nonrepudiation. *Repudiation* is defined as denial; nonrepudiation is the inability to deny. In information technology, nonrepudiation is the process of proving that a user performed an action, such as sending an email message. Nonrepudiation prevents an individual from fraudulently reneging on an action. The nonrepudiation features of cryptography can prevent a manager from claiming he never sent the list of employees to be laid off to an unauthorized third party.
- *Obfuscation.* Obfuscation is making something obscure or unclear. Cryptography can provide a degree of obfuscation by encrypting a list of employees to be laid off so that an unauthorized user cannot read it.

The security protections afforded by cryptography are summarized in Table 12-3.

Table 12-3 Information protections by cryptography

Characteristic	Description	Protection
Confidentiality	Ensures that only authorized parties can view the information	Encrypted information can only be viewed by those who have been provided the key.
Integrity	Ensures that the information is correct and no unauthorized person or malicious software has altered that data	Encrypted information cannot be changed except by authorized users who have the key.
Authentication	Provides proof of the genuineness of the user	Proof that the sender was legitimate and not an imposter can be obtained.
Nonrepudiation	Proves that a user performed an action	Individuals are prevented from fraudulently denying that they were involved in a transaction.
Obfuscation	Makes something obscure or unclear	By making obscure, the original information cannot be determined.

Applying encryption to maintain the confidentiality of data is an important control for data protection that leads to preserving user privacy.

Limiting Access to Data

It is not feasible in all instances to strictly prevent access to data. In several cases, many users, who may or may not be trustworthy, must nevertheless have the ability to access data. In cases where *preventing* access to data is not possible, it is then important to apply the control of *limiting* access to the data.

Limiting access to data often involves specific data and is not applied for more general data such as personally identifiable information (PII), personal health information (PHI), or sensitive personal information (SPI). The specific data usually includes intellectual property (IP), which is a work or invention that is the result of creativity.

NOTE 10

PII, PHI, and SPI are covered in Module 9.

The primary reason for limiting access to IP through a technical control is so that the creator of the IP can maintain specific rights over the content by limiting who can use it, how it can be used, and how it may be distributed. These limitations are necessary so that the creator can be duly compensated for his or her work, generally through earning royalties. Without these technology limitations, the creator's work would likely be freely copied and distributed, depriving the creator of any royalties.

NOTE 11

In addition to technology controls, the creator may apply for a copyright, patent, trademark, or similar legal protection. These legal protections do not by themselves limit technical access to IP. Rather, they can be applied in a civil (not criminal) court when the content is used in such a way that violates the protections.

However, IP is designed by its very nature to be accessible to a large number of users. An author of a book, for example, would generally not want the completed manuscript locked away in a vault; rather, it is intended to be published and distributed in such a way that the author receives payment (royalties) for his or her efforts. The same is true of a film, music, a poem, or other similar works. The difficulty rests in making the IP accessible—but not *too* accessible. That is, a book may be published in a specific electronic format so that it can be read on a user's mobile device but not published in a general electronic format like an unprotected Portable Document Format (PDF) file that could be easily distributed through the Internet for anyone download. This would deprive the author of the royalties for his or her efforts.

For many years, protecting IP has been attempted through digital rights management (DRM). DRM is a broad category of access control technologies that are designed to restrict the use and duplication of digital content across a wide range of devices. DRM is intended to grant control and protection over IP for the creators and content providers who own the digital media.

NOTE 12

DRM is much like a multisided prism that looks different to different individuals. To IP creators, rights holders, and publishers, DRM is all the technologies that protect their IP from illegal theft. For the average content consumer, it is sometimes seen as an inconvenient burden that gets in the way when trying to read electronic books, listen to music, or watch films that have been legitimately purchased. And for pirates who want to steal the IP, DRM is viewed as the enemy that must be destroyed.

Any number of technologies have been developed to support DRM. Table 12-4 lists several of these technologies.

Often used with DRM is watermarking. A watermark is an invisible and unique embedded piece of information added to the content. If the content is transcoded, resized, shrunk, or altered, the watermark still persists. Watermarking is a means by which pirated content can be easily traced back to the offending user. Watermarking is added in postproduction ("post") after the content is encoded but before it is protected by DRM.

Table 12-4 DRM technologies

Media	DRM name	Description	Explanation
Broadcast TV—United States	Broadcast flag	A set of status bits indicating the permission status of the TV signal or stream	Although the FCC mandated that new television receivers manufactured after July 2005 must support the broadcast flag, after numerous struggles with the Supreme Court, the FCC eliminated the broadcast flag in 2011.
Broadcast TV—Europe	DVB Content Protection and Copy Management (DVB-CPCM)	A set of flags (Usage State Information) that are transmitted with the content that describe how the content can be consumed, copied, or exported and can also specify limits on either the viewing time or the number of concurrent devices streaming the content	Similar to broadcast flags, it is concerned only with how content is handled after it is delivered.
E-books	More than 30 competing formats	Formats include EPUB, DAISY, Djvu, iBook, and TomeRaider	EPUB is the most popular e-book format but is not natively supported by the most popular e-reader, Amazon Kindle.
Computer games	Most streaming gaming services and gaming consoles support DRM	Proprietary formats	A limited number of DRM-free games are available.
Music	Apple FairPlay, Sony OpenMG	With streaming music overtaking digital music downloads, it has reduced the need for music DRM	One of the first DRMs for music was Sony's Extended Copy Protection (XCP) that installed a Sony rootkit on the user's computer and sparked a public outrage and a class action lawsuit.

 **CAUTION** Many traditional DRM technologies have been plagued by usability and legal issues. Other DRM technologies were defeated by pirates and rendered useless. As a result, many publishers in the industry developed their own proprietary DRM technology. However, this only served to segment the market, requiring users to purchase specific DRM software to run on specific DRM hardware.

Hiding Data

Another technical control for protecting data is to hide the data so that it cannot be identified and used (deidentification). These technologies include data masking and tokenization.

Data Masking When the data is used only for testing purposes, such as determining if a new app functions properly, data masking may be used. Data masking involves creating a copy of the original data but obfuscating (making unintelligible) any sensitive elements such as a user's name or Social Security number. By replacing the actual information with fictitious information, the testing can still be carried out.

Tokenization Similar to data masking, tokenization obfuscates sensitive data elements, such as an account number, into a random string of characters (token). The original sensitive data element and the corresponding token are then stored in a database called a token vault so that if the actual data element is needed, it can be retrieved. Unlike encryption, which requires the use of an algorithm and a key, tokenization can hide the data while making the retrieval process more seamless. Tokenization is illustrated in Figure 12-3.

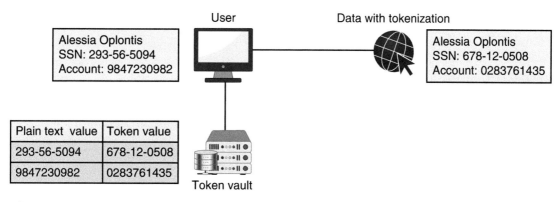

Figure 12-3 Tokenization

NOTE 13

Data deidentification is becoming increasingly important as organizations look to leverage users' private data for new purposes. In early 2021, a group of major hospital systems across 40 states announced that it is launching a company to gather and then sell access to deidentified data on millions of patients. This is to meet the demand from drug makers, insurers, and tech companies that are rushing to develop new medical treatments and tools. The data—which includes detailed information on patient histories, medical conditions, and care—will cover 13 percent of all clinical care provided in the United States.

Destroying Data

In 2013, an IT engineer in England had two identical hard drives and accidentally threw the wrong drive into his trash, which was then picked up by the local municipality and deposited into a landfill. On this hard drive was the only private key to unlocking 7,500 bitcoins of cryptocurrency that he owned. (He did not have a backup of the key.) After he realized his mistake, the engineer asked the city council for permission to search the city's landfill site for his hard drive, but his request was denied. However, since that time, the value of bitcoins has increased dramatically. His bitcoins (and the missing hard drive) are now worth almost $420 million.

NOTE 14

The engineer who threw away the hard drive returned to the city council in 2021 and offered 25 percent of his bitcoins (worth about $72 million) to set up a COVID-19 relief fund for the city's residents if he was given permission to review the landfill log records, isolate the area in which the dump was made, and then search a small area of the landfill. The engineer stated that he has already received backing from a hedge fund that is willing to make the donation to the city now before the search for the hard drive even begins.

This cautionary tale serves to illustrate that media containing valuable data can be inadvertently disposed of before the device is examined and the data erased or retrieved. It is not uncommon for media that contains sensitive user data to be disposed of but later retrieved by threat actors. Thus, destroying data is an important (albeit final) technical control for protecting data.

Because data itself is intangible, destroying data that is no longer needed involves destroying the media on which the data is stored. If data is contained on paper and is not labeled as public, that media should never be thrown away in a dumpster, recycle bin, or trash receptacle. Paper media can be destroyed by burning (lighting it on fire), shredding (cutting it into small strips or particles), pulping (breaking the paper back into wood cellulose fibers after the ink is removed), or pulverizing ("hammering" the paper into dust).

If data is on electronic media, the data should never be erased using the operating system's "delete" command (*purging*). This is because the data still could be retrieved by using third-party tools. Instead, data sanitation tools can be employed to securely remove data. One technique is called *wiping* (overwriting the disk space with zeros or random data). For a magnetic-based hard disk drive, degaussing will permanently destroy the entire drive by reducing or eliminating the magnetic field. Degaussing is normally a third-party solution because it is a specialized technique requiring special equipment.

NOTE 15

There is no universal agreement on the differences between purging and wiping.

Consideration on which data destruction technique to use may hinge upon the need to verify the destruction for regulatory purposes. Some techniques cannot provide this verification. For example, degaussing cannot provide verification that the drive was destroyed. In this instance, it may be necessary to first perform a wiping of the drive to verify that all data has been destroyed before then degaussing the drive to destroy it completely and permanently.

Nontechnical Controls

In addition to technical controls for protecting data, there are also nontechnical controls. These controls include identifying the data to be protected, addressing data retention, following data limitations, and controlling the data through legal requirements.

Identifying Data

Not all data is the same. However, organizations often treat data as being equal and give it the same level of protection. This results in critical data being underprotected and lesser-value data being overprotected. An important nontechnical control is to identify the different types of data so as to assign different levels of protection. Identifying data involves knowing the different data types, determining data ownership, and then classifying the data appropriately.

Data Types   One of the first steps in identifying data is to determine which "family" of data it belongs to (data type). There are several types of data. These types include the following:

- *High risk.* Data that is high risk means that there are serious consequences if that data is exposed. Inappropriate handling of this data could result in criminal or civil penalties, loss of federal funding, identity theft, financial loss, or invasion of privacy. High-risk data must only be accessed by those who are given specific authorization. Examples of high-risk data types include PII, PHI, and SPI.

 **CAUTION**   The fines and costs for a data breach exposing high-risk data can be in the millions of dollars.

- *Sensitive.* Due to legal, ethical, or other constraints, sensitive data may not be accessed without authorization, and only selective access should be granted. Sensitive data examples include student records, employee personal information (home address, email address, telephone), and network and system configuration documents. The fines and costs for a data breach of this type can be up to a million dollars.
- *Internal.* Internal data, which may include unpublished research data at a university or IP, is data that if released could result in reputational damage, a loss of competitive advantage, or higher costs for business processes.
- *Public.* Public data is information that can be freely shared with the public and posted on public-facing webpages.

Ownership   Data ownership defines the duties of a *data custodian* (the employee responsible for day-to-day maintenance of a set of data) and a *data owner* (the manager responsible for the business function supported by the data). For example, the data ownership policy may state that data owners shall perform a security risk assessment on an annual basis and identify, recommend, and document acceptable risk levels for data under their authority.

Classification   Once the data type and data ownership have been determined, the data can be classified. Commercial (corporate) environments have no standards for data classification. Some organizations simply use *Public* and *Confidential* as the only data classifications. However, using multiple data classification levels can help provide greater clarification of the importance of the data and prevent data that is "mostly public but a little confidential" from being mislabeled. Government data classifications have continued to evolve.

NOTE 16

Data classification is covered in Module 3.

Retaining Data

Another nontechnical control for protecting data is to not keep the data any longer than is necessary. Purging unnecessary data eliminates the risk of a threat actor accessing that data. Data retention involves determining how long data must be kept. Many regulatory bodies set specifications for the length of time that data should be retained (retention standards).

Most organizations address data retention through an internal data retention policy that outlines how to maintain information for a predetermined length of time. Different types of data may require different lengths of retention. In addition to describing how long various types of information must be maintained in the user's possession, retention policies usually describe the procedures for archiving the information and special mechanisms for handling the information when under litigation.

Basic principles for data retention include the following:

- Do not keep personal data for longer than it is needed. Personal data may be retained after the need has expired only if is kept for public interest archiving, scientific or historical research, or statistical purposes.
- Organizations must be able to justify how long they keep personal data. Although this depends on the purposes for holding the data, a solid reason must be established.
- A data retention policy setting standard retention periods must be in place.
- It is important to periodically review the data being held and erase or tokenize it when it is no longer needed.
- Any challenges to the retention of data that arise should be thoughtfully considered and not immediately dismissed.

Limiting Data

Some restrictions should be followed regarding the collection and usage of data. These include the following:

- *Data minimization.* Data minimization is limiting the collection of personal information to what is directly relevant and necessary to accomplish a specific task. In other words, the collection of privacy data should be adequate, relevant, and not excessive in relation to the designated purpose. Organizations should periodically review their privacy data collection to ensure that the collection is following the principle of data minimization.
- *Purpose limitation.* Purpose limitation is a principle that data collected for one specified purpose should not be used for a new or incompatible purpose. For example, collecting user Social Security numbers for the purpose of filing insurance claims is a justifiable action. However, using all or part of the Social Security number as a unique identifier should be prohibited.

NOTE 17

Under the European Union General Data Protection Regulation (GDPR), purpose limitation is a requirement that personal data be collected for specified, explicit, and legitimate purposes and not be processed (used) further in a manner incompatible with those purposes. The only exceptions for additional usage are if the person consents to the new usage, if the usage is on the basis of EU or an EU member state law, or if usage is for public interest purposes.

Controlling Data

The final nontechnical control is controlling the data through external mandates. Most often, stipulations outlined by legislatures (legal requirements) serve as controls to protecting data to preserve user privacy. Two legal requirements for controlling data are data sovereignty and nondisclosure agreements.

Data Sovereignty   Until recently, personal data collected by a technology company would be stored on servers that resided within the borders of the country in which that company operated (and not in the country in which the data was collected). This made the protection of that data contingent on the laws of that country. However, nation states increasingly are imposing their own country-specific government regulations that apply to the storage location of data collected from their citizens.

Data sovereignty is the country-specific requirements that apply to data, most notably that data collected from a nation's citizens must be stored on servers in that country. The argument is given that it is in the citizens (and government's) best interest to protect private data against any misuse from foreign governments, and this is not possible if the data is outside of that country's jurisdiction. Currently, Russia, China, Germany, France, Indonesia, and Vietnam all require that their citizen's data be stored on physical servers within the country's borders.

NOTE 18

Many countries have had laws on the books for decades that data of its citizens must be stored within its borders, but it was less of an issue and was not always enforced. However, new privacy laws such as the GDPR are now making this issue more prominent. And with the rising popularity of cloud computing and Software as a Service (SaaS) solutions, data sovereignty issues have taken on even greater importance.

Nondisclosure Agreement (NDA) A nondisclosure agreement (NDA), also called a confidentiality agreement, is a legally binding contract between two parties in which one party agrees to give a second party confidential information about its business or products. The second party agrees not to share this information with any other entity for a specified period of time. NDAs are generally used to protect sensitive information and IP by outlining in detail what information must remain private and what information can be shared or released to the public.

NOTE 19

The information covered by a NDA is virtually unlimited, ranging from test results to customer lists. If the NDA is broken and the information is leaked, it is treated as a breach of contract.

TWO RIGHTS & A WRONG

1. A data privacy officer (DPO) is the manager who oversees data privacy compliance and manages data risk.
2. DAC is the least restrictive access control scheme.
3. Geotagging is another name for geographic access requirements.

See Appendix C for the answer.

DATA PRIVACY

 CERTIFICATION

5.1 Understand the importance of data privacy and protection.

Privacy is defined as the state or condition of being free from public attention, observation, or interference to the degree that the person chooses. In short, privacy is the right to be left alone to the level that you want.

Prior to the current age of technology, almost all individuals (with the exception of media celebrities and politicians) could generally choose the level of privacy they desired. Those who wanted to have open and public lives could freely provide information about themselves to others. Those who wanted to live a quiet or even unknown life could limit what information was disseminated. In short, both those wanting a public life and those wanting a private life could choose to do so by controlling information about themselves.

However, today that is no longer possible. Data is collected on almost all actions and transactions that individuals perform. This includes data collected through web surfing, purchases (online and in stores), user surveys and questionnaires, and smartphone apps. It also is collected on benign activities such as the choice of movies streamed through the Internet, the location signals emitted by a smartphone, and even the path of walking as recorded by surveillance cameras.

As technology devices gather data on user behavior at an unprecedented rate, users are becoming increasingly concerned about how their private data is being collected, used, and stored. Organizations are faced with these growing user concerns and increasing government regulations over data privacy. They must wrestle with how they can make legitimate use of user data while at the same time responsibly collecting, using, and protecting that data.

Understanding data privacy includes knowing reasons for user concerns and understanding the consequences of a data breach.

NOTE 20

Sometimes a distinction is made between data protection and data privacy. Data protection involves securing data against *unauthorized* access, while data privacy is concerned with the *authorized* access of data, namely, who has it and how it is being used. Data protection is a technical issue whereas data privacy is a legal issue.

User Concerns

Users are increasingly concerned over the collection, usage, and protection of their personal data, whether that data is collected with or without their authorization. These user concerns revolve around the risks associated with the use of their private data. This falls into the following three broad categories:

- *Individual inconveniences and identity theft.* Data that has been collected on individuals is frequently used to direct ad marketing campaigns toward the person. These campaigns—which include email, direct mail marketing promotions, and telephone calls—generally are considered annoying and unwanted. In addition, personal data can be used as the basis for identity theft.
- *Associations with groups.* Another use of personal data is to place what appears to be similar individuals together into groups. One data broker has 70 distinct segments (*clusters*) within 21 consumer and demographic characteristic groups (*life stages*). These groups range from *Boomer Barons* (baby boomer–aged households with high education and income), *Hard Chargers* (well-educated and professionally successful singles), and *True Blues* (working parents who hold blue-collar jobs with teenage children about to leave home). Once a person is placed in a group, the characteristics of that group are applied, such as whether a person is a "potential inheritor" or an "adult with senior parent," or whether a household has a "diabetic focus" or "senior needs." However, these assumptions may not always be accurate for the individual that has been placed within that group. Individuals might be offered fewer or the wrong types of services based on their association with a group.
- *Statistical inferences.* Statistical inferences are often made that go beyond groupings. For example, researchers have demonstrated that by examining only four data points of credit card purchases (such as the dates and times of purchases) by 1.1 million people, they were able to correctly identify 90 percent of them. In another study, the *Likes* indicated by Facebook users can statistically reveal their sexual orientation, drug use, and political beliefs.

The concerns raised regarding how private data is gathered and used are listed in Table 12-5.

Table 12-5   Concerns regarding how private data is gathered and used

Issue	Explanation
The data is gathered and kept in secret.	Users have no formal rights to find out what private information is being gathered, who gathers it, or how it is being used.
The accuracy of the data cannot be verified.	Users do not have the right to correct or control what personal information is gathered, and inaccuracy may be suspected. In some cases, inaccurate or incomplete data may lead to erroneous decisions made about individuals without any verification.
Identity theft can impact the accuracy of data.	Victims of identity theft often have information added to their profile that was the result of actions by the identity thieves, and even the victims have no right to see or correct the information.
Unknown factors can impact overall ratings.	Ratings are often created from combining thousands of individual factors or data streams, including race, religion, age, gender, household income, zip code, presence of medical conditions, transactional purchase information from retailers, and hundreds more data points about individual consumers. How these different factors impact a person's overall rating is unknown.
Informed consent is usually missing or is misunderstood.	Statements in a privacy policy such as "We may share your information for marketing purposes with third parties" is not clearly informed consent to freely allow the use of personal data. Often users are not even asked for permission to gather their information.
Data is being used for increasingly important decisions.	Private data is being used on an ever-increasing basis to determine eligibility in significant life opportunities, such as jobs, consumer credit, insurance, and identity verification.

NOTE 21

Unlike consumer reporting agencies, which are required by federal law to give consumers free copies of their credit reports and allow them to correct errors, those who collect data are not required by federal law to show consumers information that has been collected about them or provide a means of correcting it.

Data Breach Consequences

Once a data breach occurs, specific actionable steps must be taken by the organization. When required, it must notify those impacted by the breach (public notifications and disclosures) along with relevant stakeholders. It must also outline the actions that are being taken. Depending upon the severity of the breach, a regulatory agency may even require that a breach be classified as a "major incident" and that additional steps be taken (escalation).

The consequences to an organization that has suffered a data breach are not insignificant. These consequences include the following:

- *Reputation damage*. The bad publicity surrounding an organization that has been the victim of a data breach usually results in a tarnished reputation (reputation damage). This has been evidenced by the loss of customers and a drop in the stock price of publicly traded organizations following a breach.
- *IP theft*. Another consequence of a data breach is the theft of IP that the organization or its customers may own (IP theft).
- *Fines*. A financial penalty (fine) may be assessed against the organization following a data breach. Several federal and state laws have been enacted to protect the privacy of electronic data, and businesses that fail to protect data they possess may face serious financial penalties. Some of these laws include the Health Insurance Portability and Accountability Act of 1996 (HIPAA), the Sarbanes–Oxley Act of 2002 (Sarbox), the Gramm–Leach–Bliley Act (GLBA), the Payment Card Industry Data Security Standard (PCI DSS), and various state notification and security laws. Organizations in nations who belong to the EU face two tiers of fines due to a data breach based on the GDPR. The first tier is a fine up to 10 million euros or 2 percent of the firm's worldwide annual revenue from the preceding year, whichever amount is higher. The second tier is 20 million euros or 4 percent of worldwide annual revenue.

NOTE 22

Many users are surprised to learn that the rules regarding a breach of a smaller number of medical records is not strong. The HIPAA Breach Notification Rule requires that data breaches of 500 or more records must be reported to the Secretary of the Department of Health and Human Services (HHS) no later than 60 days after the discovery of a breach. But for breaches of fewer than 500 records, these can be reported to the Secretary at any time, but no later than 60 days from the end of the calendar year in which the data breach was experienced. That means a breach of 450 records that occurred in January 2021 would not have to be reported until March 2022.

TWO RIGHTS & A WRONG

1. One of the user concerns regarding data privacy is statistical inferences.
2. Identity theft can impact the accuracy of data.
3. Data protection is a legal issue while data privacy is a technical issue.

See Appendix C for the answer.

☑ VM LAB

You're now ready to complete the live, virtual machine labs for this module. The labs can be found in the Apply It folder in each MindTap module.

MODULE SUMMARY

- Different technical controls can be applied for protecting data, particularly relating to user privacy data. One obvious control is to prevent access to the data so that a threat actor cannot reach it. Access control is granting or denying approval to use specific resources; it is limiting or controlling access to assets. While physical access control consists of fencing or hardware door locks, technical access control consists of technology restrictions that limit users on digital devices from accessing resources and data. Access control has a set of associated concepts and terminology used to describe its actions. These include identification, authentication, authorization, access, and accounting. Individuals are given different roles in relationship to access control objects or resources.

- Hardware and software have a predefined framework that the custodian can use for controlling access. This framework, called an access control scheme, is embedded in the software and hardware. The custodian/steward can use the appropriate scheme to configure the necessary level of control. The Discretionary Access Control (DAC) scheme is the least restrictive. With the DAC scheme, every object has an owner, who has total control over that object. Most importantly, owners have discretion (the choice) as to who can access their objects and can grant permissions to other subjects over these objects. The Rule-Based Access Control scheme, also called the Rule-Based Role-Based Access Control (RB-RBAC) scheme or automated provisioning, can dynamically assign roles to subjects based on a set of rules defined by a custodian (called conditional access). Each resource object contains a set of access properties based on the rules. An access control list (ACL) contains rules that administer the availability of digital assets by granting or denying access to the assets. There are two types of ACLs: a filesystem ACL that filters access to files and directories on an endpoint, and networking ACLs that filter access to a network.

- Another means of preventing access to data is to implement data loss prevention (DLP). DLP allows the owner of the data to impose restrictions on its use. DLP is a system of security tools used to recognize and identify data that is critical to the organization and ensure it is protected. Whereas DLP restricts data based on the content of the data, another control technology can be used to restrict data based on the location of the user. This requires the user to be in a specific location to access the data. This is known as geographic access requirements (geofencing).

- Another means of preventing access to data is to make the data impossible to read through cryptography. Cryptography is the practice of transforming information so that it cannot be understood by unauthorized parties and thus is protected. This is usually accomplished through "scrambling" the information in such a way that only approved recipients (either human or machine) can understand it. The process of changing the original text into a scrambled message is known as encryption. Cryptography can provide a range of security protections, including confidentiality, integrity, authentication, nonrepudiation, and obfuscation.

- Sometimes it is not possible to strictly prevent access to data. In these cases, it is important to apply the control of limiting access to the data. For many years, protecting intellectual property (IP) has been attempted through digital rights management (DRM). DRM is a broad category of access control technologies designed to restrict the use and duplication of digital content across a wide range of devices. DRM is intended to grant control and protection over IP for the creators and content providers who own the digital media. Watermarking is also used with DRM. A watermark is an invisible and unique embedded piece of information that is added to the content so that any pirated content can be easily traced back to the offending user.

- Another technical control for protecting data is to hide the data so that it cannot be identified and used, called deidentification. Data masking involves creating a copy of the original data but making unintelligible any sensitive elements such as a user's name or Social Security number. By replacing the actual information with fictitious information, testing can still be carried out without using sensitive data. Tokenization obfuscates sensitive data elements, such as an account number, into a random string of characters called a token. The original sensitive data element and the corresponding token are then stored in a database called a token vault so that if the actual data element is needed, it can be retrieved. Unlike encryption, which requires the use of an algorithm and a key, tokenization can hide the data while making the retrieval process more seamless.

- Destroying data is the final technical control for protecting data. Because data itself is intangible, destroying data that is no longer needed involves destroying the media on which the data is stored. If data contained on paper is not labeled as public, that media should never be thrown away in a dumpster, recycle bin, or trash receptacle. Paper media can be destroyed by burning (lighting it on fire), shredding (cutting it into small strips or particles), pulping (breaking the paper back into wood cellulose fibers after the ink is removed), or pulverizing ("hammering" the paper into dust). If data is on electronic media, data sanitation tools can be employed to securely remove data. One technique is wiping (overwriting the disk space with zeros or random data). For a magnetic-based hard disk drive, degaussing will permanently destroy the entire drive by reducing or eliminating the magnetic field.

- In addition to technical controls for protecting data, there are also nontechnical controls. An important nontechnical control is to identify the different types of data so as to assign different levels of protection. There are several types of data: high risk, sensitive, internal, and public. Data ownership defines the duties of a data custodian (the employee responsible for day-to-day maintenance of a set of data) and a data owner (the manager responsible for the business function supported by the data). Once the data type and data ownership have been determined, the data can be classified. Commercial (corporate) environments have no standards for data classification. Government data classifications have continued to evolve.

- Another nontechnical control for protecting data is to not keep the data any longer than is necessary. Purging unnecessary data eliminates the risk of a threat actor accessing that data. Data retention involves determining how long data must be kept. Many regulatory bodies set specifications for the length of time that data should be retained (retention standards). Some restrictions should be followed regarding the collection and usage of data. Data minimization is limiting the collection of personal information to what is directly relevant and necessary to accomplish a specific task. Purpose limitation is a principle that data collected for one specified purpose should not be used for a new or incompatible purpose. Other nontechnical controls are established through external mandates. Most often, stipulations outlined by legislatures (legal requirements) serve as controls to protecting data to preserve user privacy. Two legal requirements for controlling data are data sovereignty and nondisclosure agreements (NDAs).

- Privacy is defined as the state or condition of being free from public attention, observation, or interference to the degree that the person chooses. Today data is collected on almost all actions and transactions that individuals perform. As technology devices gather data on user behavior at an unprecedented rate, users are becoming increasingly concerned about how their private data is being collected, used, and stored. Organizations are faced with these growing user concerns and increasing government regulations over data privacy. They must wrestle with how they can make legitimate use of user data while responsibly collecting, using, and protecting that data.

- Once a data breach occurs, specific actionable steps must be taken by the organization. When required, it must notify those impacted by the breach (public notifications and disclosures) along with relevant stakeholders. It must also outline the actions that are being taken. Depending upon the severity of the breach, a regulatory agency may even require that a breach be classified as a "major incident" and that additional steps be taken (escalation). The consequences to an organization that has suffered a data breach are significant. These include reputation damage, IP theft, and fines.

Key Terms

access control	digital rights management (DRM)	purpose limitation
confidentiality	encryption	retention
data masking	geographic access requirements	retention standards
data minimization	legal requirements	tokenization
data sovereignty	nondisclosure agreement (NDA)	watermarking
data type	ownership	
deidentification	privacy	

Review Questions

1. Abby has received a request for a data set of actual data for testing a new app that is being developed. She does not want the sensitive elements of the data to be exposed. What technology should she use?
   a. Masking
   b. Tokening
   c. Data Object Obfuscation (DOO)
   d. PII Hiding

2. Braden has been asked to serve as the individual to whom day-to-day actions have been assigned by the owner. What role is Braden taking?
   a. Data custodian/steward
   b. Data privacy officer
   c. Data controller
   d. Data processor

3. Cora is researching access control schemes. Which scheme will Cora find is the least restrictive?
   a. Role-Based Access Control
   b. MAC
   c. Rule-Based Access Control
   d. DAC

4. Mia is teaching a new intern about permissions. The intern asks about a set of permissions attached to an object. Which of these will Mia tell her are permissions attached to an object?
   a. ACL
   b. SRE
   c. Object modifier
   d. Entity attribute (EnATT)

5. Gabe needs a mechanism that will provide both filesystem security and network security. Which of these will he choose?
   a. DBAs
   b. DAPs
   c. HAPs
   d. ACLs

6. Will is searching for information on geographic access requirements. What is another name for this technology that Will can search for?
   a. Geolocating
   b. Geofencing
   c. Geotagging
   d. Geoidentifying

7. Rowan is explaining to a colleague that encryption can provide a range of security protections. Which of these would Rowan NOT include in the list of protections?
   a. Nonrepudiation
   b. Accounting
   c. Integrity
   d. Confidentiality

8. Which of the following is used to protect IP?
   a. BLB
   b. ARC
   c. XLS
   d. DRM

9. Which of the following is NOT correct about watermarking?
   a. It can be erased if the content is altered.
   b. It is invisible.
   c. It allows for unauthorized duplications to be traced back to the source.
   d. It is used with DRM.

10. Which of the following allows deidentified material to be retrieved as needed?
   a. Data masking
   b. Element obfuscation
   c. Tokenization
   d. Reordering

11. Which of the following is NOT true about data sovereignty?
   a. Data sovereignty is a concept that until recently was less of an issue.
   b. Generally, data is subject to the laws of the country in which it is collected or processed.
   c. Governments cannot force companies to store data within specific countries.
   d. Data sovereignty is the country-specific requirements that apply to data.

12. Which of the following is NOT covered by DRM?
   a. E-books
   b. PHI
   c. Music
   d. Computer games

13. Which of the following techniques turns paper into dust so that any data contained on the paper is destroyed?
   a. Hammering
   b. Stoning
   c. Pulverizing
   d. Pulping

14. Which of the following permanently destroys an entire hard drive by eliminating the magnetic field?
    a. Wiping
    b. Magnetic stripping
    c. Degaussing
    d. HDD purging

15. Which of the following is NOT a nontechnical control?
    a. Identifying data
    b. Data masking
    c. Data sovereignty
    d. Nondisclosure agreements

16. Which of the following data types results in the highest risk of fines if the data is exposed?
    a. Sensitive
    b. High risk
    c. Medium value
    d. Private

17. Which of the following involves determining how long data must be kept?
    a. Data retention
    b. Data storage
    c. Data collection
    d. Data analysis

18. Which of the following is NOT a basic principle when considering the retention of data?
    a. Always retain data for six months after it is no longer used.
    b. Organizations must be able to justify their decisions.
    c. Periodic reviews of the data being held are necessary.
    d. A policy must be in place.

19. Which of the following is a principle that data collected for one specified purpose should not be used for a new purpose?
    a. Data amalgamation
    b. Reuse restriction
    c. Data specificity
    d. Purpose limitation

20. Which of the following is NOT a user concern regarding the risks associated with the usage of their private data?
    a. The inability to retrieve stolen data
    b. Individual inconveniences
    c. Associations with groups
    d. Statistical inferences

Case Projects

Case Project 12-1: Geofencing Examples

Use the Internet to research geographic access requirements (geofencing). Identify at least four examples of geofencing as it relates to cybersecurity. Then devise at least three geofencing implementations that would apply to your school or place of work. Write a one-page paper on your work.

Case Project 12-2: Digital Rights Management (DRM)

Research the current state of DRM. Select one area (e-books, music, film, TV, or games) and investigate the technologies that are currently being used and what the projects are for future use. Are these adequate? How intrusive are they for users? Can a balance be achieved? Or do you have an alternative recommendation that can protect the creator while still making the content available electronically? What do you think the future of DRM is? Why? Write a one-page paper on your findings.

Case Project 12-3: Data Masking and Tokenization

Research data masking and tokenization. Explain in detail how each is used. What are their strengths? What are their weaknesses? What alternatives are there to these technologies? Write a one-page paper on your research.

Case Project 12-4: Data Sovereignty

Use the Internet to research the current state of data sovereignty. Should today's tech platforms be forced to store and maintain data in the country in which they collect the data instead of where the company is headquartered? What are the risks for the company? What if each of the 195 nations around the world had this requirement? Is this an excessive burden on the tech platform? What happens if the government of that nation demands the tech platform to surrender information that has been collected on its citizens, even if this contradicts with the policies of the organization? Write a one-page paper on your research.

Case Project 12-5: On the Job

Suppose you work for a company that has just hired a new chief technology officer (CTO). At the first executive-level meeting in which this CTO was introduced, another senior vice president stood up and said that the previous CTO spent far too much time trying to protect the privacy of user data instead of protecting what he called "our company data." The senior vice president said that because user data breaches are so commonplace, the customer personal data the company has collected has likely already been stolen and is freely available on the Internet anyway. He went on to say that the worst that could happen if there were a data breach is that "we'd just lose a handful of customers." He pointed a finger at the CTO and said his sole priority should be the company's data instead. Write a one-page memo to the CTO stating what you think about protecting the privacy of user data compared with company data.

Reference

1. Samuely, Alex, "Visa Leverages Geo-location to Enhance Travelers' Card Payment Experiences," *Retail Dive,* accessed Feb. 20, 2021, https://www.retaildive.com/ex/mobilecommercedaily/visa-leverages-geo-targeting-to-enhance-travelers-card-payment-experiences.

PREPARING FOR THE COMPTIA CYSA+ CS0-002 CERTIFICATION EXAM

The CompTIA CySA+ CS0-002 certification exam contains two categories of questions. The first category is *knowledge-based* assessment questions (multiple choice, multiple answer, ranking and ordering, etc.). The second category is *performance-based questions (PBQs)* that are designed to assess the test taker's skills in working with different cybersecurity tools.

This appendix provides instruction and practice of both knowledge-based questions and PBQs as may be found on the CySA+ certification exam. For those who may not be taking the CySA+ certification exam, this appendix can help provide an assessment and a more detailed understanding of different cybersecurity tools and how they are used.

KNOWLEDGE-BASED ASSESSMENT QUESTIONS

1. At the SOC, Annike is suddenly seeing a wide variety of very sophisticated attacks, many of which she has not seen before. As Annike continues to observe these attacks, she finds that unlike other attacks, they do not diminish over time, but instead they continue to be "ferocious" and seemingly unending. What type of threat is Annike likely witnessing?
   A. Zero-day
   B. APT
   C. RSTS
   D. Unknown

2. Renate is working as a freelance security consultant for a small rural hospital to help secure the database of employee information. This database contains employee names, ages, contact information, employment history, Social Security numbers, and the bank account numbers for payroll direct deposit. What is the classification of this type of information?
   A. SPI
   B. PII
   C. PHI
   D. IPI

3. CFI Software has been alerted to a vulnerability that was discovered in its software's codebase by an independent researcher. CFI has just completed the patch to address the vulnerability. Your team has been tasked with testing the software to ensure the vulnerability has been remediated and the application continues to function correctly and securely. What type of test should your team perform?

   A. Stress testing

   B. User acceptance testing

   C. Security regression testing

   D. Patch verification testing

4. Ilse is tracking a particularly persistent instance of malware on the corporate network. Her analysis so far indicates that this malware is attempting to download itself from an external website through the user's web browser. Where should Ilse first focus her attention?

   A. Network appliances

   B. SOAR

   C. SIEM

   D. Endpoints

5. Kaspar works as a forensics investigator at a large organization. He has received a call that an endpoint device has been compromised and the CIO needs him to start an analysis of the malware that has infected the device. Which tool should Kaspar use first in his analysis?

   A. dd

   B. HexWin

   C. DUMP

   D. Extract-L

6. List the order of the steps of the intelligence cycle.

   A. Analysis

   B. Collection

   C. Dissemination

   D. Feedback

   E. Requirements

7. Bente has been investigating how a malicious threat actor was able to exfiltrate PII from a web server to a C&C. Upon completing her analysis, she found that the web server's UEFI had been modified by the installation of malware. After making her report, the CTO asks Bente what is the most secure type of boot that can be performed to prevent this from happening again. What would Bente tell him?

   A. Secure Boot

   B. Strong Boot

   C. Trusted Boot

   D. Measured Boot

8. An employee accessed a website, but it resulted in an attack directed at the enterprise. Your supervisor wants to know if this is an isolated security failure, part of a pattern of poor security of that website, or even underlying malicious behavior. What type of research would you perform?

   A. Behavioral research

   B. Heuristic analysis

   C. Reputational research

   D. Trend behavior

9. Betje needs to implement an automated software development process that will allow every code change that passes through all states of the production pipeline to immediately be released to customers. Which process would she choose?

   A. CI

   B. CDE

   C. CD

   D. CS

10. You have been asked to perform a vulnerability scan on a network. However, the CSO does not want additional network traffic to be sent across the network since it is already saturated. What type of scan will you perform?

   A. Active scan

   B. Passive scan

   C. Token scan

   D. Restricted scan

11. Aart has been asked to look into supplementing the threat feeds that the organization receives by adding third-party threat feeds to it. What activity is Aart performing?

   A. Feed collection

   B. Threat aggregation

   C. Threat feed combination

   D. Data enrichment

12. A vulnerability scan has returned the following results. What is the best explanation for this event?

Detailed Results

171.96.167.101 (Apache 2.4)

Windows Shares

Category: Windows

CVE ID:

Vendor Ref: Microsoft

Bugtraq ID: 0000000000

Service Modified: 2.24.2022

Enumeration Results:

print$ c:\windows\system32\spool\drivers

files c:\FileShare\Accounting

Temp c:\temp

   A. Because there is no CVE, this can be considered as a false positive by the Apache software running on the Windows server.

   B. The antimalware software has a known vulnerability that must be resolved.

   C. Connecting to the host using a null session allows the enumeration of the share names on the host.

   D. The missing Bugtraq ID indicates a zero-day vulnerability.

13. You have been presented with the result of a vulnerability scan and asked to prioritize the list. Which of the following questions would you NOT consider in your analysis?

   A. Is the vulnerability on a critical system that runs a core business process, or is it on a remote device that is rarely used?

   B. Is the data on the affected device sensitive, or is it public?

   C. Is the vulnerability a recent vulnerability or one that was identified in the past?

   D. If the vulnerability led to a threat actor infiltrating the system, would she be able to pivot to more important systems, or would she be isolated?

   E. Can the vulnerability be exploited by an external threat actor, or would exploitation require that the person be sitting at a computer in an executive's office?

   F. Can the vulnerability be addressed in a reasonable amount of time, or would it take several days or even a week to fix?

14. You are asked to remediate a vulnerability in an older web server. You first locate a patch that addresses the vulnerability. What is the next step that you would then take?

   A. Scan the server again to be sure the vulnerability still exists.

   B. Report the identified vulnerability to the incident response team in the SOC.

   C. Continuously monitor the server for at least seven days.

   D. Submit a request to the change management system.

15. Consider the following email log. Which of the following indicates that a digital signature was not used to validate the content of the email message?

Received: from BYAPR15MB3462.namprd15.prod.outlook.com (2603:10b6:a03:112::10)

by BN7PR15MB4081.namprd15.prod.outlook.com with HTTPS; Fri, 11 Dec 2020

12:42:27 +0000

Received: from BN6PR13CA0038.namprd13.prod.outlook.com (2603:10b6:404:13e::24)

by BYAPR15MB3462.namprd15.prod.outlook.com (2603:10b6:a03:112::10) with

Microsoft SMTP Server (version=TLS1_2,

cipher=TLS_ECDHE_RSA_WITH_AES_256_GCM_SHA384) id 15.20.3632.18; Fri, 11 Dec

2020 12:42:26 +0000

Received: from BN7NAM10FT025.eop-nam10.prod.protection.outlook.com

(2603:10b6:404:13e:cafe::a9) by BN6PR13CA0038.outlook.office365.com

(2603:10b6:404:13e::24) with Microsoft SMTP Server (version=TLS1_2,

cipher=TLS_ECDHE_RSA_WITH_AES_256_GCM_SHA384) id 15.20.3654.9 via Frontend

Transport; Fri, 11 Dec 2020 12:42:25 +0000

Authentication-Results: spf=softfail (sender IP is 161.6.94.39)

smtp.mailfrom=potomac1050.mktomail.com;

topperwkuedu94069.mail.onmicrosoft.com; dkim=fail (body hash did not verify)

header.d=raritan.com;topperwkuedu94069.mail.onmicrosoft.com; dmarc=none

action=none header.from=raritan.com;

Received-SPF: SoftFail (protection.outlook.com: domain of transitioning

potomac1050.mktomail.com discourages use of 161.6.94.39 as permitted sender)

   A. dkim=fail (body hash did not verify)

   B. spf=softfail

   C. dmarc=none

   D. action=none header.from=raritan.com

PERFORMANCE-BASED QUESTIONS (PBQs)

The CompTIA CySA+ certification exam contains several *performance-based questions (PBQs)* that are designed to assess the test taker's skills in working with different cybersecurity tools. CompTIA explains its PBQs as follows:

> *In addition to traditional multiple-choice questions, some CompTIA certification exams include performance-based questions (PBQs). PBQs test a candidate's ability to solve problems in a simulated environment. Please be aware that the environment is not a live lab, and therefore, it may have*

restricted system functionality. PBQs are often an approximation of a virtual environment, such as a firewall, network diagram, terminal window, or operating system.

PBQs typically do not require the test taker to *perform* a specific task; rather, the test taker is asked to *decide* which tool would be best to use in a specific situation or to *analyze* the results of using a tool. For example, a sample PBQ may include the following:

Several employees of Company X were victims of a recent phishing attack. Here are email log files, file server logins, and output from a SIEM. Indicate how many employees replied to the phishing email, the number of computers that were infected, and the type of malware that was distributed by the attack.

To be prepared for PBQs, students must understand when different cybersecurity tools should be used and how to interpret the results. Students must also know how to compare different results from different sources in order to paint a more complete picture of a cybersecurity incident. This appendix covers some of the cybersecurity tools that relate to PBQs.

Ports

Modern computers run multiple applications simultaneously. In a TCP/IP client/server network, a server in particular runs different applications while receiving different data requests from multiple client computers. The server's response back to the hosts is combined (*multiplexed*) into a single signal sent across a shared medium. When the server's response is received by the client, it must then be determined which client application (*process*) should receive the data. This requires an additional addressing element besides the client's IP address to give a more specific "location" (the software application process) to be identified within that client. In TCP/IP, this Transport layer address is called a *port*.

Because TCP and UDP port numbers are 16 bits, valid port numbers may have a value of 0 to 65535. It is necessary to manage the port number address space. The range of TCP and UDP port numbers is divided into three ranges:

- *Well-known (privileged) port numbers (0–1023)*. These port numbers are reserved for only the most universal TCP/IP applications, and are assigned only to protocols that have been or will be standardized. On most computers, only server processes run by system administrators or privileged users use well-known port numbers. These processes generally correspond to processes that implement key IP applications, such as web servers or FTP servers.
- *Registered (user) port numbers (1024–49151)*. Many applications must use TCP/IP for data transmission, but these applications are not as universally used as others, so they do not require a well-known port number. However, to ensure that these different applications do not conflict with each other, the vast majority of port number ranges are registered port numbers. Anyone who creates a viable TCP/IP server application can request to reserve one of these port numbers; if approved, the port number will be registered and assigned to the application.
- *Private/dynamic port numbers (49152–65535)*. Private port numbers can be used for any purpose. These numbers are appropriate for a private protocol that only a particular organization uses.

You should be familiar with the most commonly used ports and their corresponding applications:

- *Well-known (privileged) port numbers (0–1023)*
  - 20 FTP (Send file data)
  - 21 FTP (Session info)
  - 22 SSH, SFTP, SCP
  - 23 Telnet
  - 25 SMTP

NOTE 1

The term *port* has other definitions besides the software application process that should receive a response. For example, a physical outlet in a network device is also called a port. Generally, the context in which the term is used helps to distinguish between a hardware connection and a software application process.

NOTE 2

Well-known port numbers are sometimes called system port numbers.

NOTE 3

Because any user can generally access registered port numbers, they are called user port numbers.

- ○ 49 TACACS+
- ○ 53 UDP/TCP – DNS
- ○ 67 UDP – DHCP and BOOTP
- ○ 69 TFTP
- ○ 80 HTTP
- ○ 88 Kerberos
- ○ 110 POP3
- ○ 119 NNTP (Network News Transfer Protocol)
- ○ 123 NTP (Network Time Protocol)
- ○ 137, 138, 139 NetBIOS
- ○ 143 IMAP
- ○ 161 SNMP (Agents receive requests)
- ○ 162 SNMP (Controller receives data)
- ○ 389 LDAP (Lightweight Directory Access protocol)
- ○ 443 HTTPS over TLS
- ○ 445 SMB/SAMBA (Server Messaging Block)
- ○ 465 SMTP over TLS
- ○ 500 IKE (Internet Key Exchange)
- ○ 636 LDAPS w/ TLS
- ○ 990 FTPS
- *Registered (user) port numbers (1024–49151)*
  - ○ 1433 SQL
  - ○ 1701 L2TP, L2F
  - ○ 1720 H.323
  - ○ 1723 PPTP
  - ○ 1812, 1813 RADIUS
  - ○ 2427 MGCP (Media Gateway Control Protocol)
  - ○ 3389 RDP
  - ○ 5004 RTP
  - ○ 5005 RTP (Default)
  - ○ 5060 SIP (unencrypted)
  - ○ 5061 SIP w/TLS

Protocol IDs

The protocol ID is a number embedded into the header of a TCP/IP packet. It is used to identify a protocol that is not identified by a port number.

- 1 ICMP (Internet Control Message Protocol)
- 2 IGMP (Internet Group Management Protocol)
- 6 TCP (Transmission Control Protocol)
- 17 UDP (User Datagram Protocol)
- 50 IPsec ESP (Internet Protocol Security Encapsulating Security Payload)
- 51 IPsec AH (Internet Protocol Security Authentication Header)

Sandboxes

A sandbox is an isolated virtual machine: Anything run within a sandbox will impact only the virtual machine and not the underlying computer. Sandboxes are how antivirus software can be used with heuristic monitoring to spot the characteristics of a virus.

The Microsoft Windows Sandbox is part of the Windows 10 operating system and can help provide users a higher degree of security and flexibility. The Windows Sandbox is an isolated desktop virtual machine in which you can install software without being concerned that it will affect your computer. Although other programs are available that perform a sandbox function, the Windows Sandbox has the advantage of being included as part of Windows, so nothing has to be downloaded and installed. It relies on the Microsoft hypervisor to run a separate kernel that isolates the Windows Sandbox from the host. This makes it more efficient because it can take advantage of the Windows integrated kernel scheduler, smart memory management, and a virtual GPU. Once you close the Windows Sandbox, nothing remains on your computer; when you launch the Windows Sandbox again, it starts as a clean image.

To enable the Windows Sandbox, follow these steps.

1. You must be running Windows 10 Professional, Enterprise, or Education (not Home) Version 1903 or preferably Version 1909. To determine which version you are running, click the **Start** button, click **Settings**, click **System**, and then click **About**.

2. Next, check to make sure your system has virtualization turned on. Right-click the taskbar at the bottom of the screen, select **Task Manager**, and then click the **Performance** tab. Under Virtualization, the Enabled option must be selected. If the option is disabled, you must reboot, enter your BIOS or UEFI, and turn on virtualization. Also note that with older BIOS setups, you may need to disable other settings, such as Hyper-threading.

3. Enable Windows Sandbox. In the Windows search box, enter **Windows Features** to launch Windows Features. Click the **Windows Sandbox** box to turn on the feature.

4. To launch Windows Sandbox, click the **Start** button, scroll down, and click **Windows Sandbox**.

A protected virtual machine sandbox starts; it looks like another Windows instance. You can download a program through the Microsoft Edge application in Windows Sandbox. (Edge is included within Windows Sandbox along with a handful of other Windows applications, including access to OneDrive.) You can also copy an executable file from your normal Windows environment and then paste it into the Windows Sandbox desktop to launch it. When you are finished, close the Windows Sandbox, and everything will be discarded.

Command-Line/IP Utilities

A security professional should be familiar with several command-line and IP utilities. Some of them are explained in this section.

Ping

Ping is a command-line tool that tests the ability of the source computer to reach a specified destination computer. At its basic level, the ping command is used to verify that a computer can communicate over a network with another computer or network device. The ping command sends Internet Control Message Protocol (ICMP) Echo Request messages; the number of responses returned and how long it takes for them to return are the two items of information the command provides. Figure A-1 shows the ping command being used to determine if www.cengage.com can be accessed.

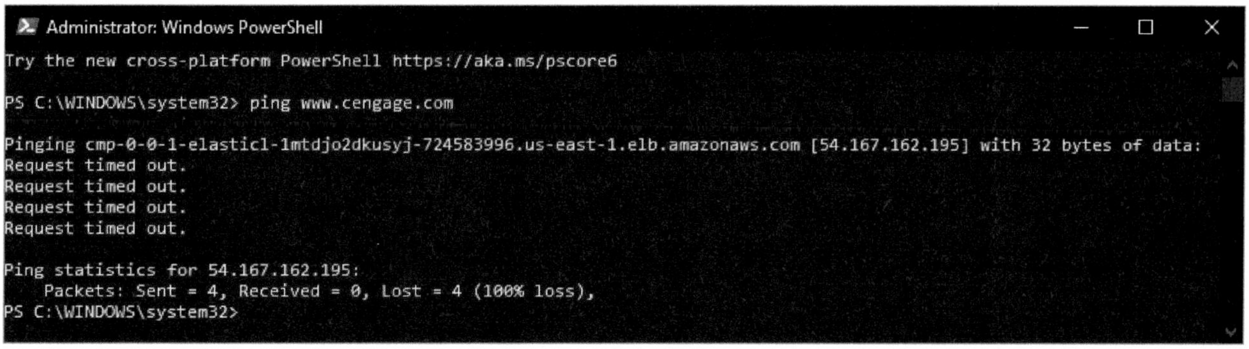

> **NOTE 4**
>
> To use command-line/IP utilities and perform the following activities, you must open a command prompt. On a Windows computer, right-click the Start button, and select Windows PowerShell (Admin).

> **NOTE 5**
>
> The word *ping* has found its way into our everyday vocabulary. For example, you can "ping" a friend (send her a message) to remind her of a meeting.

```
Administrator: Windows PowerShell                                    —    □    ✕
Try the new cross-platform PowerShell https://aka.ms/pscore6

PS C:\WINDOWS\system32> ping www.cengage.com

Pinging cmp-0-0-1-elastic1-1mtdjo2dkusyj-724583996.us-east-1.elb.amazonaws.com [54.167.162.195] with 32 bytes of data:
Request timed out.
Request timed out.
Request timed out.
Request timed out.

Ping statistics for 54.167.162.195:
    Packets: Sent = 4, Received = 0, Lost = 4 (100% loss),
PS C:\WINDOWS\system32>
```

Source: Microsoft Corporation

Figure A-1   Pinging www.cengage.com

Table A-1   Common ping switches

Switch	Explanation
-t	Force the target to respond until you press Ctrl+C.
-a	Resolve the hostname of an IP address target.
-i TTL	Set the Time to Live (TTL) value up to 255.
-R	Trace the round-trip path.
-r count	Specify the number of hops between the computer and the target computer.
-6	Use IPv6 when specifying a hostname.
-n count	Specify the number of echo requests to send (the default is 4).
-l size	Set the length in bytes of the echo request packet (32 to 65527).

NOTE 6

A switch consists of a switch specifier, either a dash (-) or a forward slash (/), followed by the name of the switch, which is usually a single alphabetic letter.

Several parameter options (called *switches*) can be used to fine-tune a command-line utility like ping. Table A-1 lists the most common switches for the ping command.

Ping Activities   Miguel is investigating suspicious activity he has noted in a log file. He is using the ping command in his investigation.

1. The log file shows the IP address as 146.18.2.91. What ping command would he use to determine the hostname of that address?
2. The ping command displays the hostname as www.xresult.io. What ping command would Miguel use to determine if that host is active by using the hostname instead of the IP address?
3. What ping command would he use to send 11 packets of 1,000 bytes each to that host?
4. As Miguel reviews the results from the ping command, he notes that ping indicates the remote device is not responding. He opens a sandbox on his computer and launches a web browser within the sandbox. He enters the address of the remote device site and finds that it can be reached through the browser. Why does the ping command indicate that the remote device is not responding when it can be reached through a browser?

Netstat

The netstat (*net*work *stat*istics) command gives detailed information about current network connections. This information includes network protocol statistics and network connections for the Transmission Control Protocol (TCP), network interfaces, and routing tables. Netstat commands can be tailored by using one or more optional parameters. Table A-2 lists some of the most commonly used netstat switches. In addition, all operating systems have their own unique netstat switches. For example, you can use the -o switch in Windows to include the process ID, and you can use the -t switch in Linux to display only TCP connections.

Table A-2   Common netstat switches

Switch	Description
-a	Show all active connections and the ports that the computer is listening on.
-e	Show Ethernet data such as number of bytes and packets sent and received.
-f	Display the fully qualified domain name (FQDN) when possible.
-g	Display multicast group membership data.
-n	Display active TCP connections. (Addresses and port numbers are displayed numerically.)
-o	Display the process identifier (PID) of the connection.
-r	Display the contents of a routing table.
-s	Display statistics by protocol.
-n	Redisplay data every *n* seconds until Ctrl+C is pressed.

Netstat Activities   After conducting a network reconnaissance, Freja notices unusual activity on the network. She decides to use the netstat command to dig deeper into this activity.

1. What netstat command would Freja use to display all active TCP connections?
2. Freja notes more than one connection that raises her suspicion. What netstat command would she use to display the FQDN computer name of those connections along with the IP address?
3. What netstat command would Freja use to display all connections along with their corresponding protocols?
4. As Freja reviews the results, she is concerned that one specific connection may be exfiltrating data. What netstat command would she use to determine if malware or even normally legitimate software is exfiltrating information? (*Hint*: This command is also useful for determining which software is utilizing a large portion of existing bandwidth.)
5. Freja needs to determine which process is responsible for exfiltrating the data. What netstat command would she use?

Ipconfig

The ipconfig utility (*ifconfig* in Linux) displays network configuration information such as the IP address, network mask, and gateway for all physical and virtual network adapters. The typical ipconfig switches are listed in Table A-3.

Table A-3   Common ipconfig switches

Switch	Explanation
-all	Displays detailed configuration information about all network interfaces
-release [adapter]	Terminates the DHCP lease on the specified adapter or on all interfaces
-renew [adapter]	Manually renews the DHCP lease on the specified adapter or on all interfaces
-displaydns	Displays the contents of the DNS resolver cache
-flushdns	Clears the DNS resolver cache
-registerdns	Renews all DHCP leases
-showcallis	Displays DHCP class IDs associated with an adapter
-setclassic [adapter][classid]	Modifies the DHCP class ID for an adapter

Ipconfig Activities   Adam is performing a basic forensics examination of a laptop computer. He is using the ipconfig command.

1. What ipconfig command would Adam use to display detailed configuration information on each of the laptop's network adapters?
2. Next, Adam needs to terminate any active TCP/IP connections on all network adapters. What ipconfig command would he use?
3. Now Adam needs to reestablish TCP/IP connections on all network adapters. What ipconfig command would he use?

Nslookup

Domain Name Service (DNS) is an essential element of TCP/IP networks. DNS allows hosts to be accessed using easily remembered names (www.cengage.com) rather than numerical IP addresses (99.15.116.1). Two different types of devices are involved in DNS: DNS name servers that store information about domains and DNS resolvers that query DNS servers to transform names into addresses.

A Windows DNS diagnostic utility is nslookup (for *name server lookup*). Although it can be used in interactive mode, the non-interactive version of nslookup is easier and therefore is used more often. Instead of typical switches, parameters are used with nslookup. The typical nslookup parameters are listed in Table A-4.

Table A-4 Common nslookup parameters

Parameter	Explanation
host	Look up the host using the default server.
host [server]	Look up the host using the specified server.
-server	Launch interactive mode using the server.
No parameter	Launch interactive mode using the default server.

Nslookup Activities Paul suspects that a security alert he just received was caused by a misconfigured DNS server that may be compromised by threat actors. He is using the nslookup utility.

1. Paul has multiple nslookup commands to enter, so he decides to use interactive lookup mode. What command would Paul use to enter interactive lookup mode and then find the IP address of www.xdnslookup.io?

2. Paul now wants to switch DNS servers to a DNS open server at 208.67.222.222. What nslookup command would he use?

3. He also suspects that the mail server at www.transfermail.io is misconfigured, and he wants to use the nslookup command to find mail servers for that domain. What command would he use?

Tracert

Tracert (*traceroute* in Linux) is a command-line utility that shows details about the path a packet takes from a computer or device to a destination. Figure A-2 shows how to trace a packet from the computer to the Cengage website.

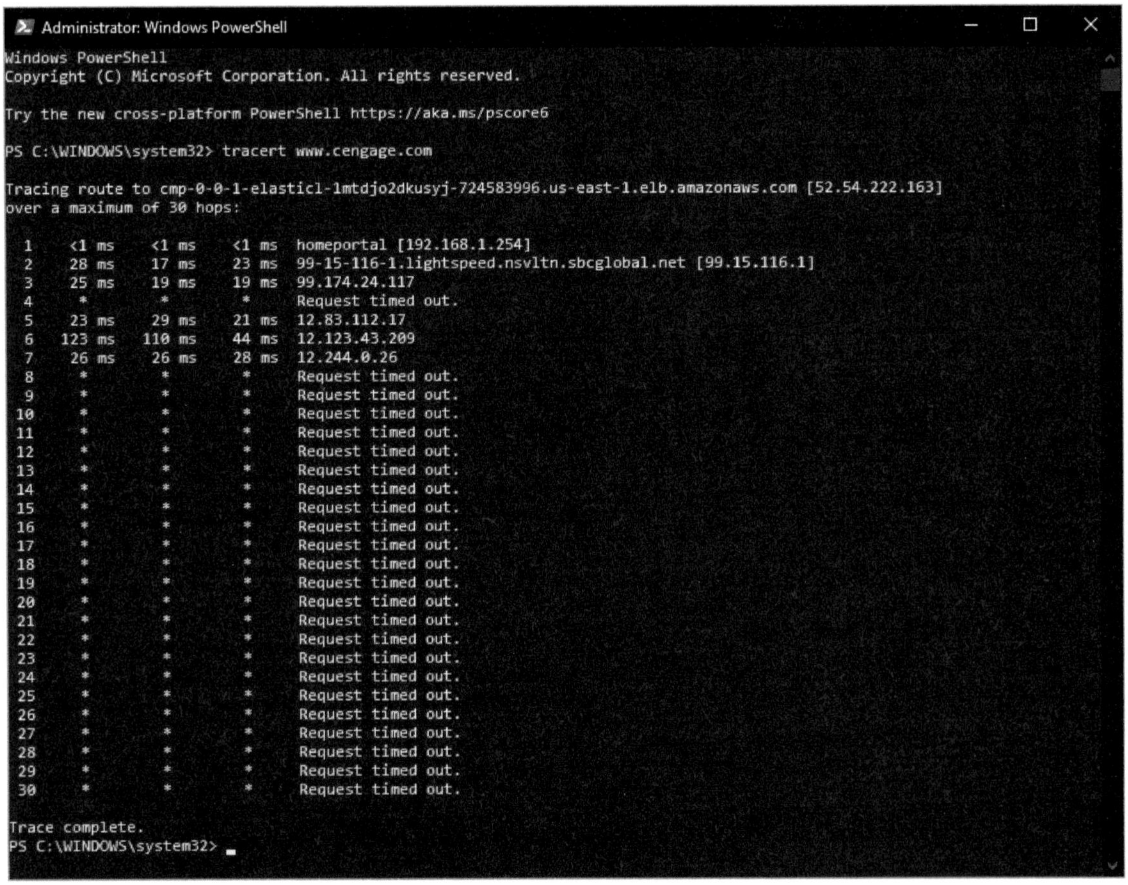

Figure A-2 Tracert www.cengage.com

Source: Microsoft Corporation

A limited number of switches are available for the tracert command; several of these are listed in Table A-5.

Table A-5   Common tracert switches

Switch	Explanation
-d	Displays the route using numeric addresses and prevents tracert from resolving IP addresses to hostnames for a faster display
-h hops	Specifies the maximum number of hops while searching for the target (the default setting is 30)
-w milliseconds	Specifies a time in milliseconds to allow each reply (the default setting is 4000)
-4	Uses IPv4 only
-6	Uses IPv6 only
target	Specifies a destination (either an IP address or hostname)

Although the ping utility is helpful for determining whether devices can communicate with each other, it provides very little information about what is going on between those two devices. If ping shows either an inability to communicate or intermittent connectivity with high loss of transmitted data, it is important to know more about what is happening to the packets as they traverse the network. When these communication problems arise, it is useful to be able to trace the route taken by the packets between devices. Tracert is a special route-tracing utility for this function.

There are several differences between the Windows tracert command and the Linux traceroute command. On modern Linux "distros," the traceroute utility uses UDP datagrams with a port number of 33434. The traceroute utility sets the Time to Live (TTL) field in the packets to a value too low to allow them to reach their destination, thus forcing each router in a route to report back to the sending device. Rather than UDP packets, tracert uses TCP Internet Control Message Protocol (ICMP) echo requests (type 8), sometimes called "ping packets." It sends ICMP Echo messages with increasing TTL values and knows it has reached the final host when it receives a final Echo Reply message.

Tracert Activities   Victor is working with Hannah, who is in the "job shadowing" program at the local community college. Hannah is enrolled in her first computer information systems course at the college. She is watching Victor perform activities using the tracert command and asking questions.

1. Victor begins by tracing a packet from the computer to the community college site southwest.cc.cc.us. What tracert command would he use?
2. Hannah looks at the results from the tracert command and asks Victor why three times are listed for each hop. What would be Victor's explanation?
3. Hannah also notes that the tracert output displays "RTT," so she asks Victor what it means. What would be Victor's explanation?
4. The tracert output displays an asterisk (*) for RTT on several lines. How would Victor explain to Hannah what this means?
5. Hannah also asks, "What does 'Request timed out' mean?" How would Victor answer this question?

NOTE 7

Tracert is an abbreviation of the name *traceroute*, which is the UNIX/Linux name of the program. The shorter version of the name was necessitated by the old eight-character filename limit for Microsoft DOS program names and has never been updated.

NOTE 8

A special ICMP traceroute message, which was intended to improve the efficiency of traceroute by eliminating the need to send several UDP messages for each route tracing, was developed in 1993. Yet, despite its technical advantages, it never became a formal Internet standard and is rarely used.

Consolidated Command-Line/IP Utility Activity

Brianna is performing network reconnaissance on a new branch location for her company. She wants to connect to the edge router of the new branch and determine which devices and networks are attached. She is only using command-line/IP utilities.

NOTE 9

It is recommended that you download and install packet analyzers using the Windows Sandbox, unless you want to have them permanently installed on your computer.

1. What command would Brianna use to verify the IP address configuration for the host device SALES?
2. Brianna discovered a new web server named 2XSERVER.IO. What command would Brianna use to determine the IP address for this server?
3. What command would she use to determine the path between SALES and 2XSERVER.IO?

Packet Analyzers

NOTE 10

WinDump was once a widely used Windows version of tcp-dump; however, it has not been updated for several years. An alternative, tcpdump for Windows, is supported and maintained by Microolap (www .microolap.com/products/ network/tcpdump/).

A packet analyzer is a very useful tool for environmental reconnaissance. It can be used to identify protocols that are running but are prohibited to identify attacks, and to determine if unencrypted data is being transmitted.

Tcpdump

Tcpdump is a command-line packet analyzer. It displays TCP/IP packets and other packets being transmitted or received over a network. Tcpdump operates on UNIX and Linux operating systems, and various forks of it are available for Windows computers.

Several switches are available for tcpdump; they are listed in Table A-6. Note that these switches are case-sensitive.

Table A-6 Common tcpdump switches

Switch	Explanation
-c count	Capture a specified number of packets and then terminate.
-A	Display each packet in ASCII.
-D	List network interfaces.
-e	Display the link-level header.
-I interface	Listen on a specific network interface.
-v, -vv, -vvv	Display increasing verbose output.
-n	Do not translate hostnames or ports.
-c number	Specify the number of packets to capture.
-XX	Display packet data in hexadecimal and ASCII.

NOTE 11

A complete list of tcpdump switches is available at www .tcpdump.org/manpages/ tcpdump.1.html.

The output from tcpdump can be voluminous and difficult to parse. Figure A-3 displays the output of only 13 packets.

Tcpdump Activities Cora suspects that unauthorized protocols are being run on the network. She needs to run tcpdump to analyze packets.

1. What tcpdump command would she use to list the available network interfaces?
2. After identifying the interface, she wants to capture HTTP packets with the highest level of detail. What tcpdump command would she use?
3. The results of Cora's command are shown in Figure A-4. Did she capture HTTP packets in order to examine them?

Figure A-3   Tcpdump output

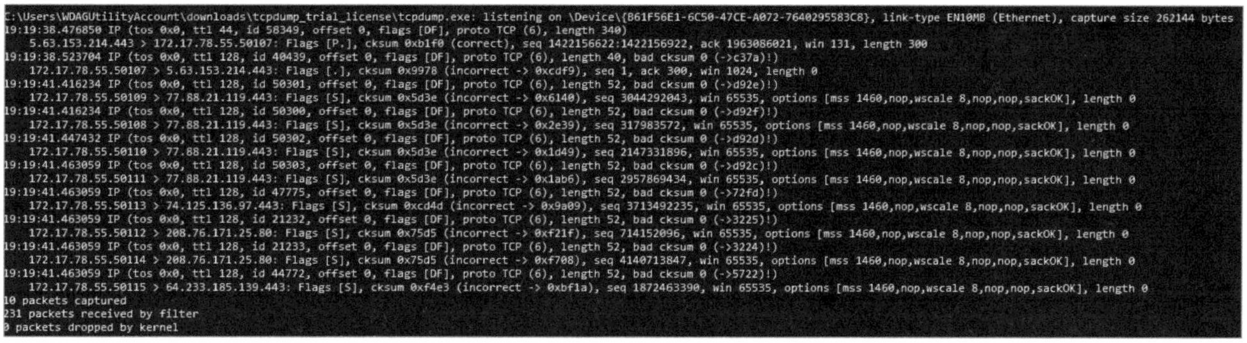

Source: Microsoft Corporation

Figure A-4   Tcpdump attempt to capture HTTP traffic

Source: Microsoft Corporation

Wireshark

Wireshark is a widely used network protocol analyzer. It enables a technician to perform deep inspection of hundreds of different protocols and provides decryption for a wide variety of protocols, such as IPsec, Kerberos, SSL/TLS, and WPA2. Figure A-5 shows the Wireshark main screen.

Wireshark Activities   Cora decides to use Wireshark to continue looking for unauthorized protocols that are being run on the network. Figure A-6 shows the Wireshark results.

1. What unauthorized protocol is running?
2. What is the IP address of the host that is running this protocol?

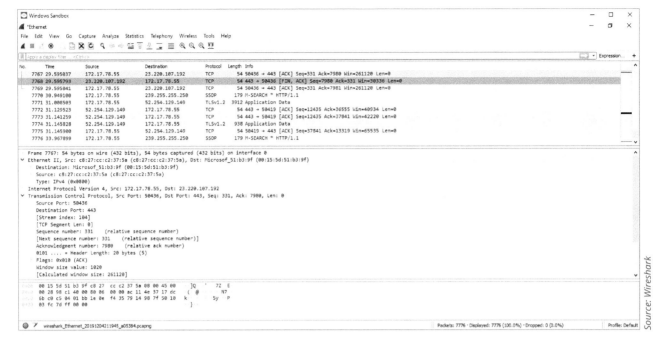

Figure A-5 Wireshark main screen

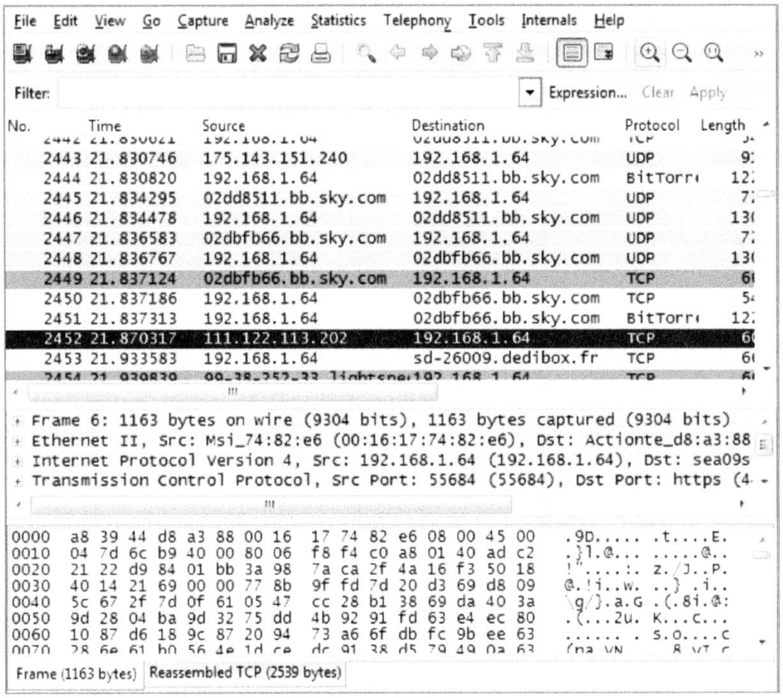

Figure A-6 Wireshark results

COMPTIA CYSA+ CS0-002 CERTIFICATION EXAM OBJECTIVES

Bloom's Taxonomy is an industry-standard classification system used to help identify the level of ability that learners need to demonstrate proficiency. It is often used to classify educational learning objectives into different levels of complexity. The Bloom's Taxonomy column in the following table reflects the level of coverage for the respective CS0-002 objective domains.

CySA+ Exam Objective Domain/Objectives	Module	Section	Bloom's Taxonomy
1.0 Threat and Vulnerability Management			
1.1 Explain the importance of threat data and intelligence.	2		

• Intelligence sources
       ○ Open-source intelligence
       ○ Proprietary/closed-source intelligence
       ○ Timeliness
       ○ Relevancy
       ○ Accuracy
    • Confidence levels
    • Indicator management
       ○ Structured Threat Information eXpression (STIX)
       ○ Trusted Automated eXchange of Indicator Information (TAXII)
       ○ OpenIoC
		Threat Data and Intelligence	Analyze

• Threat classification
       ○ Known threat vs. unknown threat
       ○ Zero-day
       ○ Advanced persistent threat
    • Threat actors
       ○ Nation-state
       ○ Hacktivist
       ○ Organized crime
       ○ Insider threat
           ▪ Intentional
		Threat Actors and Their Threats	Analyze

▪ Unintentional
    • Intelligence cycle
       ○ Requirements
       ○ Collection
       ○ Analysis
       ○ Dissemination
       ○ Feedback
    • Commodity malware
    • Information sharing and analysis communities
       ○ Healthcare
       ○ Financial
       ○ Aviation
       ○ Government
       ○ Critical infrastructure
		Threat Data and Intelligence	Understand

CySA+ Exam Objective Domain/Objectives	Module	Section	Bloom's Taxonomy
1.2 Given a scenario, utilize threat intelligence to support organizational security.	2		

• Attack frameworks
  ○ MITRE ATT&CK
  ○ The Diamond Model of Intrusion Analysis
  ○ Kill chain
• Threat research
  ○ Reputational
  ○ Behavioral
  ○ Indicator of compromise (IoC)
  ○ Common vulnerability scoring system (CVSS)
		Frameworks and Threat Research	Apply

• Threat modeling methodologies
  ○ Adversary capability
  ○ Total attack surface
  ○ Attack vector
  ○ Impact
  ○ Likelihood
		Threat Modeling	Understanding

• Threat intelligence sharing with supported functions
  ○ Incident response
  ○ Vulnerability management
  ○ Risk management
  ○ Security engineering
  ○ Detection and monitoring
		Threat Data and Intelligence	Understanding

CySA+ Exam Objective Domain/Objectives	Module	Section	Bloom's Taxonomy

1.3 Given a scenario, perform vulnerability management activities.
 	
• Vulnerability identification
  ○ Asset criticality
  ○ Active vs. passive scanning
  ○ Mapping/enumeration
• Validation
  ○ True positive
  ○ False positive
  ○ True negative
  ○ False negative
• Remediation/mitigation
  ○ Configuration baseline
  ○ Patching
  ○ Hardening
  ○ Compensating controls
  ○ Risk acceptance
  ○ Verification of mitigation
• Scanning parameters and criteria
  ○ Risks associated with scanning activities
  ○ Vulnerability feed
  ○ Scope
  ○ Credentialed vs. non-credentialed
  ○ Server-based vs. agent-based
  ○ Internal vs. external
  ○ Special considerations
    ▪ Types of data
    ▪ Technical constraints
    ▪ Workflow
    ▪ Sensitivity levels
    ▪ Regulatory requirements
    ▪ Segmentation
    ▪ Intrusion prevention system (IPS), intrusion detection system (IDS), and firewall settings
• Inhibitors to remediation
  ○ Memorandum of understanding (MOU)
  ○ Service-level agreement (SLA)
  ○ Organizational governance
  ○ Business process interruption
  ○ Degrading functionality
  ○ Legacy systems
  ○ Proprietary systems
	3	Vulnerability Scanning	Analyze

CySA+ Exam Objective Domain/Objectives	Module	Section	Bloom's Taxonomy

1.4 Given a scenario, analyze the output from common vulnerability assessment tools.
 	
• Web application scanner
  ○ OWASP Zed Attack Proxy (ZAP)
  ○ Burp suite
  ○ Nikto
  ○ Arachni
• Infrastructure vulnerability scanner
  ○ Nessus
  ○ OpenVAS
  ○ Qualys
• Software assessment tools and techniques
  ○ Static analysis
  ○ Dynamic analysis
  ○ Reverse engineering
  ○ Fuzzing
• Enumeration
  ○ Nmap
  ○ hping
  ○ Active vs. passive
  ○ Responder
• Wireless assessment tools
  ○ Aircrack-ng
  ○ Reaver
  ○ oclHashcat
• Cloud infrastructure assessment tools
  ○ ScoutSuite
  ○ Prowler
  ○ Pacu
	4	Vulnerability Diagnostic Tools	Understand

1.5 Explain the threats and vulnerabilities associated with specialized technology.
 	
• Mobile
• Internet of Things (IoT)
• Embedded
• Real-time operating system (RTOS)
• System on a chip (SoC)
• Field programmable gate array (FPGA)
• Physical access control
• Building automation systems
• Vehicles and drones
  ○ CAN bus
• Workflow and process automation systems
• Industrial control system
• Supervisory control and data acquisition (SCADA)
  ○ Modbus
	1	Threats and Vulnerabilities of Specialized Technology	Understand

CySA+ Exam Objective Domain/Objectives	Module	Section	Bloom's Taxonomy

1.6 Explain the threats and vulnerabilities associated with operating in the cloud.
 	
• Cloud service models
  ○ Software as a Service (SaaS)
  ○ Platform as a Service (PaaS)
  ○ Infrastructure as a Service (IaaS)
• Cloud deployment models
  ○ Public
  ○ Private
  ○ Community
  ○ Hybrid
• Function as a Service (FaaS)/serverless architecture
• Infrastructure as code (IaC)
• Insecure application programming interface (API)
• Improper key management
• Unprotected storage
• Logging and monitoring
  ○ Insufficient logging and monitoring
  ○ Inability to access
	4	Cloud Threats and Vulnerabilities	Analyze

1.7 Given a scenario, implement controls to mitigate attacks and software vulnerabilities.
 	
• Attack types
  ○ Extensible markup language (XML) attack
  ○ Structured query language (SQL) injection
  ○ Overflow attack
    ▪ Buffer
    ▪ Integer
    ▪ Heap
  ○ Remote code execution
  ○ Directory traversal
  ○ Privilege escalation
  ○ Password spraying
  ○ Credential stuffing
  ○ Impersonation
  ○ Man-in-the-middle attack
  ○ Session hijacking
  ○ Rootkit
  ○ Cross-site scripting
    ▪ Reflected
    ▪ Persistent
    ▪ Document object model (DOM)
	1	Types of Attacks	Apply

• Vulnerabilities
  ○ Improper error handling
  ○ Dereferencing
  ○ Insecure object reference
  ○ Race condition
  ○ Broken authentication
  ○ Sensitive data exposure
  ○ Insecure components
  ○ Insufficient logging and monitoring
  ○ Weak or default configurations
  ○ Use of insecure functions
    ▪ strcpy
	3	Common Vulnerabilities	Understand

CySA+ Exam Objective Domain/Objectives	Module	Section	Bloom's Taxonomy
2.0 Software and Systems Security			

2.1 Given a scenario, apply security solutions for infrastructure management.
 	
• Cloud vs. on-premises
• Asset management
  ◦ Asset tagging
• Segmentation
  ◦ Physical
  ◦ Virtual
  ◦ Jumpbox
  ◦ System isolation
    ▪ Air gap
• Network architecture
  ◦ Physical
  ◦ Software-defined
  ◦ Virtual private cloud (VPC)
  ◦ Virtual private network (VPN)
  ◦ Serverless
• Change management
• Virtualization
  ◦ Virtual desktop infrastructure (VDI)
• Containerization
• Identity and access management
  ◦ Privilege management
  ◦ Multifactor authentication (MFA)
  ◦ Single sign-on (SSO)
  ◦ Federation
  ◦ Role-based
  ◦ Attribute-based
  ◦ Mandatory
  ◦ Manual review
• Cloud access security broker (CASB)
• Honeypot
• Monitoring and logging
• Encryption
• Certificate management
• Active defense
	5	Infrastructure Management Solutions and Controls	Apply

CySA+ Exam Objective Domain/Objectives	Module	Section	Bloom's Taxonomy

2.2 Explain software assurance best practices.
 	
• Platforms
  ◦ Mobile
  ◦ Web application
  ◦ Client/server
  ◦ Embedded
  ◦ System on a chip (SoC)
  ◦ Firmware
• Software development life cycle (SDLC) integration
• DevSecOps
• Software assessment methods
  ◦ User acceptance testing
  ◦ Stress test application
  ◦ Security regression testing
  ◦ Code review
• Secure coding best practices
  ◦ Input validation
  ◦ Output encoding
  ◦ Session management
  ◦ Authentication
  ◦ Data protection
  ◦ Parameterized queries
• Static analysis tools
• Dynamic analysis tools
• Formal methods for verification of critical software
• Service-oriented architecture
  ◦ Security Assertions Markup Language (SAML)
  ◦ Simple Object Access Protocol (SOAP)
  ◦ Representational State Transfer (REST)
  ◦ Microservices
	6	Software Best Practices	Analyze

2.3 Explain hardware assurance best practices.
 	
• Hardware root of trust
  ◦ Trusted platform module (TPM)
  ◦ Hardware security module (HSM)
• eFuse
• Unified Extensible Firmware Interface (UEFI)
• Trusted foundry
• Secure processing
  ◦ Trusted execution
  ◦ Secure enclave
  ◦ Processor security extensions
  ◦ Atomic execution
• Anti-tamper
• Self-encrypting drive
• Trusted firmware updates
• Measured boot and attestation
• Bus encryption
	6	Hardware Best Practices	Understand

CySA+ Exam Objective Domain/Objectives	Module	Section	Bloom's Taxonomy
3.0 Security Operations and Monitoring			
3.1 Given a scenario, analyze data as part of security monitoring activities.	7		
• Heuristics • Trend analysis		Data Analytics	Analyze
• Endpoint 　○ Malware 　　▪ Reverse engineering		Monitoring Systems	Apply
○ Memory 　○ System and application behavior 　　▪ Known-good behavior 　　▪ Anomalous behavior 　　▪ Exploit techniques 　○ File system 　○ User and entity behavior analytics (UEBA) • Network 　○ Uniform Resource Locator (URL) and domain name system (DNS) analysis 　　▪ Domain generation algorithm			
○ Flow analysis 　○ Packet and protocol analysis 　　▪ Malware		Data Analytics	Analyze
• Log review 　○ Event logs 　○ Syslog 　○ Firewall logs 　○ Web application firewall (WAF) 　○ Proxy 　○ Intrusion detection system (IDS)/Intrusion prevention system (IPS) • Impact analysis 　○ Organization impact vs. localized impact 　○ Immediate vs. total • Security information and event management (SIEM) review 　○ Rule writing 　○ Known-bad Internet protocol (IP) 　○ Dashboard			
• Query writing 　○ String search 　○ Script 　○ Piping		Monitoring Systems	Analyze
• E-mail analysis 　○ Malicious payload 　○ Domain Keys Identified Mail (DKIM) 　○ Domain-based Message 　○ Authentication, Reporting, and Conformance (DMARC) 　○ Sender Policy Framework (SPF) 　○ Phishing 　○ Forwarding 　○ Digital signature 　○ E-mail signature block 　○ Embedded links 　○ Impersonation 　○ Header			

CySA+ Exam Objective Domain/Objectives	Module	Section	Bloom's Taxonomy
3.2 Given a scenario, implement configuration changes to existing controls to improve security. • Permissions • Whitelisting • Blacklisting • Firewall • Intrusion prevention system (IPS) rules • Data loss prevention (DLP) • Endpoint detection and response (EDR) • Network access control (NAC) • Sinkholing • Malware signatures ○ Development/rule writing • Sandboxing • Port security	5	Configuration Controls	Apply
3.3 Explain the importance of proactive threat hunting. • Establishing a hypothesis • Profiling threat actors and activities • Threat hunting tactics ○ Executable process analysis • Reducing the attack surface area • Bundling critical assets • Attack vectors • Integrated intelligence • Improving detection capabilities	8	Threat Hunting	Analyze

3.4 Compare and contrast automation concepts and technologies.
 	
• Workflow orchestration
  ○ Security Orchestration, Automation, and Response (SOAR)
• Scripting
• Application programming interface (API) integration
• Automated malware signature creation
• Data enrichment
• Threat feed combination
• Machine learning
• Use of automation protocols and standards
  ○ Security Content Automation Protocol (SCAP)
• Continuous integration
• Continuous deployment/delivery
	8	Automation and Orchestration	Analyze

CySA+ Exam Objective Domain/Objectives	Module	Section	Bloom's Taxonomy
4.0 Incident Response			

4.1 Explain the importance of the incident response process.
 	
• Communication plan
  ○ Limiting communication to trusted parties
  ○ Disclosing based on regulatory/legislative requirements
  ○ Preventing inadvertent release of information
  ○ Using a secure method of communication
  ○ Reporting requirements
• Response coordination with relevant entities
  ○ Legal
  ○ Human resources
  ○ Public relations
  ○ Internal and external
  ○ Law enforcement
  ○ Senior leadership
  ○ Regulatory bodies
• Factors contributing to data criticality
  ○ Personally identifiable information (PII)
  ○ Personal health information (PHI)
  ○ Sensitive personal information (SPI)
  ○ High value asset
  ○ Financial information
  ○ Intellectual property
  ○ Corporate information
	9	Incident Response Preparation	Apply

4.2 Given a scenario, apply the appropriate incident response procedure.
 	
• Preparation
  ○ Training
  ○ Testing
  ○ Documentation of procedures
• Detection and analysis
  ○ Characteristics contributing to severity level classification
  ○ Downtime
  ○ Recovery time
  ○ Data integrity
  ○ Economic
  ○ System process criticality
  ○ Reverse engineering
  ○ Data correlation
• Containment
  ○ Segmentation
  ○ Isolation
• Eradication and recovery
  ○ Vulnerability mitigation
  ○ Sanitization
  ○ Reconstruction/reimaging
  ○ Secure disposal
  ○ Patching
  ○ Restoration of permissions
  ○ Reconstitution of resources
  ○ Restoration of capabilities and services
  ○ Verification of logging/communication to security monitoring
• Post-incident activities
  ○ Evidence retention
  ○ Lessons learned report
  ○ Change control process
  ○ Incident response plan update
  ○ Incident summary report
  ○ IoC generation
  ○ Monitoring
	9	Incident Response Procedures	Apply

CySA+ Exam Objective Domain/Objectives	Module	Section	Bloom's Taxonomy

4.3 Given an incident, analyze potential indicators of compromise.
 	
• Network-related
  ○ Bandwidth consumption
  ○ Beaconing
  ○ Irregular peer-to-peer communication
  ○ Rogue device on the network
  ○ Scan/sweep
  ○ Unusual traffic spike
  ○ Common protocol over non-standard port
• Host-related
  ○ Processor consumption
  ○ Memory consumption
  ○ Drive capacity consumption
  ○ Unauthorized software
  ○ Malicious process
  ○ Unauthorized change
  ○ Unauthorized privilege
  ○ Data exfiltration
  ○ Abnormal OS process behavior
  ○ File system change or anomaly
  ○ Registry change or anomaly
  ○ Unauthorized scheduled task
• Application-related
  ○ Anomalous activity
  ○ Introduction of new accounts
  ○ Unexpected output
  ○ Unexpected outbound communication
  ○ Service interruption
  ○ Application log
	10	Indicators of Compromise (IoCs)	Analyze

4.4 Given a scenario, utilize basic digital forensics techniques.
 	
• Network
  ○ Wireshark
  ○ tcpdump
• Endpoint
  ○ Disk
  ○ Memory
• Mobile
• Cloud
• Virtualization
• Legal hold
• Procedures
• Hashing
  ○ Changes to binaries
• Data acquisition
	10	Digital Forensics	Apply

CySA+ Exam Objective Domain/Objectives	Module	Section	Bloom's Taxonomy
5.0 Compliance and Assessment			
5.1 Understand the importance of data privacy and protection.	12		

• Privacy vs. security
• Non-technical controls
  ○ Classification
  ○ Ownership
  ○ Retention
  ○ Data types
  ○ Retention standards
  ○ Confidentiality
  ○ Legal requirements
  ○ Data sovereignty
  ○ Data minimization
  ○ Purpose limitation
  ○ Non-disclosure agreement (NDA)
• Technical controls
  ○ Encryption
  ○ Data loss prevention (DLP)
  ○ Data masking
  ○ Deidentification
  ○ Tokenization
  ○ Digital rights management (DRM)
    ▪ Watermarking
  ○ Geographic access requirements
  ○ Access controls
		Data Privacy Controls for Protecting Data	Apply
			Analyze

5.2 Given a scenario, apply security concepts in support of organizational risk mitigation.	11	Minimizing Risk	Understand

• Business impact analysis
• Risk identification process
• Risk calculation
  ○ Probability
  ○ Magnitude
• Communication of risk factors
• Risk prioritization
  ○ Security controls
  ○ Engineering tradeoffs
• Systems assessment
• Documented compensating controls
• Training and exercises
  ○ Red team
  ○ Blue team
  ○ White team
  ○ Tabletop exercise
• Supply chain assessment
  ○ Vendor due diligence
  ○ Hardware source authenticity			

CySA+ Exam Objective Domain/Objectives	Module	Section	Bloom's Taxonomy

5.3 Explain the importance of frameworks, policies, procedures, and controls.
 	
• Frameworks
  ◦ Risk-based
  ◦ Prescriptive
• Policies and procedures
  ◦ Code of conduct/ethics
  ◦ Acceptable use policy (AUP)
  ◦ Password policy
  ◦ Data ownership
  ◦ Data retention
  ◦ Account management
  ◦ Continuous monitoring
  ◦ Work product retention
• Control types
  ◦ Managerial
  ◦ Operational
  ◦ Technical
  ◦ Preventative
  ◦ Detective
  ◦ Responsive
  ◦ Corrective
• Audits and assessments
  ◦ Regulatory
  ◦ Compliance
	11	Risk-Based Controls	Apply

TWO RIGHTS & A WRONG: ANSWERS

MODULE 1

Two Rights & A Wrong 1-1

1. A rootkit is malware that can hide its presence and the presence of other malware on the computer.
2. The stack is dynamic memory for the programmer to allocate as necessary.
3. A Reflected XSS attack only affects the user who entered data into the website.

Answer: The wrong statement is #2. The heap is dynamic memory for the programmer to allocate as necessary.

Two Rights & A Wrong 1-2

1. A field-programmable gate array (FPGA) is an integrated circuit (IC) that can be programmed by the user to carry out one or more logical operations.
2. A CAN bus is a network in a vehicle used for sending and receiving data.
3. Both Apple iOS and Google Android provide OTA updates for at least four years after the OS is released.

Answer: The wrong statement is #3. Only Apple iOS has OTA updates for at least four years.

MODULE 2

Two Rights & A Wrong 2-1

1. Hactivists are responsible for the class of attacks called advanced persistent threats.
2. Hactivists are strongly motivated by ideology.
3. Brokers sell their knowledge of a weakness to other attackers or a government.

Answer: The wrong statement is #1. Nation-state actors are responsible for the class of attacks called advanced persistent threats.

Two Rights & A Wrong 2-2

1. A key risk indicator (KRI) is a metric of the upper and lower bounds of specific indicators of normal network activity.
2. Two tools that facilitate the privacy of OSNIT are STIX and TAXII.
3. The adversary tactics, techniques, and procedures (TTP) is a database of the behavior of threat actors and how they orchestrate and manage attacks.

Answer: The wrong statement is #2. STIX and TAXII address timeliness concerns.

Two Rights & A Wrong 2-3

1. The focus of ATT&CK is on the tools and malware that attackers use.
2. The Cyber Kill Chain™ outlines the steps of an attack.
3. The principle of social proof is to do things we see other people doing.

Answer: The wrong statement is #1. The focus of ATT&CK is not on the tools and malware that attackers use but instead looks at how they interact with systems during an operation.

Two Rights & A Wrong 2-4

1. At its core, threat modeling is a proactive strategy for evaluating risks and involves identifying potential threats and developing tests to detect and respond to those threats.
2. The total attack surface is the sum total of the number of different attack points.
3. The threat model methodology STRIDE has its primary focus on the enterprise.

Answer: The wrong statement is #3. The focus of STRIDE is on the developer.

MODULE 3

Two Rights & A Wrong 3-1

1. A dereference is to obtain from a pointer the address of a data item held in another location.
2. A race condition in software occurs when two concurrent threads of execution access a shared resource simultaneously, resulting in unintended consequences.
3. A dynamic link library (DLL) is software that controls and operates an external hardware device that is connected to a computer.

Answer: The wrong statement is #3. A device driver is software that controls and operates an external hardware device that is connected to a computer.

Two Rights & A Wrong 3-2

1. Unlike a penetration test, a vulnerability scan is designed to identify deep vulnerabilities.
2. There are five types of vulnerability scans over assets: network, endpoint, wireless network, database, and applications.
3. Active scanning sends test traffic transmissions into the network and monitors the responses of the endpoints.

Answer: The wrong statement is #1. A penetration test is designed to identify deep vulnerabilities.

MODULE 4

Two Rights & A Wrong 4-1

1. Invisible resource pooling is an advantage of cloud computing.
2. "Serverless" means that an application is running on a virtual machine.
3. A serverless infrastructure is one in which the capacity planning, installation, setup, and management are all invisible to the user because they are handled by the cloud provider.

Answer: The wrong statement is #2. A serverless infrastructure is one in which the capacity planning, installation, setup, and management are all invisible to the user because they are handled by the cloud provider.

Two Rights & A Wrong 4-2

1. There are two types of software analysis for vulnerabilities and malware: static analysis and dynamic analysis.
2. OpenVAS is a wireless vulnerability scanner.
3. Cybersecurity enumeration is defined as the process of extracting a list of usernames, machine names, network resources, shares, and services from a network system.

Answer: The wrong statement is #2. OpenVAS is an infrastructure scanner.

MODULE 5

Two Rights & A Wrong 5-1

1. Active defense is considered too weak to be of any value in cybersecurity defenses.
2. A CASB is a set of software tools or services that resides between an enterprise's on-prem infrastructure and the cloud provider's infrastructure.
3. VDI is the process of running a user desktop inside a VM that resides on a server.

Answer: The wrong statement is #1. Active defense has value, although it is limited.

Two Rights & A Wrong 5-2

1. Blacklisting is approving in advance only specific applications to run so that any item not approved is either restricted or denied ("default-deny").
2. "Force Allow" is a firewall rule that is useful for determining if essential network services are able to communicate.
3. NAC examines the current state of an endpoint before it can connect to the network.

Answer: The wrong statement is #1. Whitelisting is approving in advance only specific applications to run so that any item not approved is either restricted or denied ("default-deny").

MODULE 6

Two Rights & A Wrong 6-1

1. A goal of software diversity is to reduce the probability that errors created by different compilers will influence the end results.
2. Provisioning is removing a resource that is no longer needed.
3. DevSecOps has elasticity and scalability.

Answer: The wrong statement is #2. Provisioning is the enterprise-wide configuration, deployment, and management of multiple types of IT system resources, of which the new application would be viewed as a new resource.

Two Rights & A Wrong 6-2

1. Firmware is a specific class of computer software that provides the low-level control for a device's specific hardware.
2. Measured Boot provides the highest degree of security and does not impact the boot process.
3. A secure enclave is a secure coprocessor that functions in addition to the regular processor.

Answer: The wrong statement is #2. Measured Boot can slow down the boot process.

MODULE 7

Two Rights & A Wrong 7-1

1. UEBA includes networks, devices, applications, and users.
2. Flow analysis (also called network traffic analysis) is the evaluation of a collection of network data: instead of examining the individual performance of a device on the network by looking at raw data packets, network traffic analysis uses an aggregate or collection of data from the network's different devices.
3. DKIM is an email authentication method that identifies who the MTA email servers are that have been authorized to send email for a domain.

Answer: The wrong statement is #3. Sender Policy Framework (SPF) is an email authentication method that identifies who the MTA email servers are that have been authorized to send email for a domain.

Two Rights & A Wrong 7-2

1. Conditional analysis seeks to uncover one or more events that violate predefined rules.
2. Trend analysis seeks to answer the question, *Will this do something harmful if it is allowed to execute?*
3. A SIEM consolidates real-time monitoring and management of security information with analysis and reporting of security events.

Answer: The wrong statement is #2. Heuristic analysis seeks to answer the question, *Will this do something harmful if it is allowed to execute?*

MODULE 8

Two Rights & A Wrong 8-1

1. An SOC houses the IT security team responsible for detecting, analyzing, and responding to cybersecurity incidents and typically uses a combination of automated and manual technology processes.
2. Data enrichment is an enhancement upon threat feed combination.
3. SCAP is an open standard that enables an automated vulnerability management, measurement, and policy compliance evaluation.

Answer: The wrong statement is #2. Threat feed combination is an enhancement upon data enrichment.

Two Rights & A Wrong 8-2

1. Threat hunting is both reactive and proactive.
2. Reducing the attack surface area is a goal of a successful threat hunt.
3. A hypothesis is a tentative assumption that is made and will then be tested to determine if it is valid.

Answer: The wrong statement is #1. Threat hunting is proactive.

MODULE 9

Two Rights & A Wrong 9-1

1. A cyber incident is the act of violating an explicit or implied security policy whether or not it is successful.
2. Most but not all states have notification laws requiring that users be promptly notified in the event of a data breach.
3. SPI is information that does not directly identify an individual.

Answer: The wrong statement is #2. All states have data notification laws.

Two Rights & A Wrong 9-2

1. The first step in incident response is to determine if an actual attack did occur.
2. If the initial analysis is one of the most difficult steps in an incident response and recovery process, prioritizing is perhaps the most critical step.
3. Recovery time is the length of time needed for the IT systems to be disinfected and to return to their normal functions.

Answer: The wrong statement is #1. Preparation is the first step in incident response.

MODULE 10

Two Rights & A Wrong 10-1

1. Traffic spikes are always an indication of data exfiltration by threat actors.
2. Beaconing occurs when infected devices attempt to contact the threat actor's external command and control (C&C) server.
3. Threat actors attempt to avoid detection by using common protocols over nonstandard ports.

Answer: The wrong statement is #1. There are several benign reasons for a data spike.

Two Rights & A Wrong 10-2

1. The amount of digital evidence, increased scrutiny by the legal profession, and the higher level of computer skill by criminals are all reasons why computer forensics is increasingly important.
2. There are two types of hardware write blockers: native and tailgate.
3. A Legal Stop Order (LSO) is a judicial requirement that once data has been identified, it cannot be modified or deleted.

Answer: The wrong statement is #3. A legal hold is the judicial requirement that prevents data from being modified or deleted.

MODULE 11

Two Rights & A Wrong 11-1

1. At a basic level, risk may be defined as a situation that involves exposure to some type of danger, while at a more advanced level, risk can be described as a function of threats, consequences of those threats, and the resulting vulnerabilities.
2. The Annualized Loss Expectancy (ALE) is the expected monetary loss that can be expected for an asset due to a risk over a one-year period.
3. Risk avoidance utilizes cybersecurity insurance.

Answer: The wrong statement is #3. Risk transference utilizes cybersecurity insurance.

Two Rights & A Wrong 11-2

1. An operational control is implemented and executed by people.
2. A preventative control is designed to identify any threat that has reached the system.
3. An assessment is an internal review of security controls that are compared against stated security objectives.

Answer: The wrong statement is #2. A preventative control works to prevent the threat from coming in contact with the vulnerability.

MODULE 12

Two Rights & A Wrong 12-1

1. A data privacy officer (DPO) is the manager who oversees data privacy compliance and manages data risk.

2. DAC is the least restrictive access control scheme.

3. Geotagging is another name for geographic access requirements.

Answer: The wrong statement is #3. Geofencing is another name for geographic access requirements.

Two Rights & A Wrong 12-2

1. One of the user concerns regarding data privacy is statistical inferences.

2. Identity theft can impact the accuracy of data.

3. Data protection is a legal issue while data privacy is a technical issue.

Answer: The wrong statement is #3. Data protection is a technical issue whereas data privacy is a legal issue.

INDEX